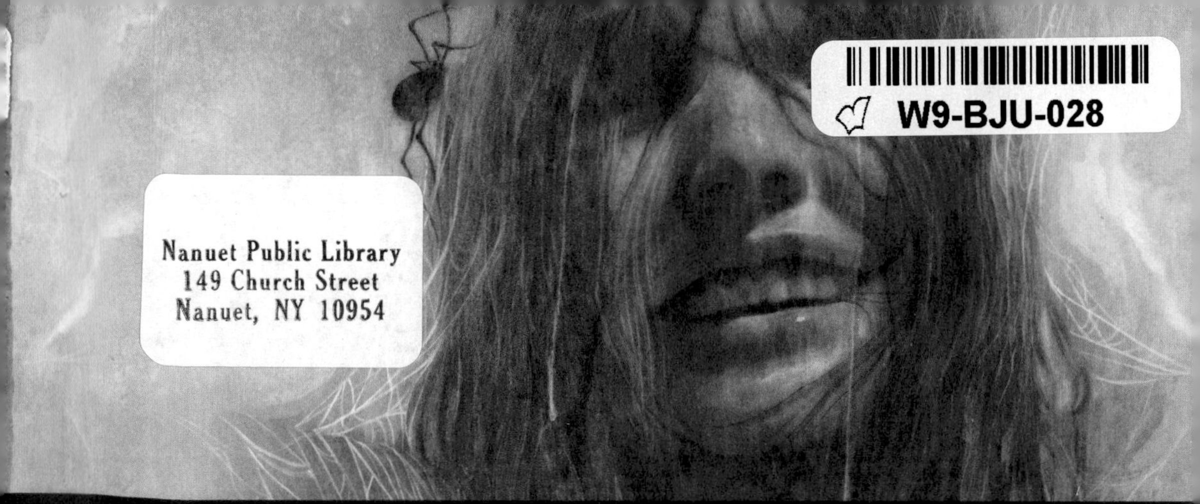

FABLES: THE DARK AGES

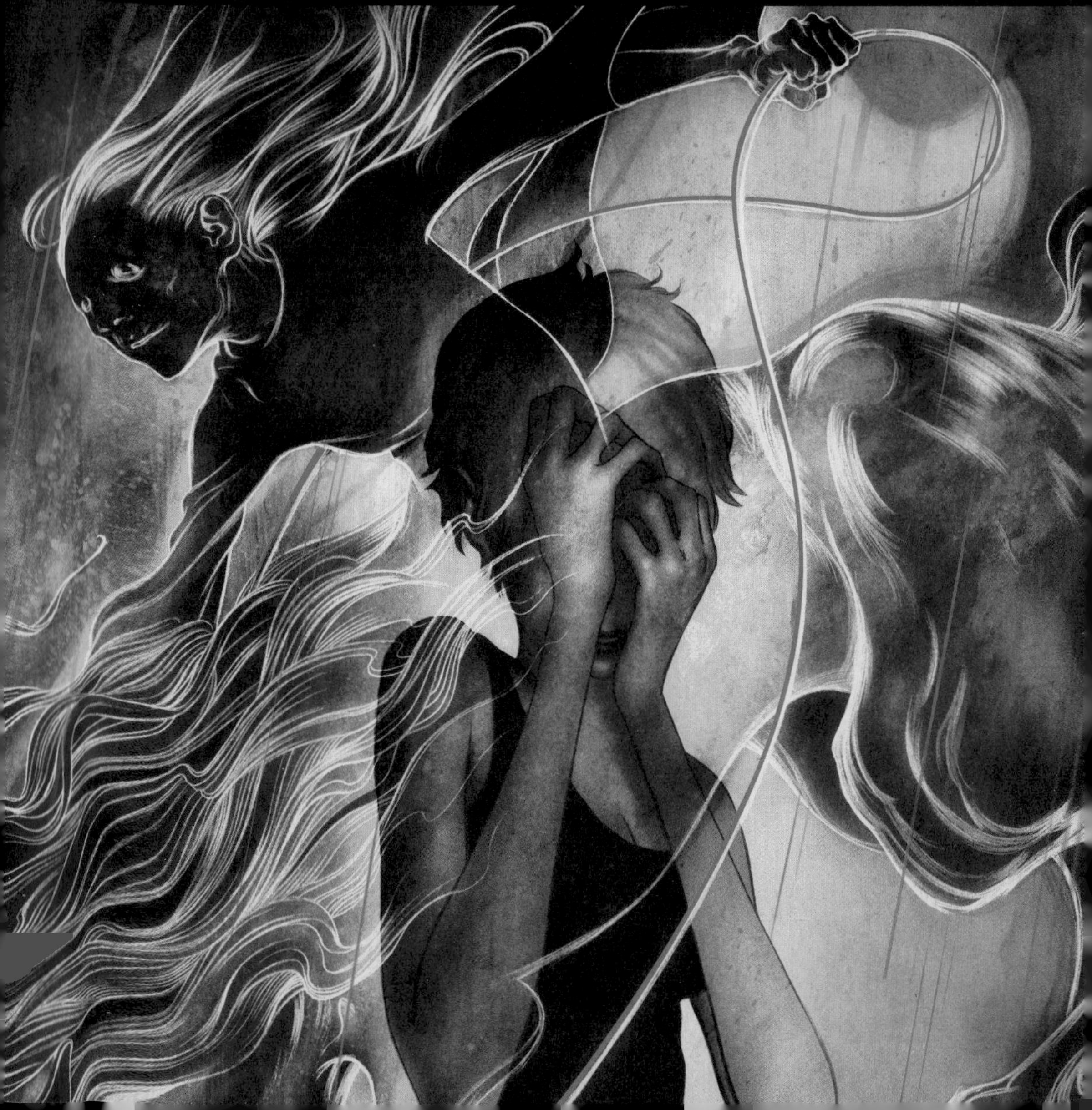

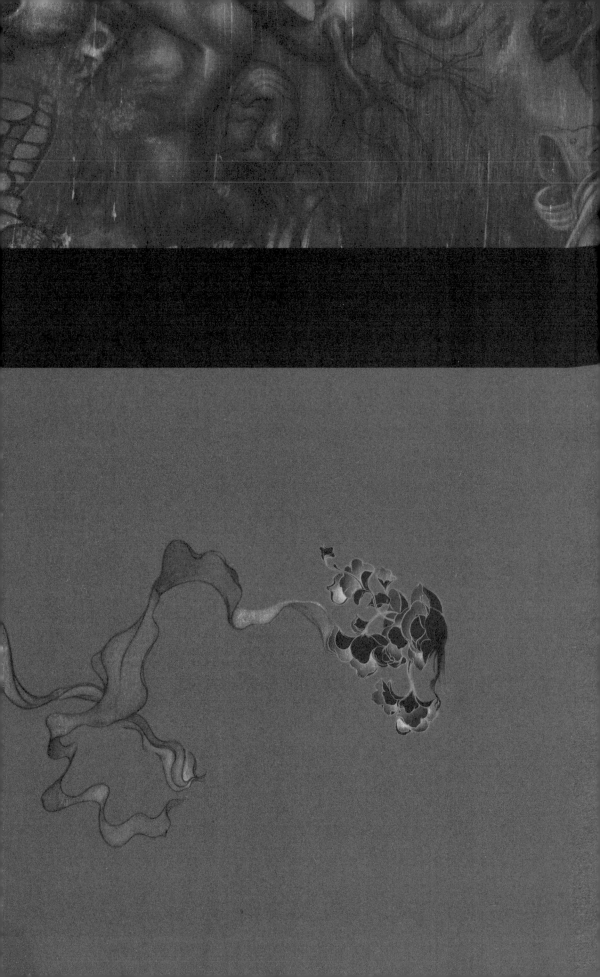

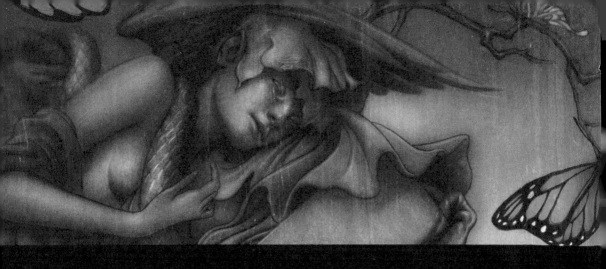

FABLES: THE DARK AGES

FABLES CREATED BY BILL WILLINGHAM

Bill Willingham
writer

Mark Buckingham
Peter Gross
Andrew Pepoy
Michael Allred
David Hahn
artists

Lee Loughridge
Laura Allred
colorists

Todd Klein
letterer

James Jean (#76-81)
Mark Buckingham (#82)
original series covers

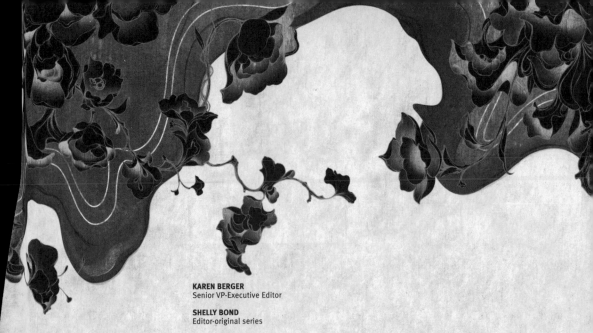

This volume is dedicated to Stacy Sinner,
who went into the woods, found my
house of many stories there,
and then built it for me.
— Bill Willingham

In loving memory of Marisa, Irma's Mum.
— Mark Buckingham

Cover illustration by James Jean
Logo design by Brainchild Studios/NYC

FABLES: THE DARK AGES

Published by DC Comics. Cover and compilation

DC Comics, 1700 Broadway, New York, NY 10019
A Warner Bros. Entertainment Company.
Printed in Canada. First Printing.
ISBN: 978-1-4012-2316-8

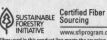

SUSTAINABLE FORESTRY INITIATIVE
Certified Fiber Sourcing
www.sfiprogram.org
Fiber used in this product line meets the sourcing requirements of the SFI program. www.sfiprogram.org PWC-SFICOC-260

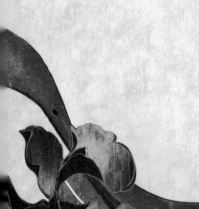

Table of Contents

WHO'S WHO IN FABLETOWN

GEPPETTO

He was once Fabletown's most terrible adversary. Now he's one of them.

PINOCCHIO

Geppetto's first son, and quite possibly the only person in hundreds of worlds who still has any love for the mean old man

BEAUTY AND BEAST

They help run Fabletown as the deputy mayor and sheriff, respectively.

GRIMBLE

The Woodland's perpetually sleepy security officer and perhaps the most famous (and infamous) of all bridge trolls.

BIGBY

The Big Bad Wolf, reformed now and happily married.

SNOW WHITE

Bigby's wife and still a power in Fabletown politics.

BAGHEERA

One of Mowgli's closest friends and advisors.

BOY BLUE

A wicked horn player and a warrior of note. One of the heroes of the war against the Empire, where he received a wound to his arm.

DOCTOR SWINEHEART

The best military surgeon in uncountable worlds, and Boy Blue's postwar physician.

NURSE SPRAT

Jack Sprat's widow, and not the nicest of ladies.

ROSE RED

She still runs the Farm and recently turned down Boy Blue's ill-timed romantic overtures.

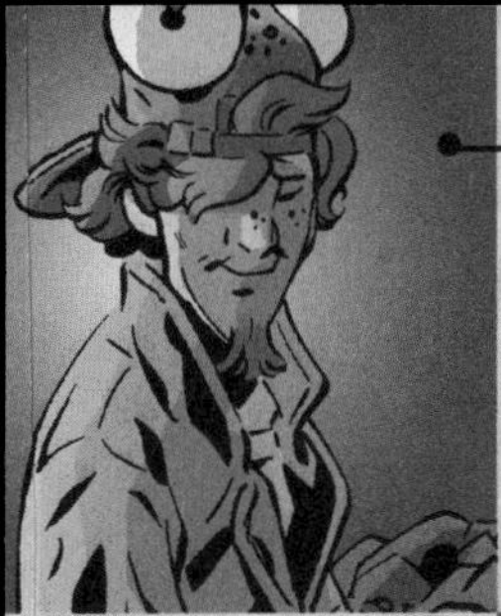

FLYCATCHER

The famous janitor king and former Frog Prince.

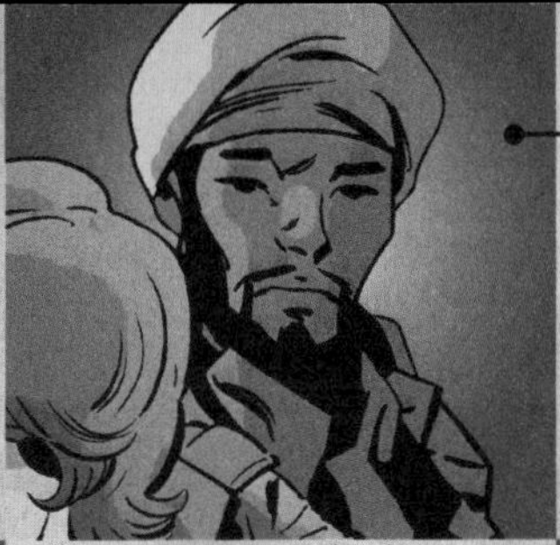

SINBAD

A leader of Fabletown East (in the Homelands' version of Baghdad) and a hero of the war against the Empire.

FRAU TOTENKINDER

The Black Forest Witch and leader of Fabletown's magic set.

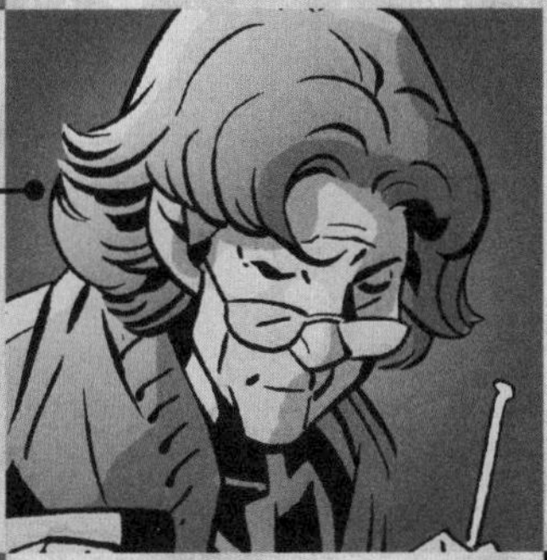

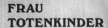

MOWGLI

A hunter of no small repute, and one of Fabletown's top secret agents.

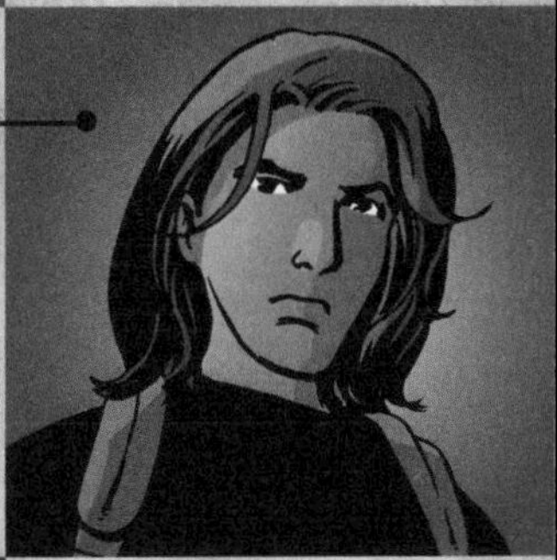

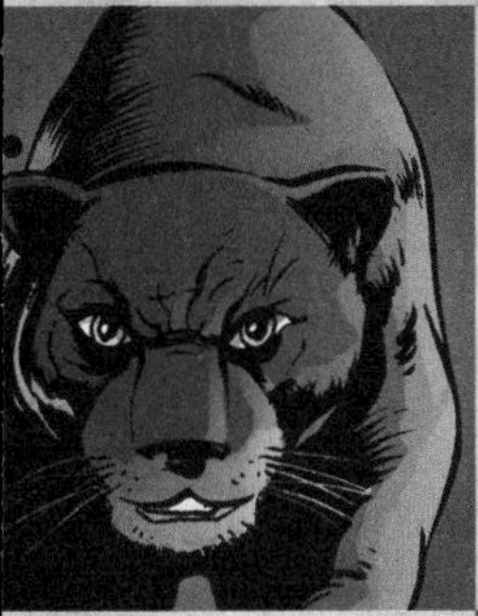

BIGBY'S BROTHERS

Six bad siblings, sometimes wolves, sometimes monsters, and sometimes fish.

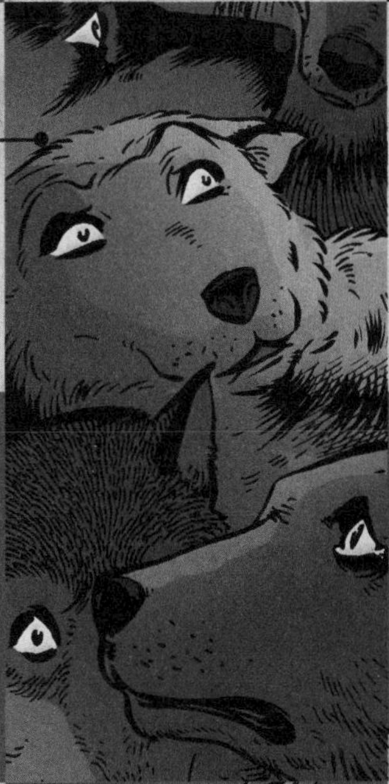

KING COLE

Once the beloved mayor of Fabletown, then not, then mayor again.

BUFKIN

A flying monkey from Oz who knows where the books go.

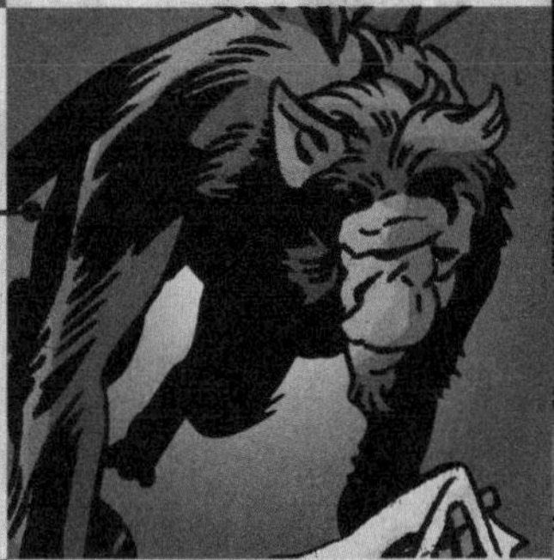

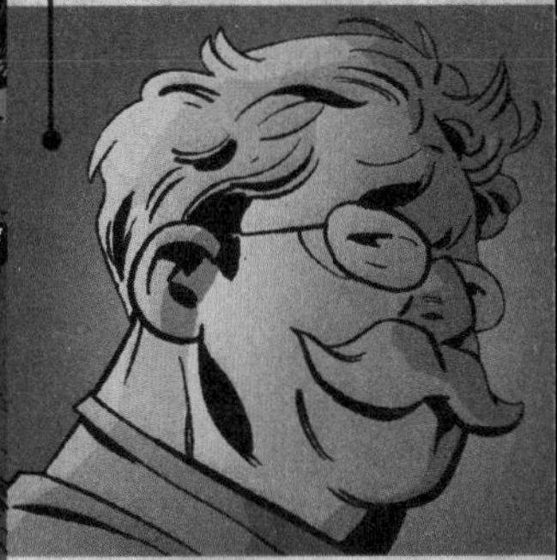

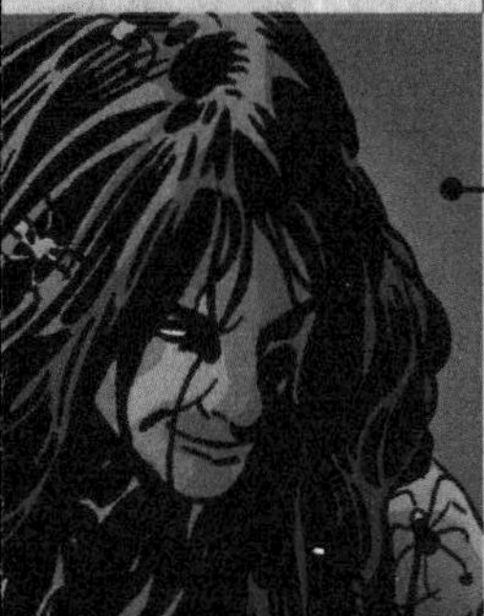

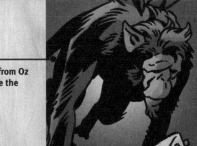

BABA YAGA

Less than a handful of Fables know she's being held captive somewhere in the back warrens of the Woodland's business office.

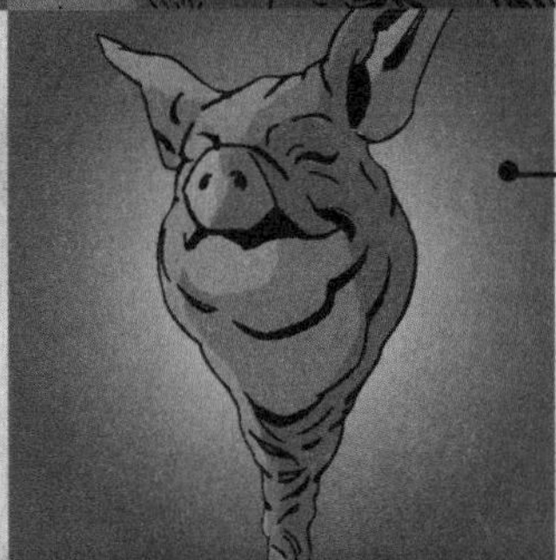

COLIN THE PIG

Once one of the Three Little Pigs, he's now just a big dead pig head on a stick, but one with some sort of oracular power.

THE STORY SO FAR

After spending centuries as a hidden community in exile, Fabletown finally rose up in righteous anger and brought down Geppetto's vast empire in a quick and nearly bloodless war — though victory did have some costs, including the loss of

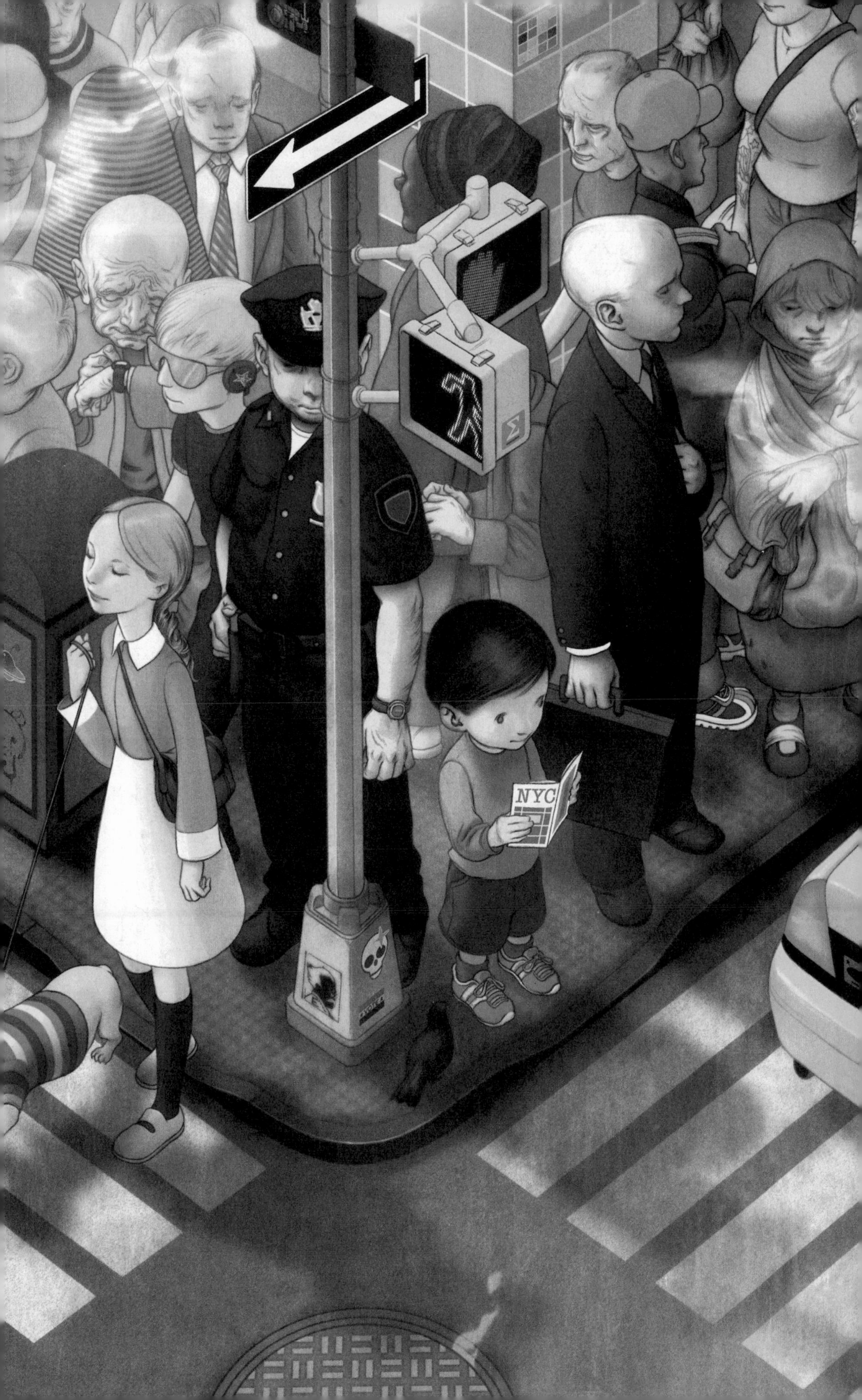
NYC

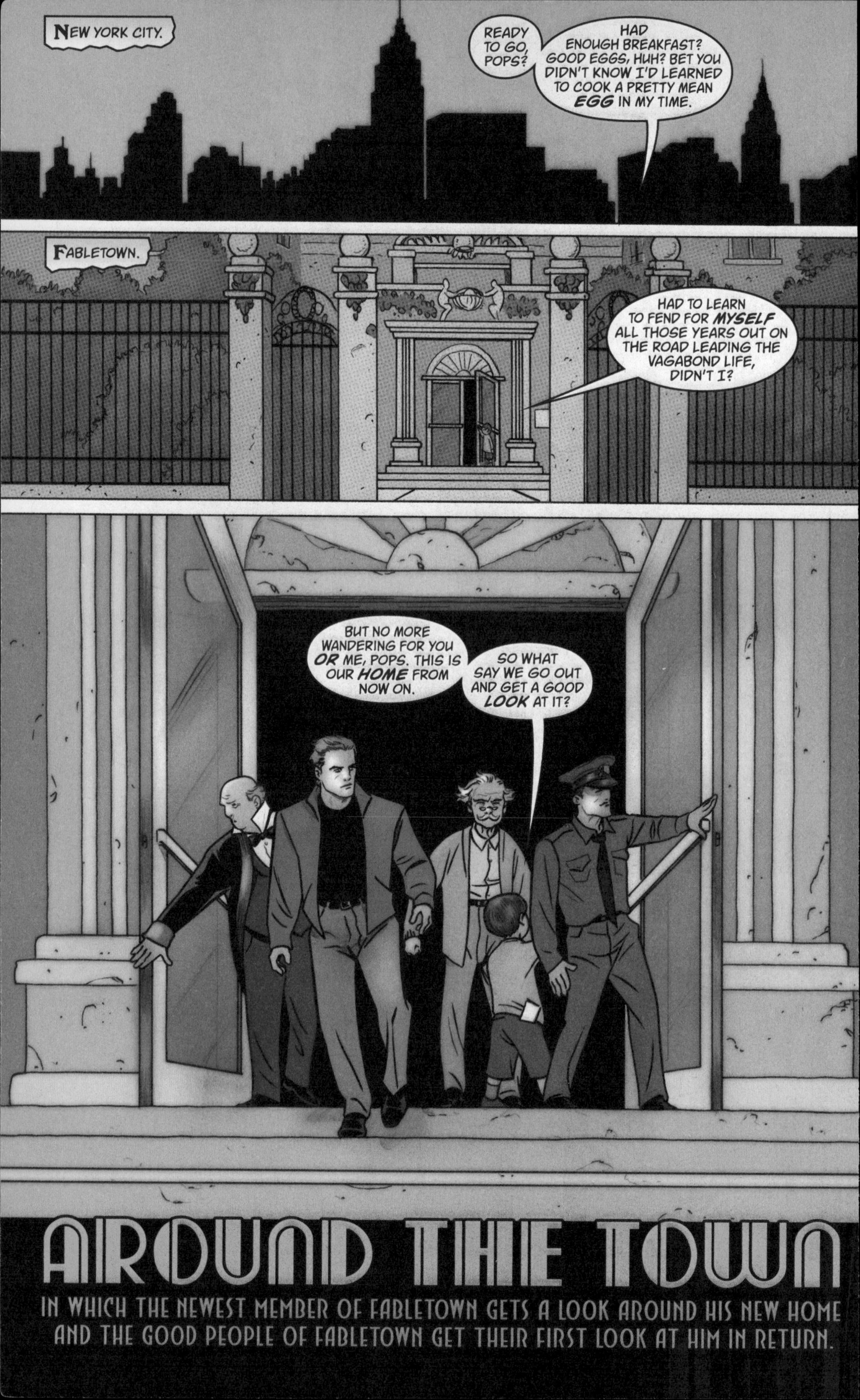

NEW YORK CITY.
READY TO GO, POPS?
HAD ENOUGH BREAKFAST? GOOD EGGS, HUH? BET YOU DIDN'T KNOW I'D LEARNED TO COOK A PRETTY MEAN EGG IN MY TIME.
FABLETOWN.
HAD TO LEARN TO FEND FOR MYSELF ALL THOSE YEARS OUT ON THE ROAD LEADING THE VAGABOND LIFE, DIDN'T I?
BUT NO MORE WANDERING FOR YOU OR ME, POPS. THIS IS OUR HOME FROM NOW ON.
SO WHAT SAY WE GO OUT AND GET A GOOD LOOK AT IT?
AROUND THE TOWN
IN WHICH THE NEWEST MEMBER OF FABLETOWN GETS A LOOK AROUND HIS NEW HOME AND THE GOOD PEOPLE OF FABLETOWN GET THEIR FIRST LOOK AT HIM IN RETURN.

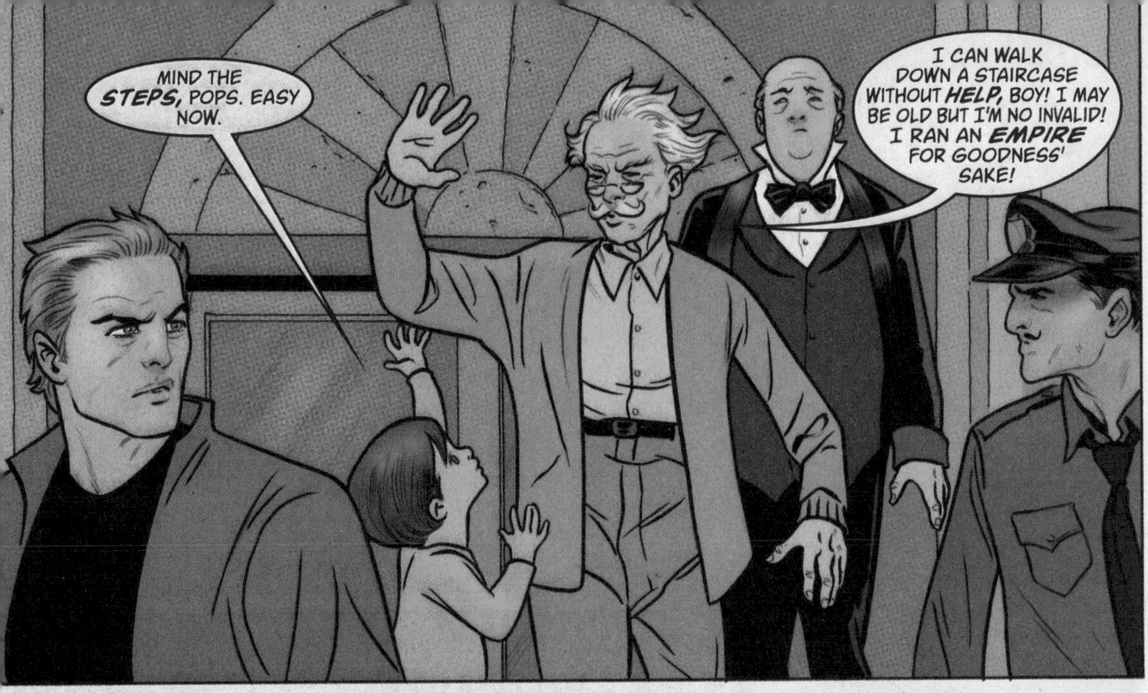
MIND THE STEPS, POPS. EASY NOW.
I CAN WALK DOWN A STAIRCASE WITHOUT HELP, BOY! I MAY BE OLD BUT I'M NO INVALID! I RAN AN EMPIRE FOR GOODNESS' SAKE!

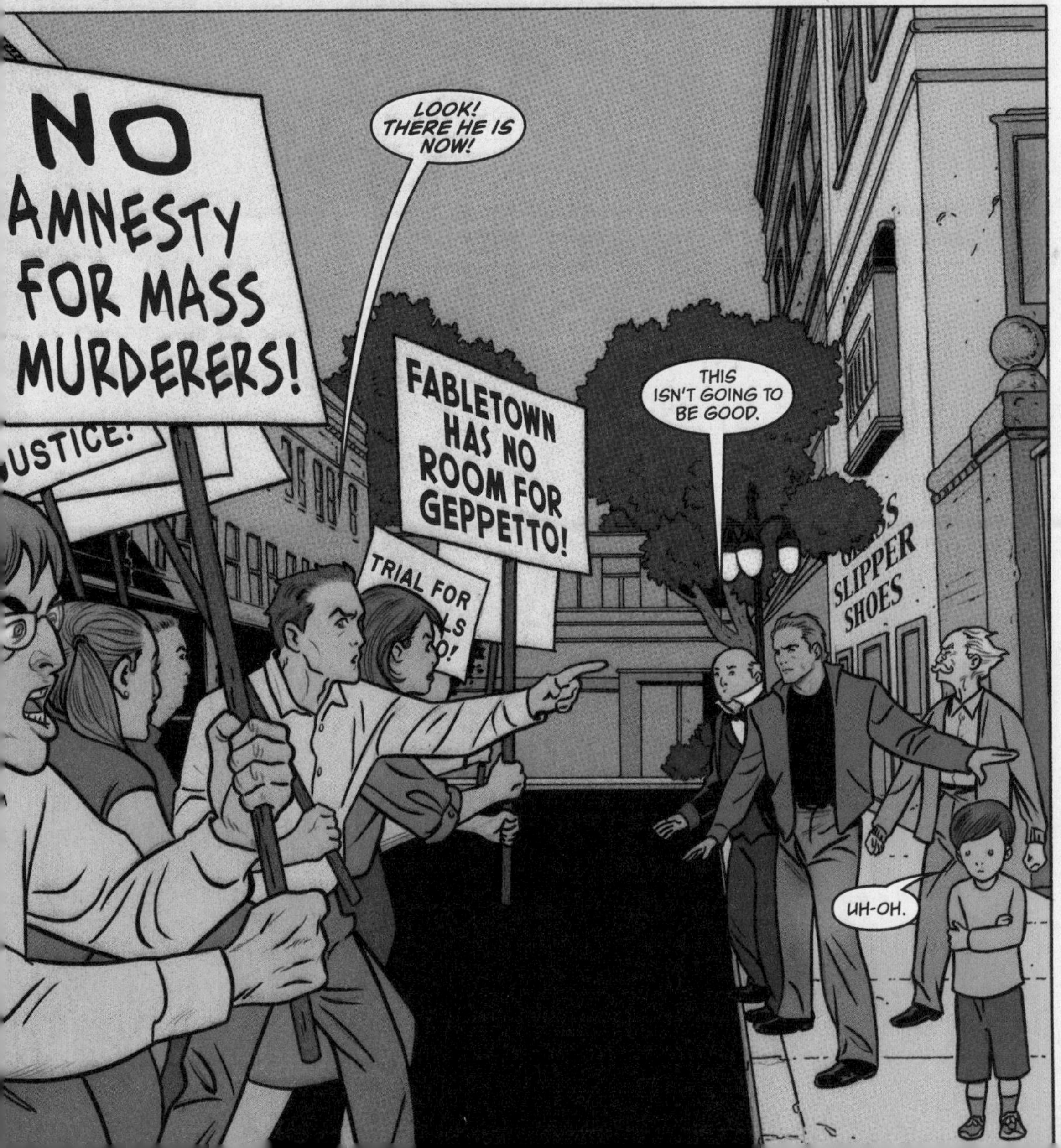
NO AMNESTY FOR MASS MURDERERS!
USTICE!
FABLETOWN HAS NO ROOM FOR GEPPETTO!
TRIAL FOR
LOOK! THERE HE IS NOW!
THIS ISN'T GOING TO BE GOOD.
SLIPPER SHOES
UH-OH.

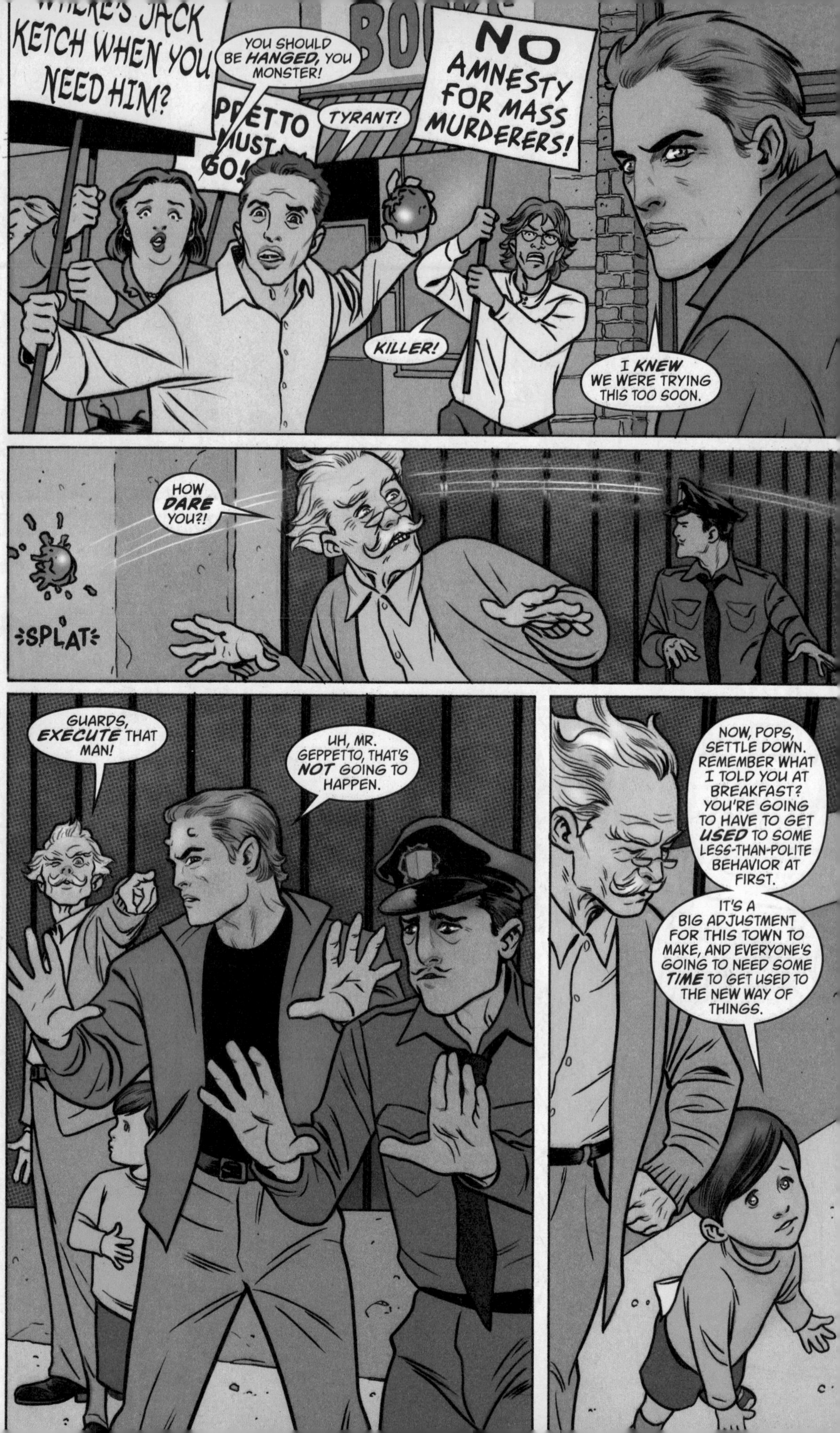

WHERE'S JACK KETCH WHEN YOU NEED HIM?
YOU SHOULD BE HANGED, YOU MONSTER!
PPETTO MUST GO!
TYRANT!
NO AMNESTY FOR MASS MURDERERS!
KILLER!
I KNEW WE WERE TRYING THIS TOO SOON.
HOW DARE YOU?!
SPLAT
GUARDS, EXECUTE THAT MAN!
UH, MR. GEPPETTO, THAT'S NOT GOING TO HAPPEN.
NOW, POPS, SETTLE DOWN. REMEMBER WHAT I TOLD YOU AT BREAKFAST? YOU'RE GOING TO HAVE TO GET USED TO SOME LESS-THAN-POLITE BEHAVIOR AT FIRST.
IT'S A BIG ADJUSTMENT FOR THIS TOWN TO MAKE, AND EVERYONE'S GOING TO NEED SOME TIME TO GET USED TO THE NEW WAY OF THINGS.

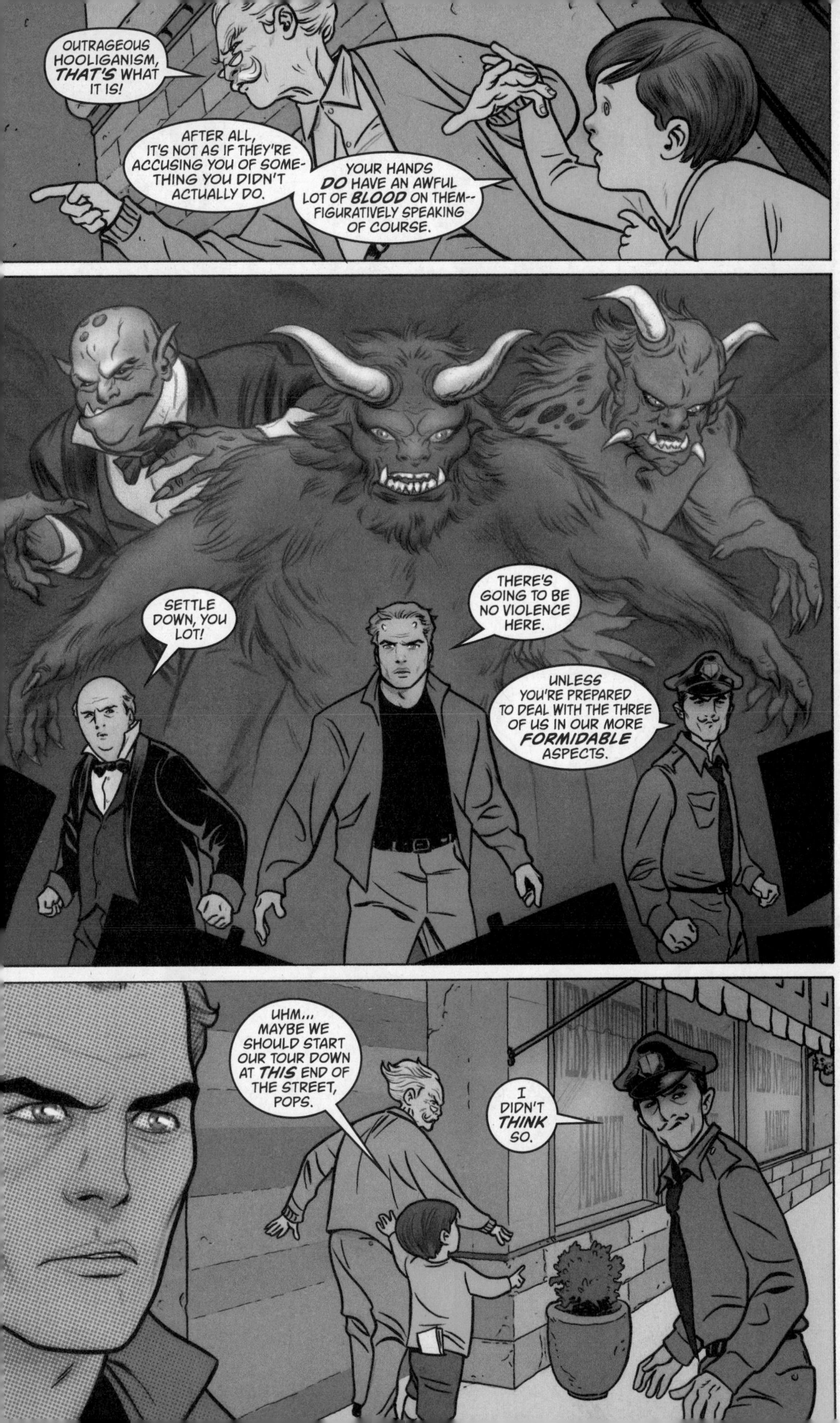
OUTRAGEOUS HOOLIGANISM, THAT'S WHAT IT IS!
AFTER ALL, IT'S NOT AS IF THEY'RE ACCUSING YOU OF SOMETHING YOU DIDN'T ACTUALLY DO.
YOUR HANDS DO HAVE AN AWFUL LOT OF BLOOD ON THEM-- FIGURATIVELY SPEAKING OF COURSE.
SETTLE DOWN, YOU LOT!
THERE'S GOING TO BE NO VIOLENCE HERE.
UNLESS YOU'RE PREPARED TO DEAL WITH THE THREE OF US IN OUR MORE FORMIDABLE ASPECTS.
UHM... MAYBE WE SHOULD START OUR TOUR DOWN AT THIS END OF THE STREET, POPS.
I DIDN'T THINK SO.

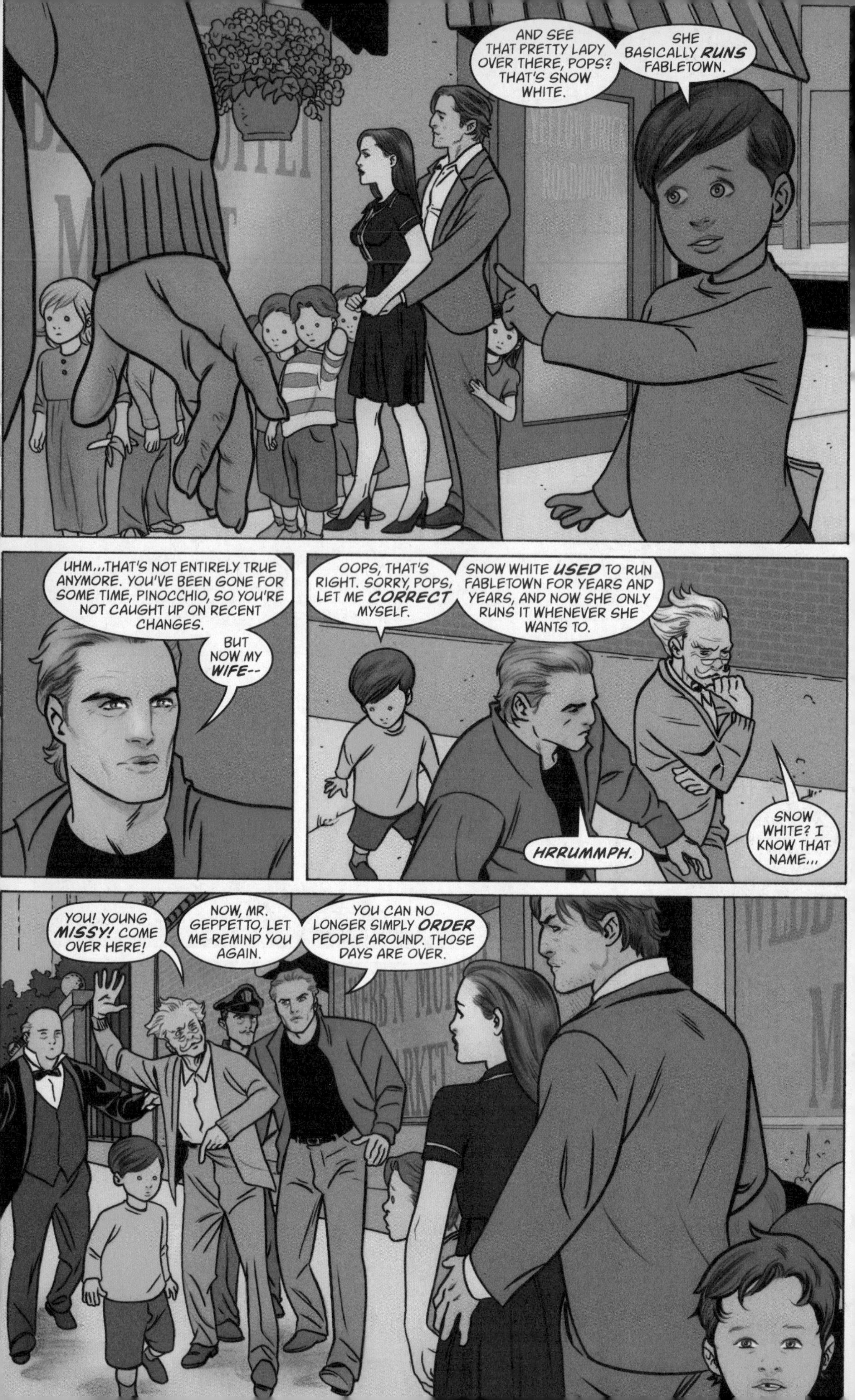
AND SEE THAT PRETTY LADY OVER THERE, POPS? THAT'S SNOW WHITE.
SHE BASICALLY RUNS FABLETOWN.
UHM...THAT'S NOT ENTIRELY TRUE ANYMORE. YOU'VE BEEN GONE FOR SOME TIME, PINOCCHIO, SO YOU'RE NOT CAUGHT UP ON RECENT CHANGES.
BUT NOW MY WIFE--
OOPS, THAT'S RIGHT. SORRY, POPS, LET ME CORRECT MYSELF.
SNOW WHITE USED TO RUN FABLETOWN FOR YEARS AND YEARS, AND NOW SHE ONLY RUNS IT WHENEVER SHE WANTS TO.
HRRUMMPH.
SNOW WHITE? I KNOW THAT NAME...
YOU! YOUNG MISSY! COME OVER HERE!
NOW, MR. GEPPETTO, LET ME REMIND YOU AGAIN.
YOU CAN NO LONGER SIMPLY ORDER PEOPLE AROUND. THOSE DAYS ARE OVER.

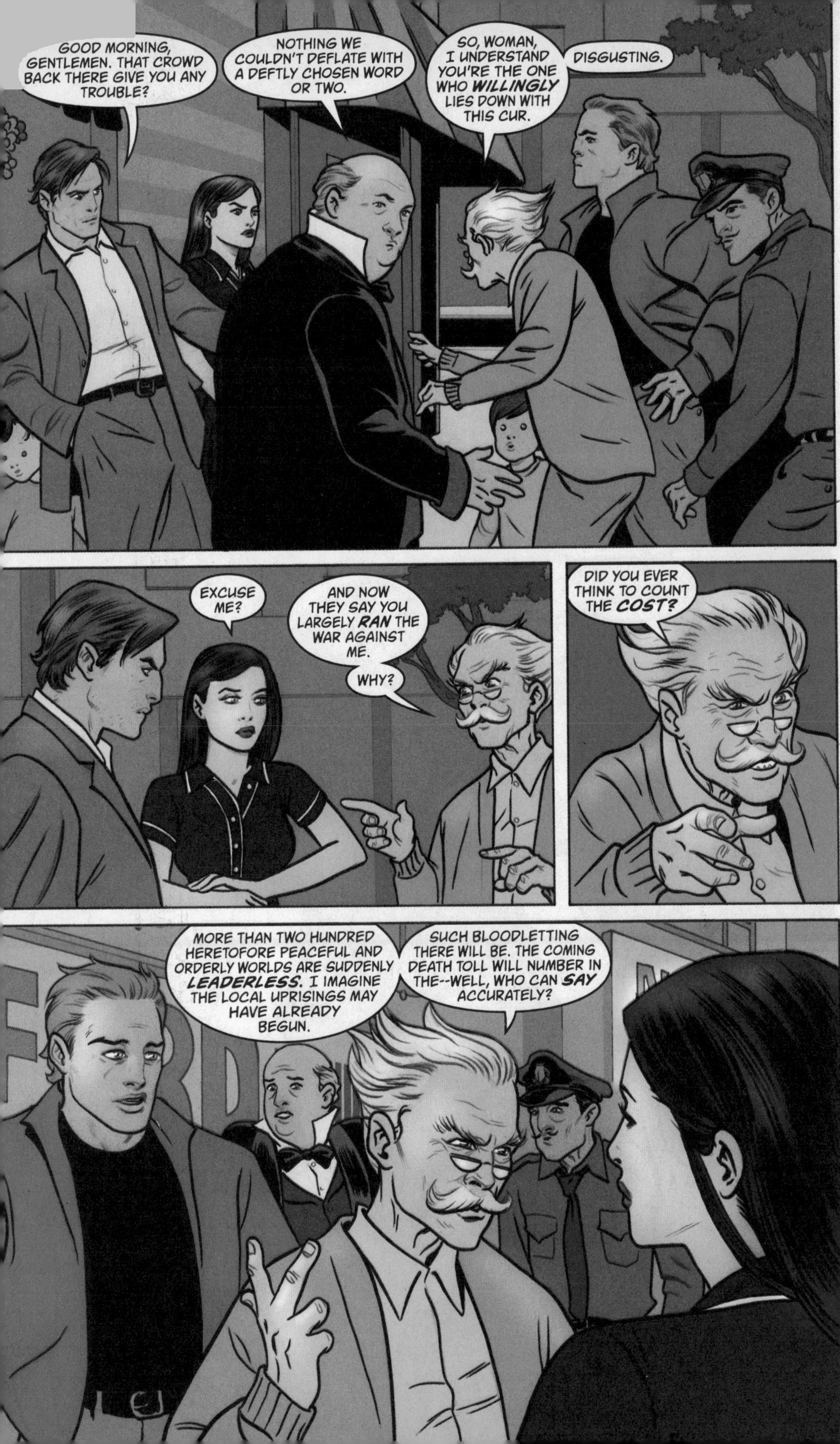
GOOD MORNING, GENTLEMEN. THAT CROWD BACK THERE GIVE YOU ANY TROUBLE?
NOTHING WE COULDN'T DEFLATE WITH A DEFTLY CHOSEN WORD OR TWO.
SO, WOMAN, I UNDERSTAND YOU'RE THE ONE WHO WILLINGLY LIES DOWN WITH THIS CUR.
DISGUSTING.
EXCUSE ME?
AND NOW THEY SAY YOU LARGELY RAN THE WAR AGAINST ME.
WHY?
DID YOU EVER THINK TO COUNT THE COST?
MORE THAN TWO HUNDRED HERETOFORE PEACEFUL AND ORDERLY WORLDS ARE SUDDENLY LEADERLESS. I IMAGINE THE LOCAL UPRISINGS MAY HAVE ALREADY BEGUN.
SUCH BLOODLETTING THERE WILL BE. THE COMING DEATH TOLL WILL NUMBER IN THE--WELL, WHO CAN SAY ACCURATELY?

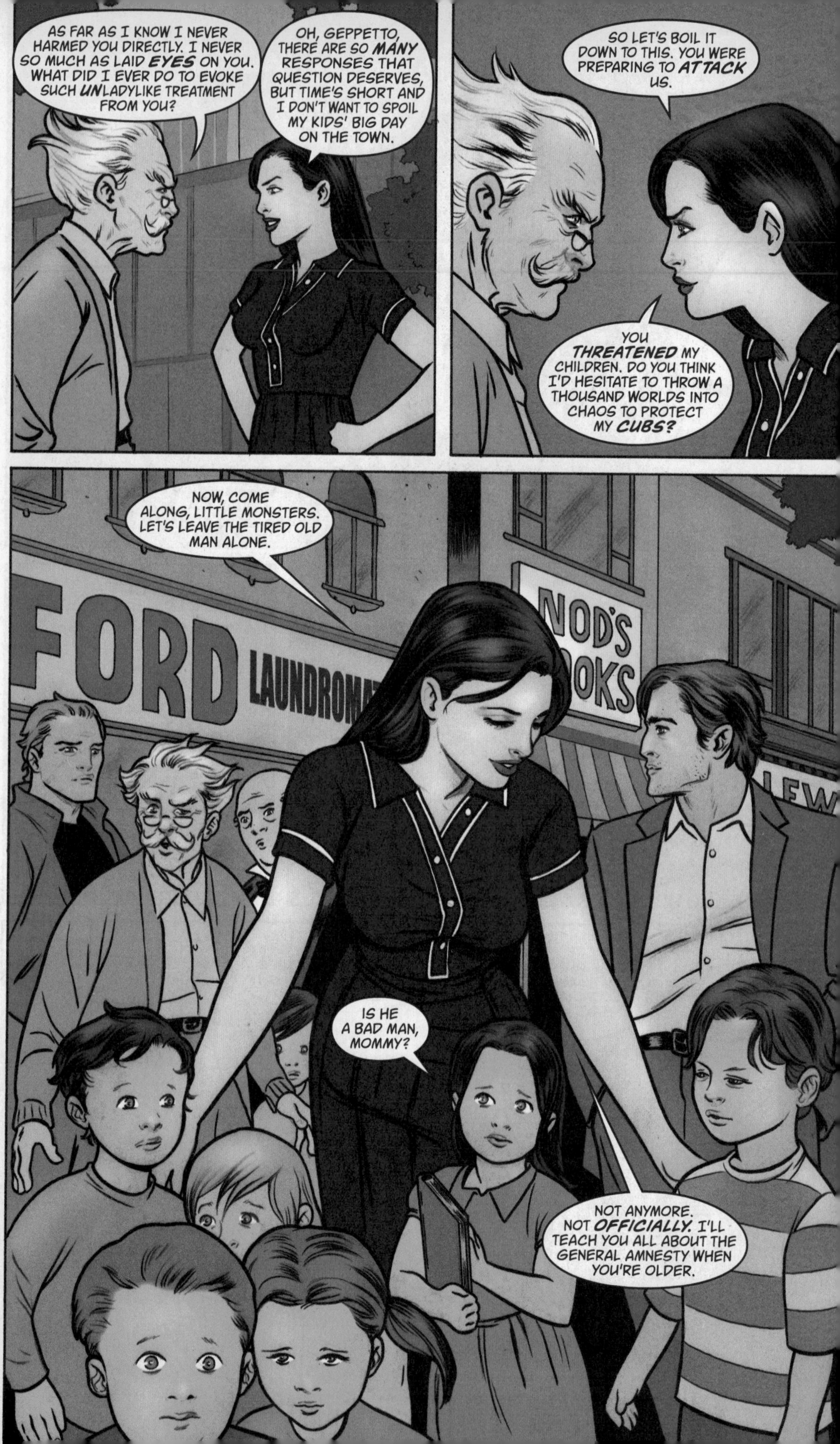

AS FAR AS I KNOW I NEVER HARMED YOU DIRECTLY. I NEVER SO MUCH AS LAID EYES ON YOU. WHAT DID I EVER DO TO EVOKE SUCH UNLADYLIKE TREATMENT FROM YOU?
OH, GEPPETTO, THERE ARE SO MANY RESPONSES THAT QUESTION DESERVES, BUT TIME'S SHORT AND I DON'T WANT TO SPOIL MY KIDS' BIG DAY ON THE TOWN.
SO LET'S BOIL IT DOWN TO THIS. YOU WERE PREPARING TO ATTACK US.
YOU THREATENED MY CHILDREN. DO YOU THINK I'D HESITATE TO THROW A THOUSAND WORLDS INTO CHAOS TO PROTECT MY CUBS?
NOW, COME ALONG, LITTLE MONSTERS. LET'S LEAVE THE TIRED OLD MAN ALONE.
FORD LAUNDROMA
NOD'S OOKS
IS HE A BAD MAN, MOMMY?
NOT ANYMORE. NOT OFFICIALLY. I'LL TEACH YOU ALL ABOUT THE GENERAL AMNESTY WHEN YOU'RE OLDER.

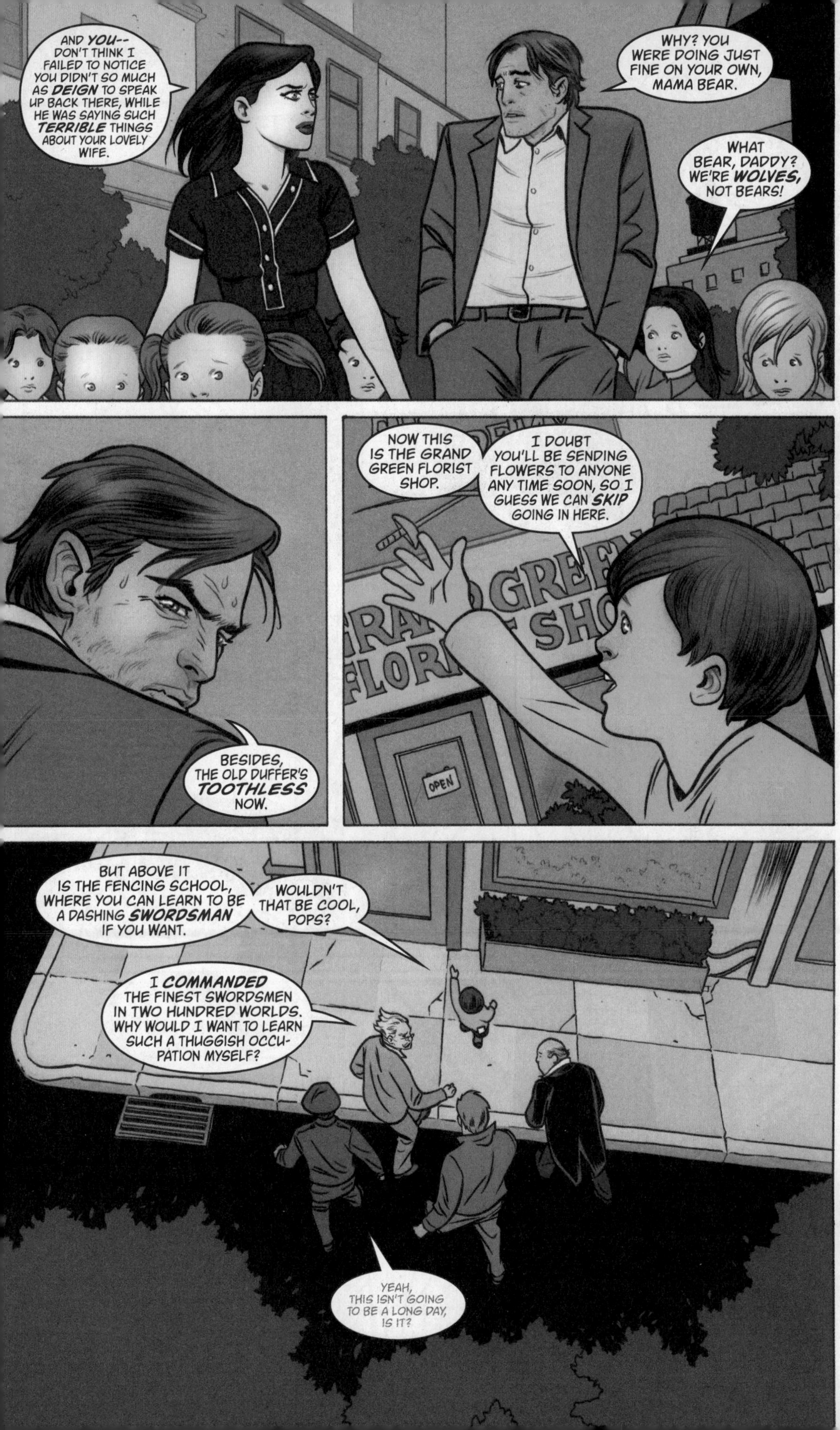
AND YOU-- DON'T THINK I FAILED TO NOTICE YOU DIDN'T SO MUCH AS DEIGN TO SPEAK UP BACK THERE, WHILE HE WAS SAYING SUCH TERRIBLE THINGS ABOUT YOUR LOVELY WIFE.
WHY? YOU WERE DOING JUST FINE ON YOUR OWN, MAMA BEAR.
WHAT BEAR, DADDY? WE'RE WOLVES, NOT BEARS!
BESIDES, THE OLD DUFFER'S TOOTHLESS NOW.
NOW THIS IS THE GRAND GREEN FLORIST SHOP.
I DOUBT YOU'LL BE SENDING FLOWERS TO ANYONE ANY TIME SOON, SO I GUESS WE CAN SKIP GOING IN HERE.
OPEN
BUT ABOVE IT IS THE FENCING SCHOOL, WHERE YOU CAN LEARN TO BE A DASHING SWORDSMAN IF YOU WANT.
WOULDN'T THAT BE COOL, POPS?
I COMMANDED THE FINEST SWORDSMEN IN TWO HUNDRED WORLDS. WHY WOULD I WANT TO LEARN SUCH A THUGGISH OCCU-PATION MYSELF?
YEAH, THIS ISN'T GOING TO BE A LONG DAY, IS IT?

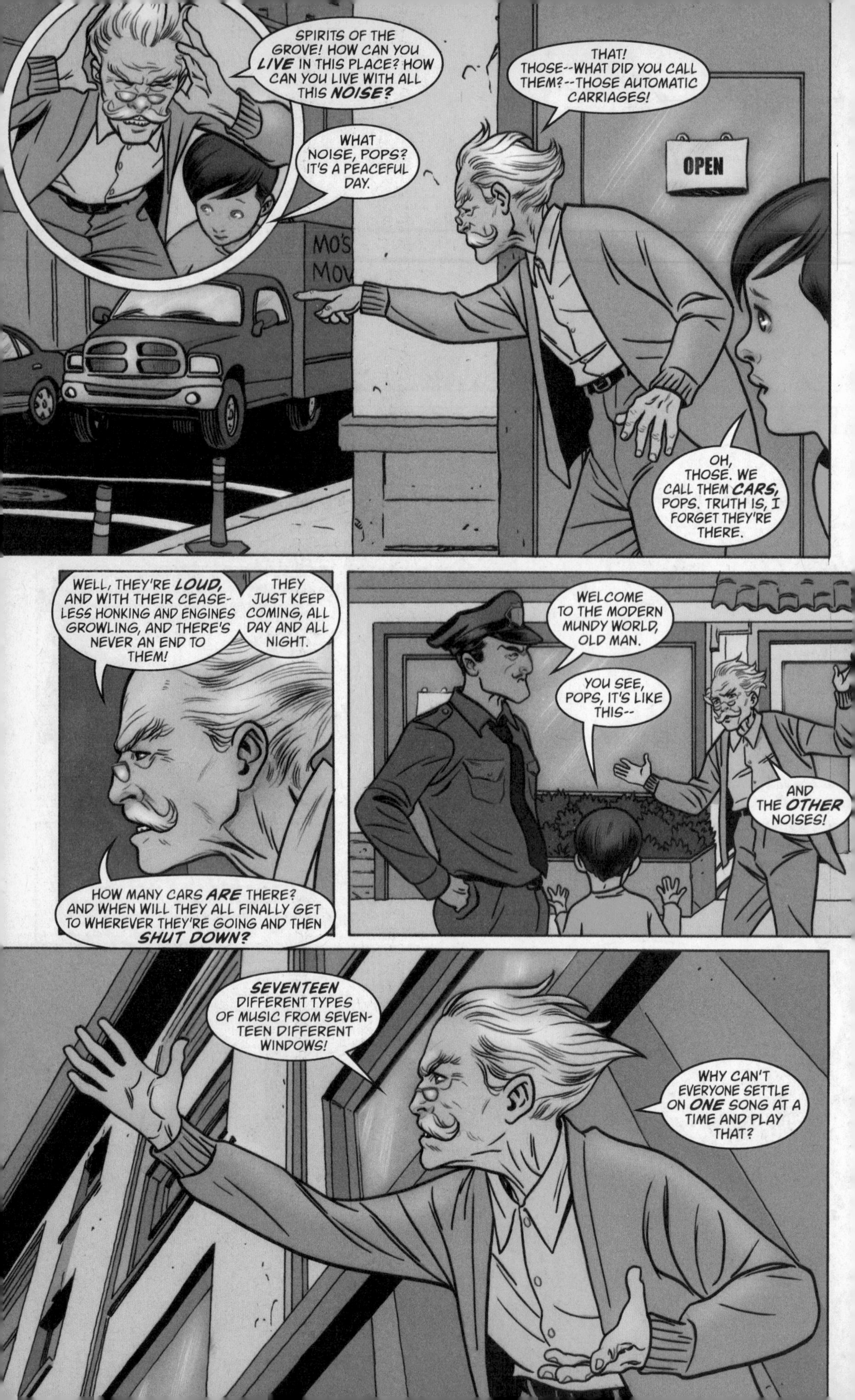
SPIRITS OF THE GROVE! HOW CAN YOU LIVE IN THIS PLACE? HOW CAN YOU LIVE WITH ALL THIS NOISE?
WHAT NOISE, POPS? IT'S A PEACEFUL DAY.
THAT! THOSE--WHAT DID YOU CALL THEM?--THOSE AUTOMATIC CARRIAGES!
OPEN
MO'S MOV
OH, THOSE. WE CALL THEM CARS, POPS. TRUTH IS, I FORGET THEY'RE THERE.
WELL, THEY'RE LOUD, AND WITH THEIR CEASE-LESS HONKING AND ENGINES GROWLING, AND THERE'S NEVER AN END TO THEM!
THEY JUST KEEP COMING, ALL DAY AND ALL NIGHT.
HOW MANY CARS ARE THERE? AND WHEN WILL THEY ALL FINALLY GET TO WHEREVER THEY'RE GOING AND THEN SHUT DOWN?
WELCOME TO THE MODERN MUNDY WORLD, OLD MAN.
YOU SEE, POPS, IT'S LIKE THIS--
AND THE OTHER NOISES!
SEVENTEEN DIFFERENT TYPES OF MUSIC FROM SEVEN-TEEN DIFFERENT WINDOWS!
WHY CAN'T EVERYONE SETTLE ON ONE SONG AT A TIME AND PLAY THAT?

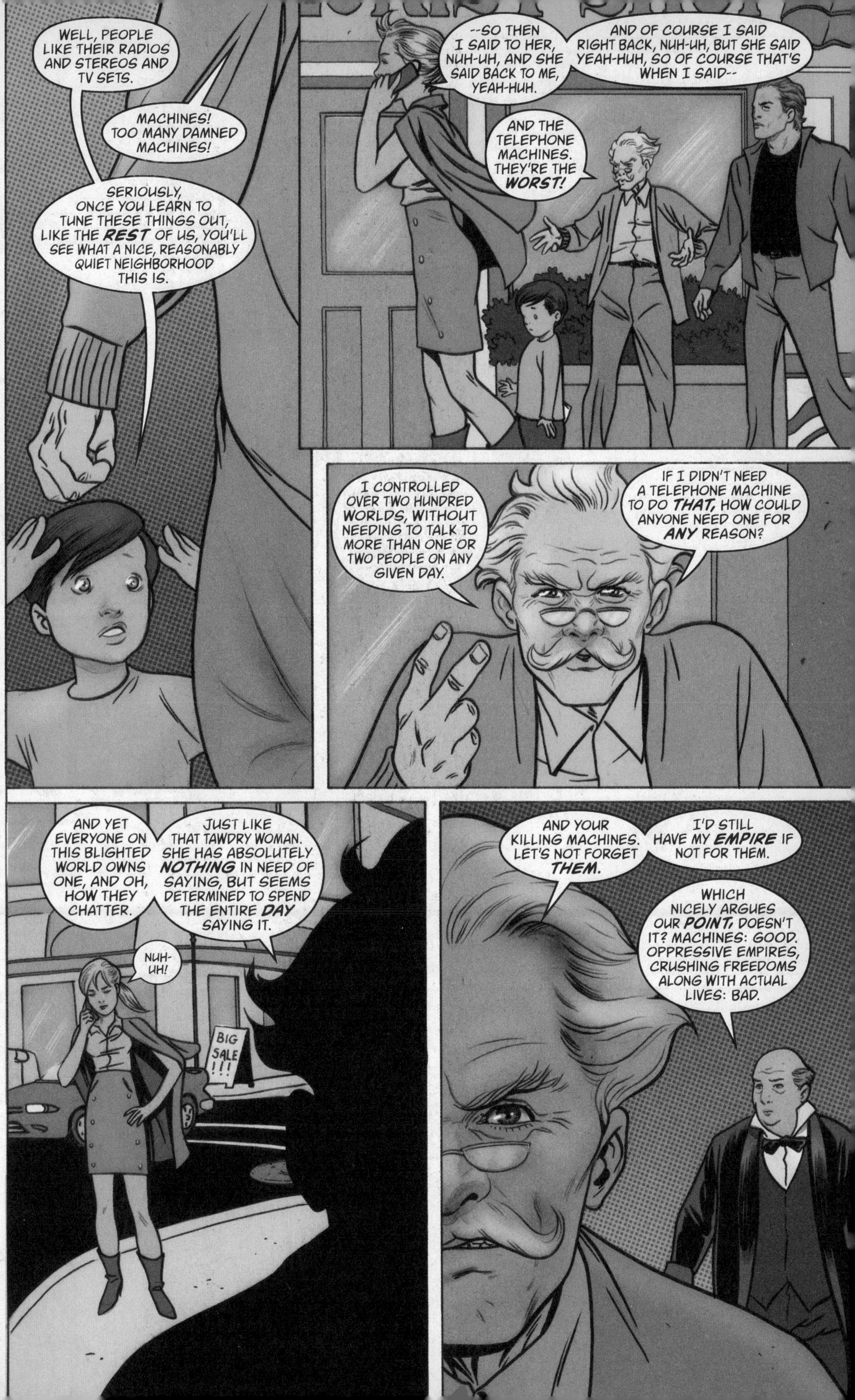
WELL, PEOPLE LIKE THEIR RADIOS AND STEREOS AND TV SETS.
MACHINES! TOO MANY DAMNED MACHINES!
SERIOUSLY, ONCE YOU LEARN TO TUNE THESE THINGS OUT, LIKE THE REST OF US, YOU'LL SEE WHAT A NICE, REASONABLY QUIET NEIGHBORHOOD THIS IS.
--SO THEN I SAID TO HER, NUH-UH, AND SHE SAID BACK TO ME, YEAH-HUH.
AND OF COURSE I SAID RIGHT BACK, NUH-UH, BUT SHE SAID YEAH-HUH, SO OF COURSE THAT'S WHEN I SAID--
AND THE TELEPHONE MACHINES. THEY'RE THE WORST!
I CONTROLLED OVER TWO HUNDRED WORLDS, WITHOUT NEEDING TO TALK TO MORE THAN ONE OR TWO PEOPLE ON ANY GIVEN DAY.
IF I DIDN'T NEED A TELEPHONE MACHINE TO DO THAT, HOW COULD ANYONE NEED ONE FOR ANY REASON?
AND YET EVERYONE ON THIS BLIGHTED WORLD OWNS ONE, AND OH, HOW THEY CHATTER.
JUST LIKE THAT TAWDRY WOMAN. SHE HAS ABSOLUTELY NOTHING IN NEED OF SAYING, BUT SEEMS DETERMINED TO SPEND THE ENTIRE DAY SAYING IT.
NUH-UH!
BIG SALE !!!
AND YOUR KILLING MACHINES. LET'S NOT FORGET THEM.
I'D STILL HAVE MY EMPIRE IF NOT FOR THEM.
WHICH NICELY ARGUES OUR POINT, DOESN'T IT? MACHINES: GOOD. OPPRESSIVE EMPIRES, CRUSHING FREEDOMS ALONG WITH ACTUAL LIVES: BAD.

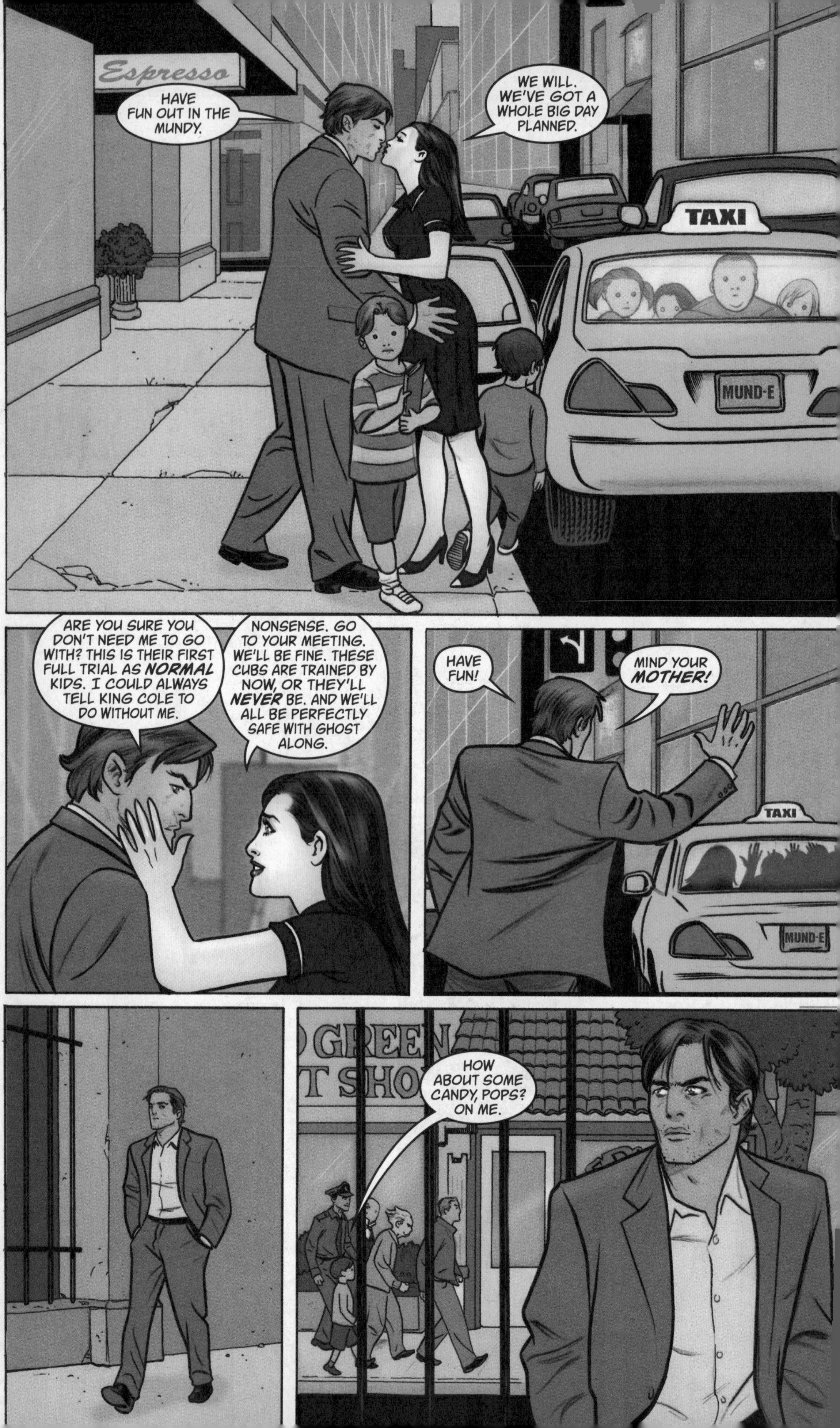
Espresso
HAVE FUN OUT IN THE MUNDY.
WE WILL. WE'VE GOT A WHOLE BIG DAY PLANNED.
TAXI
MUND-E
ARE YOU SURE YOU DON'T NEED ME TO GO WITH? THIS IS THEIR FIRST FULL TRIAL AS NORMAL KIDS. I COULD ALWAYS TELL KING COLE TO DO WITHOUT ME.
NONSENSE. GO TO YOUR MEETING. WE'LL BE FINE. THESE CUBS ARE TRAINED BY NOW, OR THEY'LL NEVER BE. AND WE'LL ALL BE PERFECTLY SAFE WITH GHOST ALONG.
HAVE FUN!
MIND YOUR MOTHER!
TAXI
MUND-E
HOW ABOUT SOME CANDY, POPS? ON ME.

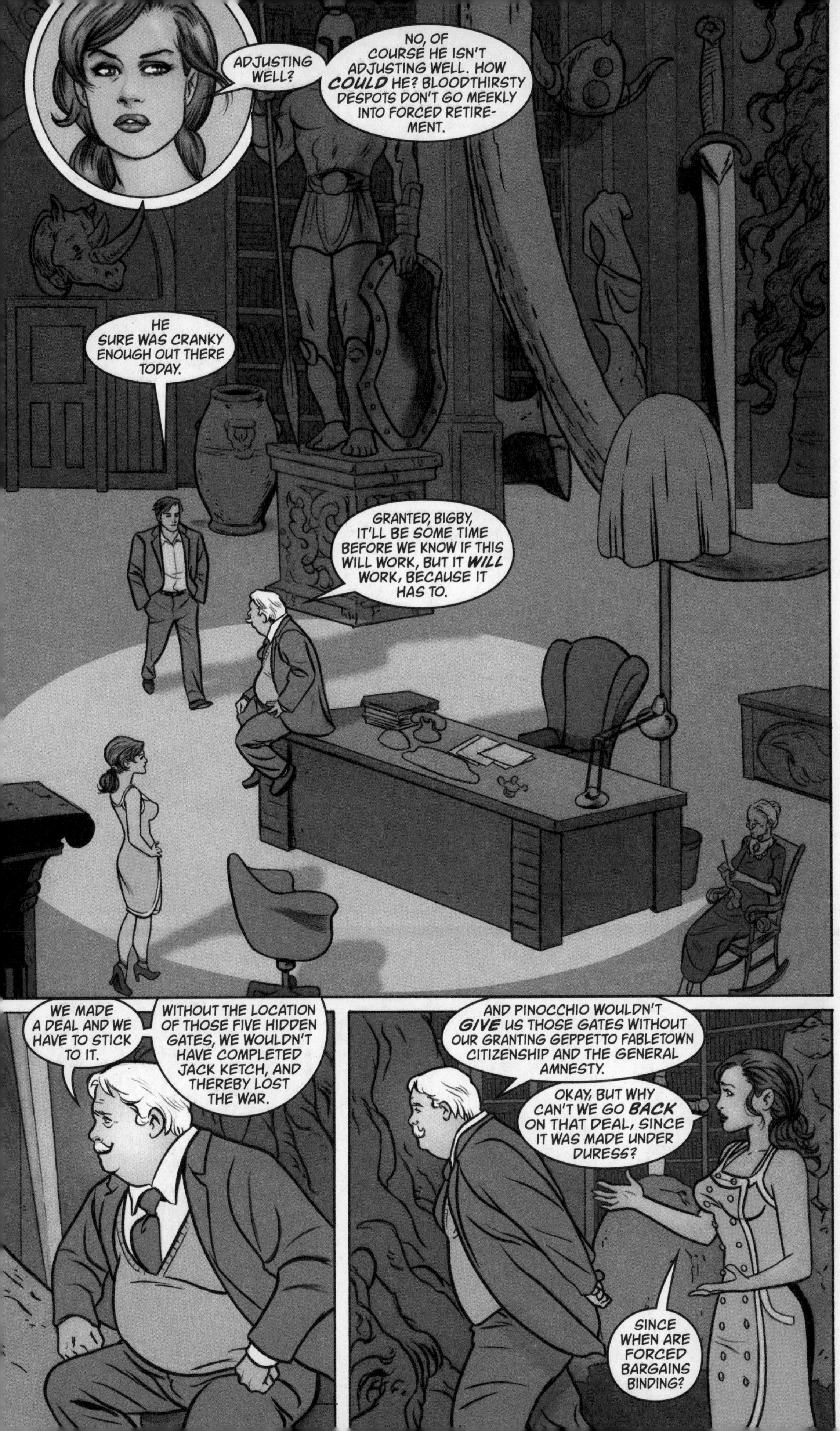
ADJUSTING WELL?
NO, OF COURSE HE ISN'T ADJUSTING WELL. HOW COULD HE? BLOODTHIRSTY DESPOTS DON'T GO MEEKLY INTO FORCED RETIREMENT.
HE SURE WAS CRANKY ENOUGH OUT THERE TODAY.
GRANTED, BIGBY, IT'LL BE SOME TIME BEFORE WE KNOW IF THIS WILL WORK, BUT IT WILL WORK, BECAUSE IT HAS TO.
WE MADE A DEAL AND WE HAVE TO STICK TO IT.
WITHOUT THE LOCATION OF THOSE FIVE HIDDEN GATES, WE WOULDN'T HAVE COMPLETED JACK KETCH, AND THEREBY LOST THE WAR.
AND PINOCCHIO WOULDN'T GIVE US THOSE GATES WITHOUT OUR GRANTING GEPPETTO FABLETOWN CITIZENSHIP AND THE GENERAL AMNESTY.
OKAY, BUT WHY CAN'T WE GO BACK ON THAT DEAL, SINCE IT WAS MADE UNDER DURESS?
SINCE WHEN ARE FORCED BARGAINS BINDING?

OH, I WOULDN'T WORRY TOO MUCH ABOUT THAT, BEAUTY.

THE AMNESTY ONLY COVERS THE ATROCITIES HE'S COMMITTED SO FAR.

SOONER RATHER THAN LATER, HE'LL COMMIT SOME *NEW* CRIME. BY NOW IT'S IN HIS NATURE.

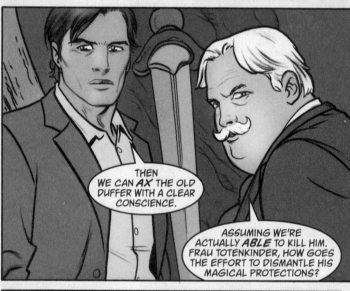

SLOWLY, KING COLE. SLOWLY.

SINCE IT'S IMPORTANT THAT HE NEVER SUSPECT WE'RE DOING IT, WE HAVE TO TREAD CAREFULLY, MY COLLEAGUES AND I.

THEN WE CAN *AX* THE OLD DUFFER WITH A CLEAR CONSCIENCE.

ASSUMING WE'RE ACTUALLY *ABLE* TO KILL HIM. FRAU TOTENKINDER, HOW GOES THE EFFORT TO DISMANTLE HIS MAGICAL PROTECTIONS?

SPEAKING OF THINGS HE SHOULD NEVER SUSPECT, WHEN IS OUR ALL-SEEING *BLIND MAN* GOING TO GET A LOOK AT HIM?

AMNESTY OR NOT, WE NEED TO KNOW THE FULL EXTENT OF HIS PAST MISDEEDS.

AND THE NATURE OF ANY SURVIVING IMPERIAL POWERS ARRAYING AGAINST US.

THE BOYS SHOULD BE ACCIDENTALLY RUNNING INTO KAY ANY MINUTE NOW.

SEE? THAT DIDN'T GO SO BADLY. EVEN THOUGH THEY OPENLY *DESPISED* YOU, THEY STILL SERVED YOU.

AND THEY DIDN'T EVEN SPIT IN YOUR BAG--AT LEAST NOT WHILE I WAS LOOKING. WASN'T THAT NICE OF THEM?

GOOD CHOICE GETTING THE HONEY CLUSTERS, POPS. THEY'RE THE BEST.

WHERE WAS THE BEAR?

HUH?

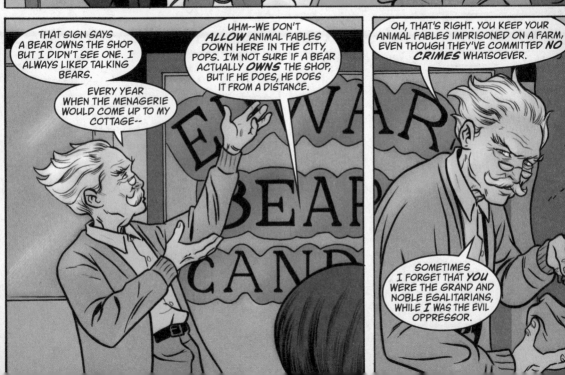

THAT SIGN SAYS A BEAR OWNS THE SHOP BUT I DIDN'T SEE ONE. I ALWAYS LIKED TALKING BEARS.

EVERY YEAR WHEN THE MENAGERIE WOULD COME UP TO MY COTTAGE--

UHM--WE DON'T *ALLOW* ANIMAL FABLES DOWN HERE IN THE CITY, POPS. I'M NOT SURE IF A BEAR ACTUALLY *OWNS* THE SHOP, BUT IF HE DOES, HE DOES IT FROM A DISTANCE.

OH, THAT'S RIGHT. YOU KEEP YOUR ANIMAL FABLES IMPRISONED ON A FARM, EVEN THOUGH THEY'VE COMMITTED *NO CRIMES* WHATSOEVER.

SOMETIMES I FORGET THAT *YOU* WERE THE GRAND AND NOBLE EGALITARIANS, WHILE *I* WAS THE EVIL OPPRESSOR.

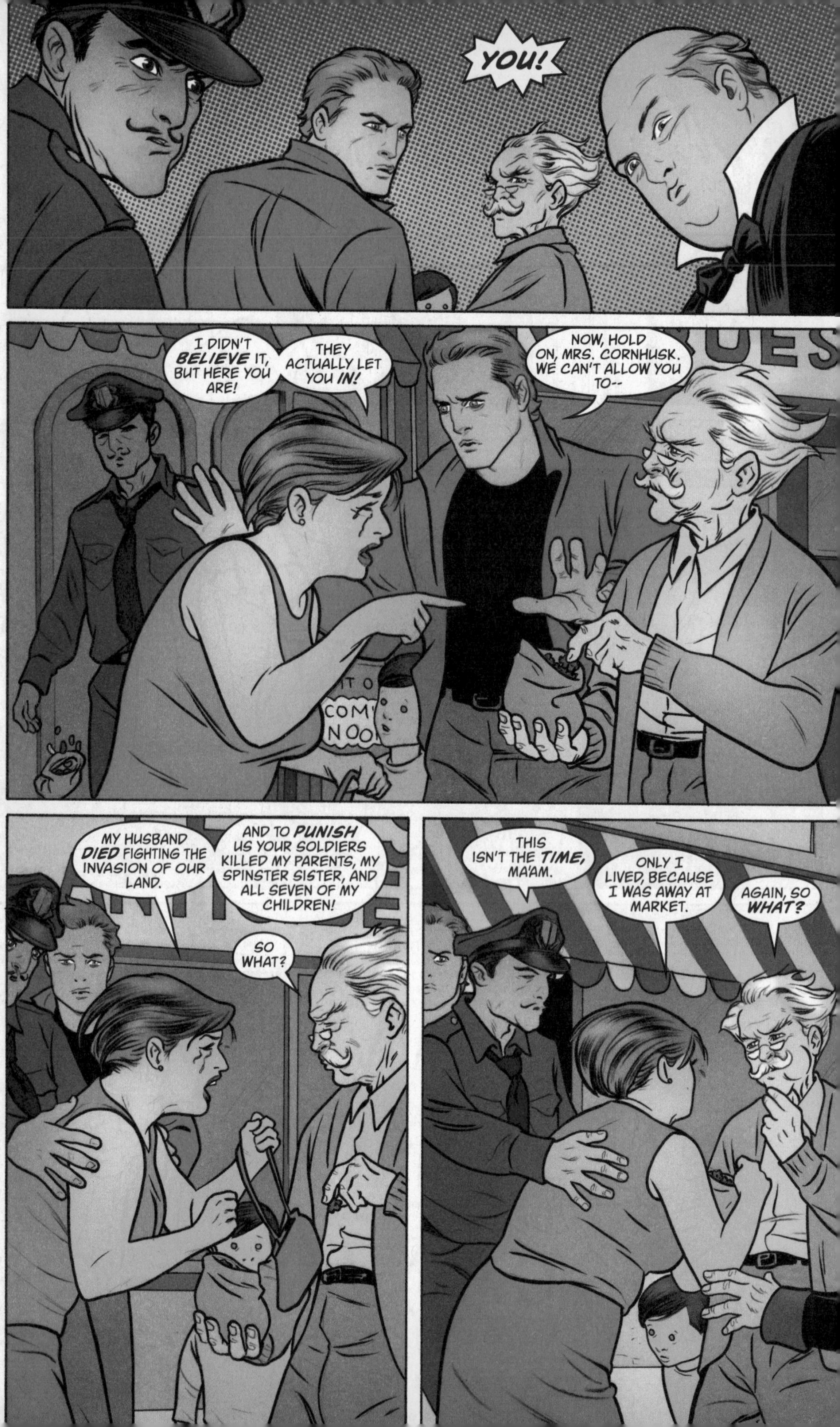
YOU!
I DIDN'T BELIEVE IT, BUT HERE YOU ARE!
THEY ACTUALLY LET YOU IN!
NOW, HOLD ON, MRS. CORNHUSK. WE CAN'T ALLOW YOU TO--
MY HUSBAND DIED FIGHTING THE INVASION OF OUR LAND.
AND TO PUNISH US YOUR SOLDIERS KILLED MY PARENTS, MY SPINSTER SISTER, AND ALL SEVEN OF MY CHILDREN!
SO WHAT?
THIS ISN'T THE TIME, MA'AM.
ONLY I LIVED, BECAUSE I WAS AWAY AT MARKET.
AGAIN, SO WHAT?

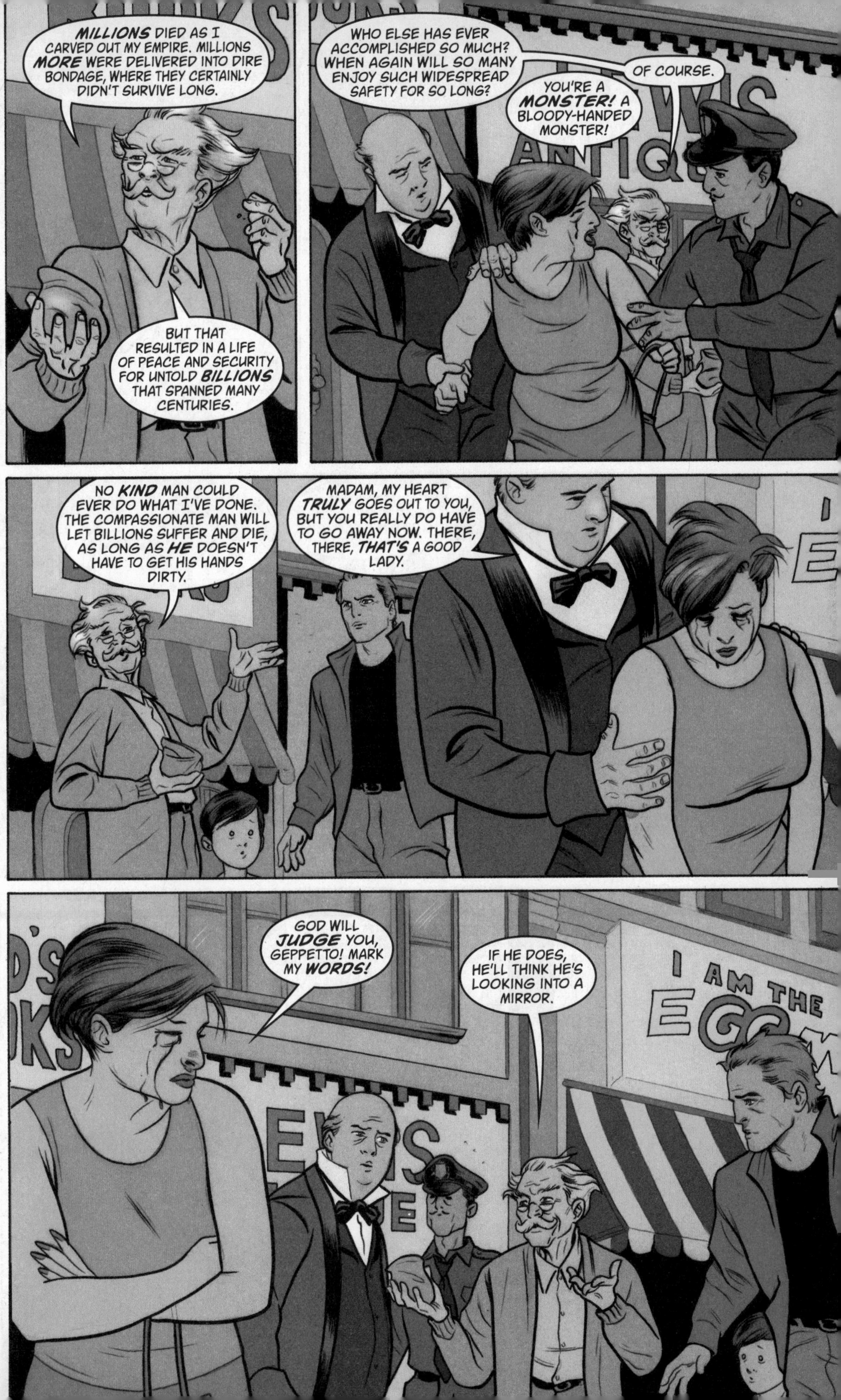
MILLIONS DIED AS I CARVED OUT MY EMPIRE. MILLIONS MORE WERE DELIVERED INTO DIRE BONDAGE, WHERE THEY CERTAINLY DIDN'T SURVIVE LONG.
BUT THAT RESULTED IN A LIFE OF PEACE AND SECURITY FOR UNTOLD BILLIONS THAT SPANNED MANY CENTURIES.
WHO ELSE HAS EVER ACCOMPLISHED SO MUCH? WHEN AGAIN WILL SO MANY ENJOY SUCH WIDESPREAD SAFETY FOR SO LONG?
OF COURSE.
YOU'RE A MONSTER! A BLOODY-HANDED MONSTER!
ANTIQU
NO KIND MAN COULD EVER DO WHAT I'VE DONE. THE COMPASSIONATE MAN WILL LET BILLIONS SUFFER AND DIE, AS LONG AS HE DOESN'T HAVE TO GET HIS HANDS DIRTY.
MADAM, MY HEART TRULY GOES OUT TO YOU, BUT YOU REALLY DO HAVE TO GO AWAY NOW. THERE, THERE, THAT'S A GOOD LADY.
GOD WILL JUDGE YOU, GEPPETTO! MARK MY WORDS!
IF HE DOES, HE'LL THINK HE'S LOOKING INTO A MIRROR.
I AM THE EGO

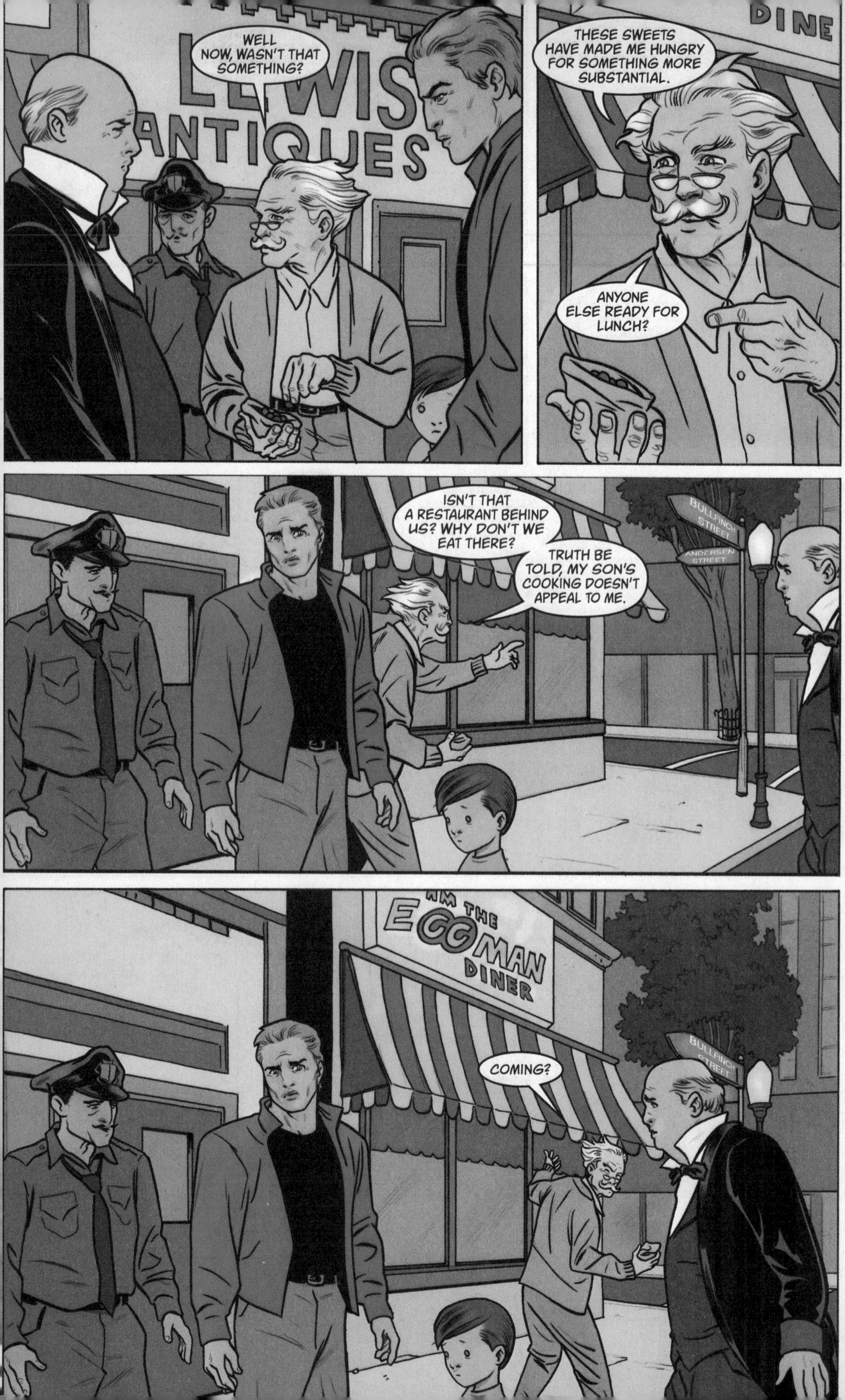
LEWIS ANTIQUES
WELL NOW, WASN'T THAT SOMETHING?
DINE
THESE SWEETS HAVE MADE ME HUNGRY FOR SOMETHING MORE SUBSTANTIAL.
ANYONE ELSE READY FOR LUNCH?
ISN'T THAT A RESTAURANT BEHIND US? WHY DON'T WE EAT THERE?
TRUTH BE TOLD, MY SON'S COOKING DOESN'T APPEAL TO ME.
BULLFINCH STREET
ANDERSEN STREET
EGGMAN DINER
BULLFINCH STREET
COMING?

ABSOLUTELY **NOT**!

BUT, VULCO! HE'S A MEMBER OF FABLETOWN NOW!

SO WHAT?

MANAGEMENT RESE RIGHT TO REFUSE S R ANY REAS

ALL THAT MEANS IS I HAVE TO PUT UP WITH HIM LIVING IN OUR COMMUNITY, AND I'M NOT SUPPOSED TO **BRING UP** HIS PAST CRIMES. YOU'LL NOTICE I DIDN'T MENTION ONE OF THEM.

BUT NOTHING IN FABLETOWN LAW REQUIRES ME TO **FEED** HIM, OR EVEN **ALLOW** HIM INTO MY DINER.

SEE THAT NOTICE? "THE MANAGEMENT"--THAT'S ME-- "RESERVES THE RIGHT TO REFUSE SERVICE FOR ANY REASON."

MANAGEMENT RESERVES THE RIGHT TO REFUSE SERVICE R ANY REASON

AND UNLIKE OUT IN THE MUNDY, OUR PRIVATE POLICIES STILL HAVE SOME **TOOTH** BEHIND THEM. YOU CAN'T SUE ME FOR MAKING YOU **FEEL** BAD.

AND DON'T BOTHER TRYING THE BRANSTOCK, OR THE YELLOW BRICK ROADHOUSE NEITHER.

WE'VE ALREADY PLEDGED TO STAND **TOGETHER** ON THIS.

GO OUT INTO THE **MUNDY** IF YOU'RE HUNGRY, OLD MAN. YOU'LL NEVER FIND SO MUCH AS A **CRUMB** TO EAT HERE--NOT AS LONG AS **I** OWN THE EGGMAN.

BRANSTOCK TAVERN

GLASS SLIPPER SLIPPER

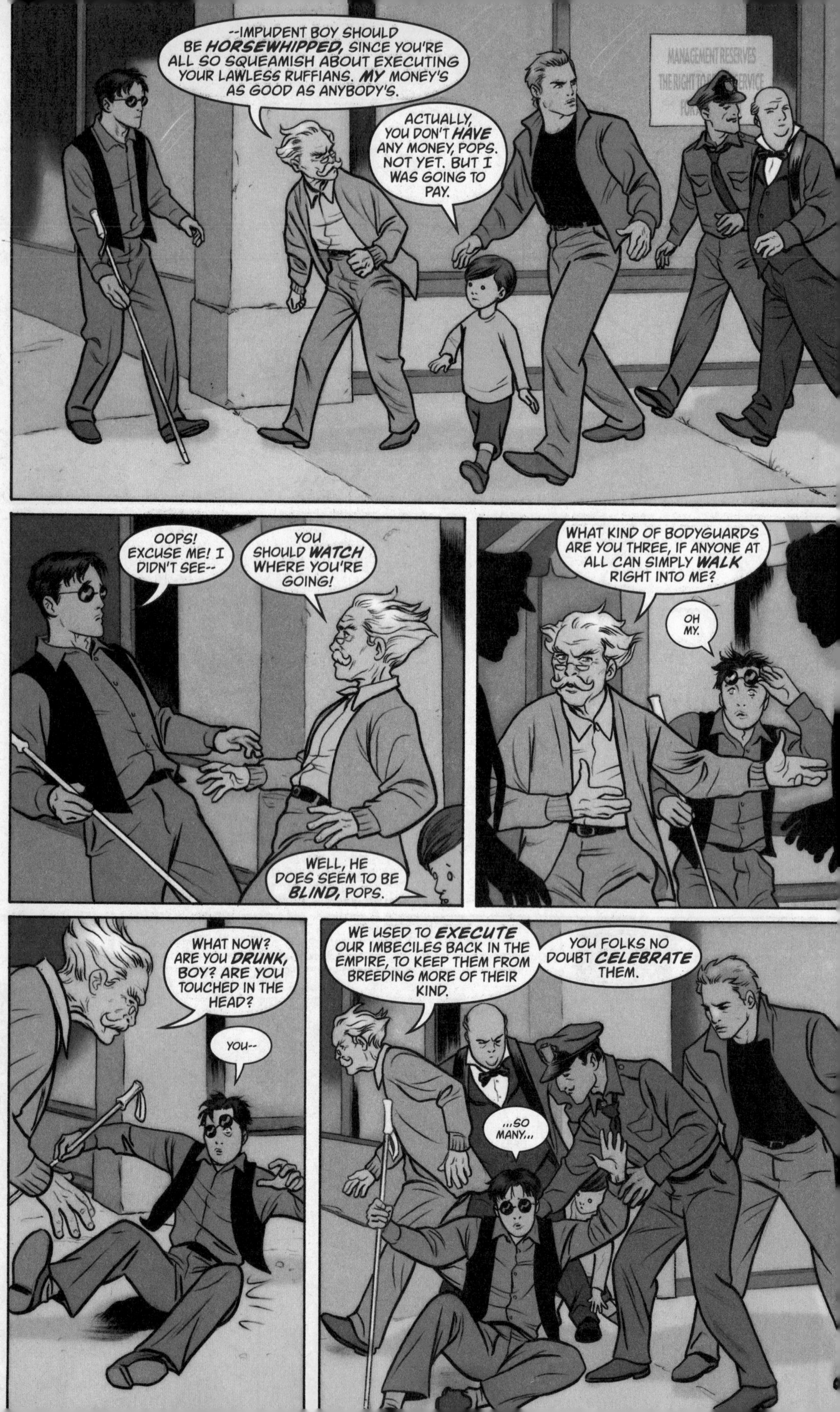
--IMPUDENT BOY SHOULD BE HORSEWHIPPED, SINCE YOU'RE ALL SO SQUEAMISH ABOUT EXECUTING YOUR LAWLESS RUFFIANS. MY MONEY'S AS GOOD AS ANYBODY'S.
MANAGEMENT RESERVES
ACTUALLY, YOU DON'T HAVE ANY MONEY, POPS. NOT YET. BUT I WAS GOING TO PAY.
OOPS! EXCUSE ME! I DIDN'T SEE--
YOU SHOULD WATCH WHERE YOU'RE GOING!
WELL, HE DOES SEEM TO BE BLIND, POPS.
WHAT KIND OF BODYGUARDS ARE YOU THREE, IF ANYONE AT ALL CAN SIMPLY WALK RIGHT INTO ME?
OH MY.
WHAT NOW? ARE YOU DRUNK, BOY? ARE YOU TOUCHED IN THE HEAD?
YOU--
WE USED TO EXECUTE OUR IMBECILES BACK IN THE EMPIRE, TO KEEP THEM FROM BREEDING MORE OF THEIR KIND.
YOU FOLKS NO DOUBT CELEBRATE THEM.
...SO MANY...

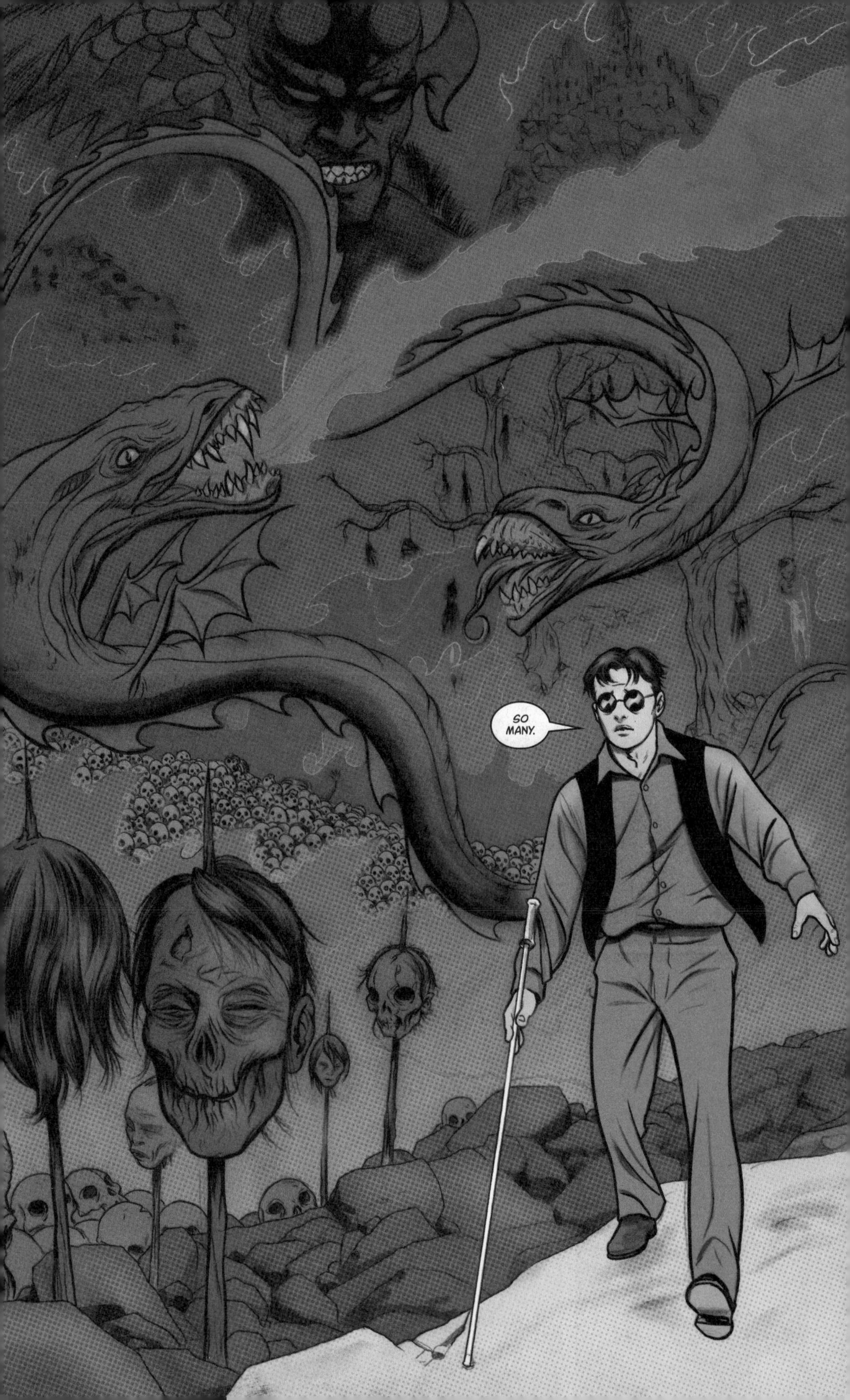
SO MANY.

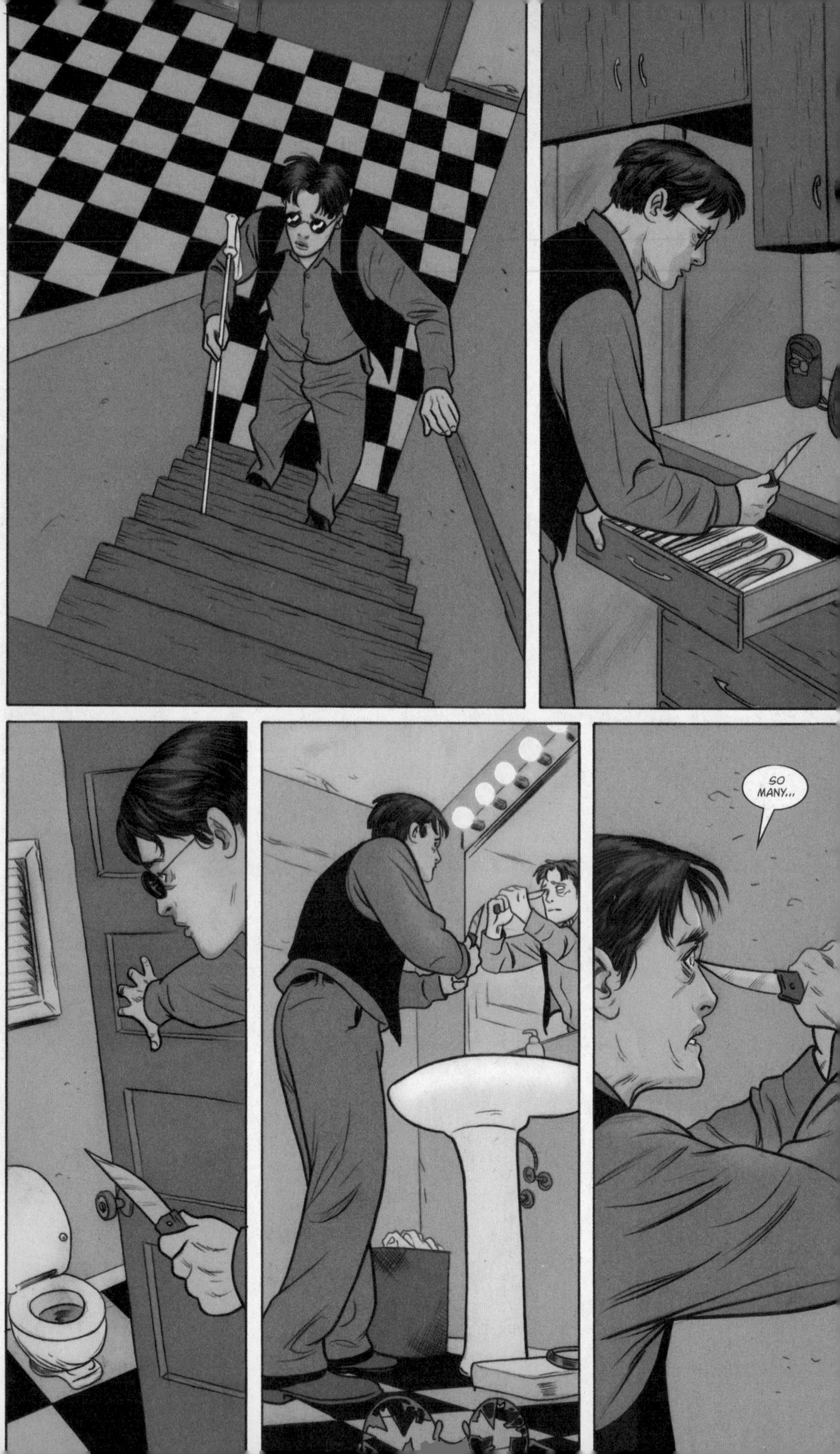
SO MANY...

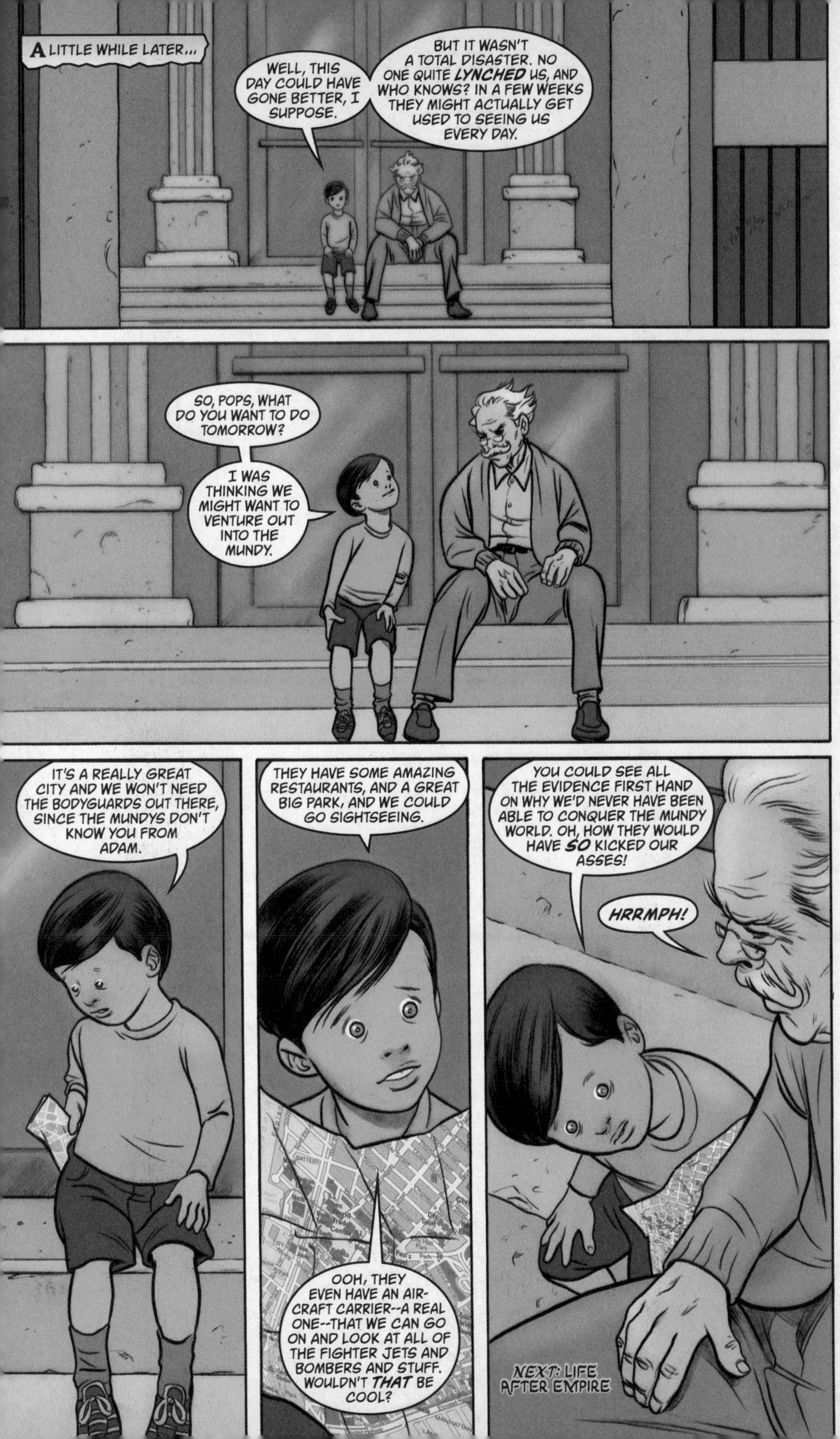
A LITTLE WHILE LATER...
WELL, THIS DAY COULD HAVE GONE BETTER, I SUPPOSE.
BUT IT WASN'T A TOTAL DISASTER. NO ONE QUITE LYNCHED US, AND WHO KNOWS? IN A FEW WEEKS THEY MIGHT ACTUALLY GET USED TO SEEING US EVERY DAY.
SO, POPS, WHAT DO YOU WANT TO DO TOMORROW?
I WAS THINKING WE MIGHT WANT TO VENTURE OUT INTO THE MUNDY.
IT'S A REALLY GREAT CITY AND WE WON'T NEED THE BODYGUARDS OUT THERE, SINCE THE MUNDYS DON'T KNOW YOU FROM ADAM.
THEY HAVE SOME AMAZING RESTAURANTS, AND A GREAT BIG PARK, AND WE COULD GO SIGHTSEEING.
OOH, THEY EVEN HAVE AN AIR-CRAFT CARRIER--A REAL ONE--THAT WE CAN GO ON AND LOOK AT ALL OF THE FIGHTER JETS AND BOMBERS AND STUFF. WOULDN'T THAT BE COOL?
YOU COULD SEE ALL THE EVIDENCE FIRST HAND ON WHY WE'D NEVER HAVE BEEN ABLE TO CONQUER THE MUNDY WORLD. OH, HOW THEY WOULD HAVE SO KICKED OUR ASSES!
HRRMPH!
NEXT: LIFE AFTER EMPIRE

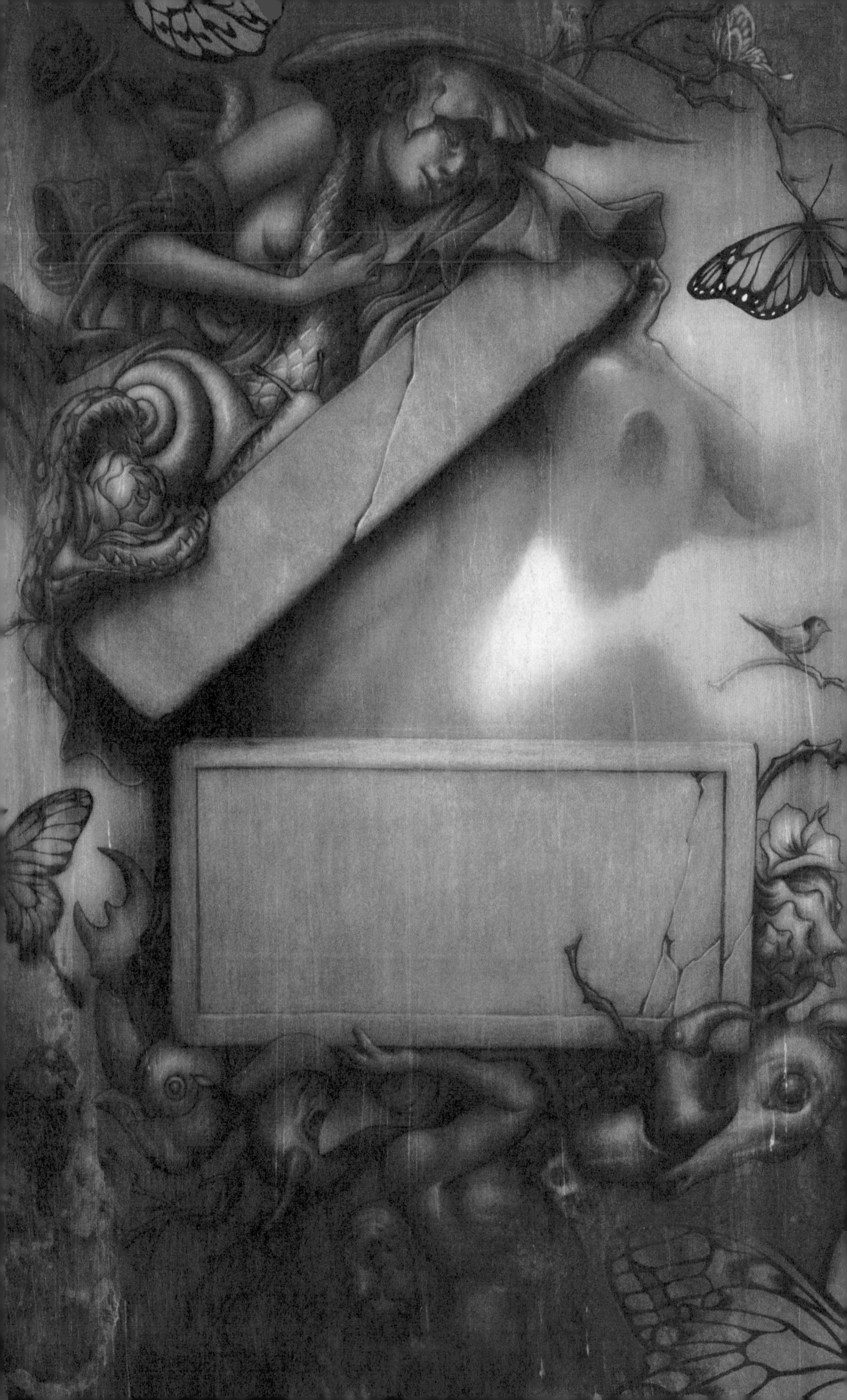

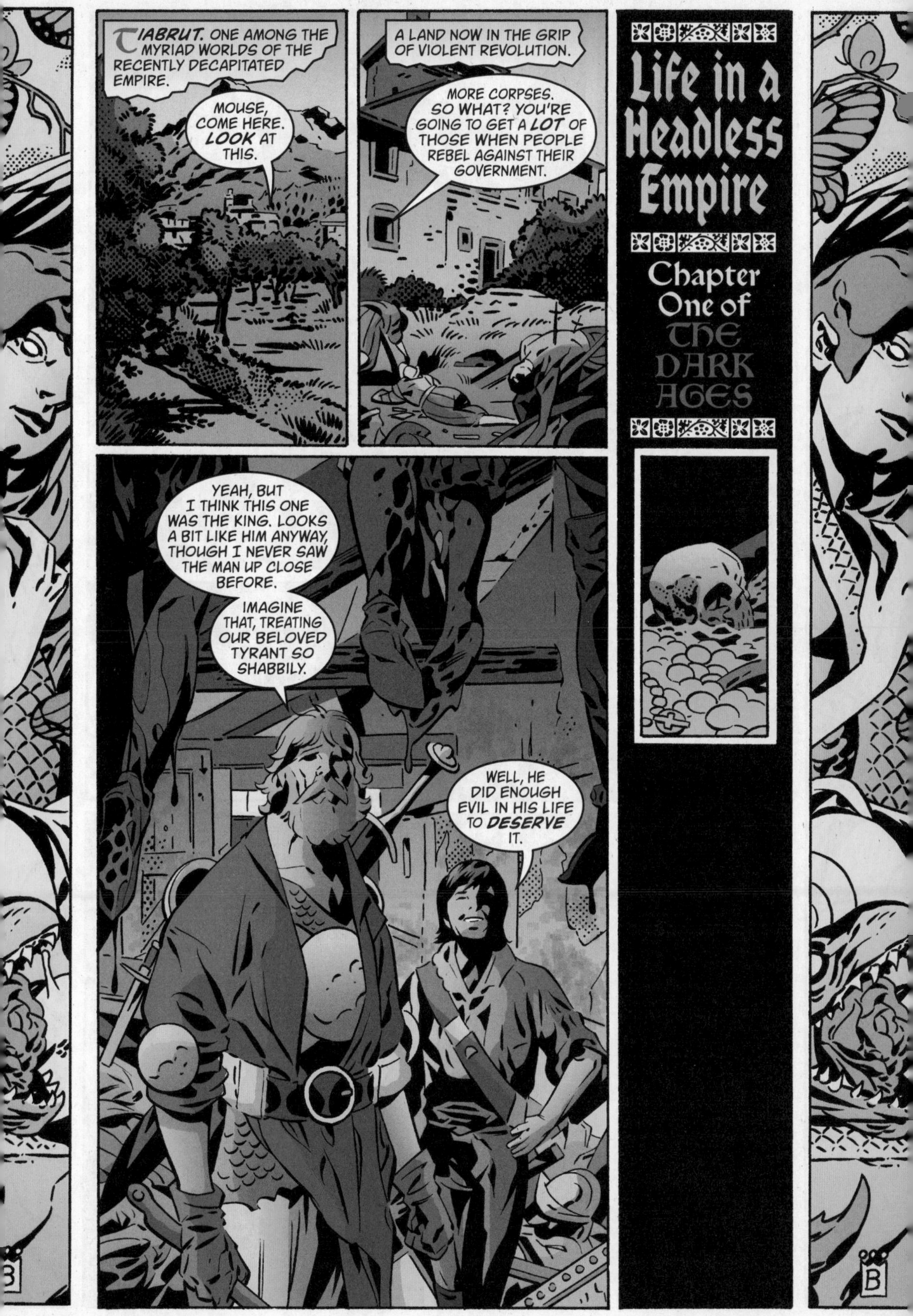
TIABRUT. ONE AMONG THE MYRIAD WORLDS OF THE RECENTLY DECAPITATED EMPIRE.
MOUSE, COME HERE. LOOK AT THIS.
A LAND NOW IN THE GRIP OF VIOLENT REVOLUTION.
MORE CORPSES. SO WHAT? YOU'RE GOING TO GET A LOT OF THOSE WHEN PEOPLE REBEL AGAINST THEIR GOVERNMENT.
Life in a Headless Empire
Chapter One of THE DARK AGES
YEAH, BUT I THINK THIS ONE WAS THE KING. LOOKS A BIT LIKE HIM ANYWAY, THOUGH I NEVER SAW THE MAN UP CLOSE BEFORE.
IMAGINE THAT, TREATING OUR BELOVED TYRANT SO SHABBILY.
WELL, HE DID ENOUGH EVIL IN HIS LIFE TO DESERVE IT.

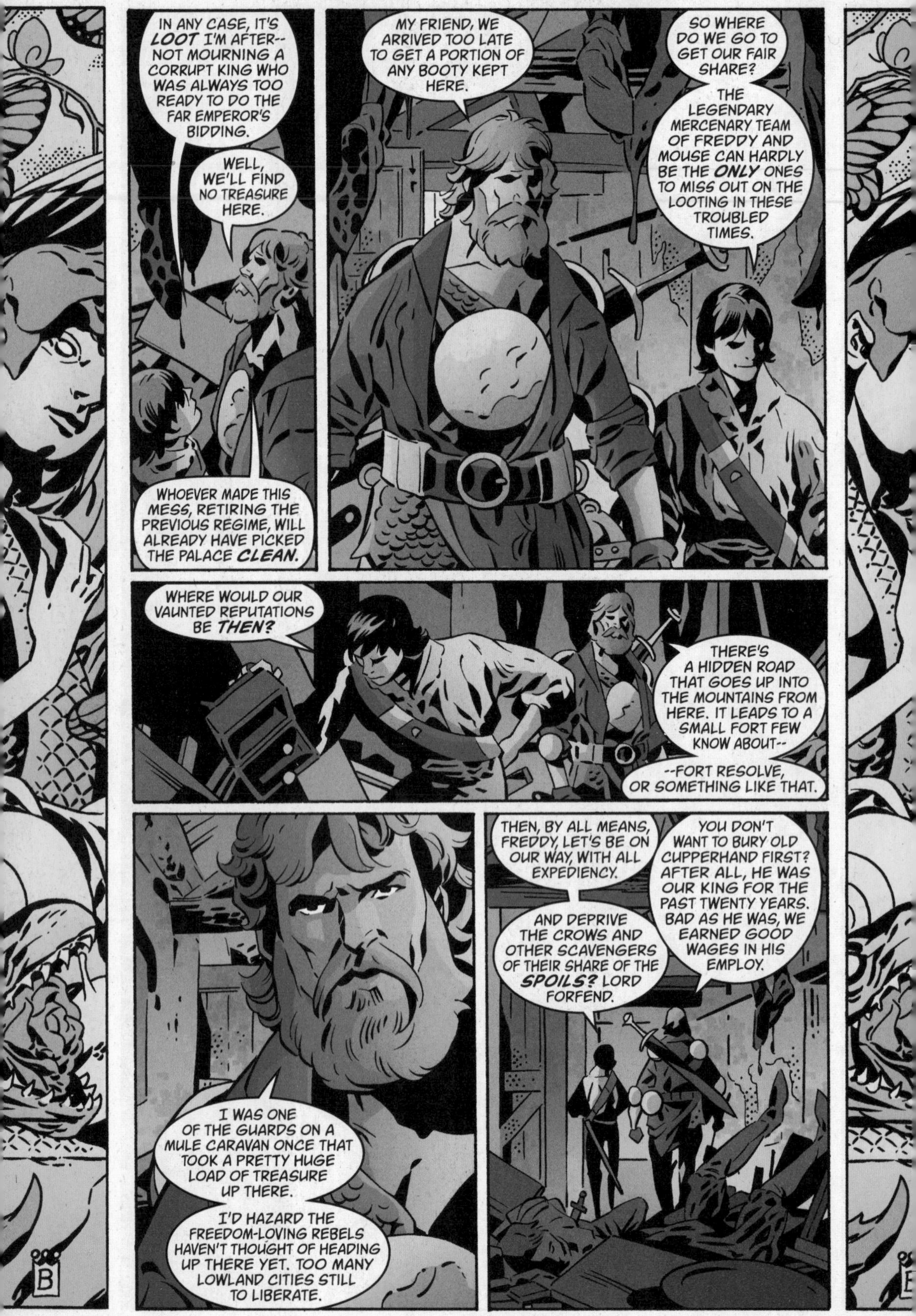
IN ANY CASE, IT'S LOOT I'M AFTER-- NOT MOURNING A CORRUPT KING WHO WAS ALWAYS TOO READY TO DO THE FAR EMPEROR'S BIDDING.
WELL, WE'LL FIND NO TREASURE HERE.
WHOEVER MADE THIS MESS, RETIRING THE PREVIOUS REGIME, WILL ALREADY HAVE PICKED THE PALACE CLEAN.
MY FRIEND, WE ARRIVED TOO LATE TO GET A PORTION OF ANY BOOTY KEPT HERE.
SO WHERE DO WE GO TO GET OUR FAIR SHARE?
THE LEGENDARY MERCENARY TEAM OF FREDDY AND MOUSE CAN HARDLY BE THE ONLY ONES TO MISS OUT ON THE LOOTING IN THESE TROUBLED TIMES.
WHERE WOULD OUR VAUNTED REPUTATIONS BE THEN?
THERE'S A HIDDEN ROAD THAT GOES UP INTO THE MOUNTAINS FROM HERE. IT LEADS TO A SMALL FORT FEW KNOW ABOUT--
--FORT RESOLVE, OR SOMETHING LIKE THAT.
I WAS ONE OF THE GUARDS ON A MULE CARAVAN ONCE THAT TOOK A PRETTY HUGE LOAD OF TREASURE UP THERE.
I'D HAZARD THE FREEDOM-LOVING REBELS HAVEN'T THOUGHT OF HEADING UP THERE YET. TOO MANY LOWLAND CITIES STILL TO LIBERATE.
THEN, BY ALL MEANS, FREDDY, LET'S BE ON OUR WAY, WITH ALL EXPEDIENCY.
AND DEPRIVE THE CROWS AND OTHER SCAVENGERS OF THEIR SHARE OF THE SPOILS? LORD FORFEND.
YOU DON'T WANT TO BURY OLD CUPPERHAND FIRST? AFTER ALL, HE WAS OUR KING FOR THE PAST TWENTY YEARS. BAD AS HE WAS, WE EARNED GOOD WAGES IN HIS EMPLOY.

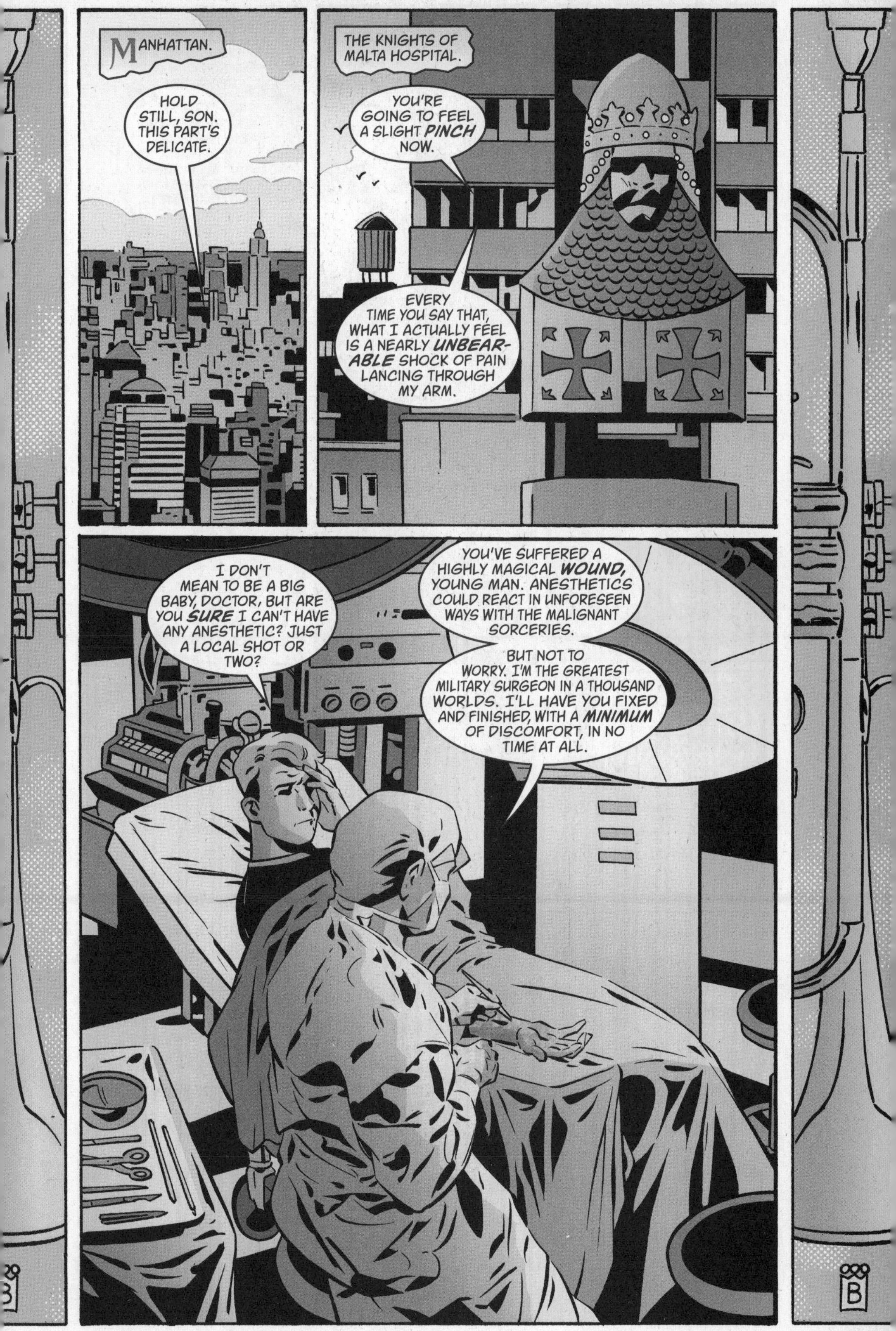
MANHATTAN.
HOLD STILL, SON. THIS PART'S DELICATE.
THE KNIGHTS OF MALTA HOSPITAL.
YOU'RE GOING TO FEEL A SLIGHT PINCH NOW.
EVERY TIME YOU SAY THAT, WHAT I ACTUALLY FEEL IS A NEARLY UNBEARABLE SHOCK OF PAIN LANCING THROUGH MY ARM.
I DON'T MEAN TO BE A BIG BABY, DOCTOR, BUT ARE YOU SURE I CAN'T HAVE ANY ANESTHETIC? JUST A LOCAL SHOT OR TWO?
YOU'VE SUFFERED A HIGHLY MAGICAL WOUND, YOUNG MAN. ANESTHETICS COULD REACT IN UNFORESEEN WAYS WITH THE MALIGNANT SORCERIES.
BUT NOT TO WORRY. I'M THE GREATEST MILITARY SURGEON IN A THOUSAND WORLDS. I'LL HAVE YOU FIXED AND FINISHED, WITH A MINIMUM OF DISCOMFORT, IN NO TIME AT ALL.

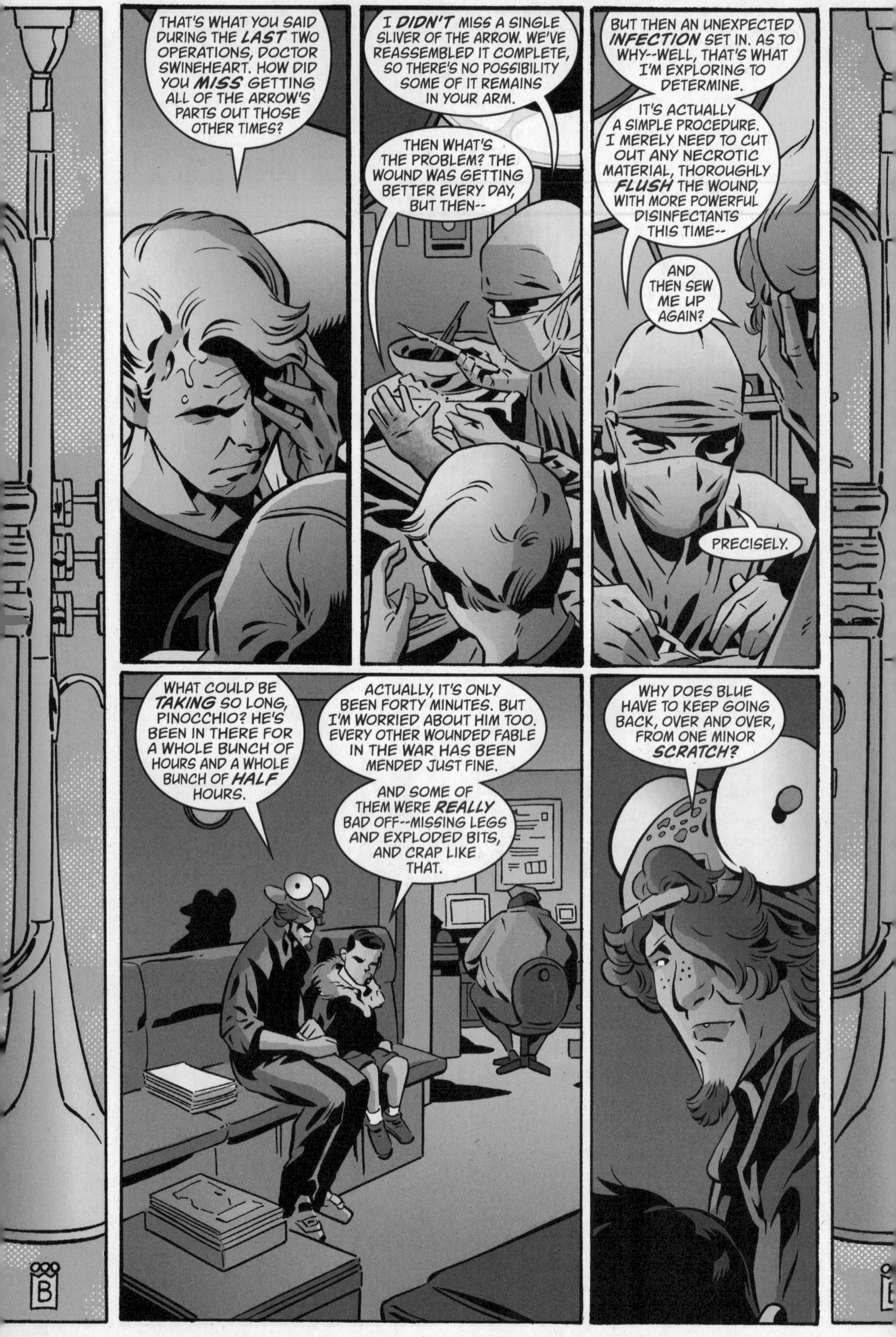
THAT'S WHAT YOU SAID DURING THE LAST TWO OPERATIONS, DOCTOR SWINEHEART. HOW DID YOU MISS GETTING ALL OF THE ARROW'S PARTS OUT THOSE OTHER TIMES?
I DIDN'T MISS A SINGLE SLIVER OF THE ARROW. WE'VE REASSEMBLED IT COMPLETE, SO THERE'S NO POSSIBILITY SOME OF IT REMAINS IN YOUR ARM.
THEN WHAT'S THE PROBLEM? THE WOUND WAS GETTING BETTER EVERY DAY, BUT THEN--
BUT THEN AN UNEXPECTED INFECTION SET IN. AS TO WHY--WELL, THAT'S WHAT I'M EXPLORING TO DETERMINE.
IT'S ACTUALLY A SIMPLE PROCEDURE. I MERELY NEED TO CUT OUT ANY NECROTIC MATERIAL, THOROUGHLY FLUSH THE WOUND, WITH MORE POWERFUL DISINFECTANTS THIS TIME--
AND THEN SEW ME UP AGAIN?
PRECISELY.
WHAT COULD BE TAKING SO LONG, PINOCCHIO? HE'S BEEN IN THERE FOR A WHOLE BUNCH OF HOURS AND A WHOLE BUNCH OF HALF HOURS.
ACTUALLY, IT'S ONLY BEEN FORTY MINUTES. BUT I'M WORRIED ABOUT HIM TOO. EVERY OTHER WOUNDED FABLE IN THE WAR HAS BEEN MENDED JUST FINE.
AND SOME OF THEM WERE REALLY BAD OFF--MISSING LEGS AND EXPLODED BITS, AND CRAP LIKE THAT.
WHY DOES BLUE HAVE TO KEEP GOING BACK, OVER AND OVER, FROM ONE MINOR SCRATCH?

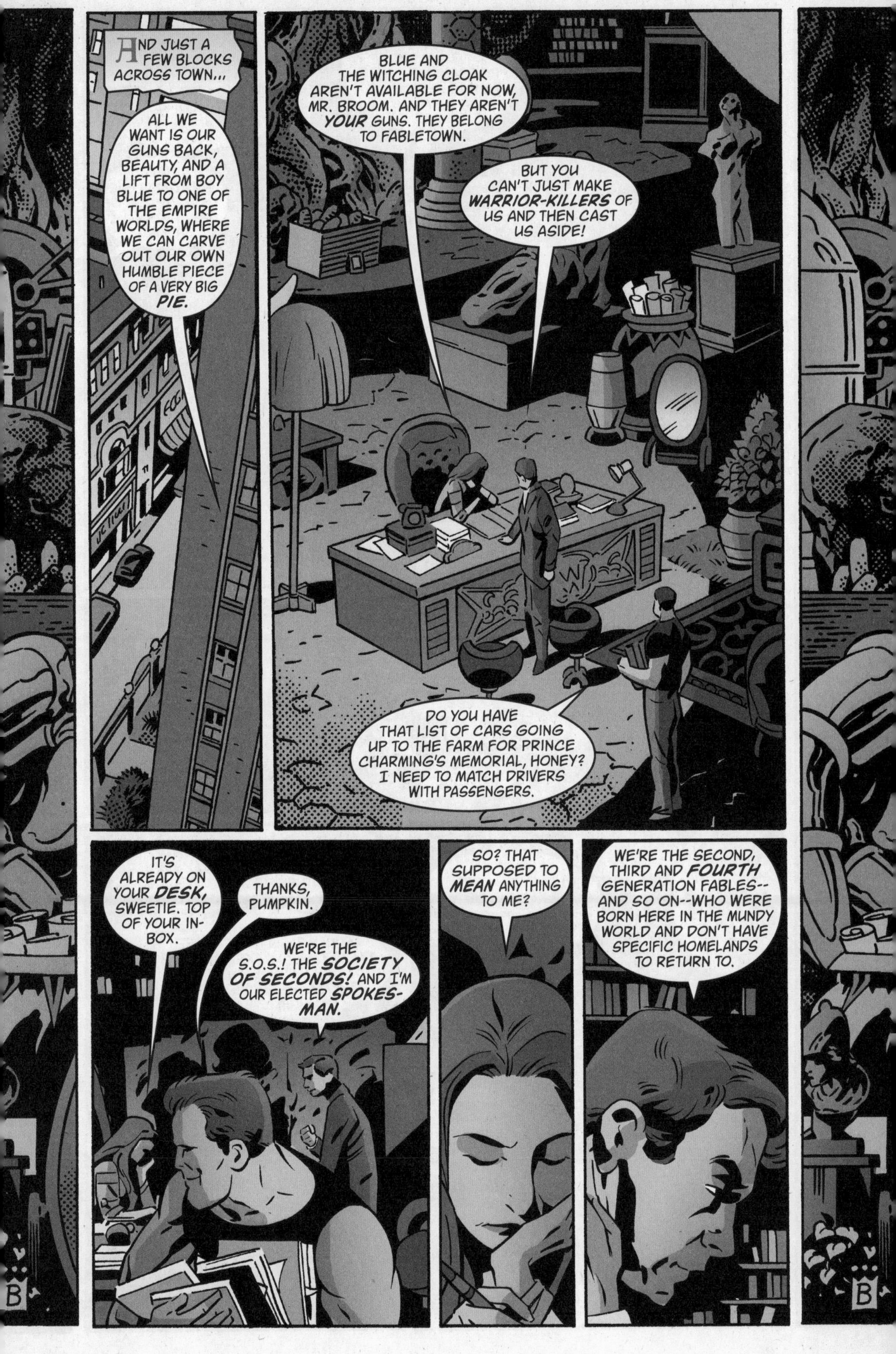
AND JUST A FEW BLOCKS ACROSS TOWN...
ALL WE WANT IS OUR GUNS BACK, BEAUTY, AND A LIFT FROM BOY BLUE TO ONE OF THE EMPIRE WORLDS, WHERE WE CAN CARVE OUT OUR OWN HUMBLE PIECE OF A VERY BIG PIE.
BLUE AND THE WITCHING CLOAK AREN'T AVAILABLE FOR NOW, MR. BROOM. AND THEY AREN'T YOUR GUNS. THEY BELONG TO FABLETOWN.
BUT YOU CAN'T JUST MAKE WARRIOR-KILLERS OF US AND THEN CAST US ASIDE!
DO YOU HAVE THAT LIST OF CARS GOING UP TO THE FARM FOR PRINCE CHARMING'S MEMORIAL, HONEY? I NEED TO MATCH DRIVERS WITH PASSENGERS.
IT'S ALREADY ON YOUR DESK, SWEETIE. TOP OF YOUR IN-BOX.
THANKS, PUMPKIN.
WE'RE THE S.O.S.! THE SOCIETY OF SECONDS! AND I'M OUR ELECTED SPOKES-MAN.
SO? THAT SUPPOSED TO MEAN ANYTHING TO ME?
WE'RE THE SECOND, THIRD AND FOURTH GENERATION FABLES--AND SO ON--WHO WERE BORN HERE IN THE MUNDY WORLD AND DON'T HAVE SPECIFIC HOMELANDS TO RETURN TO.

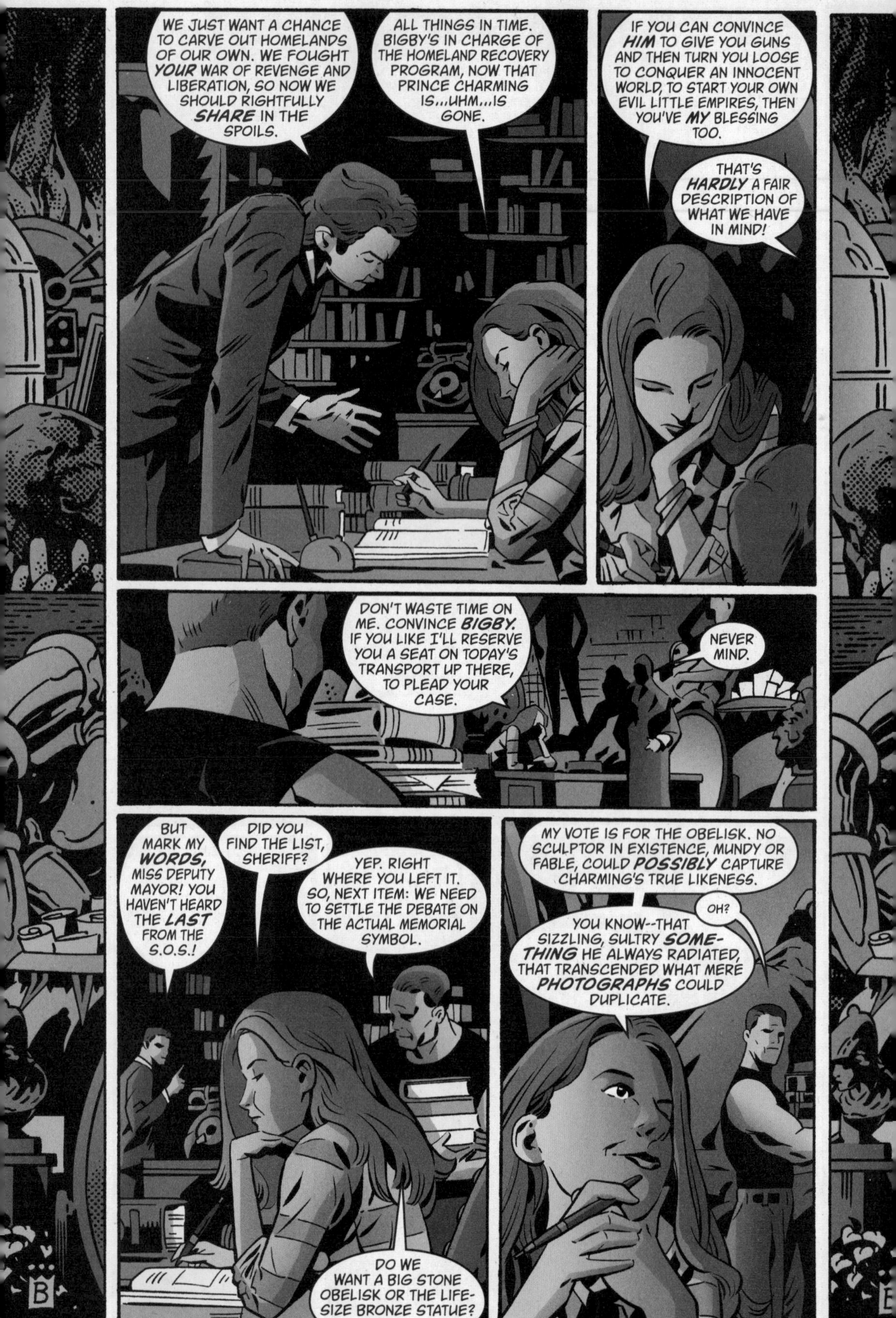
WE JUST WANT A CHANCE TO CARVE OUT HOMELANDS OF OUR OWN. WE FOUGHT YOUR WAR OF REVENGE AND LIBERATION, SO NOW WE SHOULD RIGHTFULLY SHARE IN THE SPOILS.
ALL THINGS IN TIME. BIGBY'S IN CHARGE OF THE HOMELAND RECOVERY PROGRAM, NOW THAT PRINCE CHARMING IS...UHM...IS GONE.
IF YOU CAN CONVINCE HIM TO GIVE YOU GUNS AND THEN TURN YOU LOOSE TO CONQUER AN INNOCENT WORLD, TO START YOUR OWN EVIL LITTLE EMPIRES, THEN YOU'VE MY BLESSING TOO.
THAT'S HARDLY A FAIR DESCRIPTION OF WHAT WE HAVE IN MIND!
DON'T WASTE TIME ON ME. CONVINCE BIGBY. IF YOU LIKE I'LL RESERVE YOU A SEAT ON TODAY'S TRANSPORT UP THERE, TO PLEAD YOUR CASE.
NEVER MIND.
BUT MARK MY WORDS, MISS DEPUTY MAYOR! YOU HAVEN'T HEARD THE LAST FROM THE S.O.S.!
DID YOU FIND THE LIST, SHERIFF?
YEP. RIGHT WHERE YOU LEFT IT. SO, NEXT ITEM: WE NEED TO SETTLE THE DEBATE ON THE ACTUAL MEMORIAL SYMBOL.
DO WE WANT A BIG STONE OBELISK OR THE LIFE-SIZE BRONZE STATUE?
MY VOTE IS FOR THE OBELISK. NO SCULPTOR IN EXISTENCE, MUNDY OR FABLE, COULD POSSIBLY CAPTURE CHARMING'S TRUE LIKENESS.
OH?
YOU KNOW--THAT SIZZLING, SULTRY SOME-THING HE ALWAYS RADIATED, THAT TRANSCENDED WHAT MERE PHOTOGRAPHS COULD DUPLICATE.

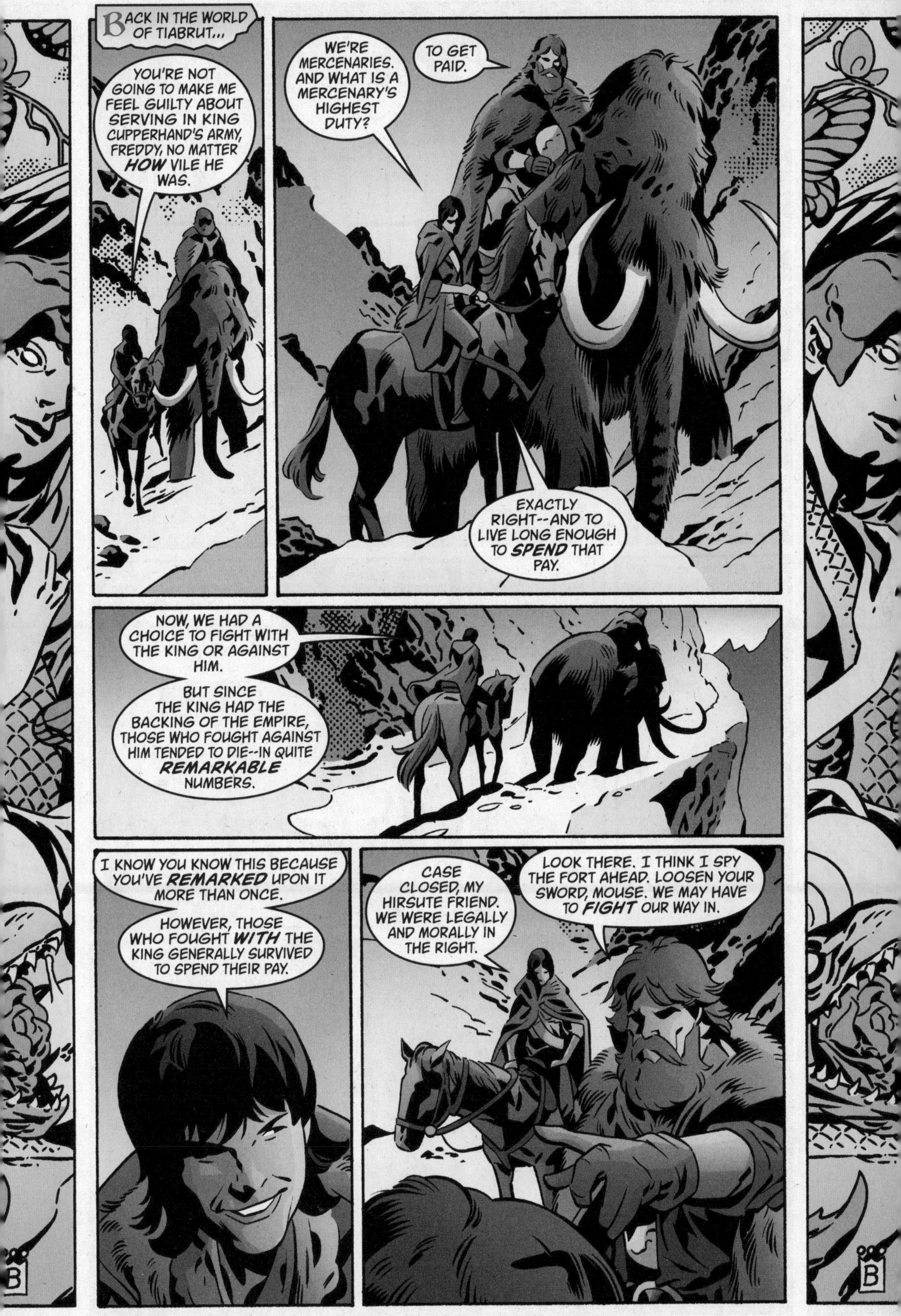
BACK IN THE WORLD OF TIABRUT...
YOU'RE NOT GOING TO MAKE ME FEEL GUILTY ABOUT SERVING IN KING CUPPERHAND'S ARMY, FREDDY, NO MATTER HOW VILE HE WAS.
WE'RE MERCENARIES. AND WHAT IS A MERCENARY'S HIGHEST DUTY?
TO GET PAID.
EXACTLY RIGHT--AND TO LIVE LONG ENOUGH TO SPEND THAT PAY.
NOW, WE HAD A CHOICE TO FIGHT WITH THE KING OR AGAINST HIM.
BUT SINCE THE KING HAD THE BACKING OF THE EMPIRE, THOSE WHO FOUGHT AGAINST HIM TENDED TO DIE--IN QUITE REMARKABLE NUMBERS.
I KNOW YOU KNOW THIS BECAUSE YOU'VE REMARKED UPON IT MORE THAN ONCE.
HOWEVER, THOSE WHO FOUGHT WITH THE KING GENERALLY SURVIVED TO SPEND THEIR PAY.
CASE CLOSED, MY HIRSUTE FRIEND. WE WERE LEGALLY AND MORALLY IN THE RIGHT.
LOOK THERE. I THINK I SPY THE FORT AHEAD. LOOSEN YOUR SWORD, MOUSE. WE MAY HAVE TO FIGHT OUR WAY IN.

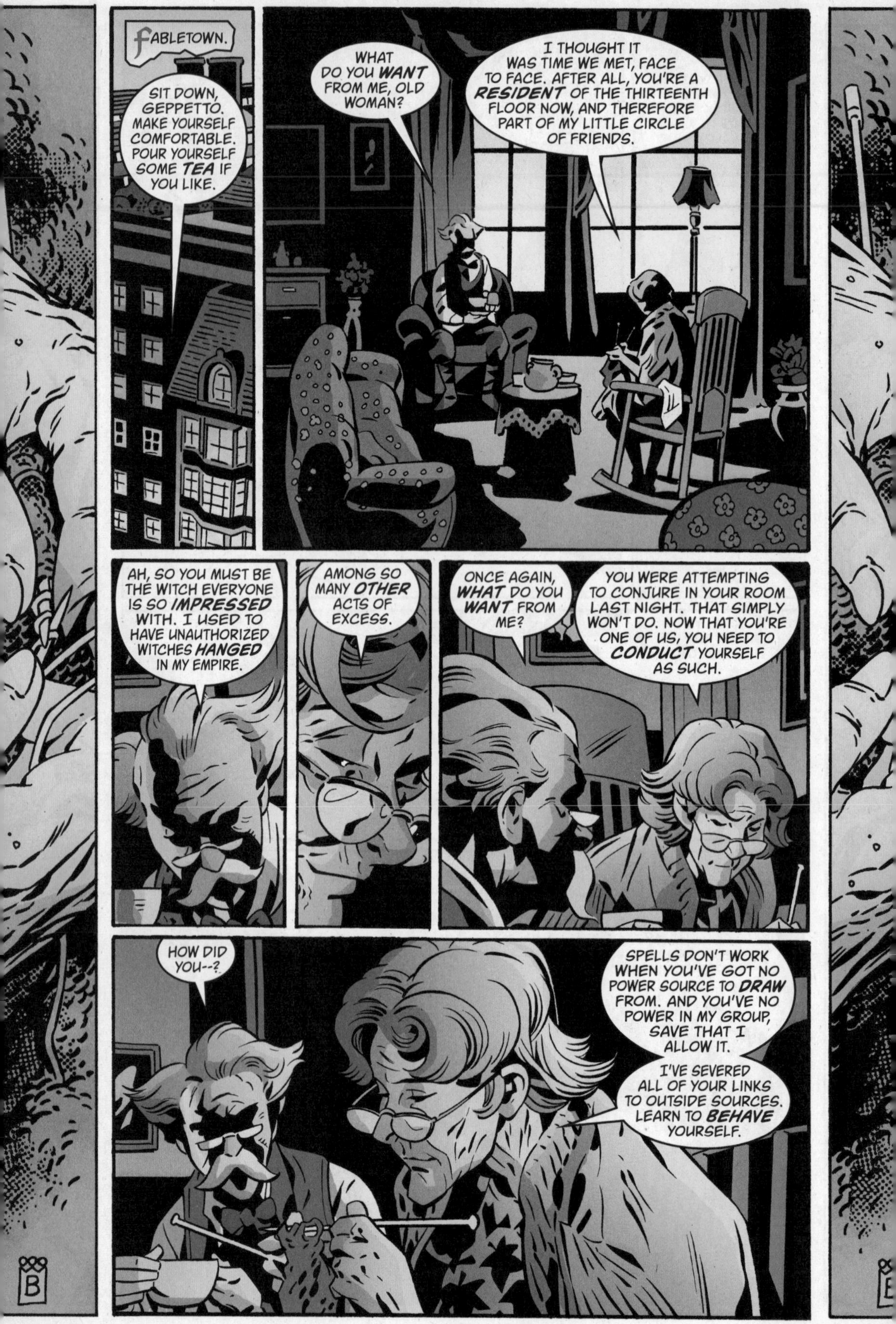
FABLETOWN.
SIT DOWN, GEPPETTO. MAKE YOURSELF COMFORTABLE. POUR YOURSELF SOME TEA IF YOU LIKE.
WHAT DO YOU WANT FROM ME, OLD WOMAN?
I THOUGHT IT WAS TIME WE MET, FACE TO FACE. AFTER ALL, YOU'RE A RESIDENT OF THE THIRTEENTH FLOOR NOW, AND THEREFORE PART OF MY LITTLE CIRCLE OF FRIENDS.
AH, SO YOU MUST BE THE WITCH EVERYONE IS SO IMPRESSED WITH. I USED TO HAVE UNAUTHORIZED WITCHES HANGED IN MY EMPIRE.
AMONG SO MANY OTHER ACTS OF EXCESS.
ONCE AGAIN, WHAT DO YOU WANT FROM ME?
YOU WERE ATTEMPTING TO CONJURE IN YOUR ROOM LAST NIGHT. THAT SIMPLY WON'T DO. NOW THAT YOU'RE ONE OF US, YOU NEED TO CONDUCT YOURSELF AS SUCH.
HOW DID YOU--?
SPELLS DON'T WORK WHEN YOU'VE GOT NO POWER SOURCE TO DRAW FROM. AND YOU'VE NO POWER IN MY GROUP, SAVE THAT I ALLOW IT.
I'VE SEVERED ALL OF YOUR LINKS TO OUTSIDE SOURCES. LEARN TO BEHAVE YOURSELF.

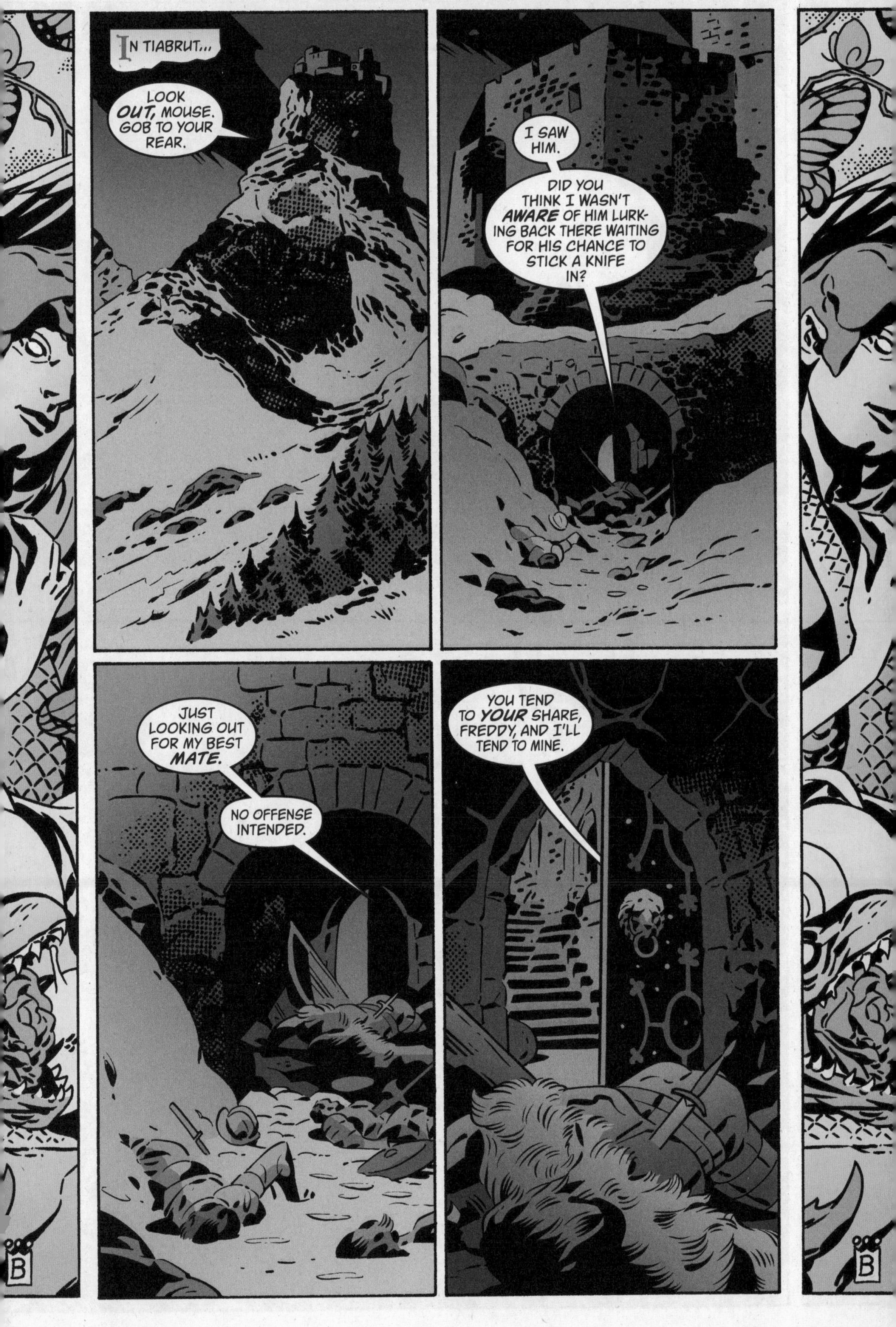
IN TIABRUT...
LOOK OUT, MOUSE. GOB TO YOUR REAR.
I SAW HIM.
DID YOU THINK I WASN'T AWARE OF HIM LURKING BACK THERE WAITING FOR HIS CHANCE TO STICK A KNIFE IN?
JUST LOOKING OUT FOR MY BEST MATE.
NO OFFENSE INTENDED.
YOU TEND TO YOUR SHARE, FREDDY, AND I'LL TEND TO MINE.

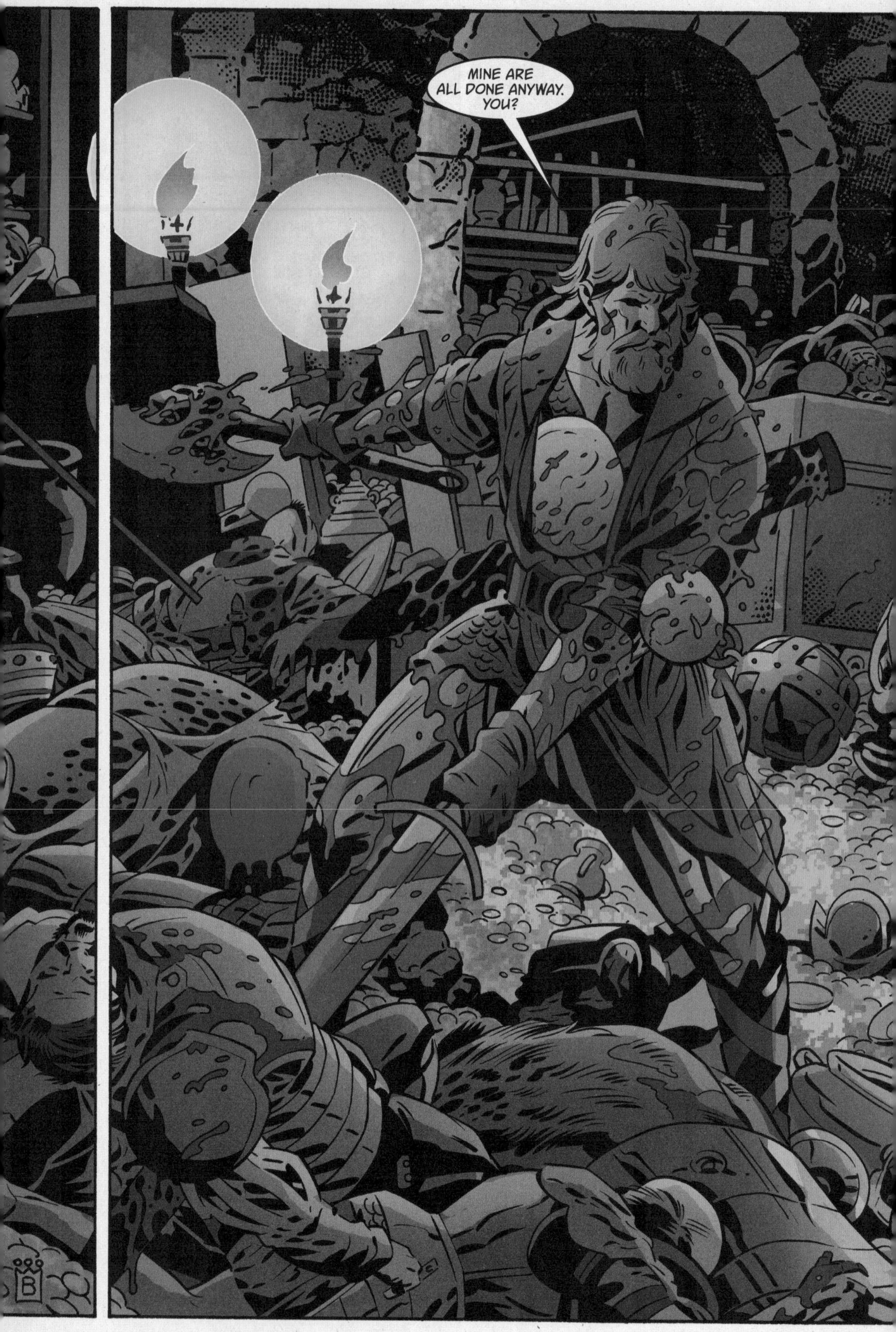
MINE ARE ALL DONE ANYWAY. YOU?

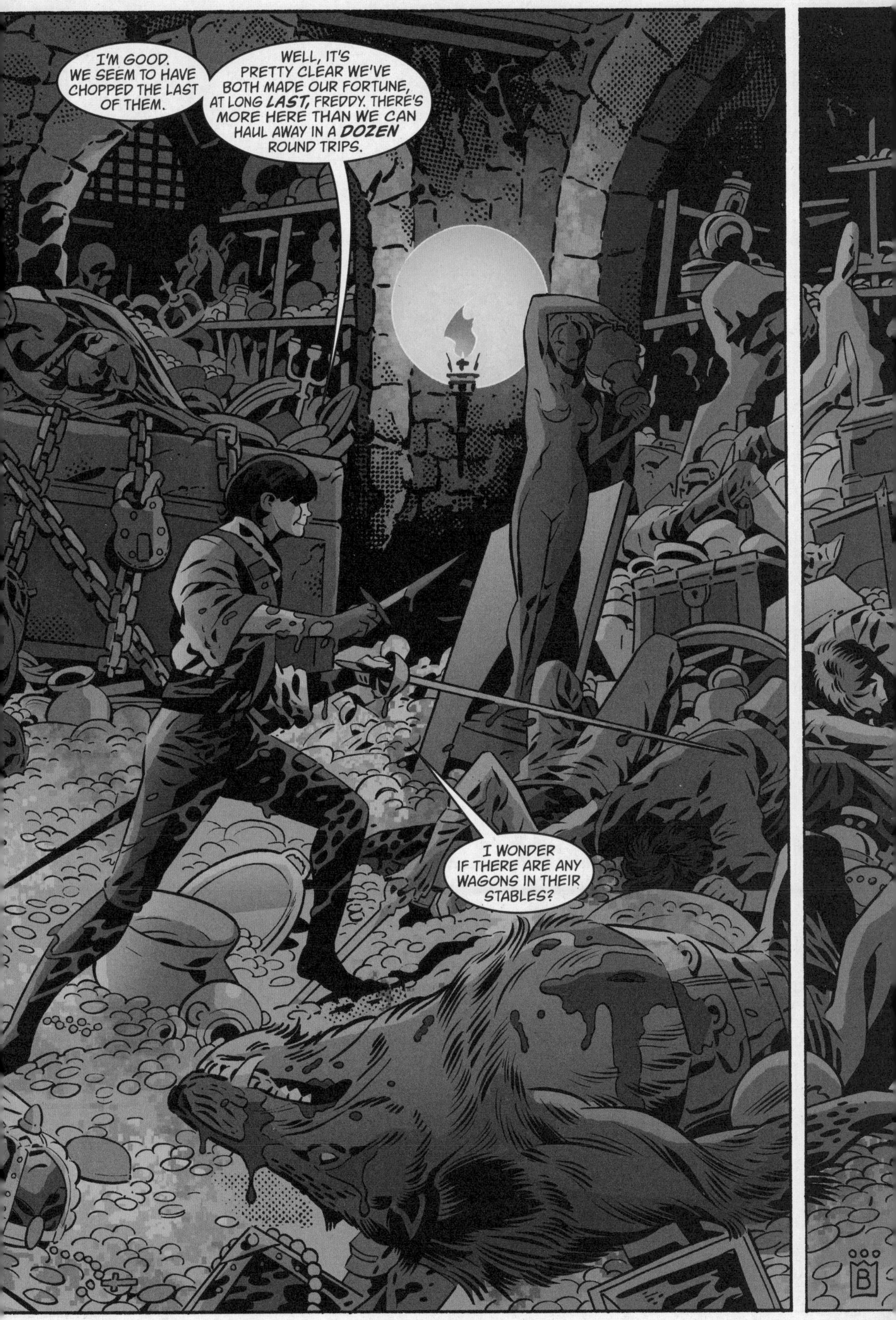
I'M GOOD. WE SEEM TO HAVE CHOPPED THE LAST OF THEM.
WELL, IT'S PRETTY CLEAR WE'VE BOTH MADE OUR FORTUNE, AT LONG LAST, FREDDY. THERE'S MORE HERE THAN WE CAN HAUL AWAY IN A DOZEN ROUND TRIPS.
I WONDER IF THERE ARE ANY WAGONS IN THEIR STABLES?

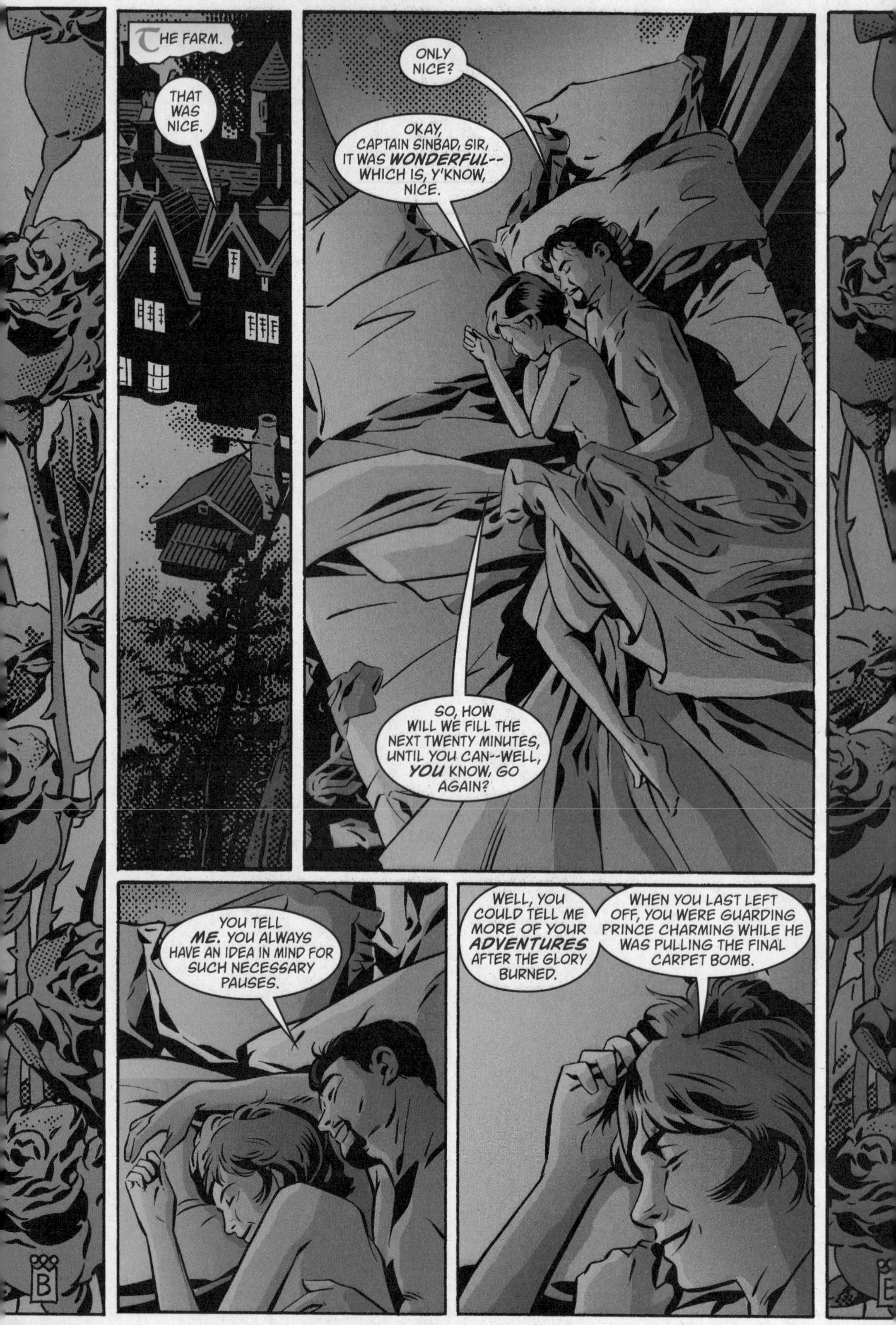
THE FARM.
THAT WAS NICE.
ONLY NICE?
OKAY, CAPTAIN SINBAD, SIR, IT WAS WONDERFUL--WHICH IS, Y'KNOW, NICE.
SO, HOW WILL WE FILL THE NEXT TWENTY MINUTES, UNTIL YOU CAN--WELL, YOU KNOW, GO AGAIN?
YOU TELL ME. YOU ALWAYS HAVE AN IDEA IN MIND FOR SUCH NECESSARY PAUSES.
WELL, YOU COULD TELL ME MORE OF YOUR ADVENTURES AFTER THE GLORY BURNED.
WHEN YOU LAST LEFT OFF, YOU WERE GUARDING PRINCE CHARMING WHILE HE WAS PULLING THE FINAL CARPET BOMB.

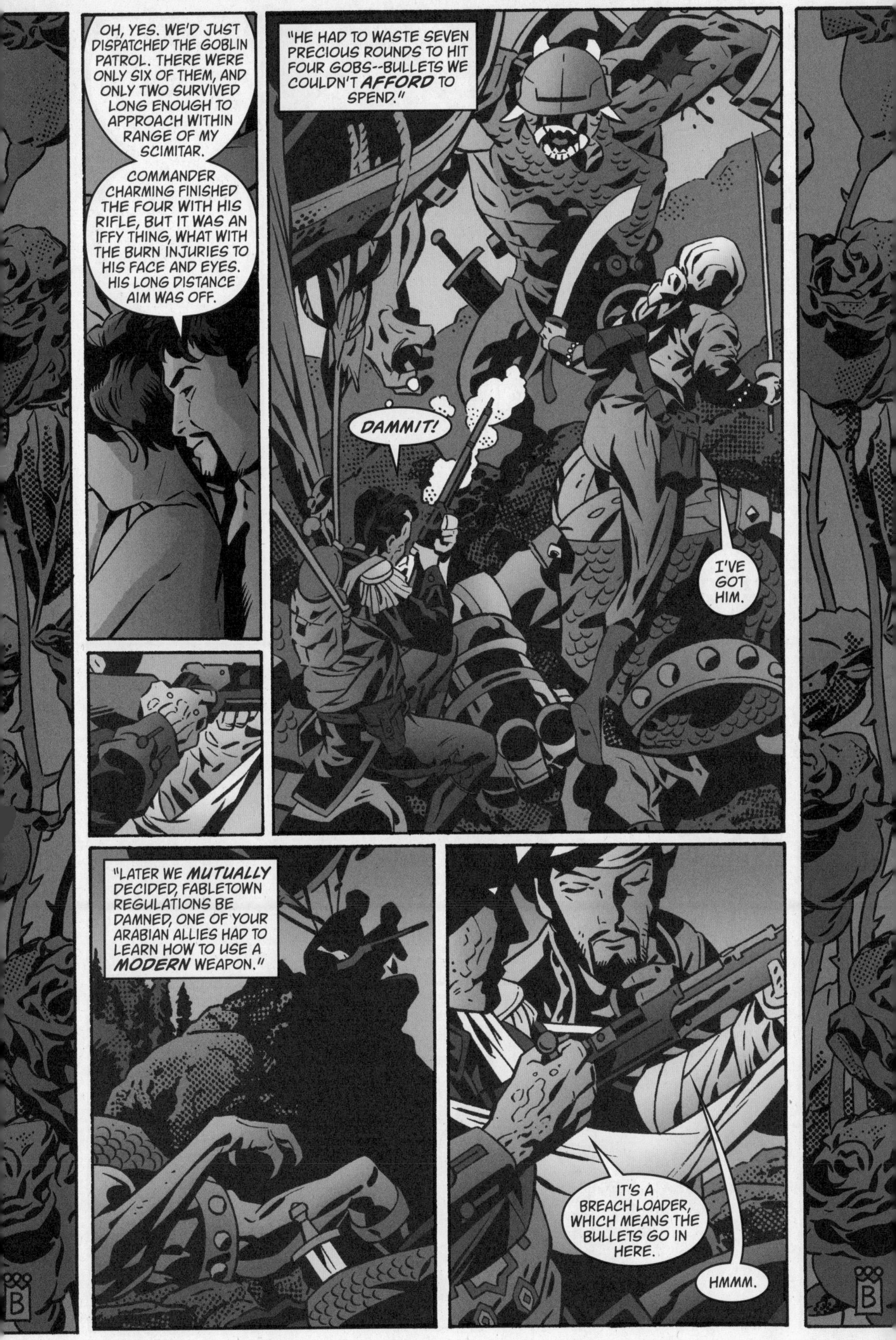
OH, YES. WE'D JUST DISPATCHED THE GOBLIN PATROL. THERE WERE ONLY SIX OF THEM, AND ONLY TWO SURVIVED LONG ENOUGH TO APPROACH WITHIN RANGE OF MY SCIMITAR.
COMMANDER CHARMING FINISHED THE FOUR WITH HIS RIFLE, BUT IT WAS AN IFFY THING, WHAT WITH THE BURN INJURIES TO HIS FACE AND EYES. HIS LONG DISTANCE AIM WAS OFF.
"HE HAD TO WASTE SEVEN PRECIOUS ROUNDS TO HIT FOUR GOBS--BULLETS WE COULDN'T AFFORD TO SPEND."
DAMMIT!
I'VE GOT HIM.
"LATER WE MUTUALLY DECIDED, FABLETOWN REGULATIONS BE DAMNED, ONE OF YOUR ARABIAN ALLIES HAD TO LEARN HOW TO USE A MODERN WEAPON."
IT'S A BREACH LOADER, WHICH MEANS THE BULLETS GO IN HERE.
HMMM.

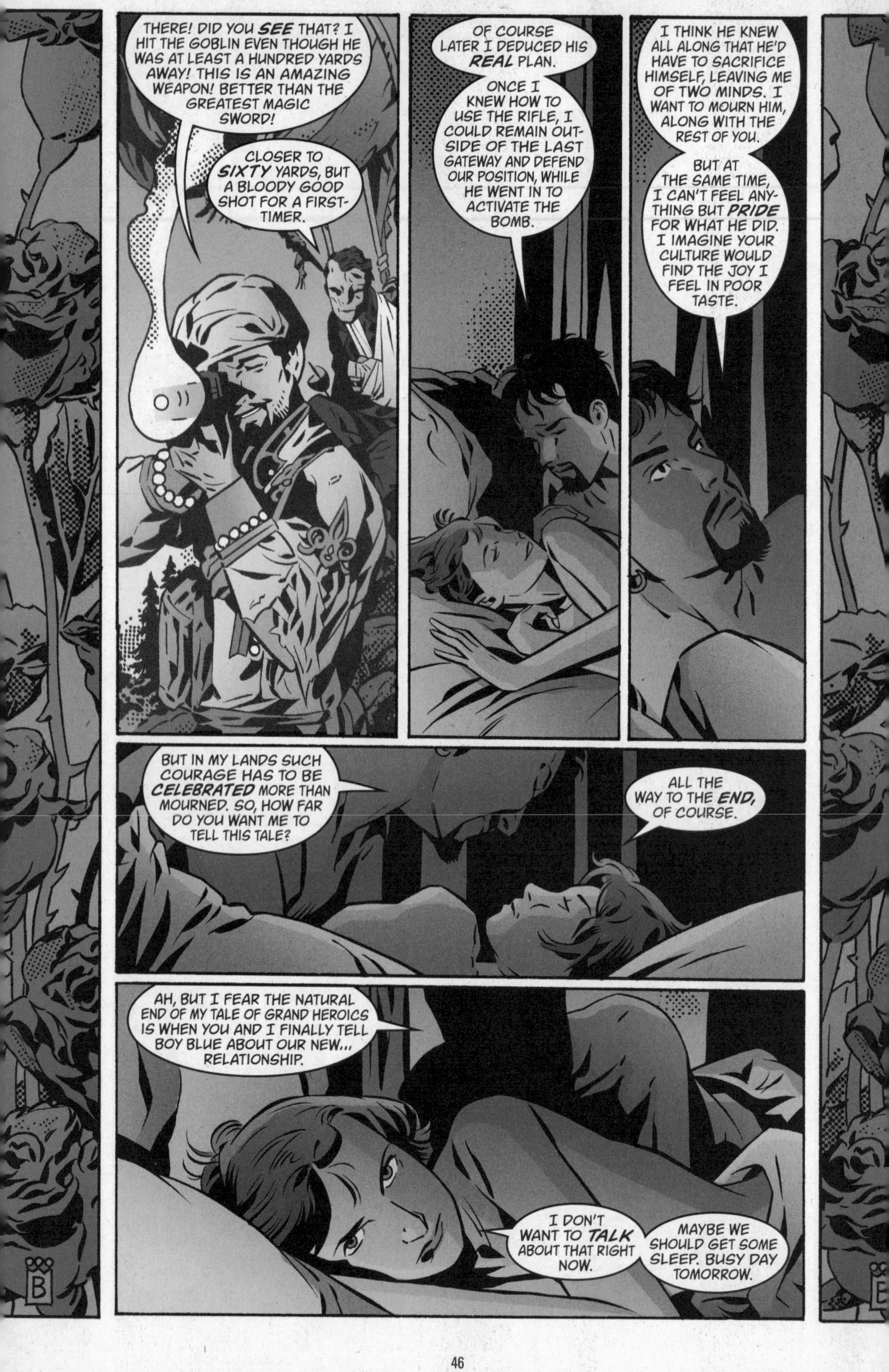

THERE! DID YOU SEE THAT? I HIT THE GOBLIN EVEN THOUGH HE WAS AT LEAST A HUNDRED YARDS AWAY! THIS IS AN AMAZING WEAPON! BETTER THAN THE GREATEST MAGIC SWORD!
CLOSER TO SIXTY YARDS, BUT A BLOODY GOOD SHOT FOR A FIRST-TIMER.
OF COURSE LATER I DEDUCED HIS REAL PLAN.
ONCE I KNEW HOW TO USE THE RIFLE, I COULD REMAIN OUTSIDE OF THE LAST GATEWAY AND DEFEND OUR POSITION, WHILE HE WENT IN TO ACTIVATE THE BOMB.
I THINK HE KNEW ALL ALONG THAT HE'D HAVE TO SACRIFICE HIMSELF, LEAVING ME OF TWO MINDS. I WANT TO MOURN HIM, ALONG WITH THE REST OF YOU.
BUT AT THE SAME TIME, I CAN'T FEEL ANYTHING BUT PRIDE FOR WHAT HE DID. I IMAGINE YOUR CULTURE WOULD FIND THE JOY I FEEL IN POOR TASTE.
BUT IN MY LANDS SUCH COURAGE HAS TO BE CELEBRATED MORE THAN MOURNED. SO, HOW FAR DO YOU WANT ME TO TELL THIS TALE?
ALL THE WAY TO THE END, OF COURSE.
AH, BUT I FEAR THE NATURAL END OF MY TALE OF GRAND HEROICS IS WHEN YOU AND I FINALLY TELL BOY BLUE ABOUT OUR NEW... RELATIONSHIP.
I DON'T WANT TO TALK ABOUT THAT RIGHT NOW.
MAYBE WE SHOULD GET SOME SLEEP. BUSY DAY TOMORROW.

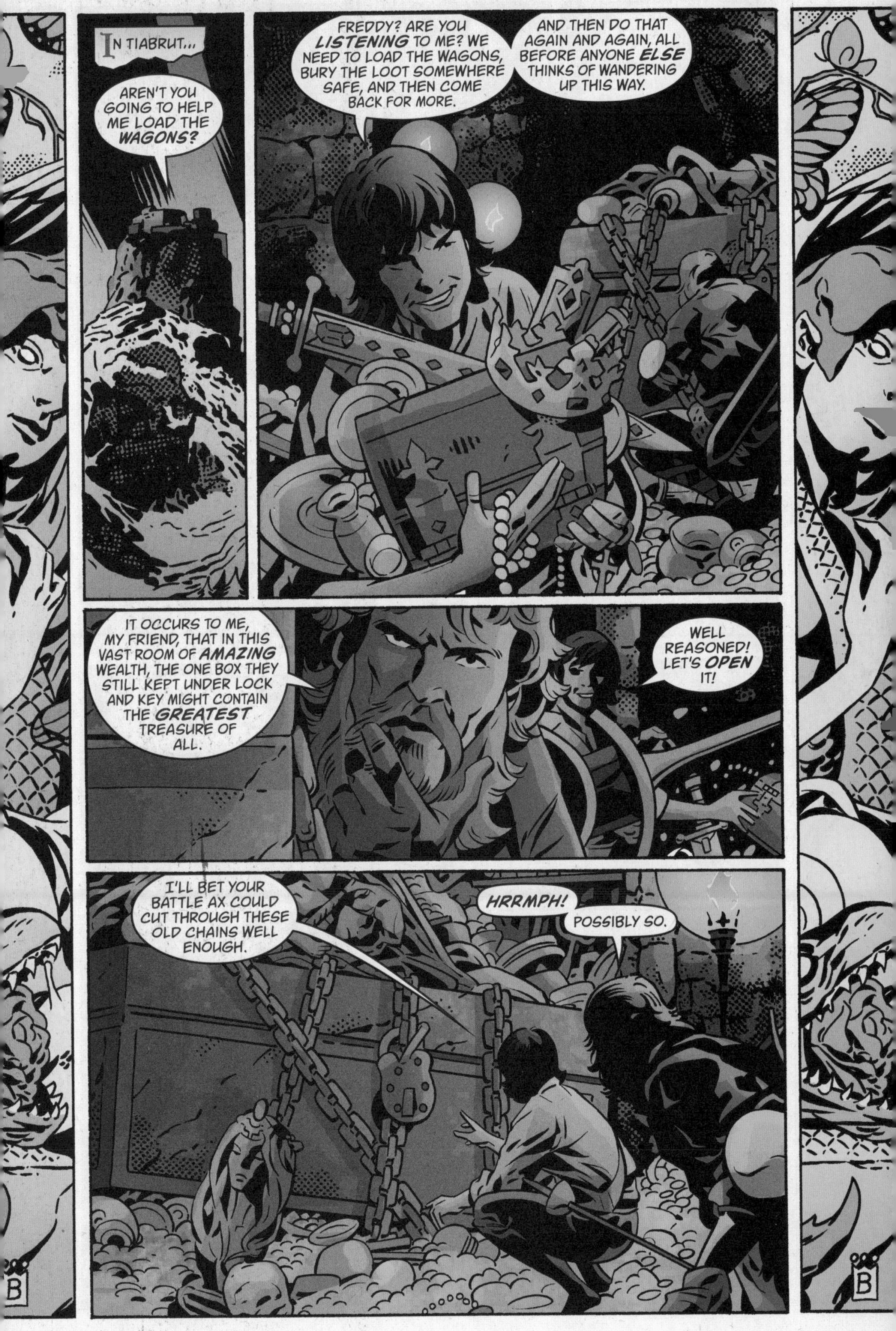
IN TIABRUT...
AREN'T YOU GOING TO HELP ME LOAD THE WAGONS?
FREDDY? ARE YOU LISTENING TO ME? WE NEED TO LOAD THE WAGONS, BURY THE LOOT SOMEWHERE SAFE, AND THEN COME BACK FOR MORE.
AND THEN DO THAT AGAIN AND AGAIN, ALL BEFORE ANYONE ELSE THINKS OF WANDERING UP THIS WAY.
IT OCCURS TO ME, MY FRIEND, THAT IN THIS VAST ROOM OF AMAZING WEALTH, THE ONE BOX THEY STILL KEPT UNDER LOCK AND KEY MIGHT CONTAIN THE GREATEST TREASURE OF ALL.
WELL REASONED! LET'S OPEN IT!
I'LL BET YOUR BATTLE AX COULD CUT THROUGH THESE OLD CHAINS WELL ENOUGH.
HRRMPH!
POSSIBLY SO.

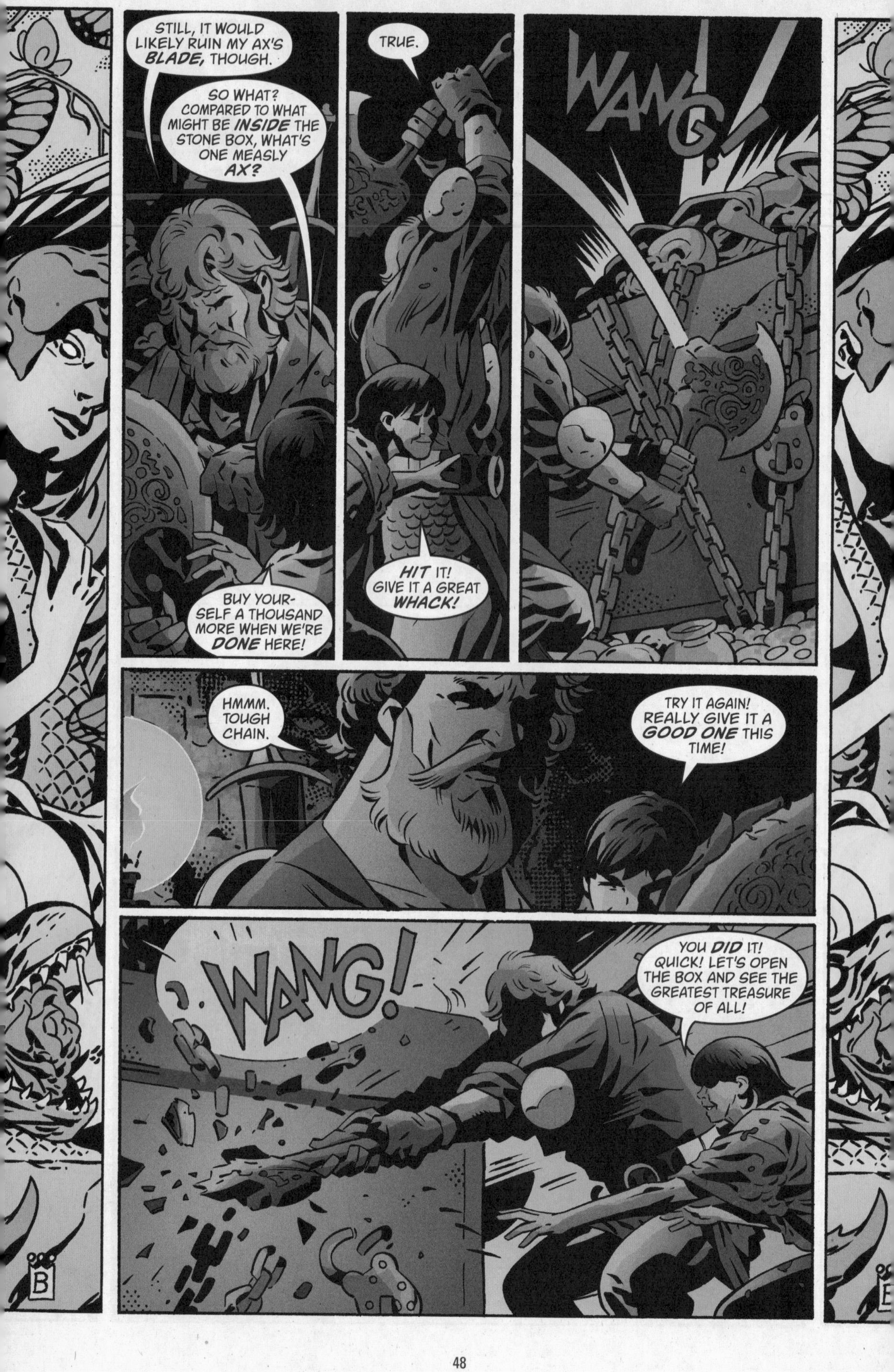
STILL, IT WOULD LIKELY RUIN MY AX'S BLADE, THOUGH.
SO WHAT? COMPARED TO WHAT MIGHT BE INSIDE THE STONE BOX, WHAT'S ONE MEASLY AX?
BUY YOURSELF A THOUSAND MORE WHEN WE'RE DONE HERE!
TRUE.
HIT IT! GIVE IT A GREAT WHACK!
WANG!
HMMM. TOUGH CHAIN.
TRY IT AGAIN! REALLY GIVE IT A GOOD ONE THIS TIME!
WANG!
YOU DID IT! QUICK! LET'S OPEN THE BOX AND SEE THE GREATEST TREASURE OF ALL!

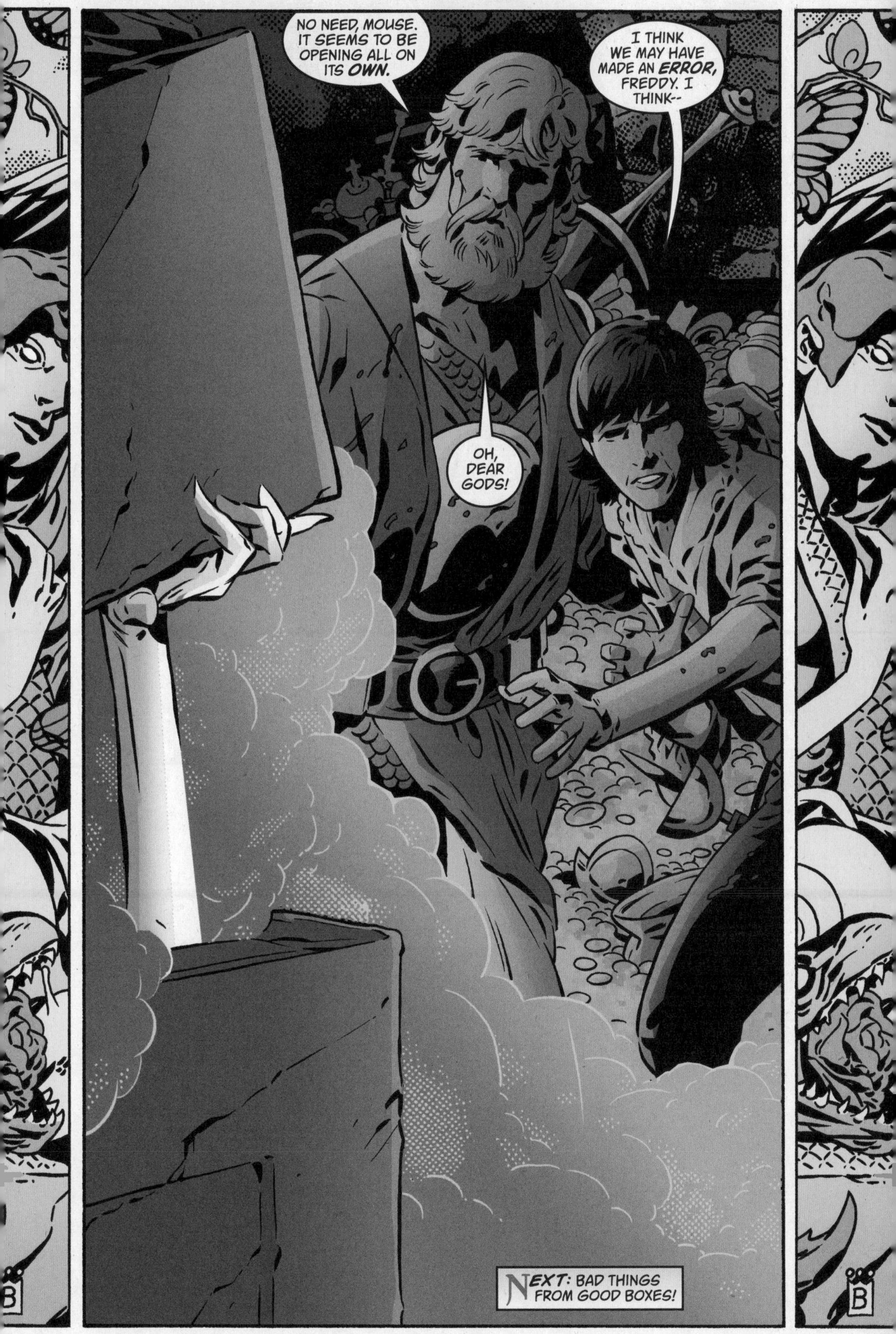
NO NEED, MOUSE. IT SEEMS TO BE OPENING ALL ON ITS OWN.
I THINK WE MAY HAVE MADE AN ERROR, FREDDY. I THINK--
OH, DEAR GODS!
NEXT: BAD THINGS FROM GOOD BOXES!

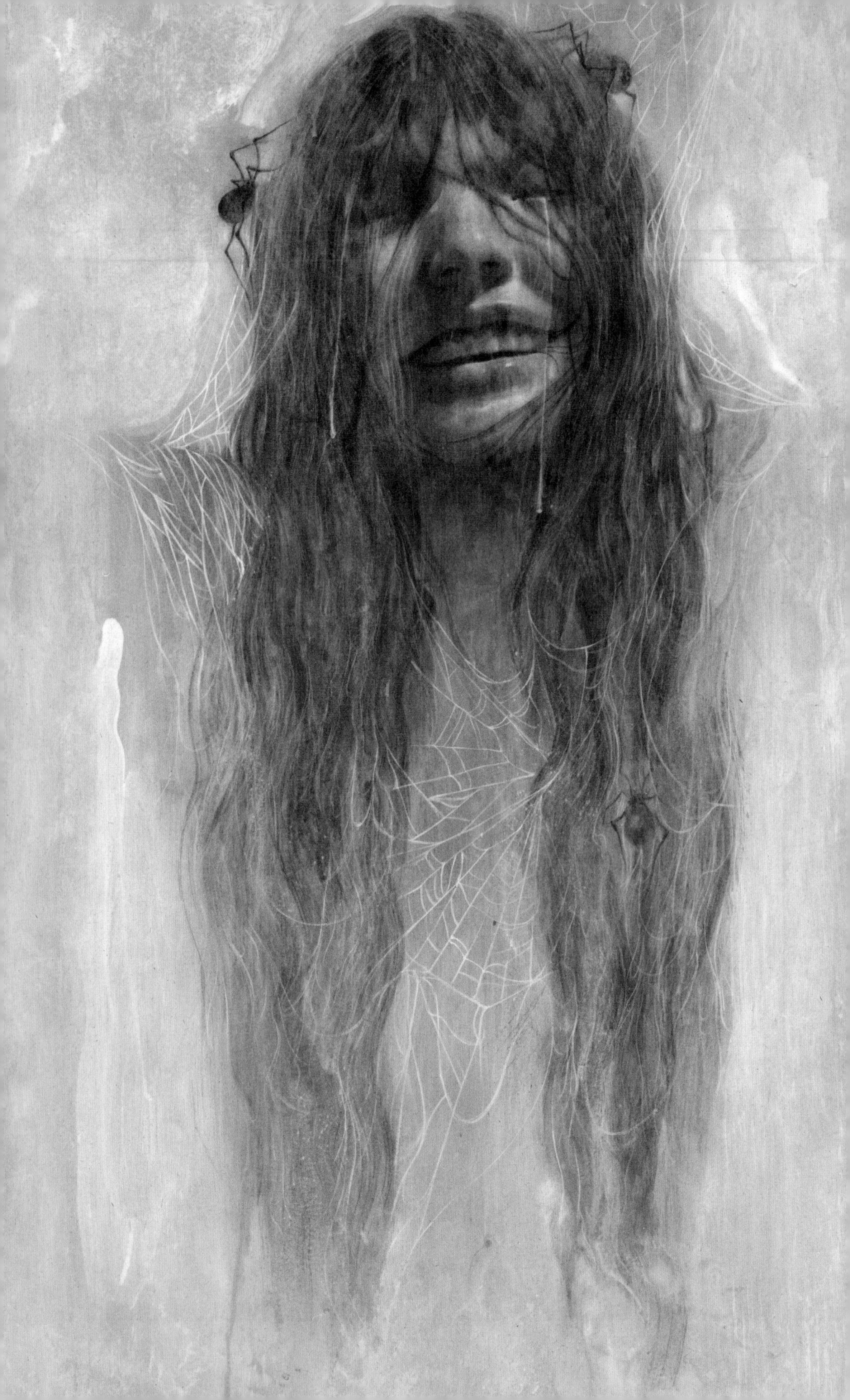

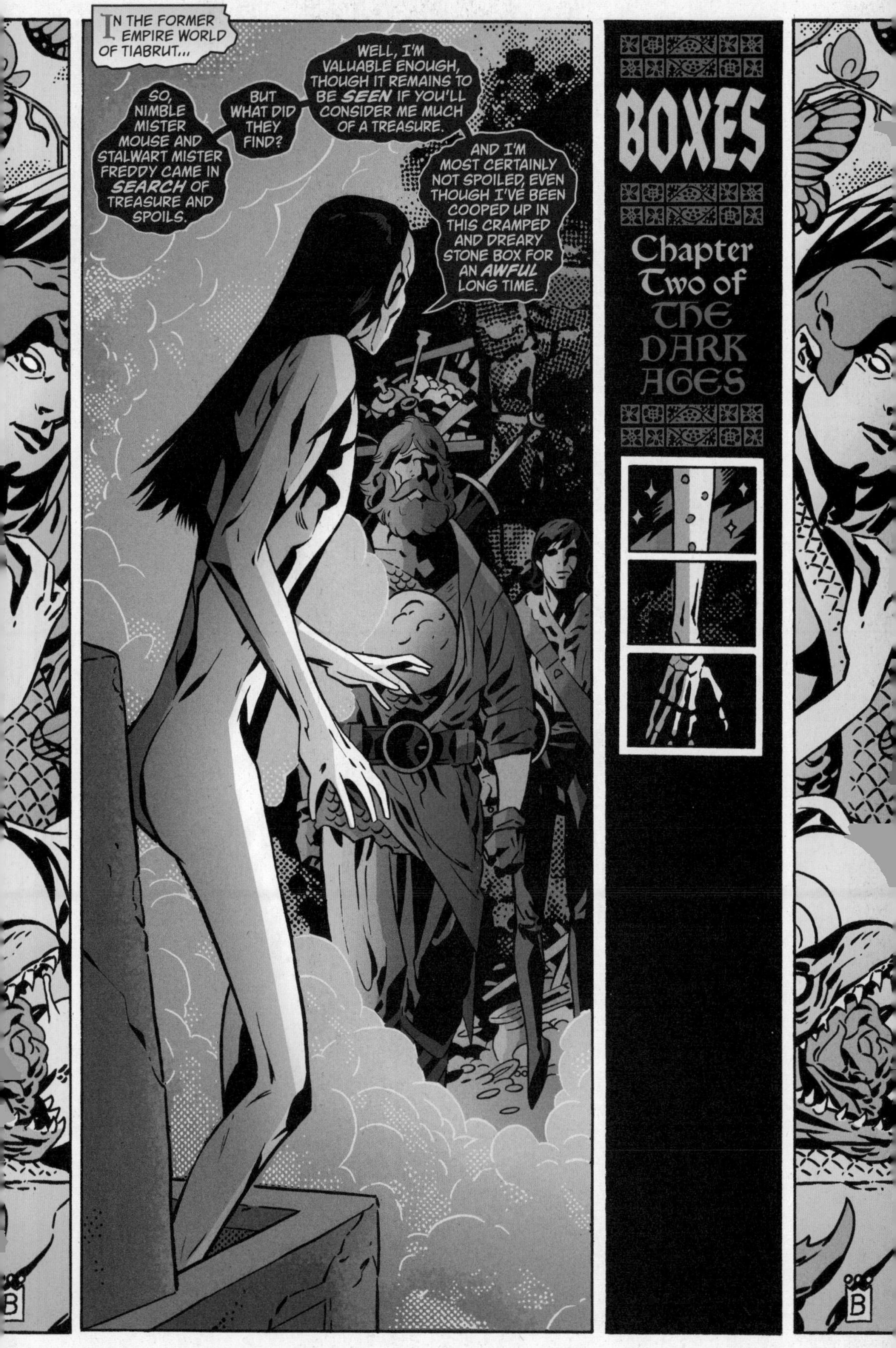
IN THE FORMER EMPIRE WORLD OF TIABRUT...
SO, NIMBLE MISTER MOUSE AND STALWART MISTER FREDDY CAME IN SEARCH OF TREASURE AND SPOILS.
BUT WHAT DID THEY FIND?
WELL, I'M VALUABLE ENOUGH, THOUGH IT REMAINS TO BE SEEN IF YOU'LL CONSIDER ME MUCH OF A TREASURE.
AND I'M MOST CERTAINLY NOT SPOILED, EVEN THOUGH I'VE BEEN COOPED UP IN THIS CRAMPED AND DREARY STONE BOX FOR AN AWFUL LONG TIME.
BOXES
Chapter Two of THE DARK AGES

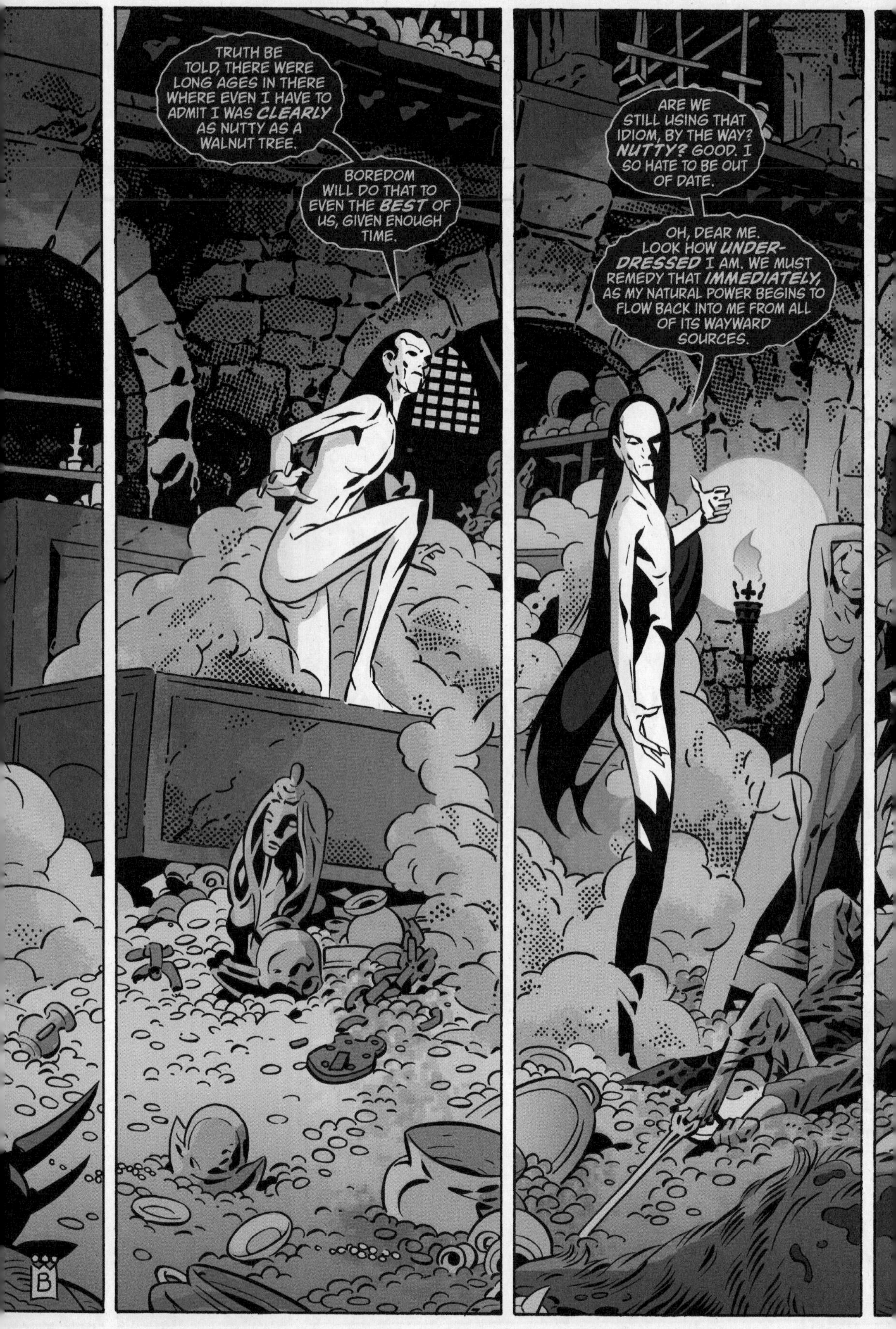
TRUTH BE TOLD, THERE WERE LONG AGES IN THERE WHERE EVEN I HAVE TO ADMIT I WAS CLEARLY AS NUTTY AS A WALNUT TREE.
BOREDOM WILL DO THAT TO EVEN THE BEST OF US, GIVEN ENOUGH TIME.
ARE WE STILL USING THAT IDIOM, BY THE WAY? NUTTY? GOOD. I SO HATE TO BE OUT OF DATE.
OH, DEAR ME. LOOK HOW UNDER-DRESSED I AM. WE MUST REMEDY THAT IMMEDIATELY, AS MY NATURAL POWER BEGINS TO FLOW BACK INTO ME FROM ALL OF ITS WAYWARD SOURCES.

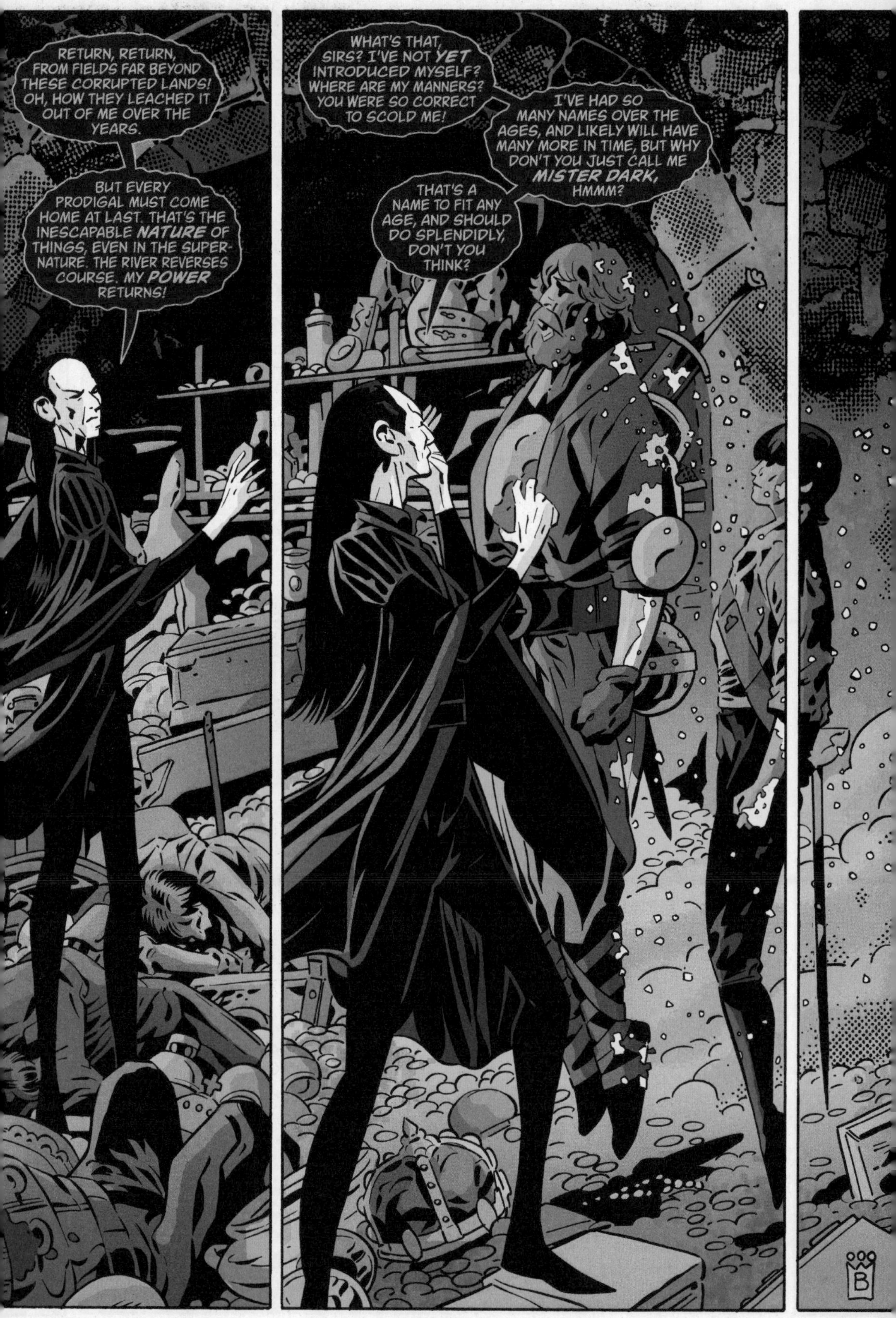
RETURN, RETURN, FROM FIELDS FAR BEYOND THESE CORRUPTED LANDS! OH, HOW THEY LEACHED IT OUT OF ME OVER THE YEARS.
BUT EVERY PRODIGAL MUST COME HOME AT LAST. THAT'S THE INESCAPABLE NATURE OF THINGS, EVEN IN THE SUPER-NATURE. THE RIVER REVERSES COURSE. MY POWER RETURNS!
WHAT'S THAT, SIRS? I'VE NOT YET INTRODUCED MYSELF? WHERE ARE MY MANNERS? YOU WERE SO CORRECT TO SCOLD ME!
I'VE HAD SO MANY NAMES OVER THE AGES, AND LIKELY WILL HAVE MANY MORE IN TIME, BUT WHY DON'T YOU JUST CALL ME MISTER DARK, HMMM?
THAT'S A NAME TO FIT ANY AGE, AND SHOULD DO SPLENDIDLY, DON'T YOU THINK?

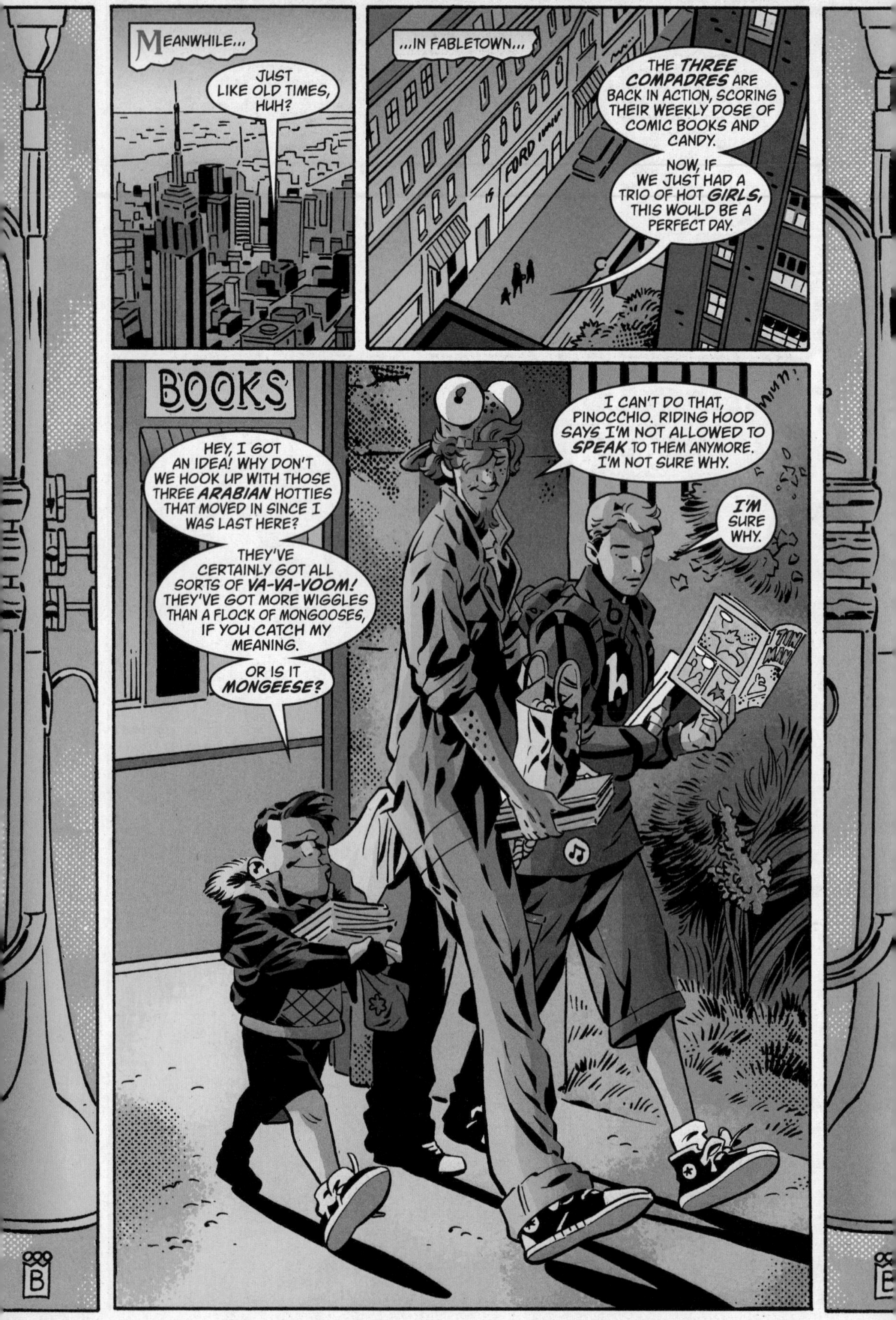
MEANWHILE...
JUST LIKE OLD TIMES, HUH?
...IN FABLETOWN...
THE THREE COMPADRES ARE BACK IN ACTION, SCORING THEIR WEEKLY DOSE OF COMIC BOOKS AND CANDY.
NOW, IF WE JUST HAD A TRIO OF HOT GIRLS, THIS WOULD BE A PERFECT DAY.
BOOKS
HEY, I GOT AN IDEA! WHY DON'T WE HOOK UP WITH THOSE THREE ARABIAN HOTTIES THAT MOVED IN SINCE I WAS LAST HERE?
THEY'VE CERTAINLY GOT ALL SORTS OF VA-VA-VOOM! THEY'VE GOT MORE WIGGLES THAN A FLOCK OF MONGOOSES, IF YOU CATCH MY MEANING.
OR IS IT MONGEESE?
I CAN'T DO THAT, PINOCCHIO. RIDING HOOD SAYS I'M NOT ALLOWED TO SPEAK TO THEM ANYMORE. I'M NOT SURE WHY.
I'M SURE WHY.

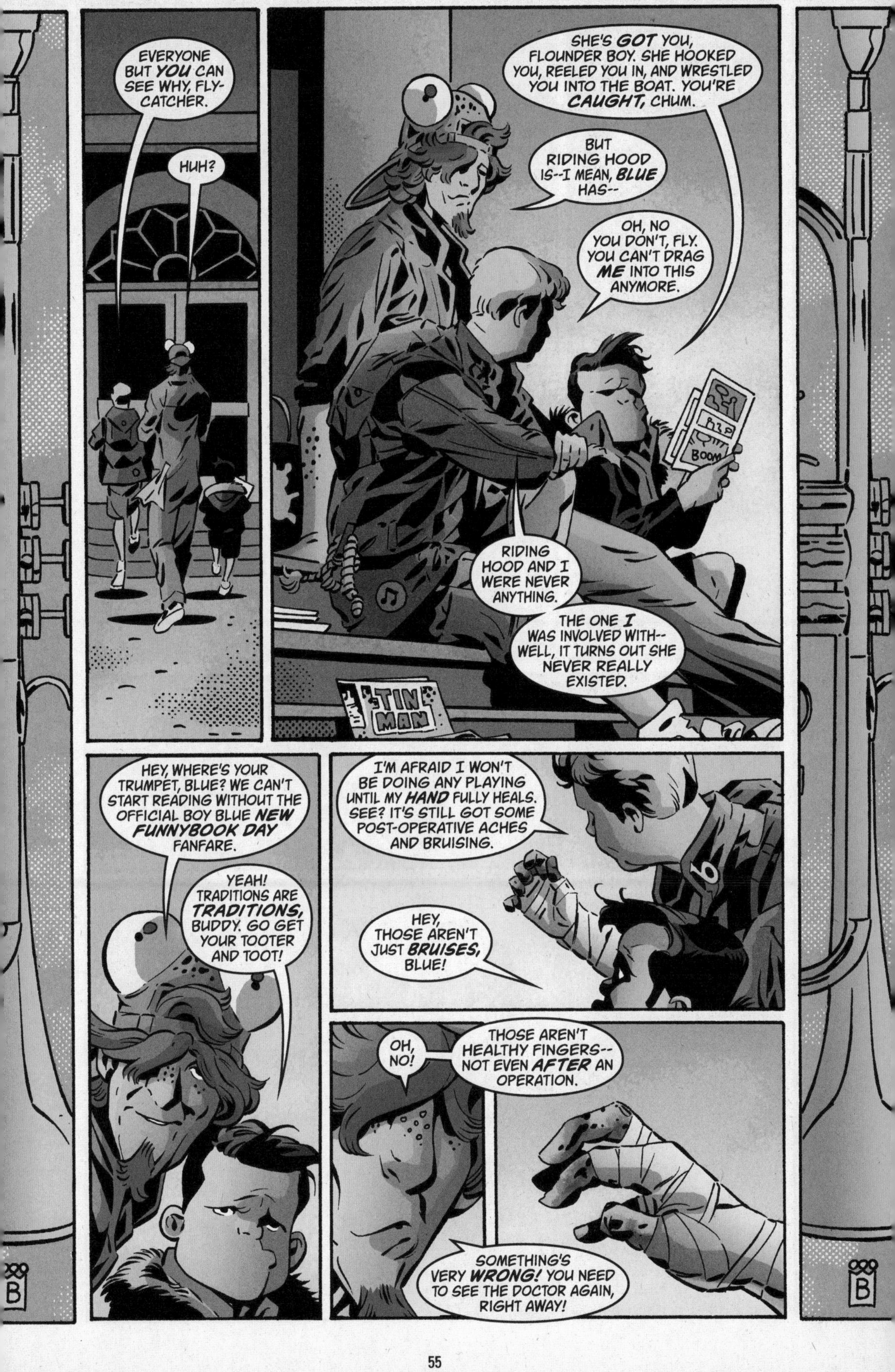
EVERYONE BUT YOU CAN SEE WHY, FLY-CATCHER.
HUH?
SHE'S GOT YOU, FLOUNDER BOY. SHE HOOKED YOU, REELED YOU IN, AND WRESTLED YOU INTO THE BOAT. YOU'RE CAUGHT, CHUM.
BUT RIDING HOOD IS--I MEAN, BLUE HAS--
OH, NO YOU DON'T, FLY. YOU CAN'T DRAG ME INTO THIS ANYMORE.
RIDING HOOD AND I WERE NEVER ANYTHING.
THE ONE I WAS INVOLVED WITH--WELL, IT TURNS OUT SHE NEVER REALLY EXISTED.
TIN MAN
BOOM
HEY, WHERE'S YOUR TRUMPET, BLUE? WE CAN'T START READING WITHOUT THE OFFICIAL BOY BLUE NEW FUNNYBOOK DAY FANFARE.
YEAH! TRADITIONS ARE TRADITIONS, BUDDY. GO GET YOUR TOOTER AND TOOT!
I'M AFRAID I WON'T BE DOING ANY PLAYING UNTIL MY HAND FULLY HEALS. SEE? IT'S STILL GOT SOME POST-OPERATIVE ACHES AND BRUISING.
HEY, THOSE AREN'T JUST BRUISES, BLUE!
OH, NO!
THOSE AREN'T HEALTHY FINGERS--NOT EVEN AFTER AN OPERATION.
SOMETHING'S VERY WRONG! YOU NEED TO SEE THE DOCTOR AGAIN, RIGHT AWAY!

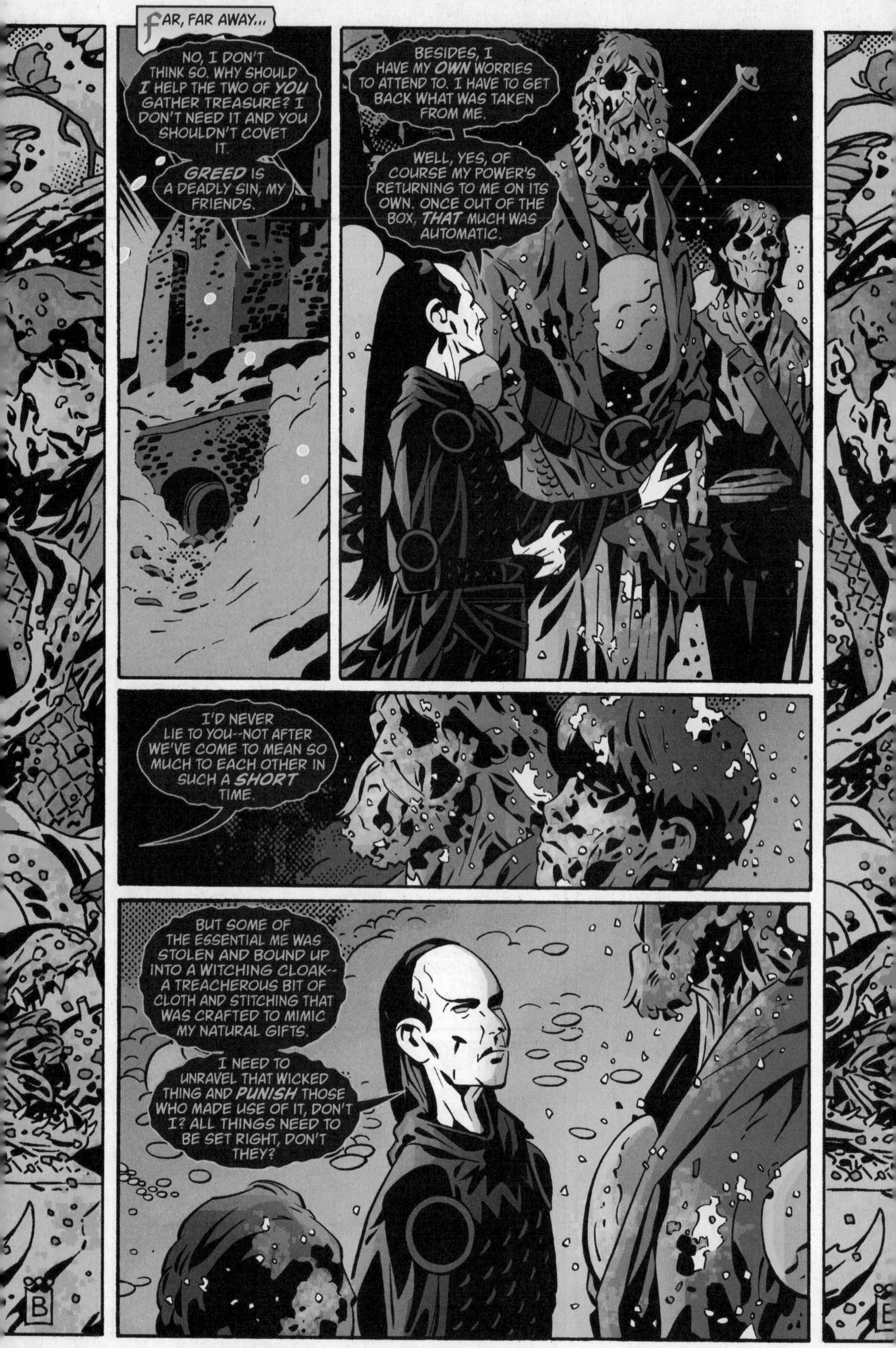
FAR, FAR AWAY...
NO, I DON'T THINK SO. WHY SHOULD I HELP THE TWO OF YOU GATHER TREASURE? I DON'T NEED IT AND YOU SHOULDN'T COVET IT.
GREED IS A DEADLY SIN, MY FRIENDS.
BESIDES, I HAVE MY OWN WORRIES TO ATTEND TO. I HAVE TO GET BACK WHAT WAS TAKEN FROM ME.
WELL, YES, OF COURSE MY POWER'S RETURNING TO ME ON ITS OWN. ONCE OUT OF THE BOX, THAT MUCH WAS AUTOMATIC.
I'D NEVER LIE TO YOU--NOT AFTER WE'VE COME TO MEAN SO MUCH TO EACH OTHER IN SUCH A SHORT TIME.
BUT SOME OF THE ESSENTIAL ME WAS STOLEN AND BOUND UP INTO A WITCHING CLOAK-- A TREACHEROUS BIT OF CLOTH AND STITCHING THAT WAS CRAFTED TO MIMIC MY NATURAL GIFTS.
I NEED TO UNRAVEL THAT WICKED THING AND PUNISH THOSE WHO MADE USE OF IT, DON'T I? ALL THINGS NEED TO BE SET RIGHT, DON'T THEY?

EVEN THOUGH YOU'VE CUT OFF MY ABILITY TO CONJURE, I STILL HAVE **CONNECTIONS** IN PLACE TO MY OLD EMPIRE.

I CAN SENSE WHEN CERTAIN THINGS HAVE BEEN DISRUPTED, AND THEY HAVE. ONE OF THE **BROADCAST BOXES** HAS BEEN OPENED.

AND WHAT MIGHT THEY BE?

AH, SO YOU DON'T KNOW **EVERYTHING**, DO YOU?

THE BOXES WERE USED TO POWER MY **SORCERERS CORPS** BY BROADCASTING WHATEVER MAGICAL SOURCE WAS CONTAINED WITHIN.

ONE OR MORE PER WORLD WOULD BE ENOUGH TO SUPPLY--

WELL, SUFFICE IT TO SAY, THEY CONTAIN GREAT OLD POWERS. NOW AT LEAST **ONE** OF THOSE OLD POWERS HAS BEEN RELEASED BACK INTO THE WORLDS.

YOU **SERIOUSLY** OVERSTEPPED IN DESTROYING MY EMPIRE. BY ANY MEASURE, WE **SOLVED** MORE PROBLEMS THAN WE CREATED.

SOMETHING THAT TOOK CENTURIES AND ENTIRE ARMIES TO SAFELY LOCK AWAY IS LOOSE AGAIN AND **YOU** CAUSED IT.

I WONDER HOW LONG WE'LL BE ABLE TO SURVIVE THE RESULTS OF YOUR NOBLE **MEDDLING**.

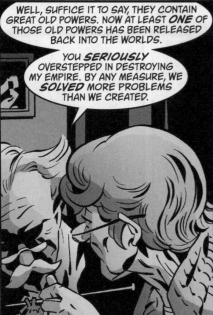

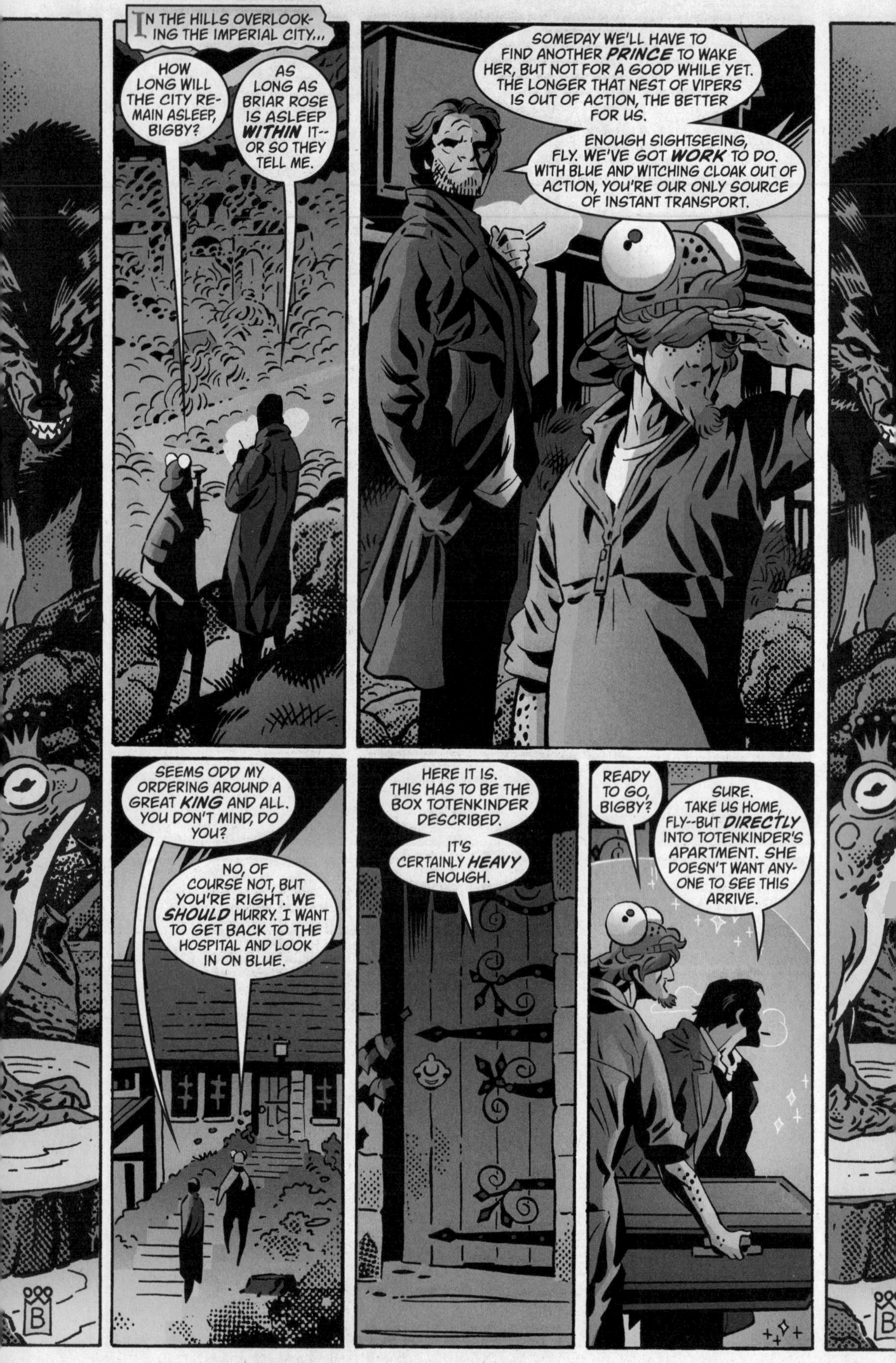
IN THE HILLS OVERLOOKING THE IMPERIAL CITY...
HOW LONG WILL THE CITY REMAIN ASLEEP, BIGBY?
AS LONG AS BRIAR ROSE IS ASLEEP WITHIN IT--OR SO THEY TELL ME.
SOMEDAY WE'LL HAVE TO FIND ANOTHER PRINCE TO WAKE HER, BUT NOT FOR A GOOD WHILE YET. THE LONGER THAT NEST OF VIPERS IS OUT OF ACTION, THE BETTER FOR US.
ENOUGH SIGHTSEEING, FLY. WE'VE GOT WORK TO DO. WITH BLUE AND WITCHING CLOAK OUT OF ACTION, YOU'RE OUR ONLY SOURCE OF INSTANT TRANSPORT.
SEEMS ODD MY ORDERING AROUND A GREAT KING AND ALL. YOU DON'T MIND, DO YOU?
NO, OF COURSE NOT, BUT YOU'RE RIGHT. WE SHOULD HURRY. I WANT TO GET BACK TO THE HOSPITAL AND LOOK IN ON BLUE.
HERE IT IS. THIS HAS TO BE THE BOX TOTENKINDER DESCRIBED.
IT'S CERTAINLY HEAVY ENOUGH.
READY TO GO, BIGBY?
SURE. TAKE US HOME, FLY--BUT DIRECTLY INTO TOTENKINDER'S APARTMENT. SHE DOESN'T WANT ANYONE TO SEE THIS ARRIVE.

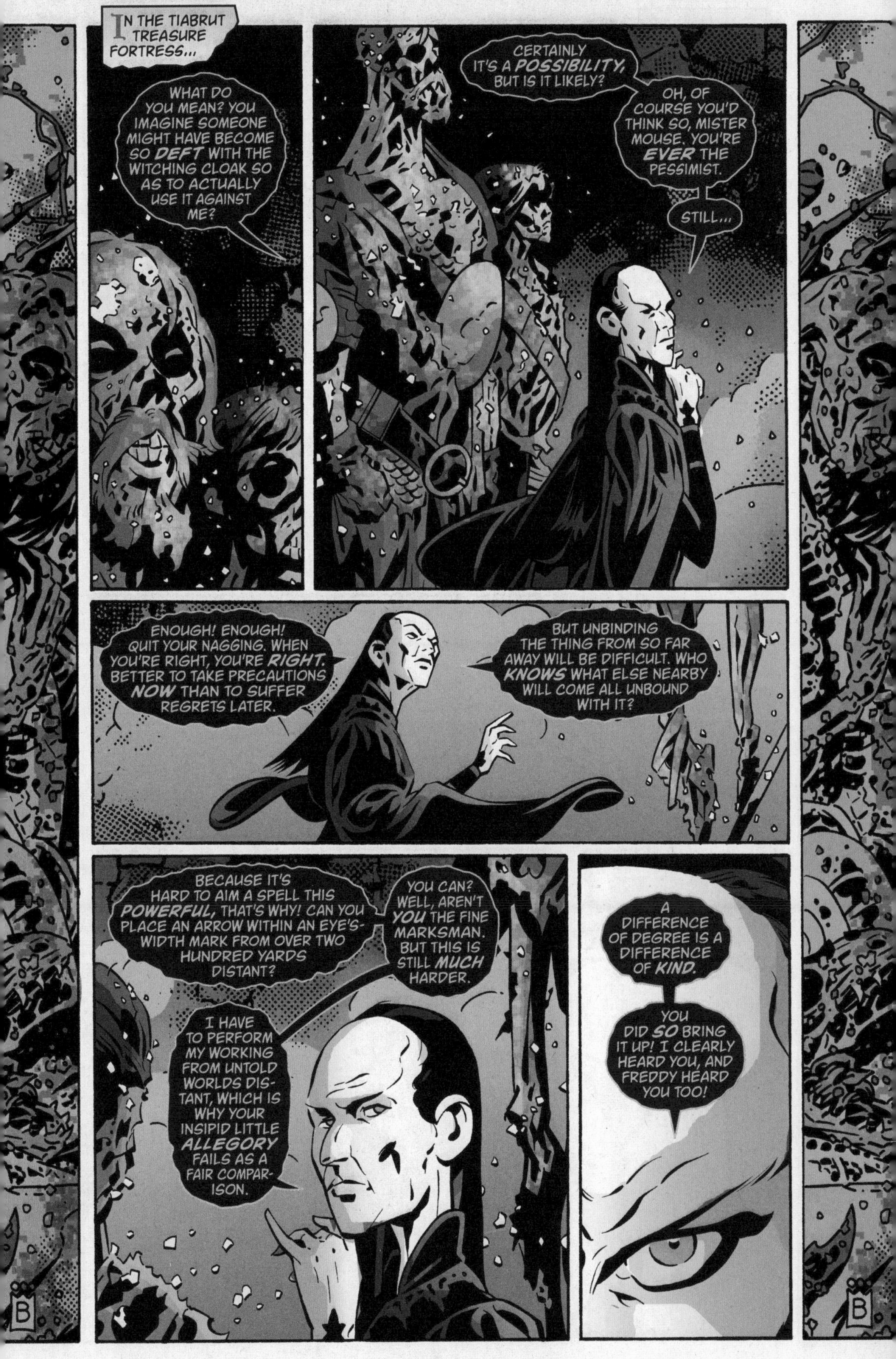
IN THE TIABRUT TREASURE FORTRESS...
WHAT DO YOU MEAN? YOU IMAGINE SOMEONE MIGHT HAVE BECOME SO DEFT WITH THE WITCHING CLOAK SO AS TO ACTUALLY USE IT AGAINST ME?
CERTAINLY IT'S A POSSIBILITY, BUT IS IT LIKELY?
OH, OF COURSE YOU'D THINK SO, MISTER MOUSE. YOU'RE EVER THE PESSIMIST.
STILL...
ENOUGH! ENOUGH! QUIT YOUR NAGGING. WHEN YOU'RE RIGHT, YOU'RE RIGHT. BETTER TO TAKE PRECAUTIONS NOW THAN TO SUFFER REGRETS LATER.
BUT UNBINDING THE THING FROM SO FAR AWAY WILL BE DIFFICULT. WHO KNOWS WHAT ELSE NEARBY WILL COME ALL UNBOUND WITH IT?
BECAUSE IT'S HARD TO AIM A SPELL THIS POWERFUL, THAT'S WHY! CAN YOU PLACE AN ARROW WITHIN AN EYE'S-WIDTH MARK FROM OVER TWO HUNDRED YARDS DISTANT?
YOU CAN? WELL, AREN'T YOU THE FINE MARKSMAN. BUT THIS IS STILL MUCH HARDER.
I HAVE TO PERFORM MY WORKING FROM UNTOLD WORLDS DISTANT, WHICH IS WHY YOUR INSIPID LITTLE ALLEGORY FAILS AS A FAIR COMPARISON.
A DIFFERENCE OF DEGREE IS A DIFFERENCE OF KIND.
YOU DID SO BRING IT UP! I CLEARLY HEARD YOU, AND FREDDY HEARD YOU TOO!

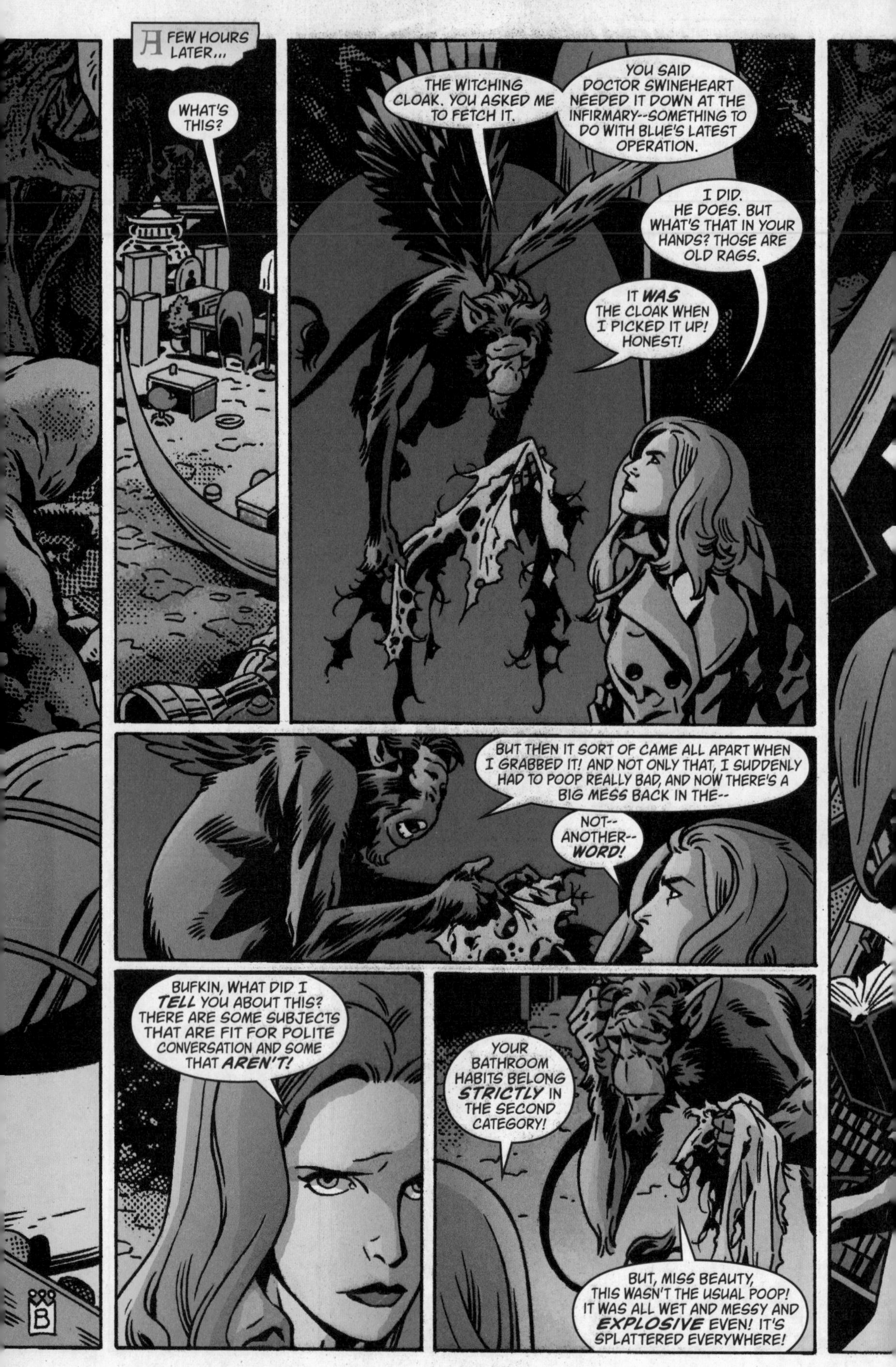

A FEW HOURS LATER...
WHAT'S THIS?
THE WITCHING CLOAK. YOU ASKED ME TO FETCH IT.
YOU SAID DOCTOR SWINEHEART NEEDED IT DOWN AT THE INFIRMARY--SOMETHING TO DO WITH BLUE'S LATEST OPERATION.
I DID. HE DOES. BUT WHAT'S THAT IN YOUR HANDS? THOSE ARE OLD RAGS.
IT WAS THE CLOAK WHEN I PICKED IT UP! HONEST!
BUT THEN IT SORT OF CAME ALL APART WHEN I GRABBED IT! AND NOT ONLY THAT, I SUDDENLY HAD TO POOP REALLY BAD, AND NOW THERE'S A BIG MESS BACK IN THE--
NOT-- ANOTHER-- WORD!
BUFKIN, WHAT DID I TELL YOU ABOUT THIS? THERE ARE SOME SUBJECTS THAT ARE FIT FOR POLITE CONVERSATION AND SOME THAT AREN'T!
YOUR BATHROOM HABITS BELONG STRICTLY IN THE SECOND CATEGORY!
BUT, MISS BEAUTY, THIS WASN'T THE USUAL POOP! IT WAS ALL WET AND MESSY AND EXPLOSIVE EVEN! IT'S SPLATTERED EVERYWHERE!

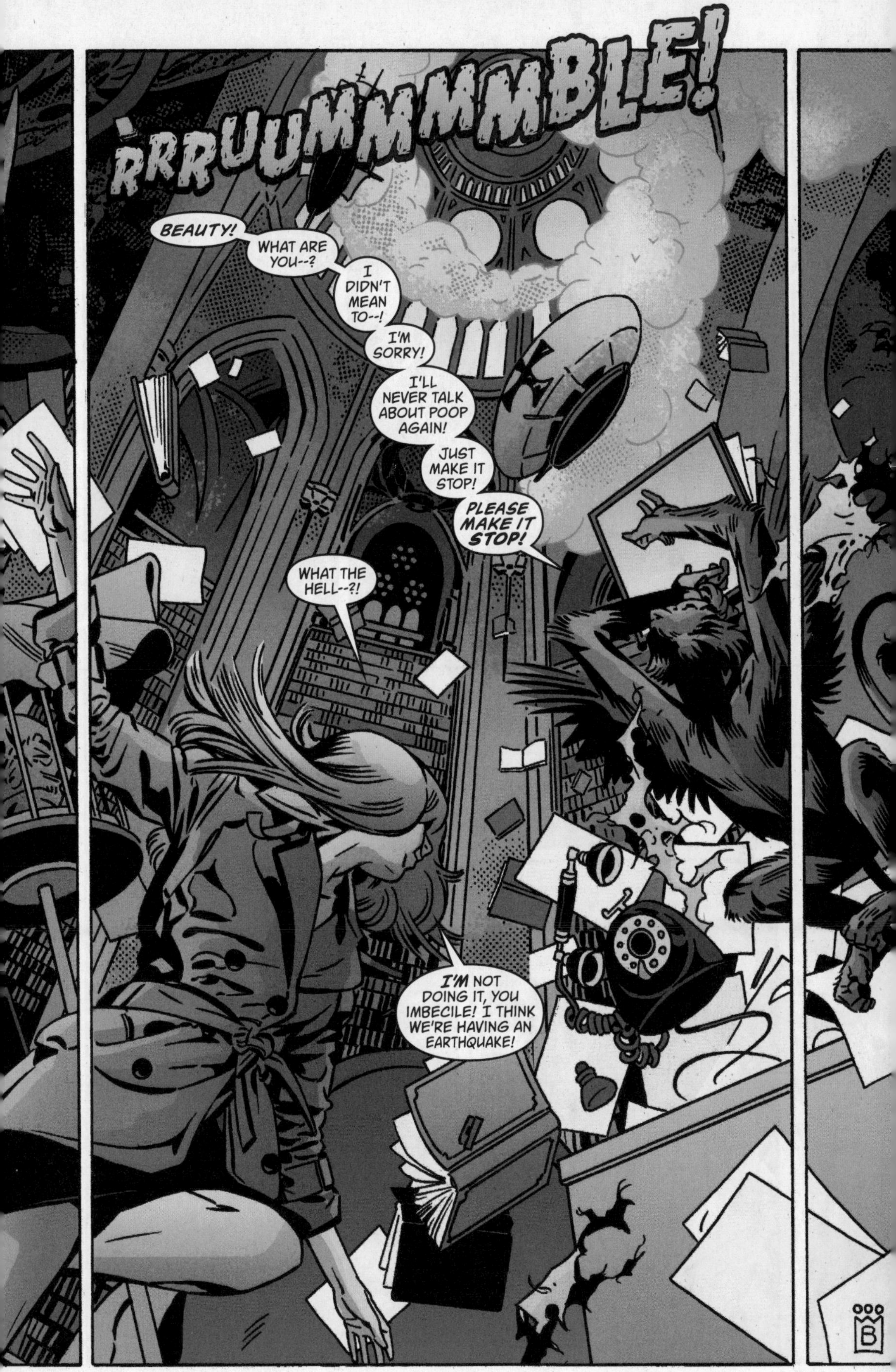
RRRUUMMMMMBLE!
BEAUTY!
WHAT ARE YOU--?
I DIDN'T MEAN TO--!
I'M SORRY!
I'LL NEVER TALK ABOUT POOP AGAIN!
JUST MAKE IT STOP!
PLEASE MAKE IT STOP!
WHAT THE HELL--?!
I'M NOT DOING IT, YOU IMBECILE! I THINK WE'RE HAVING AN EARTHQUAKE!

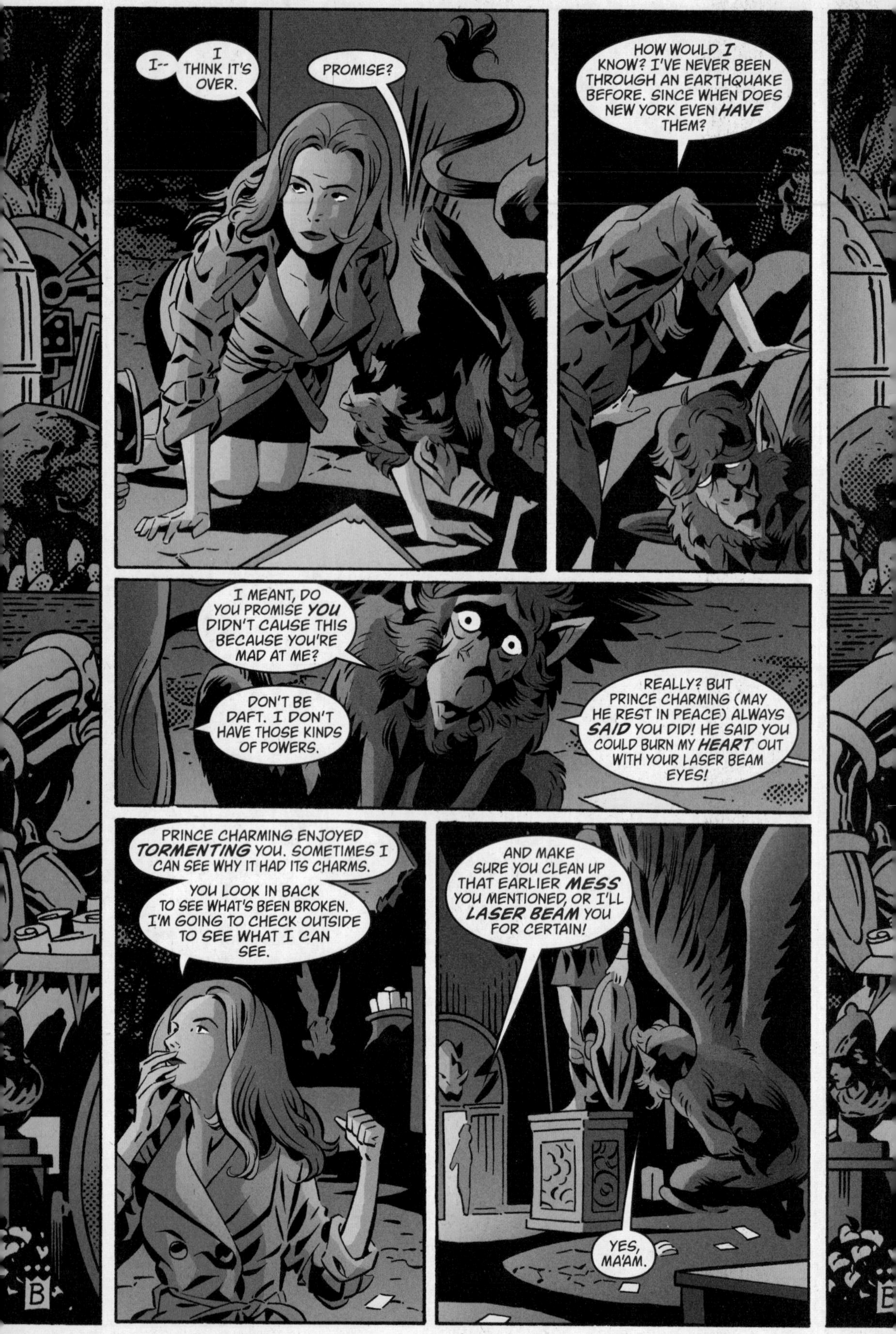
I--
I THINK IT'S OVER.
PROMISE?
HOW WOULD *I* KNOW? I'VE NEVER BEEN THROUGH AN EARTHQUAKE BEFORE. SINCE WHEN DOES NEW YORK EVEN *HAVE* THEM?
I MEANT, DO YOU PROMISE *YOU* DIDN'T CAUSE THIS BECAUSE YOU'RE MAD AT ME?
DON'T BE DAFT. I DON'T HAVE THOSE KINDS OF POWERS.
REALLY? BUT PRINCE CHARMING (MAY HE REST IN PEACE) ALWAYS *SAID* YOU DID! HE SAID YOU COULD BURN MY *HEART* OUT WITH YOUR LASER BEAM EYES!
PRINCE CHARMING ENJOYED *TORMENTING* YOU. SOMETIMES I CAN SEE WHY IT HAD ITS CHARMS.
YOU LOOK IN BACK TO SEE WHAT'S BEEN BROKEN. I'M GOING TO CHECK OUTSIDE TO SEE WHAT I CAN SEE.
AND MAKE SURE YOU CLEAN UP THAT EARLIER *MESS* YOU MENTIONED, OR I'LL *LASER BEAM* YOU FOR CERTAIN!
YES, MA'AM.

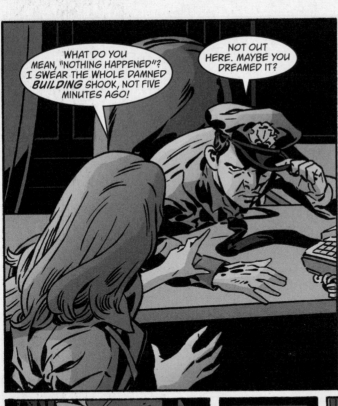

WHAT DO YOU MEAN, "NOTHING HAPPENED"? I SWEAR THE WHOLE DAMNED *BUILDING* SHOOK, NOT FIVE MINUTES AGO!

NOT OUT HERE. MAYBE YOU DREAMED IT?

THIS MAKES *NO* SENSE!

"I WASN'T DREAMING, GRIMBLE! I WASN'T EVEN ASLEEP! *YOU'RE* THE ONE WHO NAPS THE DAY AWAY!"

"I *DEMAND* THAT YOU GET OFF YOUR ASS AND SEE IF ANYONE ELSE NOTICED THE EARTHQUAKE!

"YOU'RE SUPPOSED TO BE THE WOODLAND'S SECURITY OFFICER, SO *ACT* LIKE IT! CHECK TO SEE IF WE'RE SECURE!"

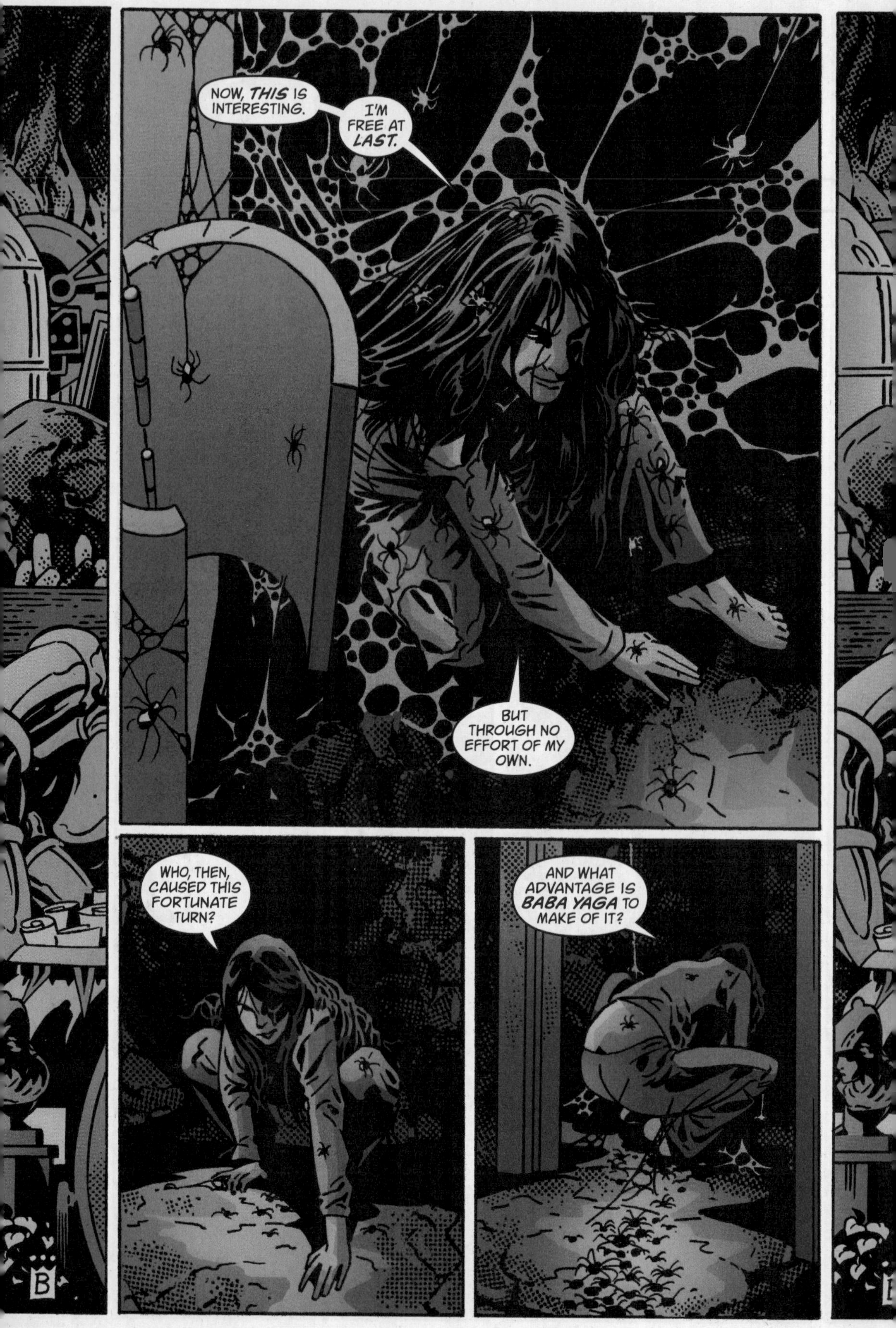
NOW, THIS IS INTERESTING.
I'M FREE AT LAST.
BUT THROUGH NO EFFORT OF MY OWN.
WHO, THEN, CAUSED THIS FORTUNATE TURN?
AND WHAT ADVANTAGE IS BABA YAGA TO MAKE OF IT?

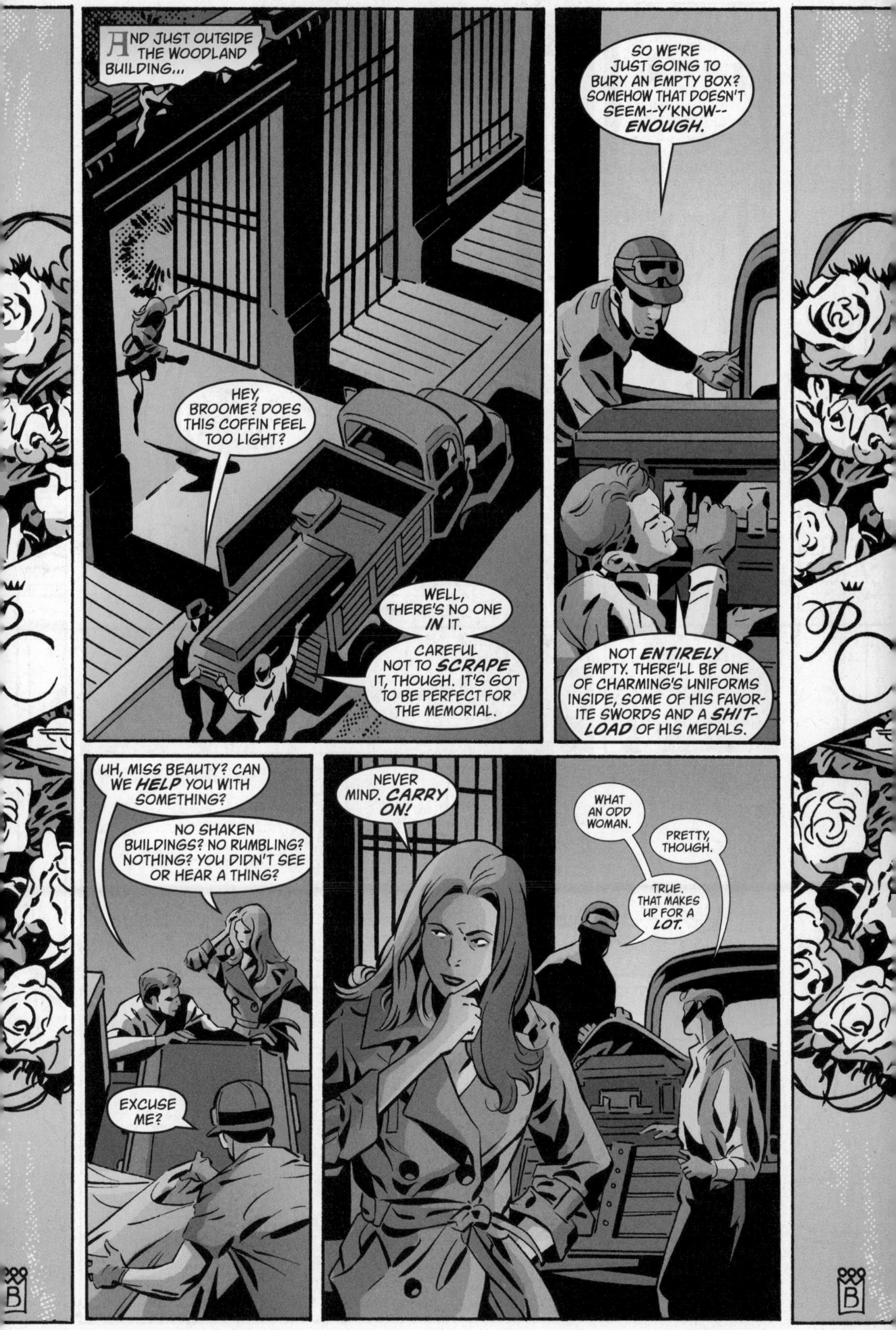
AND JUST OUTSIDE THE WOODLAND BUILDING...
HEY, BROOME? DOES THIS COFFIN FEEL TOO LIGHT?
WELL, THERE'S NO ONE IN IT.
CAREFUL NOT TO SCRAPE IT, THOUGH. IT'S GOT TO BE PERFECT FOR THE MEMORIAL.
SO WE'RE JUST GOING TO BURY AN EMPTY BOX? SOMEHOW THAT DOESN'T SEEM--Y'KNOW-- ENOUGH.
NOT ENTIRELY EMPTY. THERE'LL BE ONE OF CHARMING'S UNIFORMS INSIDE, SOME OF HIS FAVORITE SWORDS AND A SHIT-LOAD OF HIS MEDALS.
UH, MISS BEAUTY? CAN WE HELP YOU WITH SOMETHING?
NO SHAKEN BUILDINGS? NO RUMBLING? NOTHING? YOU DIDN'T SEE OR HEAR A THING?
EXCUSE ME?
NEVER MIND. CARRY ON!
WHAT AN ODD WOMAN.
PRETTY, THOUGH.
TRUE. THAT MAKES UP FOR A LOT.

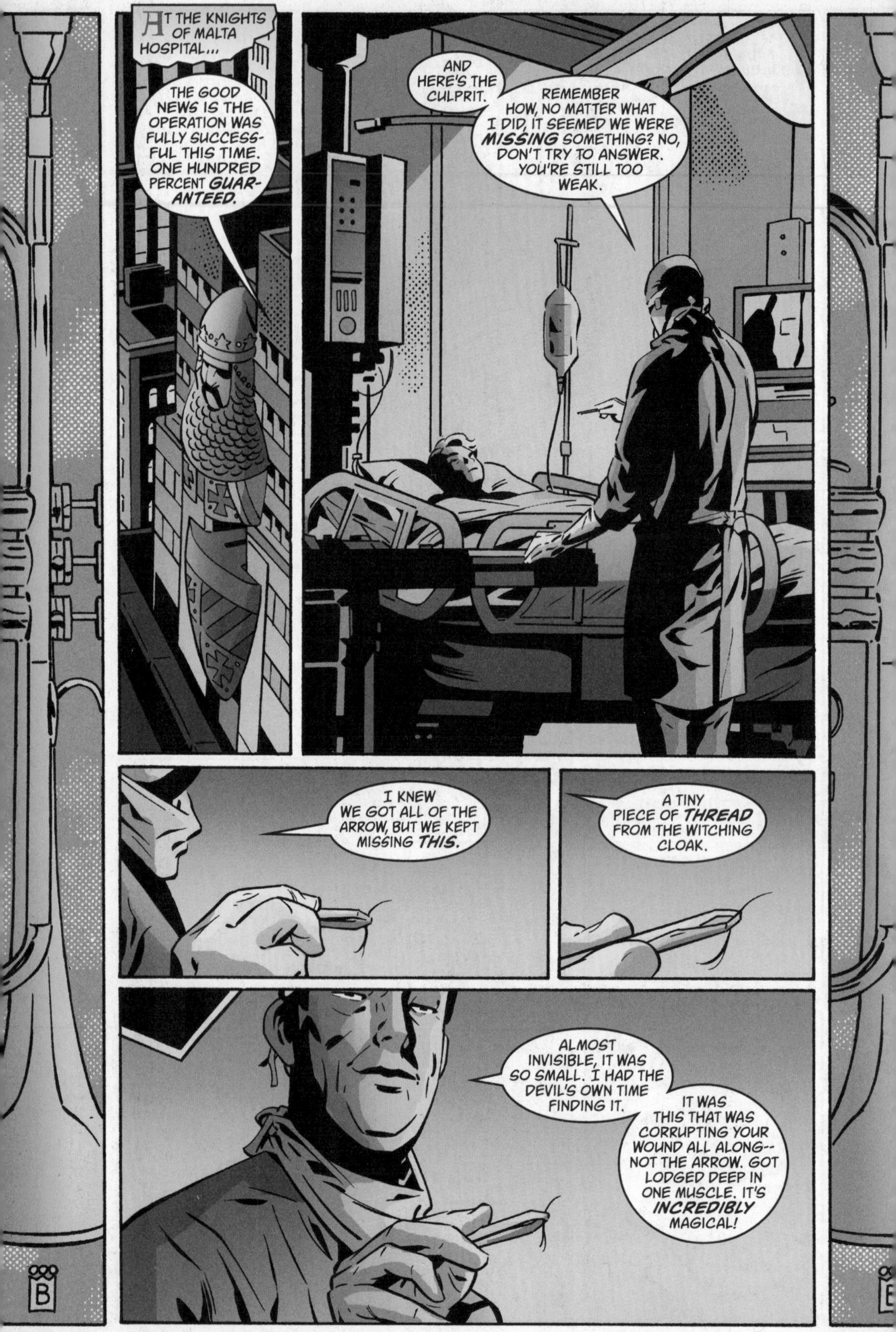

AT THE KNIGHTS OF MALTA HOSPITAL...
THE GOOD NEWS IS THE OPERATION WAS FULLY SUCCESSFUL THIS TIME. ONE HUNDRED PERCENT GUARANTEED.
AND HERE'S THE CULPRIT.
REMEMBER HOW, NO MATTER WHAT I DID, IT SEEMED WE WERE MISSING SOMETHING? NO, DON'T TRY TO ANSWER. YOU'RE STILL TOO WEAK.
I KNEW WE GOT ALL OF THE ARROW, BUT WE KEPT MISSING THIS.
A TINY PIECE OF THREAD FROM THE WITCHING CLOAK.
ALMOST INVISIBLE, IT WAS SO SMALL. I HAD THE DEVIL'S OWN TIME FINDING IT.
IT WAS THIS THAT WAS CORRUPTING YOUR WOUND ALL ALONG-- NOT THE ARROW. GOT LODGED DEEP IN ONE MUSCLE. IT'S INCREDIBLY MAGICAL!

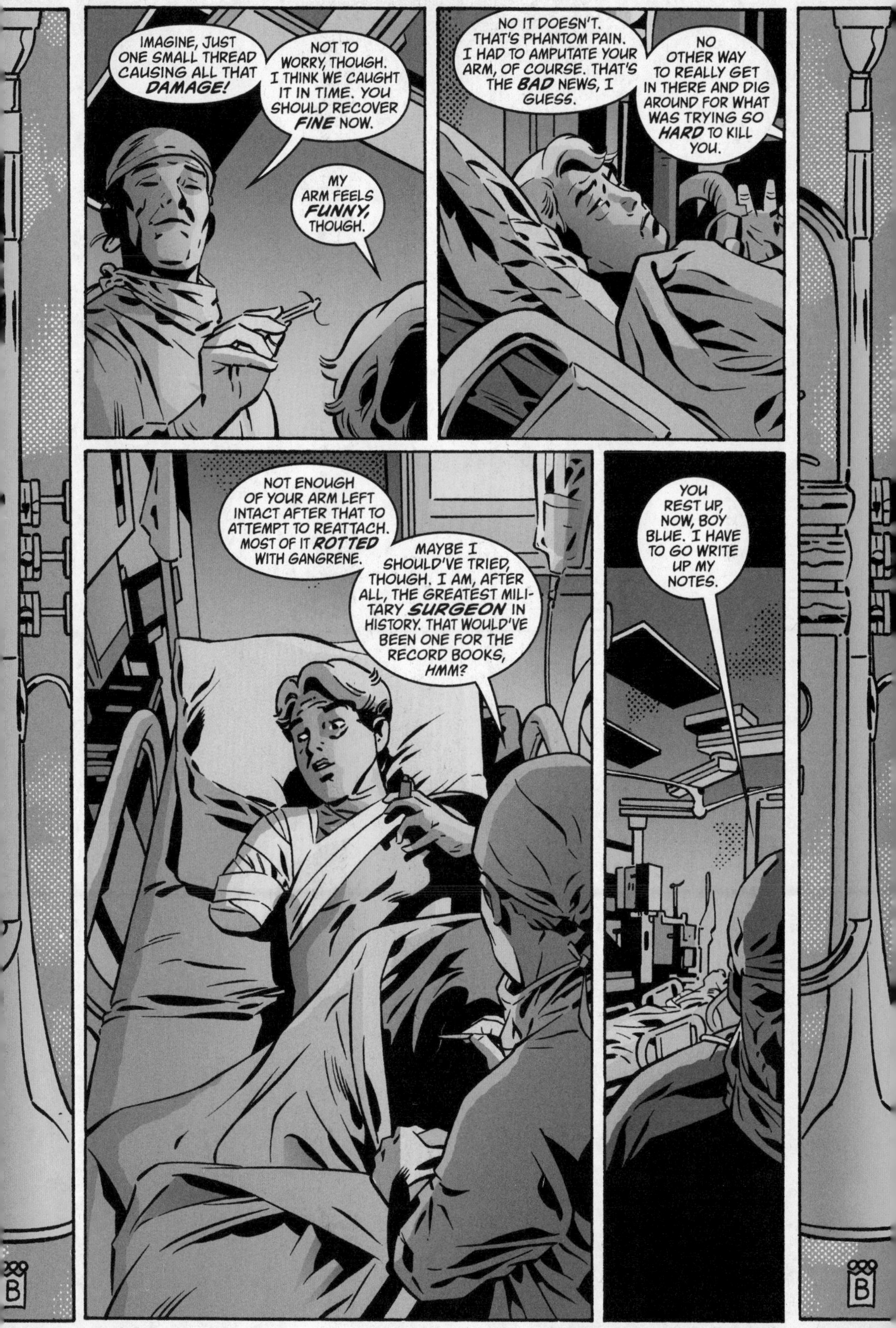
IMAGINE, JUST ONE SMALL THREAD CAUSING ALL THAT DAMAGE!
NOT TO WORRY, THOUGH. I THINK WE CAUGHT IT IN TIME. YOU SHOULD RECOVER FINE NOW.
MY ARM FEELS FUNNY, THOUGH.
NO IT DOESN'T. THAT'S PHANTOM PAIN. I HAD TO AMPUTATE YOUR ARM, OF COURSE. THAT'S THE BAD NEWS, I GUESS.
NO OTHER WAY TO REALLY GET IN THERE AND DIG AROUND FOR WHAT WAS TRYING SO HARD TO KILL YOU.
NOT ENOUGH OF YOUR ARM LEFT INTACT AFTER THAT TO ATTEMPT TO REATTACH. MOST OF IT ROTTED WITH GANGRENE.
MAYBE I SHOULD'VE TRIED, THOUGH. I AM, AFTER ALL, THE GREATEST MILI-TARY SURGEON IN HISTORY. THAT WOULD'VE BEEN ONE FOR THE RECORD BOOKS, HMM?
YOU REST UP, NOW, BOY BLUE. I HAVE TO GO WRITE UP MY NOTES.

NEXT: THE GREAT UNBINDING

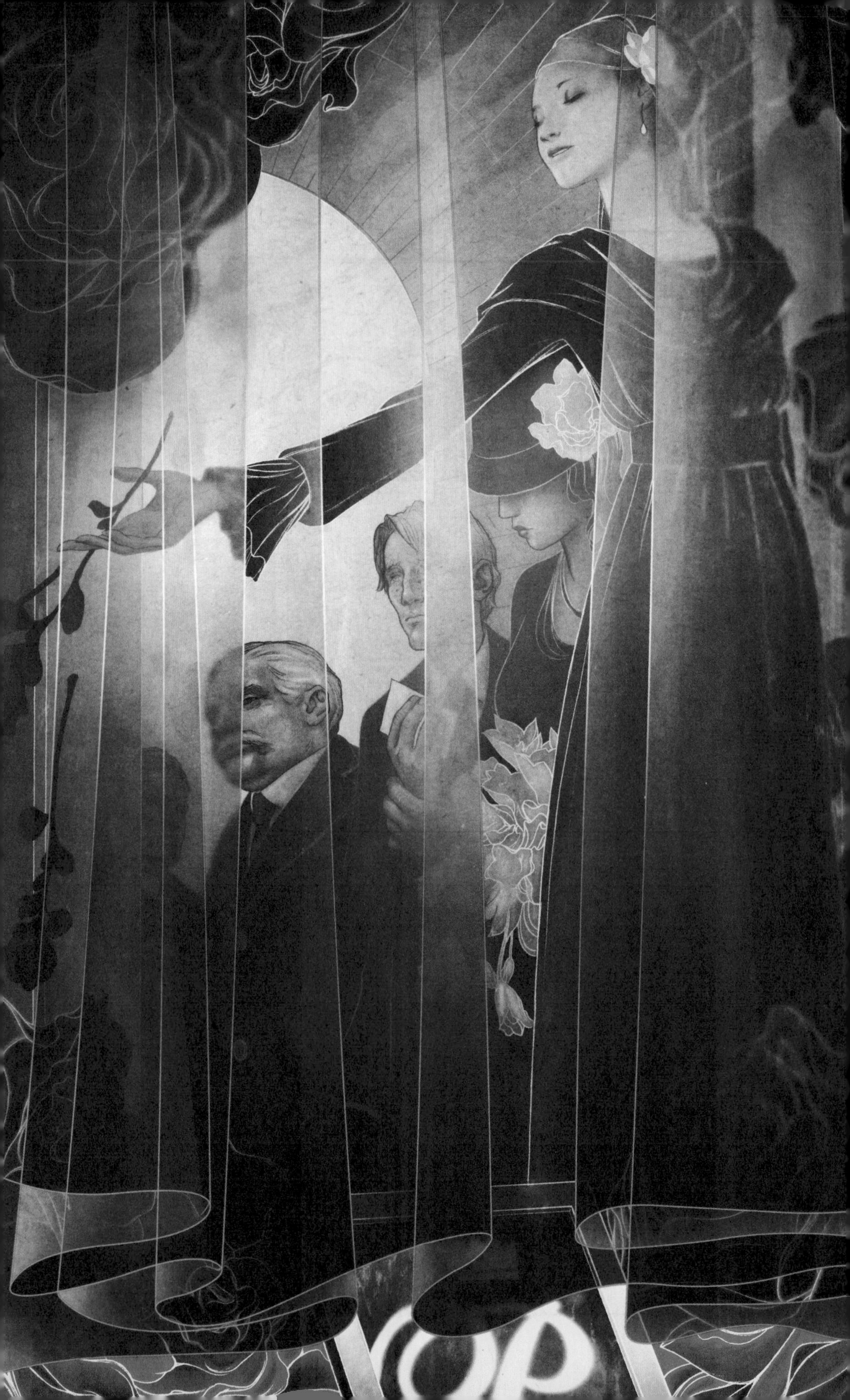

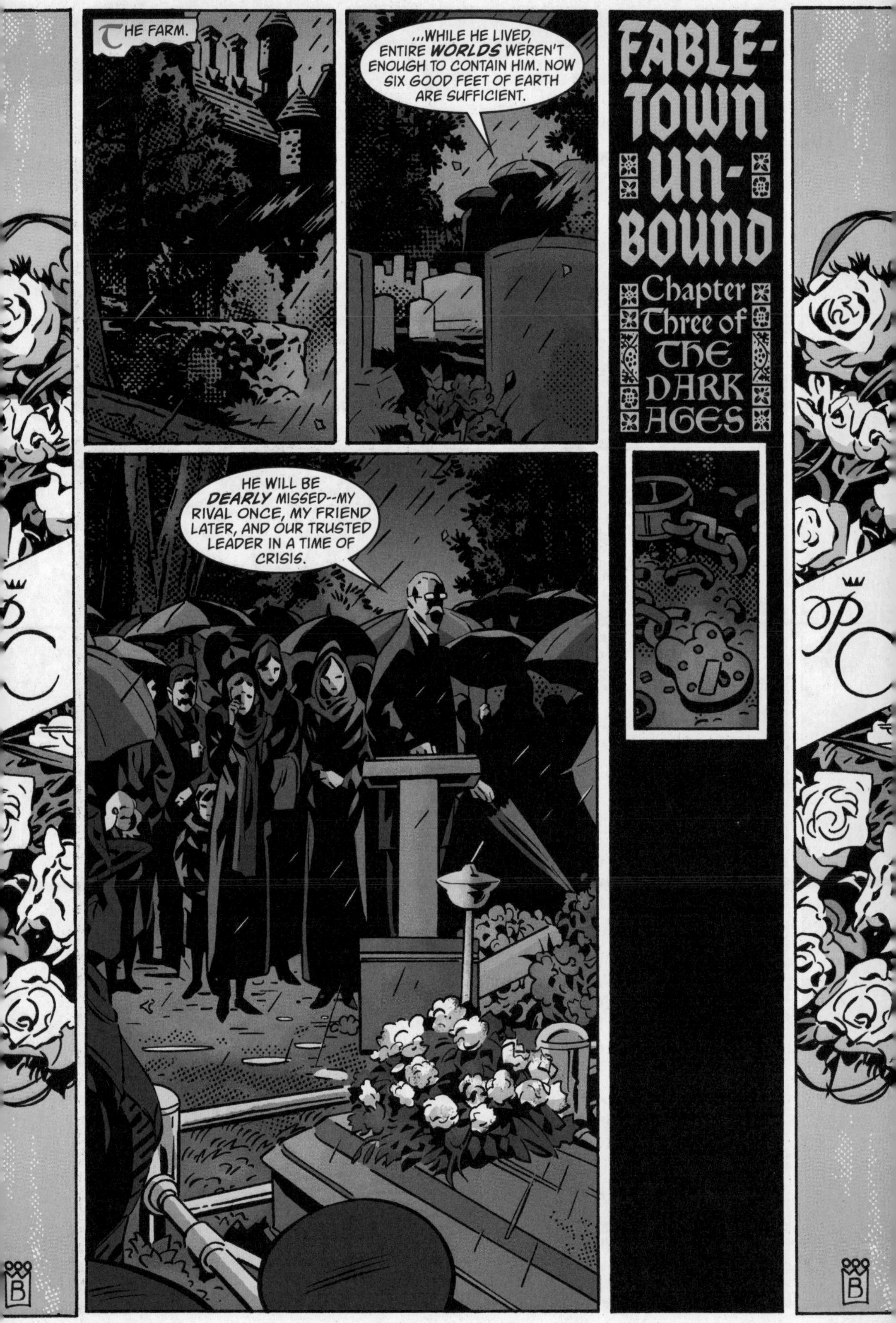
THE FARM.
...WHILE HE LIVED, ENTIRE WORLDS WEREN'T ENOUGH TO CONTAIN HIM. NOW SIX GOOD FEET OF EARTH ARE SUFFICIENT.
FABLE-TOWN UN-BOUND
Chapter Three of THE DARK AGES
HE WILL BE DEARLY MISSED--MY RIVAL ONCE, MY FRIEND LATER, AND OUR TRUSTED LEADER IN A TIME OF CRISIS.

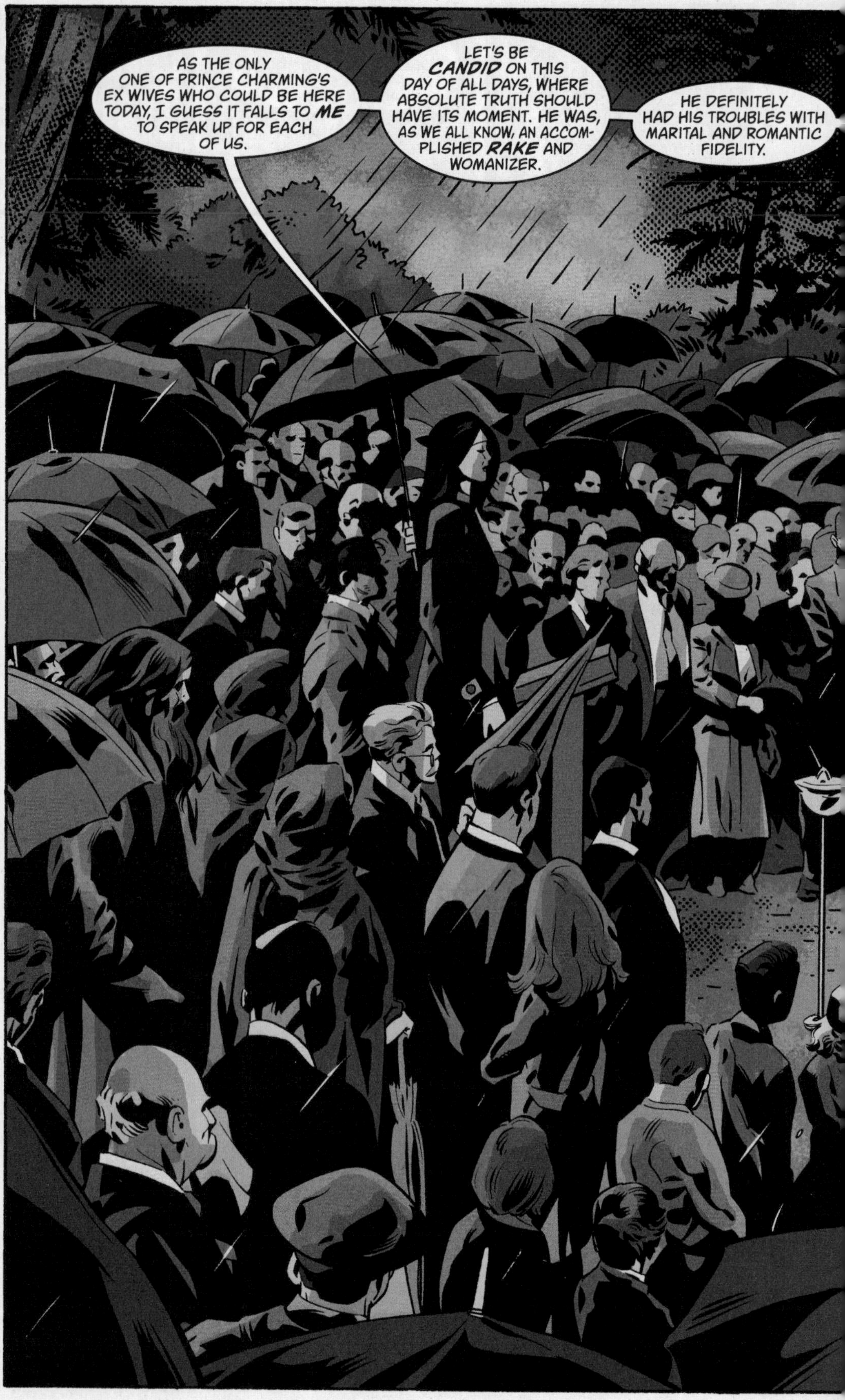
AS THE ONLY ONE OF PRINCE CHARMING'S EX WIVES WHO COULD BE HERE TODAY, I GUESS IT FALLS TO ME TO SPEAK UP FOR EACH OF US.
LET'S BE CANDID ON THIS DAY OF ALL DAYS, WHERE ABSOLUTE TRUTH SHOULD HAVE ITS MOMENT. HE WAS, AS WE ALL KNOW, AN ACCOMPLISHED RAKE AND WOMANIZER.
HE DEFINITELY HAD HIS TROUBLES WITH MARITAL AND ROMANTIC FIDELITY.

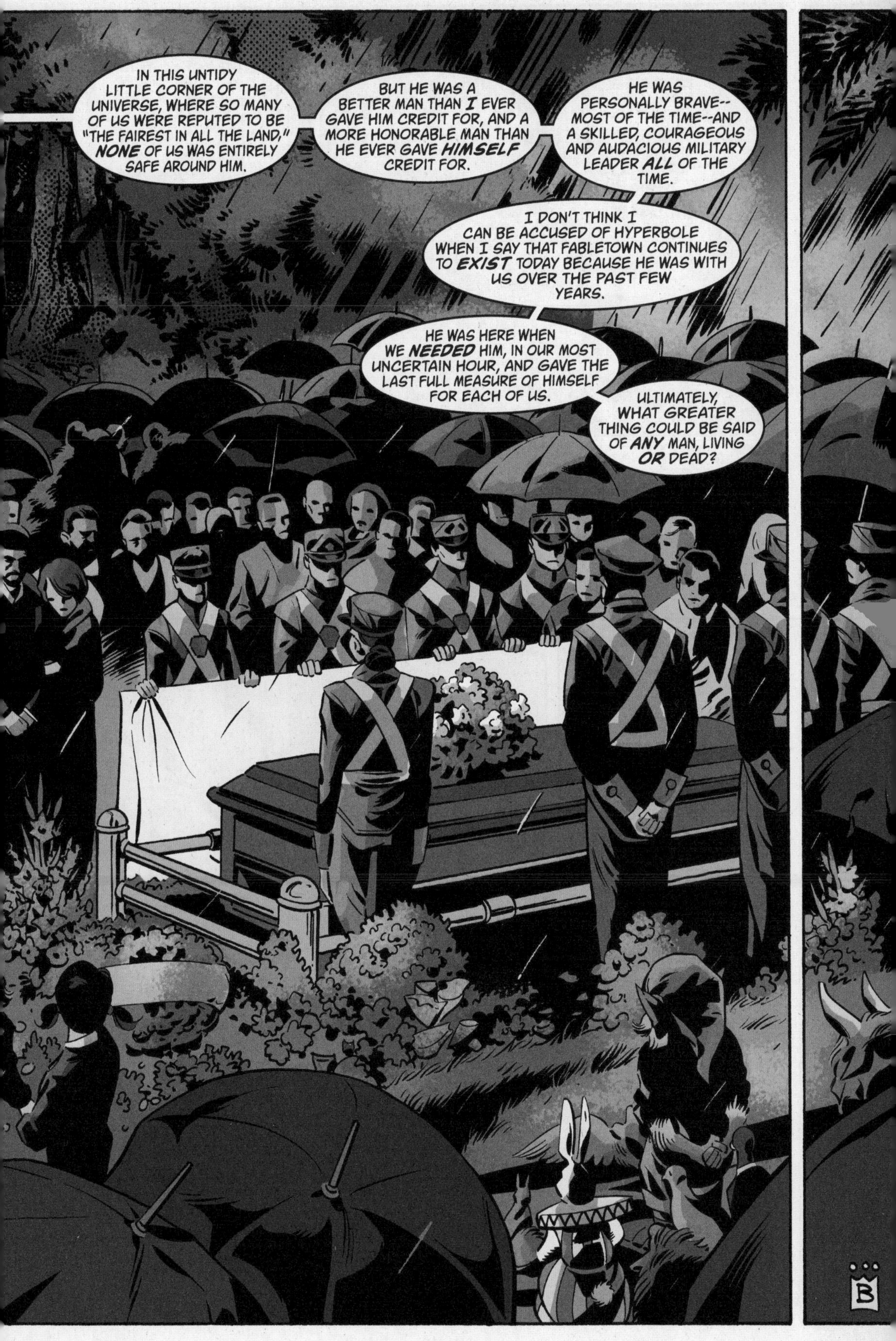
IN THIS UNTIDY LITTLE CORNER OF THE UNIVERSE, WHERE SO MANY OF US WERE REPUTED TO BE "THE FAIREST IN ALL THE LAND," NONE OF US WAS ENTIRELY SAFE AROUND HIM.
BUT HE WAS A BETTER MAN THAN I EVER GAVE HIM CREDIT FOR, AND A MORE HONORABLE MAN THAN HE EVER GAVE HIMSELF CREDIT FOR.
HE WAS PERSONALLY BRAVE-- MOST OF THE TIME--AND A SKILLED, COURAGEOUS AND AUDACIOUS MILITARY LEADER ALL OF THE TIME.
I DON'T THINK I CAN BE ACCUSED OF HYPERBOLE WHEN I SAY THAT FABLETOWN CONTINUES TO EXIST TODAY BECAUSE HE WAS WITH US OVER THE PAST FEW YEARS.
HE WAS HERE WHEN WE NEEDED HIM, IN OUR MOST UNCERTAIN HOUR, AND GAVE THE LAST FULL MEASURE OF HIMSELF FOR EACH OF US.
ULTIMATELY, WHAT GREATER THING COULD BE SAID OF ANY MAN, LIVING OR DEAD?

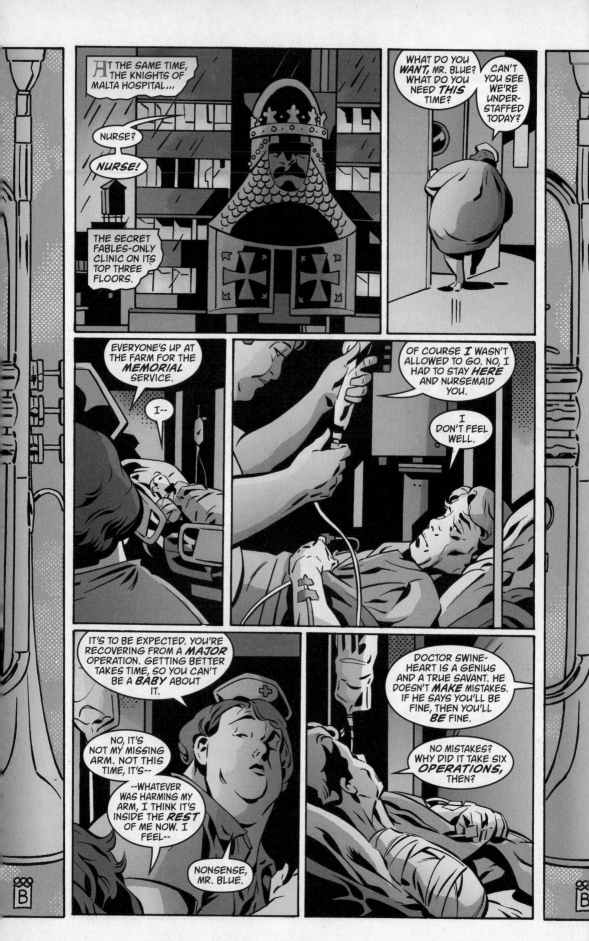

AT THE SAME TIME, THE KNIGHTS OF MALTA HOSPITAL...

NURSE?

NURSE!

THE SECRET FABLES-ONLY CLINIC ON ITS TOP THREE FLOORS.

WHAT DO YOU *WANT*, MR. BLUE? WHAT DO YOU NEED *THIS* TIME?

CAN'T YOU SEE WE'RE UNDER-STAFFED TODAY?

EVERYONE'S UP AT THE FARM FOR THE *MEMORIAL* SERVICE.

I--

OF COURSE *I* WASN'T ALLOWED TO GO. NO, I HAD TO STAY *HERE* AND NURSEMAID YOU.

I DON'T FEEL WELL.

IT'S TO BE EXPECTED. YOU'RE RECOVERING FROM A *MAJOR* OPERATION. GETTING BETTER TAKES TIME, SO YOU CAN'T BE A *BABY* ABOUT IT.

NO, IT'S NOT MY MISSING ARM. NOT THIS TIME, IT'S--

--WHATEVER WAS HARMING MY ARM, I THINK IT'S INSIDE THE *REST* OF ME NOW. I FEEL--

NONSENSE, MR. BLUE.

DOCTOR SWINE-HEART IS A GENIUS AND A TRUE SAVANT. HE DOESN'T *MAKE* MISTAKES. IF HE SAYS YOU'LL BE FINE, THEN YOU'LL *BE* FINE.

NO MISTAKES? WHY DID IT TAKE SIX *OPERATIONS*, THEN?

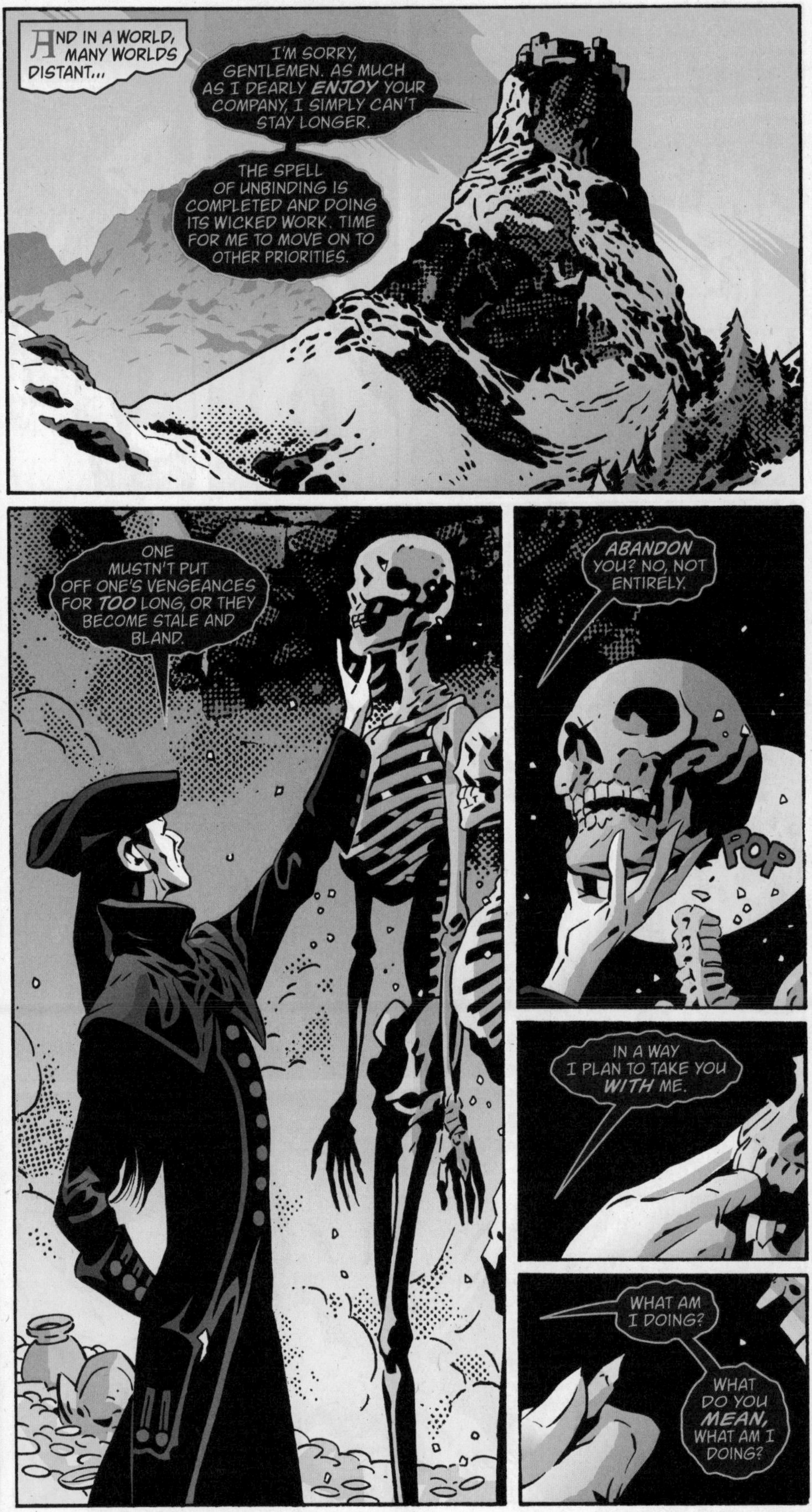
AND IN A WORLD, MANY WORLDS DISTANT...
I'M SORRY, GENTLEMEN. AS MUCH AS I DEARLY ENJOY YOUR COMPANY, I SIMPLY CAN'T STAY LONGER.
THE SPELL OF UNBINDING IS COMPLETED AND DOING ITS WICKED WORK. TIME FOR ME TO MOVE ON TO OTHER PRIORITIES.
ONE MUSTN'T PUT OFF ONE'S VENGEANCES FOR TOO LONG, OR THEY BECOME STALE AND BLAND.
ABANDON YOU? NO, NOT ENTIRELY.
POP
IN A WAY I PLAN TO TAKE YOU WITH ME.
WHAT AM I DOING?
WHAT DO YOU MEAN, WHAT AM I DOING?

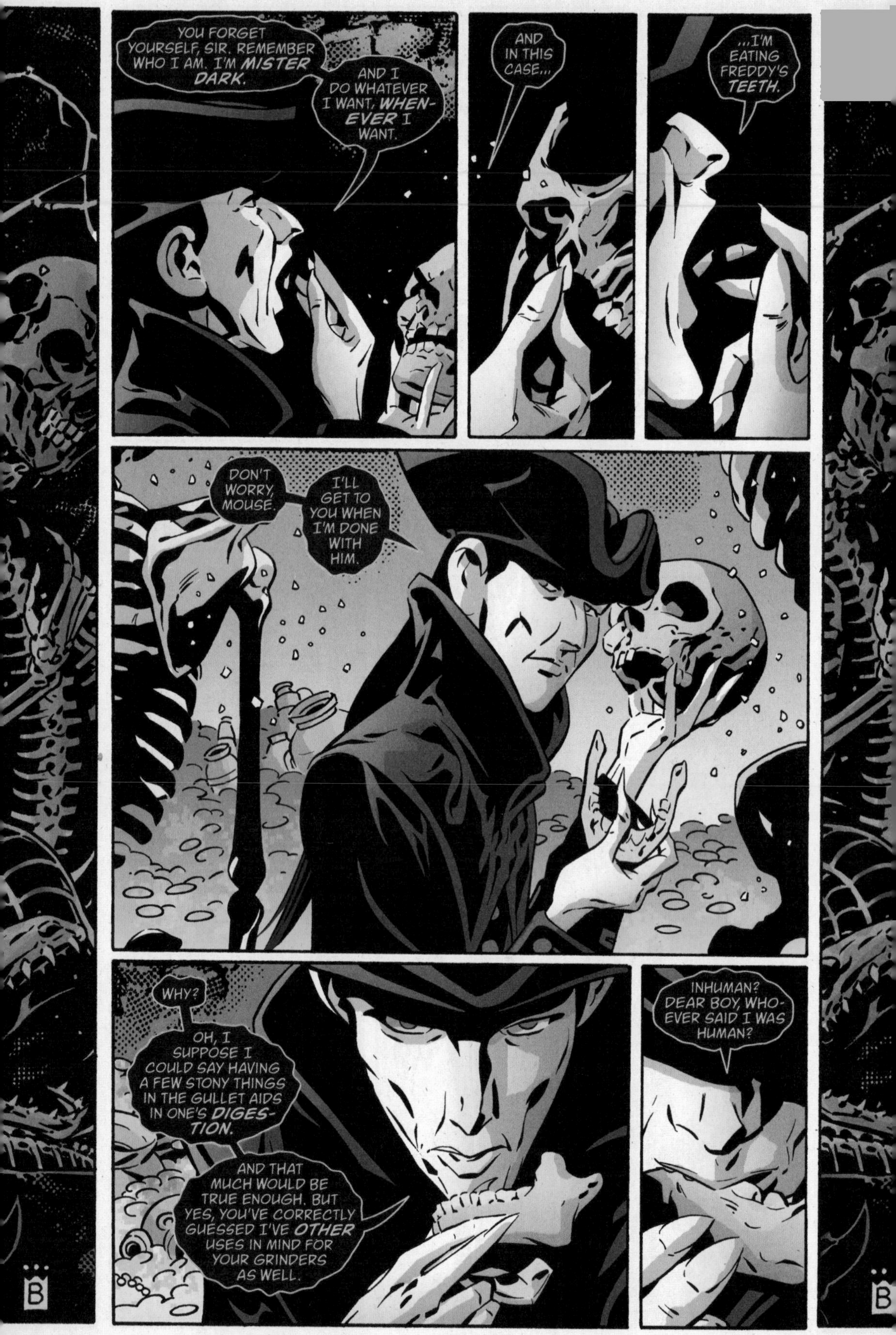

YOU FORGET YOURSELF, SIR. REMEMBER WHO I AM. I'M MISTER DARK.
AND I DO WHATEVER I WANT, WHENEVER I WANT.
AND IN THIS CASE...
...I'M EATING FREDDY'S TEETH.
DON'T WORRY, MOUSE.
I'LL GET TO YOU WHEN I'M DONE WITH HIM.
WHY?
OH, I SUPPOSE I COULD SAY HAVING A FEW STONY THINGS IN THE GULLET AIDS IN ONE'S DIGESTION.
AND THAT MUCH WOULD BE TRUE ENOUGH. BUT YES, YOU'VE CORRECTLY GUESSED I'VE OTHER USES IN MIND FOR YOUR GRINDERS AS WELL.
INHUMAN? DEAR BOY, WHOEVER SAID I WAS HUMAN?

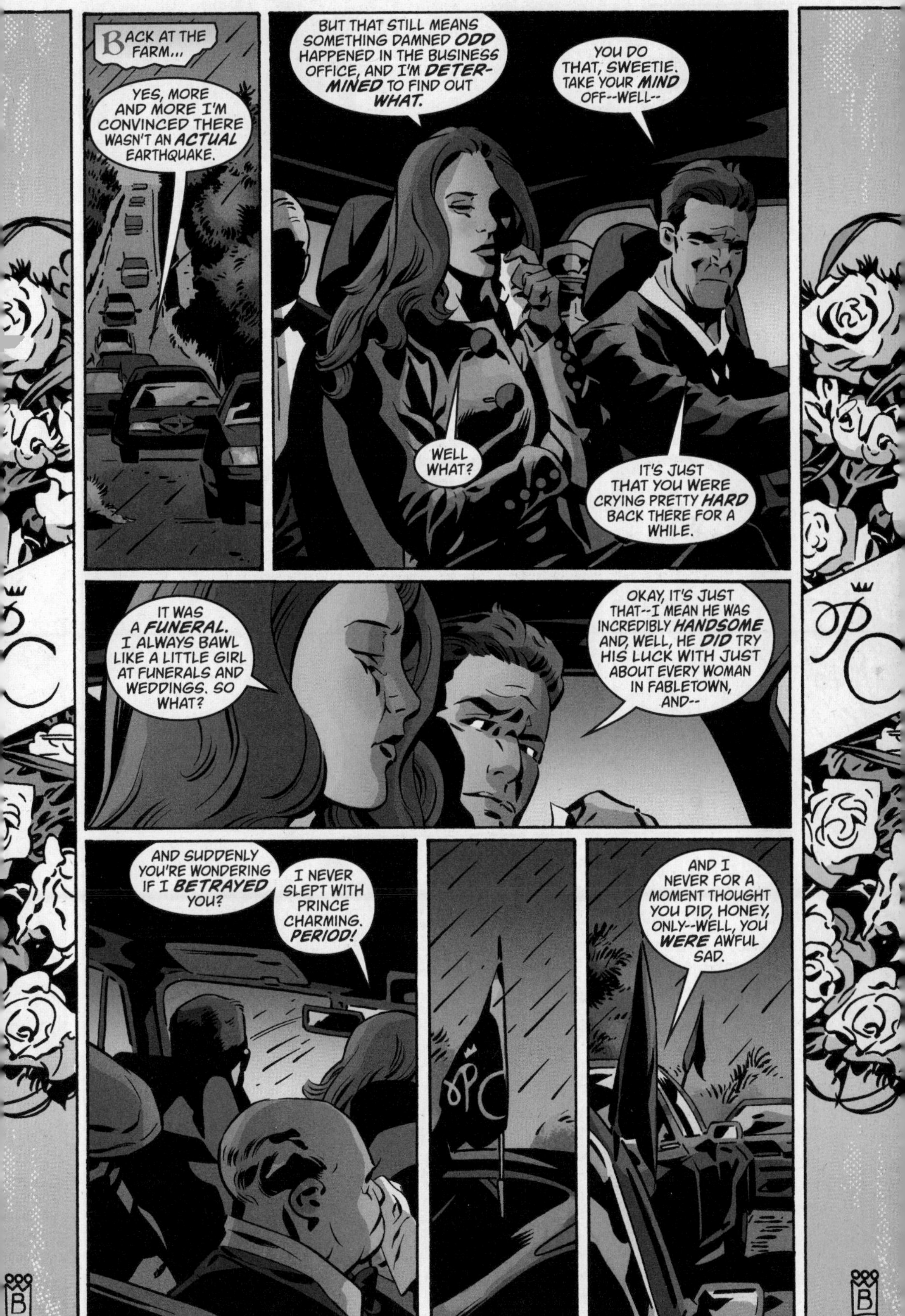
BACK AT THE FARM...
YES, MORE AND MORE I'M CONVINCED THERE WASN'T AN ACTUAL EARTHQUAKE.
BUT THAT STILL MEANS SOMETHING DAMNED ODD HAPPENED IN THE BUSINESS OFFICE, AND I'M DETERMINED TO FIND OUT WHAT.
YOU DO THAT, SWEETIE. TAKE YOUR MIND OFF--WELL--
WELL WHAT?
IT'S JUST THAT YOU WERE CRYING PRETTY HARD BACK THERE FOR A WHILE.
IT WAS A FUNERAL. I ALWAYS BAWL LIKE A LITTLE GIRL AT FUNERALS AND WEDDINGS. SO WHAT?
OKAY, IT'S JUST THAT--I MEAN HE WAS INCREDIBLY HANDSOME AND, WELL, HE DID TRY HIS LUCK WITH JUST ABOUT EVERY WOMAN IN FABLETOWN, AND--
AND SUDDENLY YOU'RE WONDERING IF I BETRAYED YOU?
I NEVER SLEPT WITH PRINCE CHARMING. PERIOD!
AND I NEVER FOR A MOMENT THOUGHT YOU DID, HONEY, ONLY--WELL, YOU WERE AWFUL SAD.

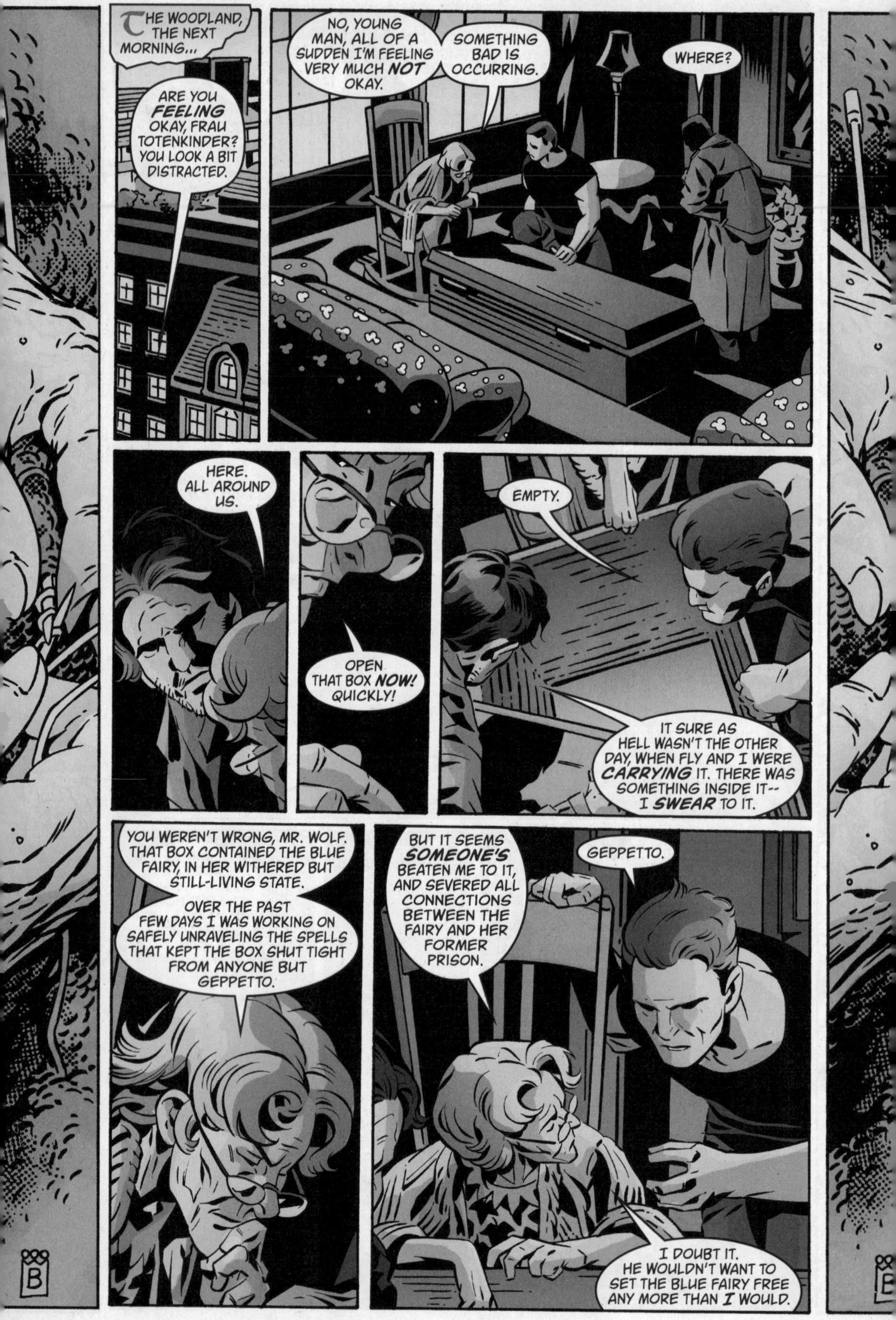
THE WOODLAND, THE NEXT MORNING...
ARE YOU FEELING OKAY, FRAU TOTENKINDER? YOU LOOK A BIT DISTRACTED.
NO, YOUNG MAN, ALL OF A SUDDEN I'M FEELING VERY MUCH NOT OKAY.
SOMETHING BAD IS OCCURRING.
WHERE?
HERE. ALL AROUND US.
OPEN THAT BOX NOW! QUICKLY!
EMPTY.
IT SURE AS HELL WASN'T THE OTHER DAY, WHEN FLY AND I WERE CARRYING IT. THERE WAS SOMETHING INSIDE IT-- I SWEAR TO IT.
YOU WEREN'T WRONG, MR. WOLF. THAT BOX CONTAINED THE BLUE FAIRY, IN HER WITHERED BUT STILL-LIVING STATE.
OVER THE PAST FEW DAYS I WAS WORKING ON SAFELY UNRAVELING THE SPELLS THAT KEPT THE BOX SHUT TIGHT FROM ANYONE BUT GEPPETTO.
BUT IT SEEMS SOMEONE'S BEATEN ME TO IT, AND SEVERED ALL CONNECTIONS BETWEEN THE FAIRY AND HER FORMER PRISON.
GEPPETTO.
I DOUBT IT. HE WOULDN'T WANT TO SET THE BLUE FAIRY FREE ANY MORE THAN I WOULD.

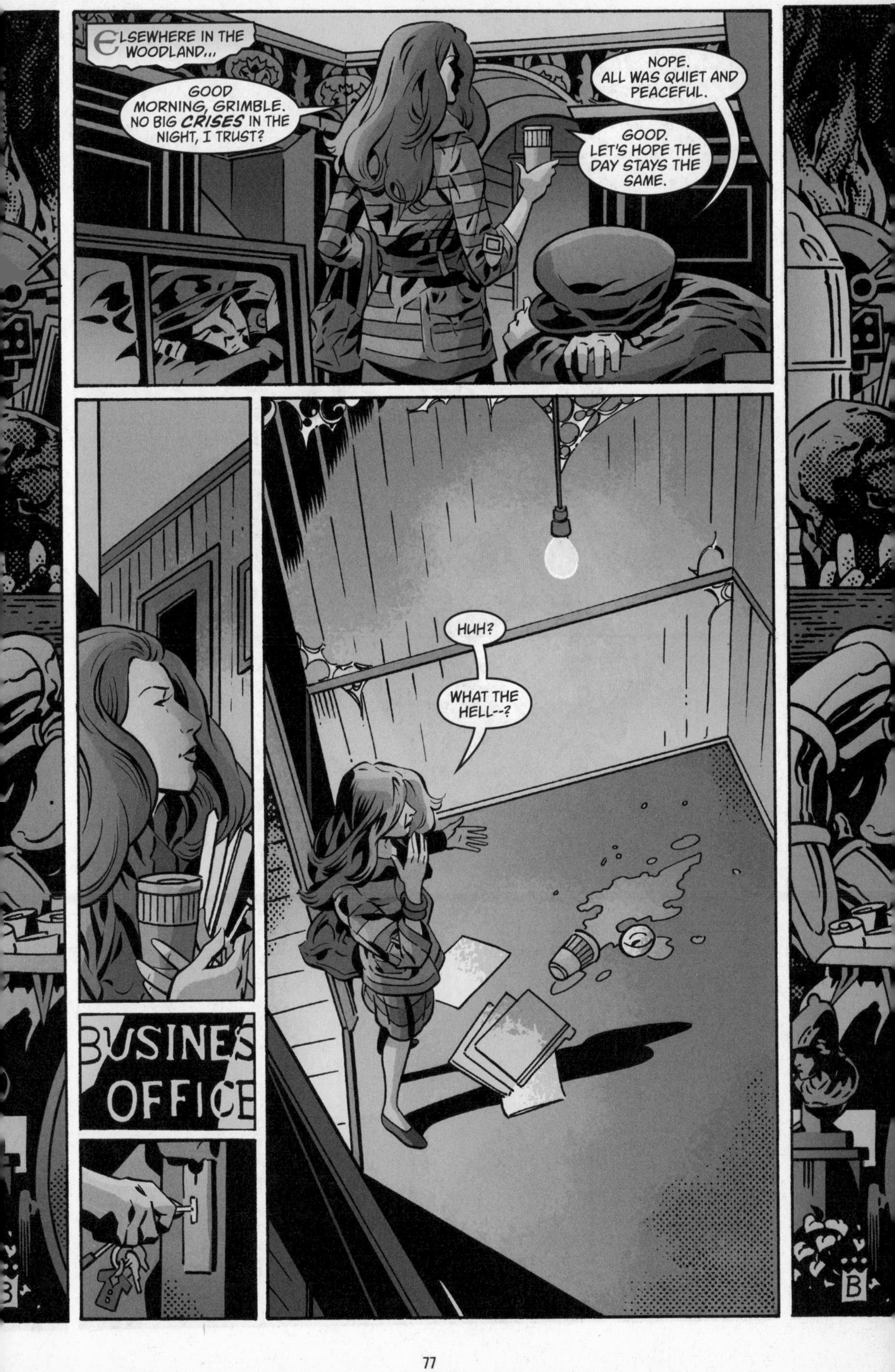
ELSEWHERE IN THE WOODLAND...
GOOD MORNING, GRIMBLE. NO BIG CRISES IN THE NIGHT, I TRUST?
NOPE. ALL WAS QUIET AND PEACEFUL.
GOOD. LET'S HOPE THE DAY STAYS THE SAME.
BUSINES OFFICE
HUH?
WHAT THE HELL--?

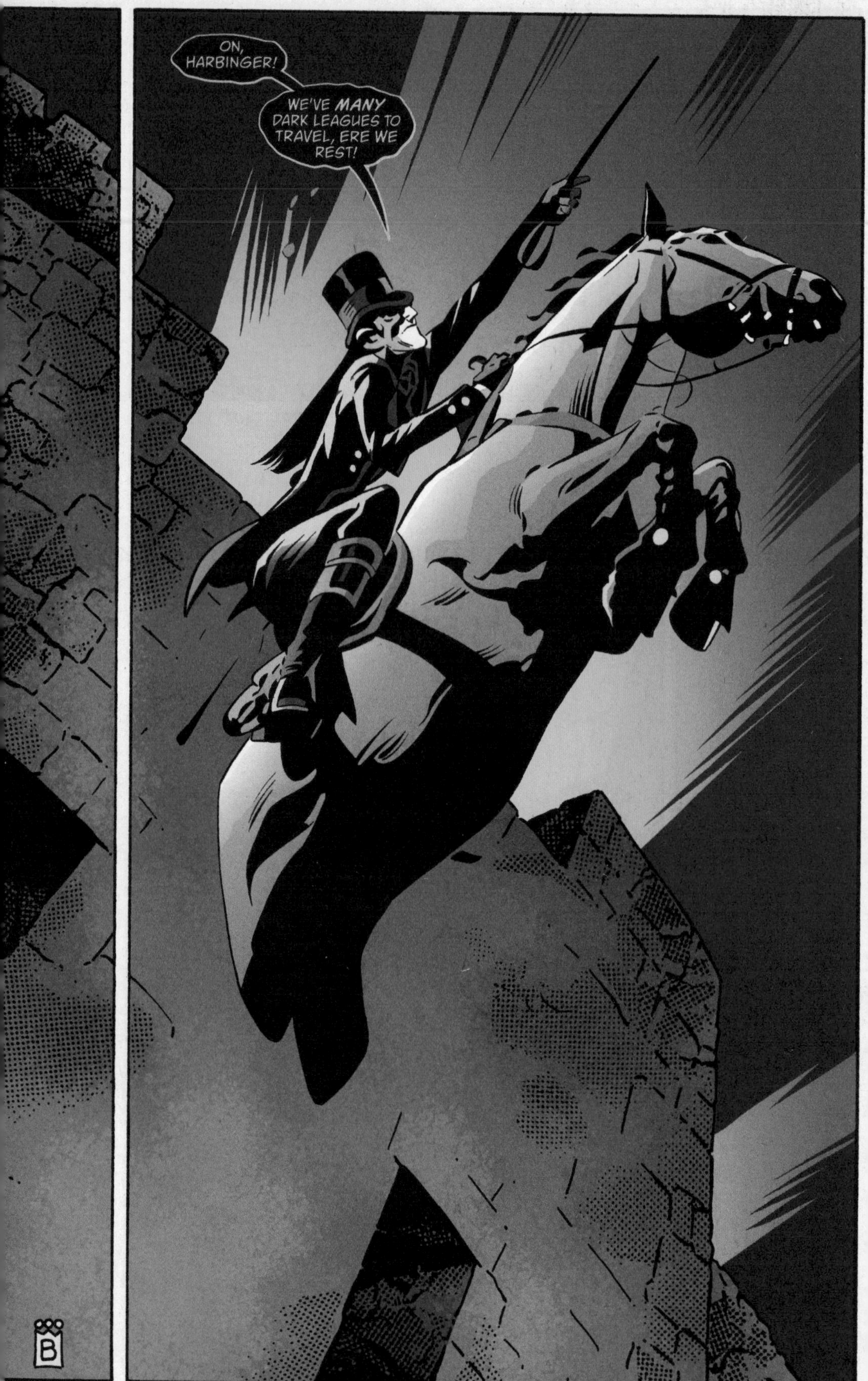
ON, HARBINGER!
WE'VE MANY DARK LEAGUES TO TRAVEL, ERE WE REST!

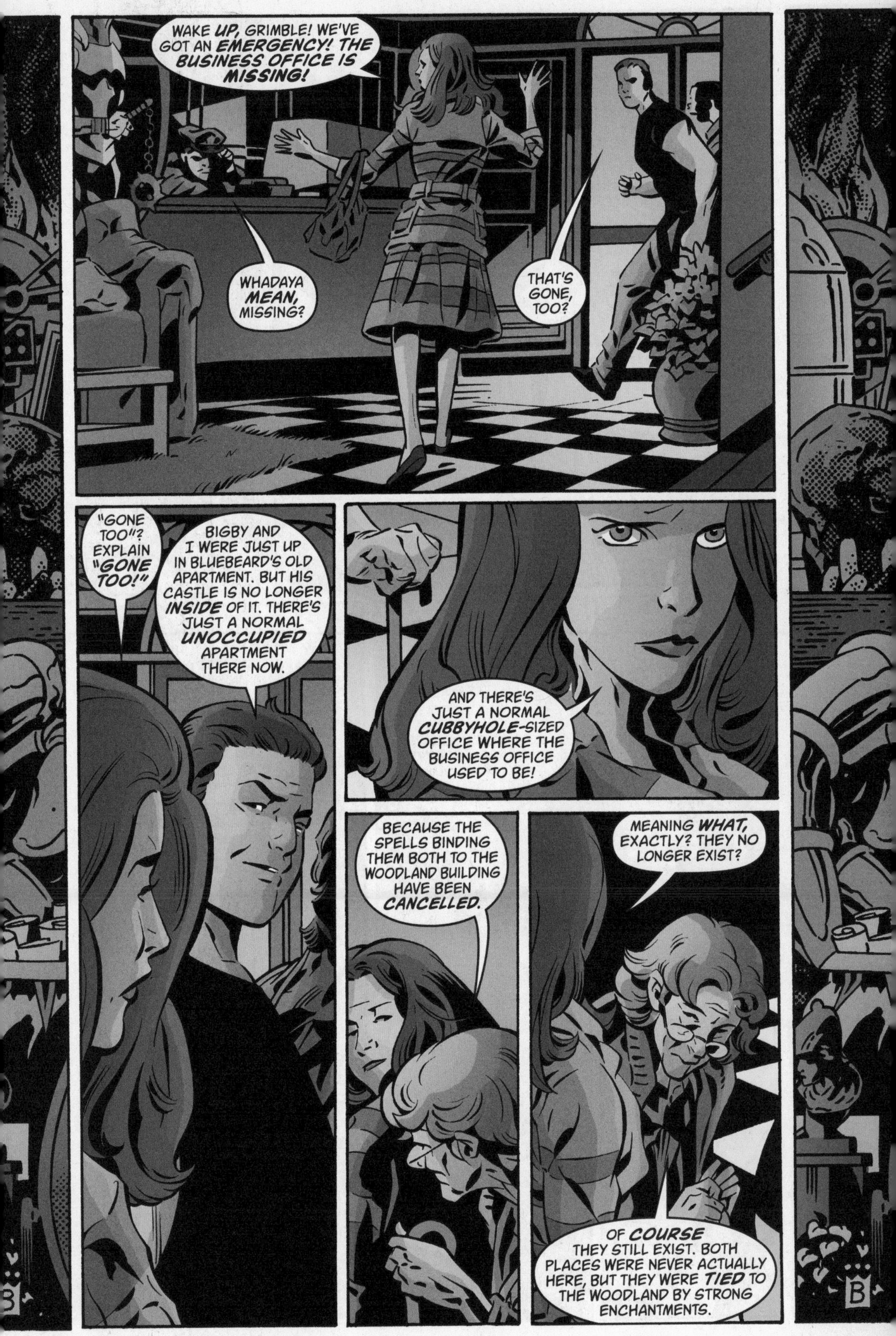
WAKE UP, GRIMBLE! WE'VE GOT AN EMERGENCY! THE BUSINESS OFFICE IS MISSING!
WHADAYA MEAN, MISSING?
THAT'S GONE, TOO?
"GONE TOO"? EXPLAIN "GONE TOO!"
BIGBY AND I WERE JUST UP IN BLUEBEARD'S OLD APARTMENT. BUT HIS CASTLE IS NO LONGER INSIDE OF IT. THERE'S JUST A NORMAL UNOCCUPIED APARTMENT THERE NOW.
AND THERE'S JUST A NORMAL CUBBYHOLE-SIZED OFFICE WHERE THE BUSINESS OFFICE USED TO BE!
BECAUSE THE SPELLS BINDING THEM BOTH TO THE WOODLAND BUILDING HAVE BEEN CANCELLED.
MEANING WHAT, EXACTLY? THEY NO LONGER EXIST?
OF COURSE THEY STILL EXIST. BOTH PLACES WERE NEVER ACTUALLY HERE, BUT THEY WERE TIED TO THE WOODLAND BY STRONG ENCHANTMENTS.

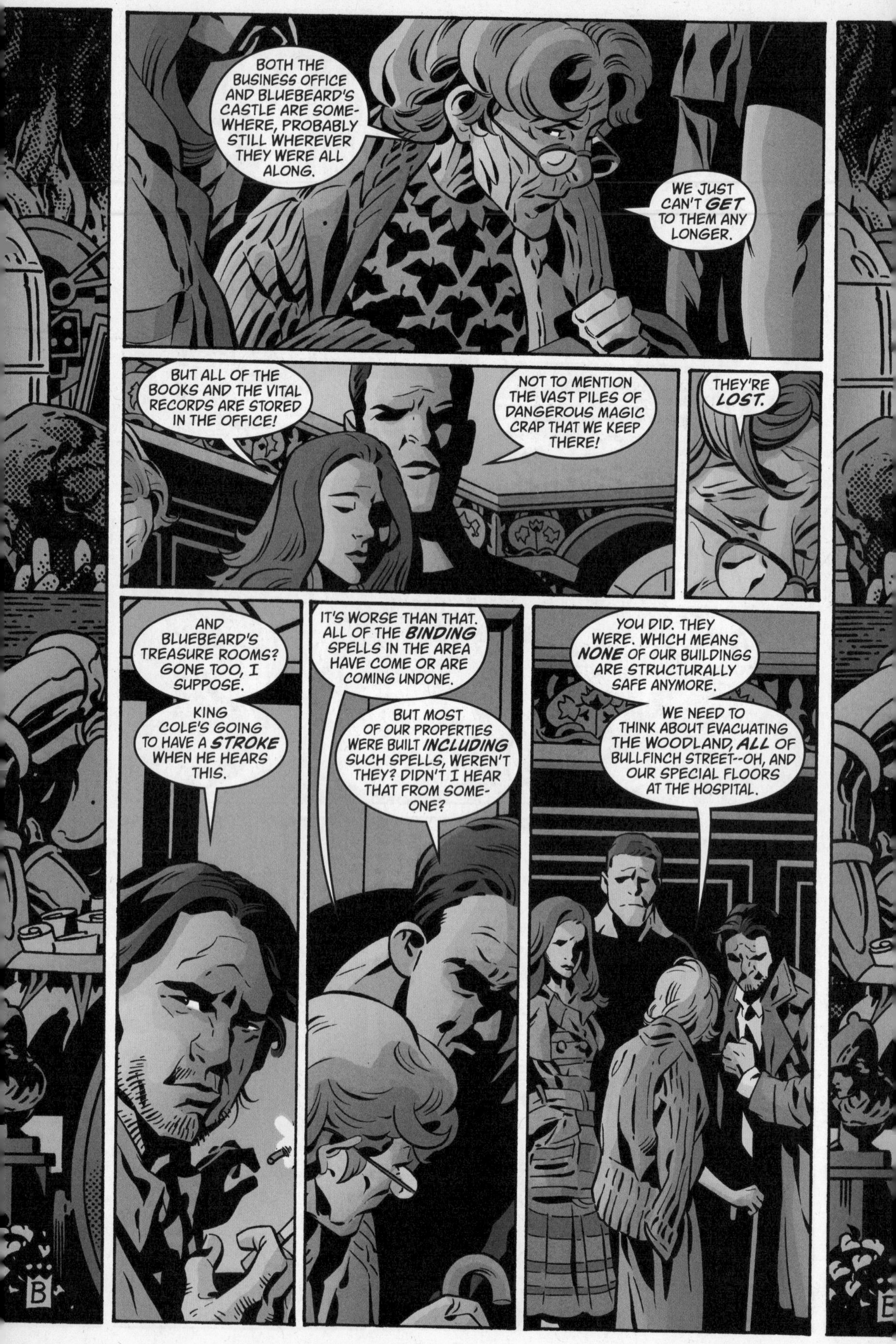
BOTH THE BUSINESS OFFICE AND BLUEBEARD'S CASTLE ARE SOME-WHERE, PROBABLY STILL WHEREVER THEY WERE ALL ALONG.
WE JUST CAN'T GET TO THEM ANY LONGER.
BUT ALL OF THE BOOKS AND THE VITAL RECORDS ARE STORED IN THE OFFICE!
NOT TO MENTION THE VAST PILES OF DANGEROUS MAGIC CRAP THAT WE KEEP THERE!
THEY'RE LOST.
AND BLUEBEARD'S TREASURE ROOMS? GONE TOO, I SUPPOSE.
KING COLE'S GOING TO HAVE A STROKE WHEN HE HEARS THIS.
IT'S WORSE THAN THAT. ALL OF THE BINDING SPELLS IN THE AREA HAVE COME OR ARE COMING UNDONE.
BUT MOST OF OUR PROPERTIES WERE BUILT INCLUDING SUCH SPELLS, WEREN'T THEY? DIDN'T I HEAR THAT FROM SOME-ONE?
YOU DID. THEY WERE. WHICH MEANS NONE OF OUR BUILDINGS ARE STRUCTURALLY SAFE ANYMORE.
WE NEED TO THINK ABOUT EVACUATING THE WOODLAND, ALL OF BULLFINCH STREET--OH, AND OUR SPECIAL FLOORS AT THE HOSPITAL.
B
B

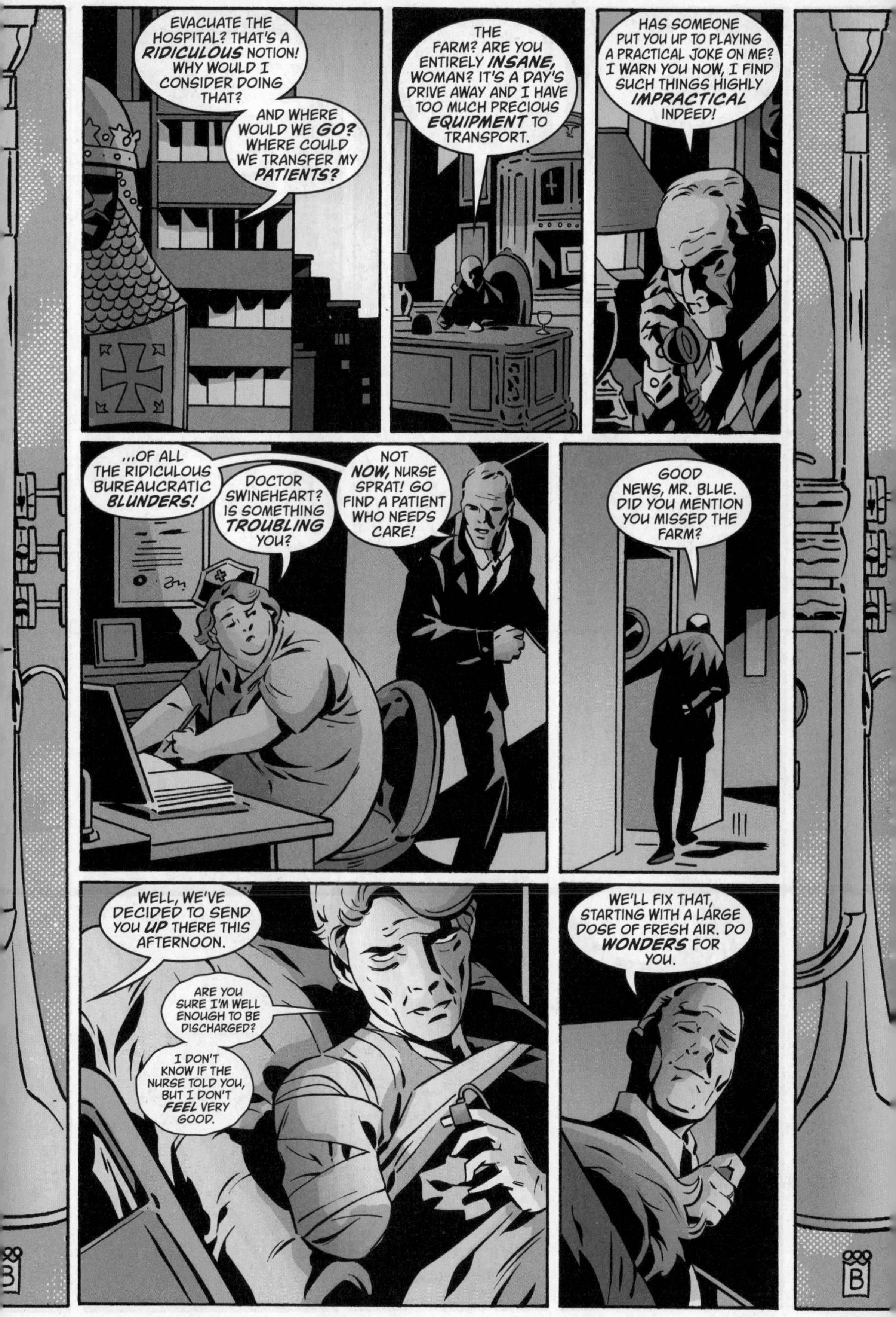
EVACUATE THE HOSPITAL? THAT'S A RIDICULOUS NOTION! WHY WOULD I CONSIDER DOING THAT?
AND WHERE WOULD WE GO? WHERE COULD WE TRANSFER MY PATIENTS?
THE FARM? ARE YOU ENTIRELY INSANE, WOMAN? IT'S A DAY'S DRIVE AWAY AND I HAVE TOO MUCH PRECIOUS EQUIPMENT TO TRANSPORT.
HAS SOMEONE PUT YOU UP TO PLAYING A PRACTICAL JOKE ON ME? I WARN YOU NOW, I FIND SUCH THINGS HIGHLY IMPRACTICAL INDEED!
...OF ALL THE RIDICULOUS BUREAUCRATIC BLUNDERS!
DOCTOR SWINEHEART? IS SOMETHING TROUBLING YOU?
NOT NOW, NURSE SPRAT! GO FIND A PATIENT WHO NEEDS CARE!
GOOD NEWS, MR. BLUE. DID YOU MENTION YOU MISSED THE FARM?
WELL, WE'VE DECIDED TO SEND YOU UP THERE THIS AFTERNOON.
ARE YOU SURE I'M WELL ENOUGH TO BE DISCHARGED?
I DON'T KNOW IF THE NURSE TOLD YOU, BUT I DON'T FEEL VERY GOOD.
WE'LL FIX THAT, STARTING WITH A LARGE DOSE OF FRESH AIR. DO WONDERS FOR YOU.

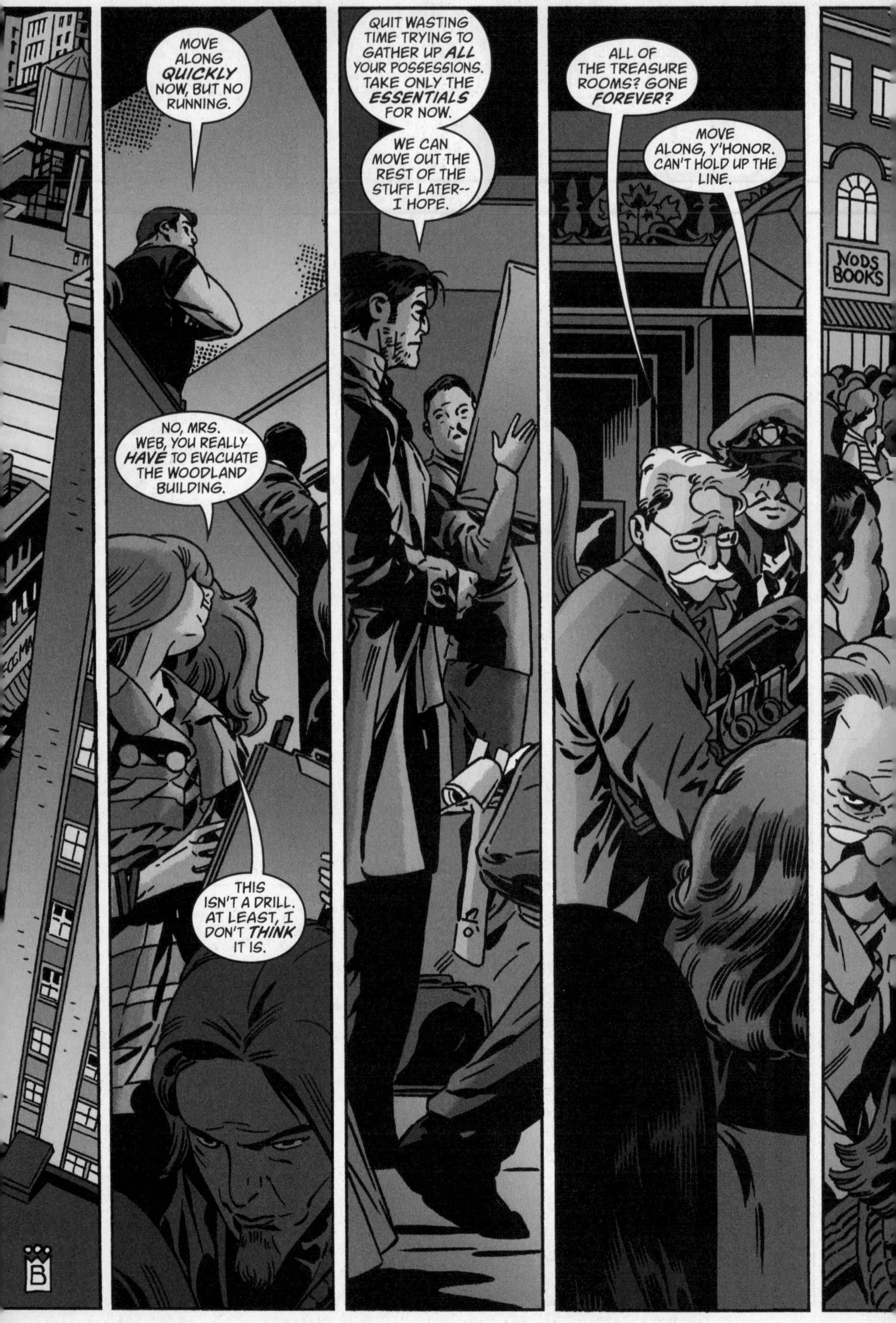
MOVE ALONG QUICKLY NOW, BUT NO RUNNING.
NO, MRS. WEB, YOU REALLY HAVE TO EVACUATE THE WOODLAND BUILDING.
THIS ISN'T A DRILL. AT LEAST, I DON'T THINK IT IS.
QUIT WASTING TIME TRYING TO GATHER UP ALL YOUR POSSESSIONS. TAKE ONLY THE ESSENTIALS FOR NOW.
WE CAN MOVE OUT THE REST OF THE STUFF LATER-- I HOPE.
ALL OF THE TREASURE ROOMS? GONE FOREVER?
MOVE ALONG, Y'HONOR. CAN'T HOLD UP THE LINE.
NODS BOOKS

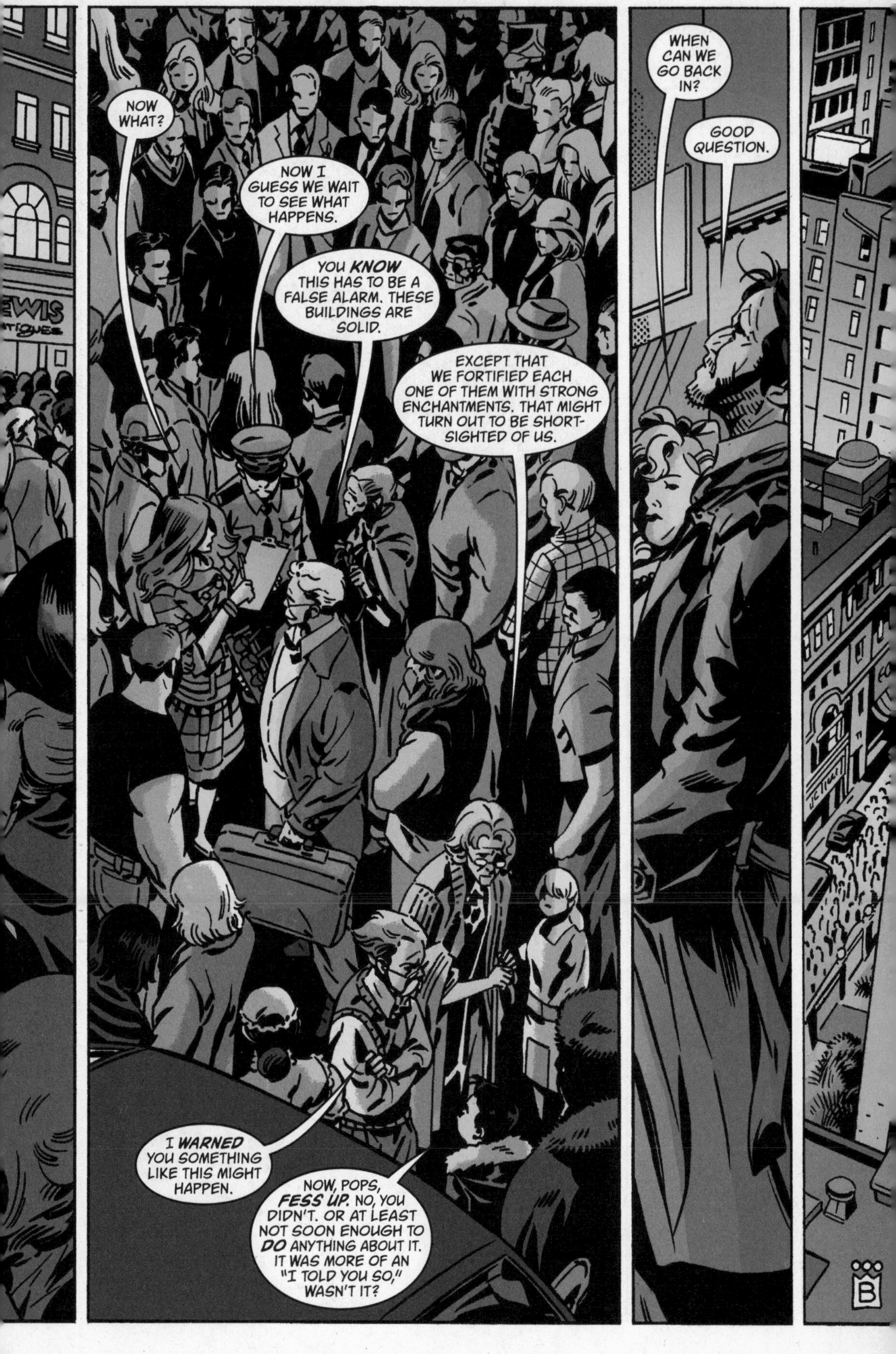
NOW WHAT?
NOW I GUESS WE WAIT TO SEE WHAT HAPPENS.
YOU KNOW THIS HAS TO BE A FALSE ALARM. THESE BUILDINGS ARE SOLID.
EXCEPT THAT WE FORTIFIED EACH ONE OF THEM WITH STRONG ENCHANTMENTS. THAT MIGHT TURN OUT TO BE SHORT-SIGHTED OF US.
I WARNED YOU SOMETHING LIKE THIS MIGHT HAPPEN.
NOW, POPS, FESS UP. NO, YOU DIDN'T. OR AT LEAST NOT SOON ENOUGH TO DO ANYTHING ABOUT IT. IT WAS MORE OF AN "I TOLD YOU SO," WASN'T IT?
WHEN CAN WE GO BACK IN?
GOOD QUESTION.

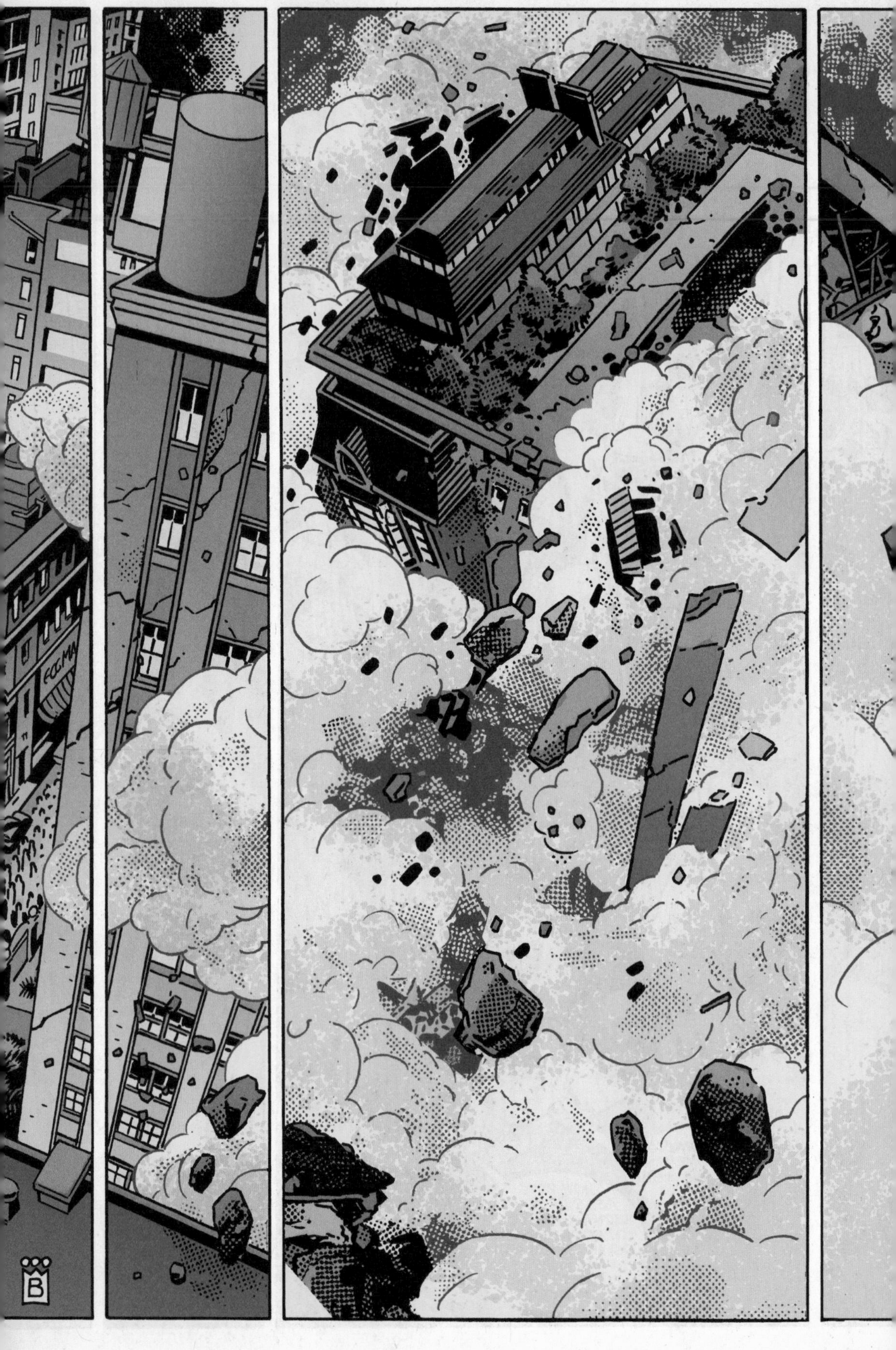

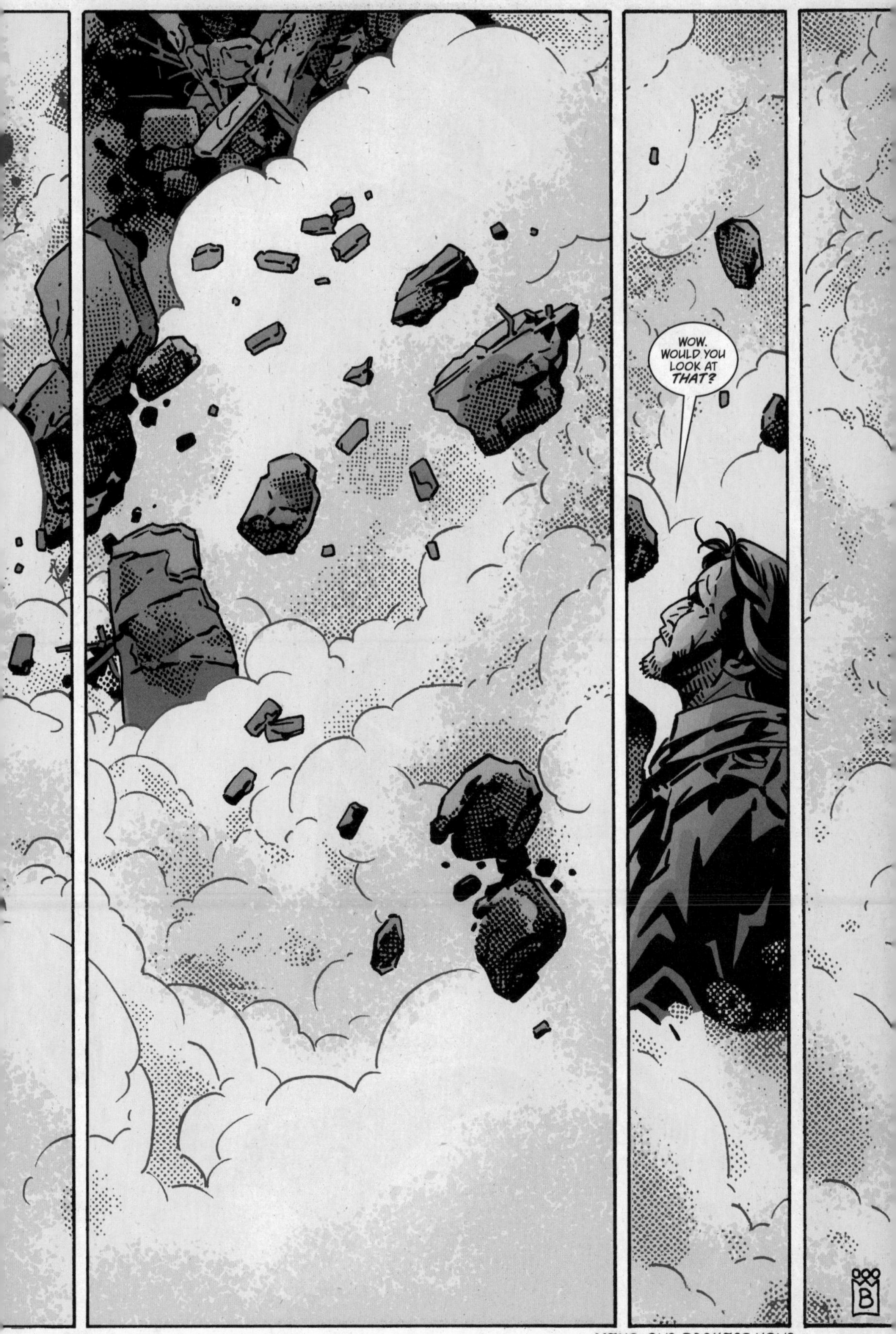
WOW. WOULD YOU LOOK AT *THAT?*

NEXT: OUR DARKEST HOUR

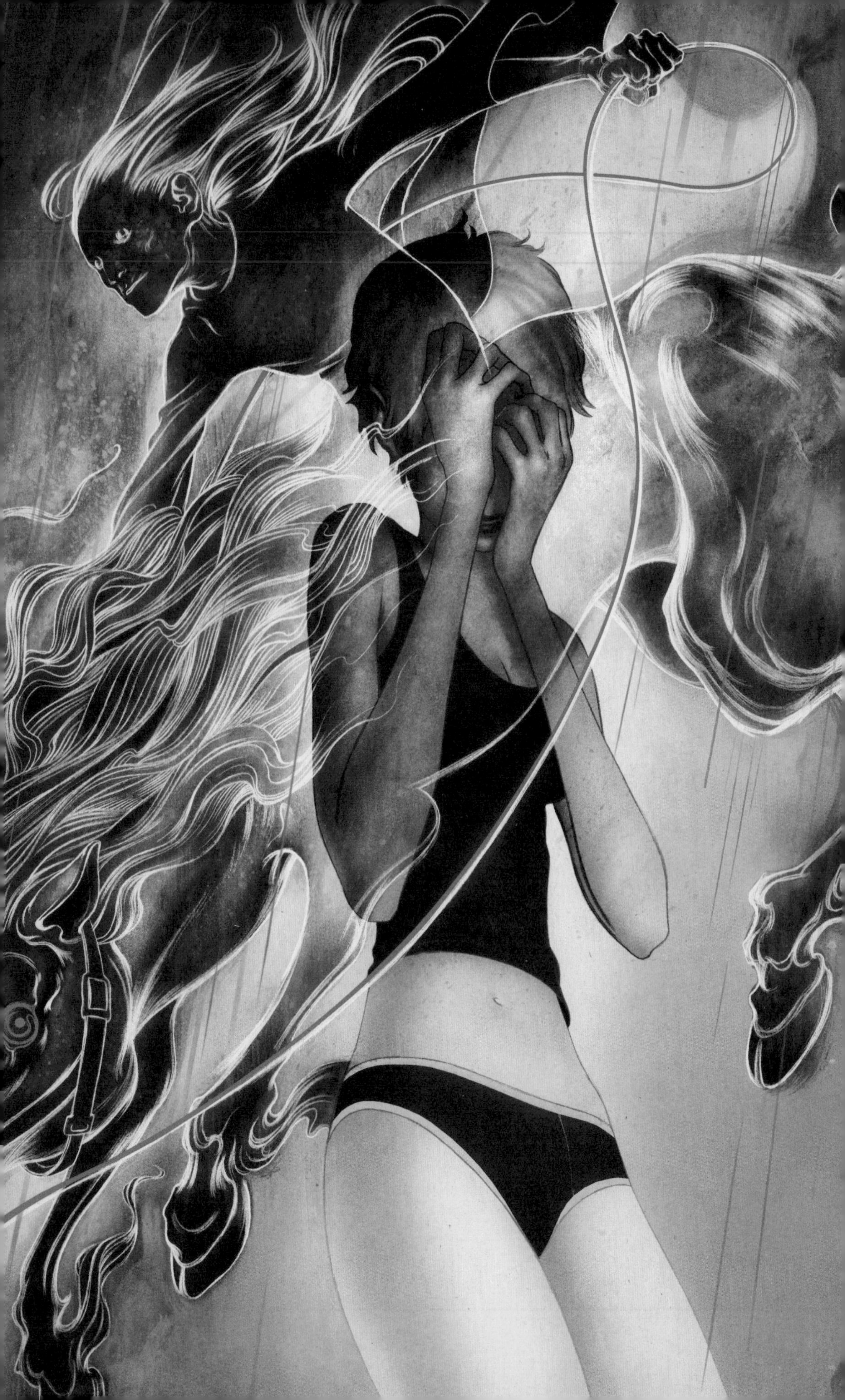

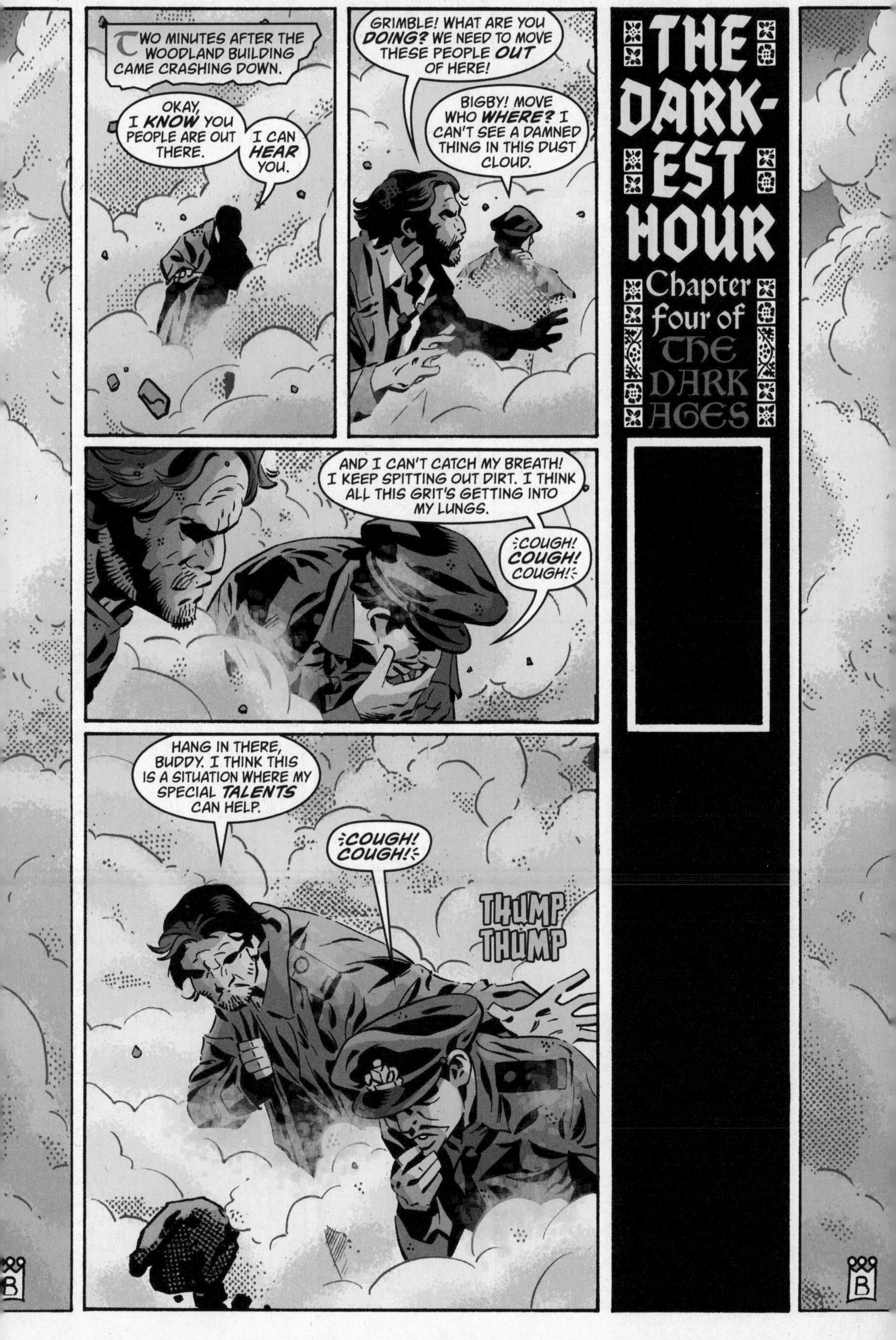

TWO MINUTES AFTER THE WOODLAND BUILDING CAME CRASHING DOWN.
OKAY, I KNOW YOU PEOPLE ARE OUT THERE.
I CAN HEAR YOU.
GRIMBLE! WHAT ARE YOU DOING? WE NEED TO MOVE THESE PEOPLE OUT OF HERE!
BIGBY! MOVE WHO WHERE? I CAN'T SEE A DAMNED THING IN THIS DUST CLOUD.
THE DARK-EST HOUR
Chapter four of THE DARK AGES
AND I CAN'T CATCH MY BREATH! I KEEP SPITTING OUT DIRT. I THINK ALL THIS GRIT'S GETTING INTO MY LUNGS.
COUGH! COUGH! COUGH!
HANG IN THERE, BUDDY. I THINK THIS IS A SITUATION WHERE MY SPECIAL TALENTS CAN HELP.
COUGH! COUGH!
THUMP THUMP

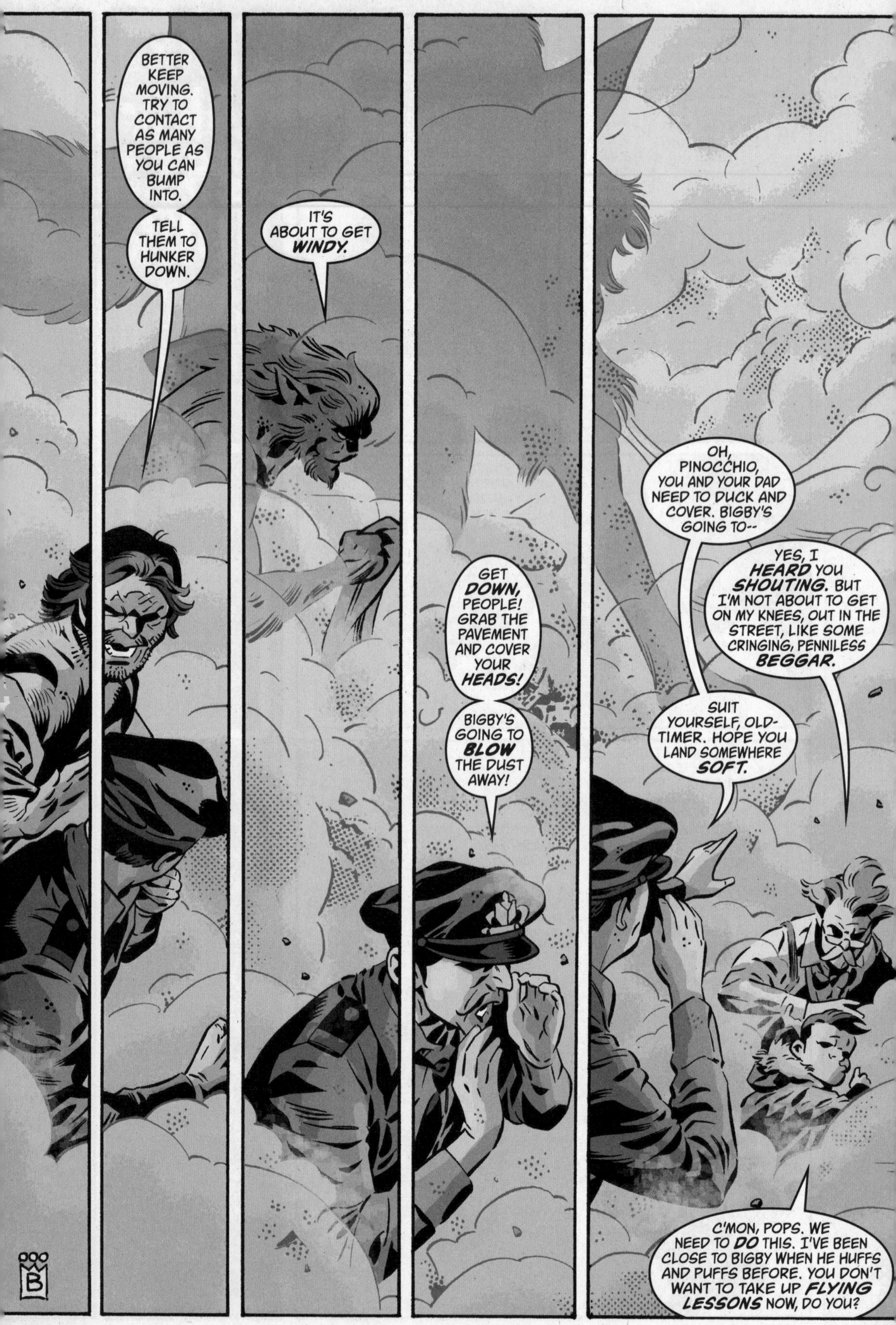
BETTER KEEP MOVING. TRY TO CONTACT AS MANY PEOPLE AS YOU CAN BUMP INTO.
TELL THEM TO HUNKER DOWN.
IT'S ABOUT TO GET WINDY.
GET DOWN, PEOPLE! GRAB THE PAVEMENT AND COVER YOUR HEADS!
BIGBY'S GOING TO BLOW THE DUST AWAY!
OH, PINOCCHIO, YOU AND YOUR DAD NEED TO DUCK AND COVER. BIGBY'S GOING TO--
YES, I HEARD YOU SHOUTING. BUT I'M NOT ABOUT TO GET ON MY KNEES, OUT IN THE STREET, LIKE SOME CRINGING, PENNILESS BEGGAR.
SUIT YOURSELF, OLD-TIMER. HOPE YOU LAND SOMEWHERE SOFT.
C'MON, POPS. WE NEED TO DO THIS. I'VE BEEN CLOSE TO BIGBY WHEN HE HUFFS AND PUFFS BEFORE. YOU DON'T WANT TO TAKE UP FLYING LESSONS NOW, DO YOU?

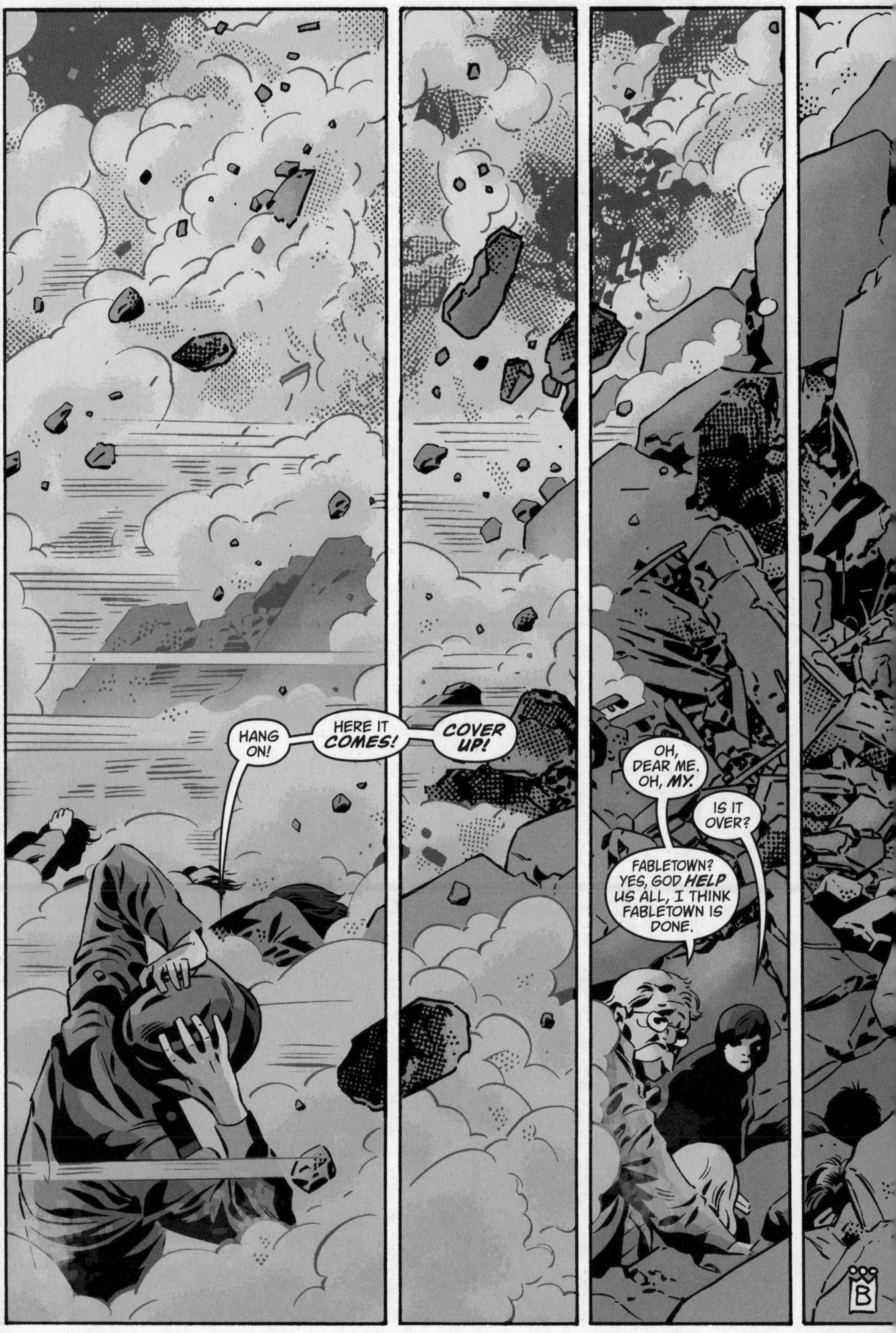
HANG ON!
HERE IT COMES!
COVER UP!
OH, DEAR ME. OH, MY.
IS IT OVER?
FABLETOWN? YES, GOD HELP US ALL, I THINK FABLETOWN IS DONE.
B

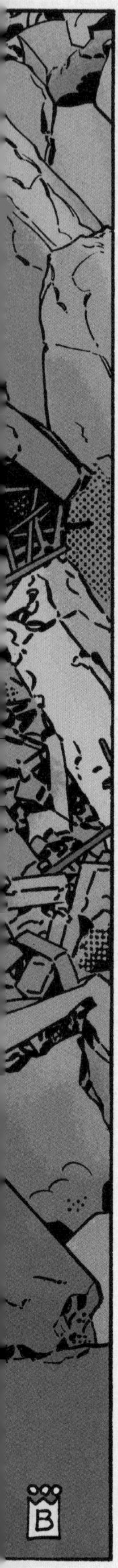
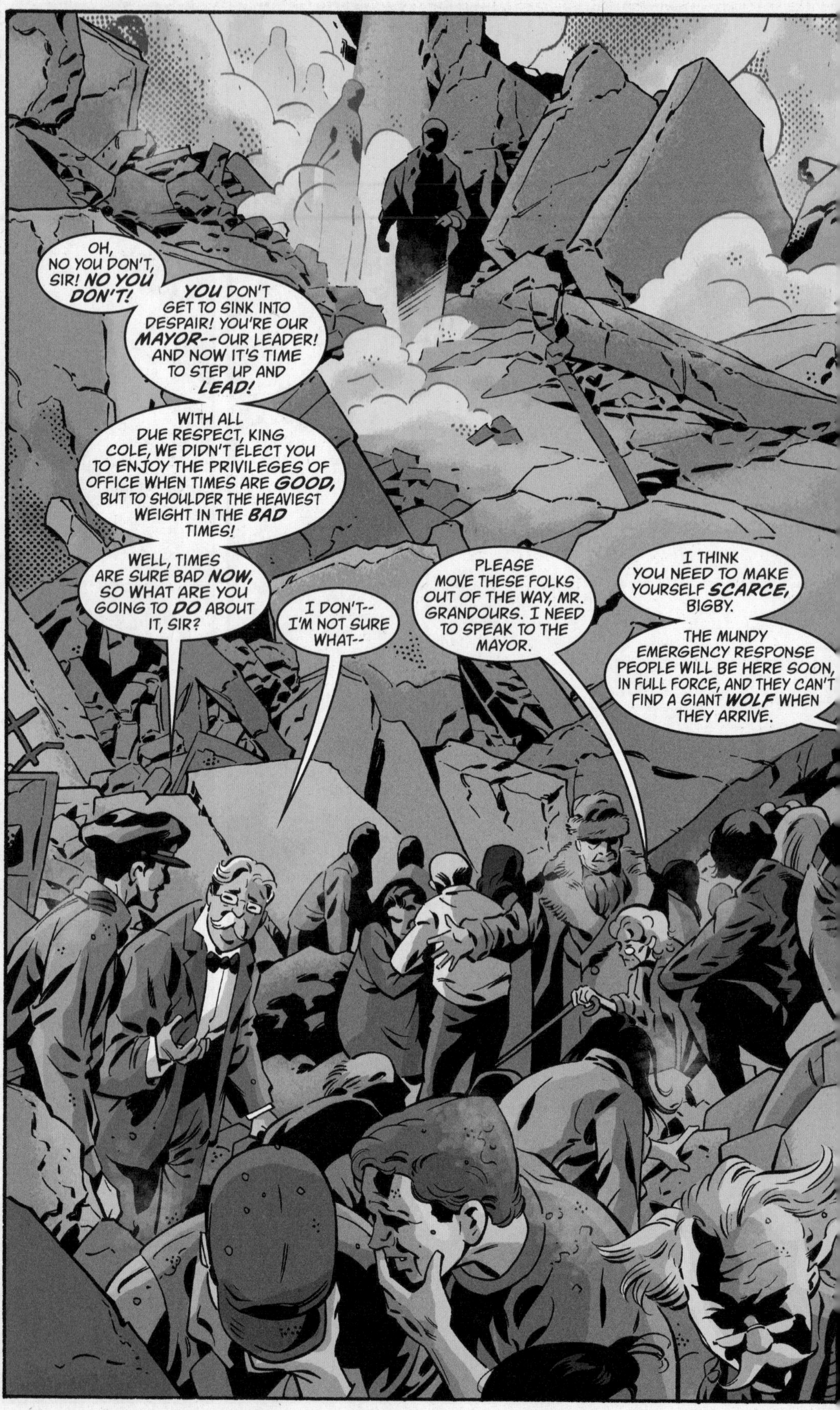
OH, NO YOU DON'T, SIR! NO YOU DON'T!
YOU DON'T GET TO SINK INTO DESPAIR! YOU'RE OUR MAYOR--OUR LEADER! AND NOW IT'S TIME TO STEP UP AND LEAD!
WITH ALL DUE RESPECT, KING COLE, WE DIDN'T ELECT YOU TO ENJOY THE PRIVILEGES OF OFFICE WHEN TIMES ARE GOOD, BUT TO SHOULDER THE HEAVIEST WEIGHT IN THE BAD TIMES!
WELL, TIMES ARE SURE BAD NOW, SO WHAT ARE YOU GOING TO DO ABOUT IT, SIR?
I DON'T-- I'M NOT SURE WHAT--
PLEASE MOVE THESE FOLKS OUT OF THE WAY, MR. GRANDOURS. I NEED TO SPEAK TO THE MAYOR.
I THINK YOU NEED TO MAKE YOURSELF SCARCE, BIGBY.
THE MUNDY EMERGENCY RESPONSE PEOPLE WILL BE HERE SOON, IN FULL FORCE, AND THEY CAN'T FIND A GIANT WOLF WHEN THEY ARRIVE.
B

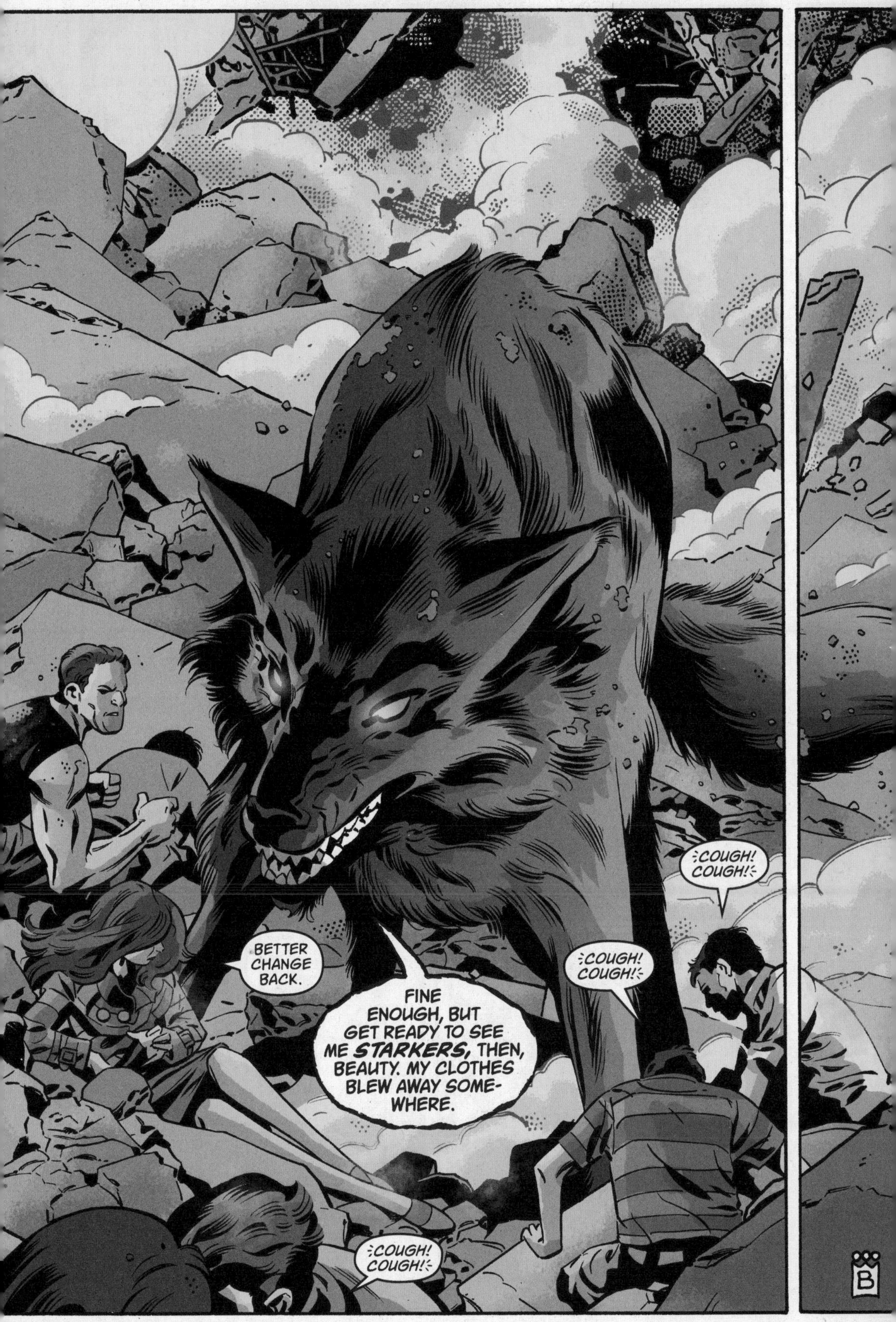
COUGH! COUGH!
BETTER CHANGE BACK.
FINE ENOUGH, BUT GET READY TO SEE ME STARKERS, THEN, BEAUTY. MY CLOTHES BLEW AWAY SOME-WHERE.
COUGH! COUGH!
COUGH! COUGH!

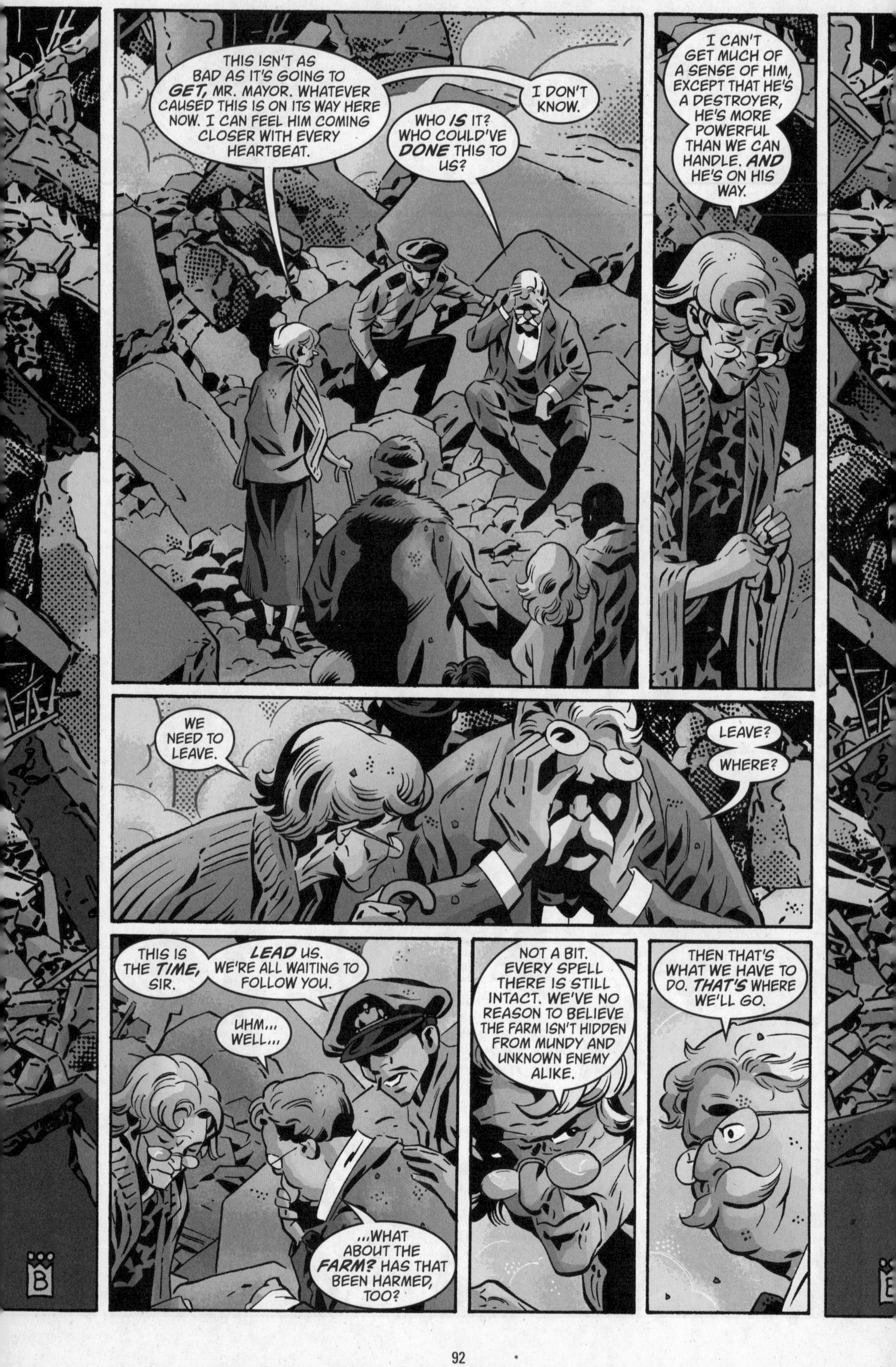
THIS ISN'T AS BAD AS IT'S GOING TO GET, MR. MAYOR. WHATEVER CAUSED THIS IS ON ITS WAY HERE NOW. I CAN FEEL HIM COMING CLOSER WITH EVERY HEARTBEAT.
WHO IS IT? WHO COULD'VE DONE THIS TO US?
I DON'T KNOW.
I CAN'T GET MUCH OF A SENSE OF HIM, EXCEPT THAT HE'S A DESTROYER, HE'S MORE POWERFUL THAN WE CAN HANDLE. AND HE'S ON HIS WAY.
WE NEED TO LEAVE.
LEAVE?
WHERE?
THIS IS THE TIME, SIR.
LEAD US. WE'RE ALL WAITING TO FOLLOW YOU.
UHM... WELL...
...WHAT ABOUT THE FARM? HAS THAT BEEN HARMED, TOO?
NOT A BIT. EVERY SPELL THERE IS STILL INTACT. WE'VE NO REASON TO BELIEVE THE FARM ISN'T HIDDEN FROM MUNDY AND UNKNOWN ENEMY ALIKE.
THEN THAT'S WHAT WE HAVE TO DO. THAT'S WHERE WE'LL GO.

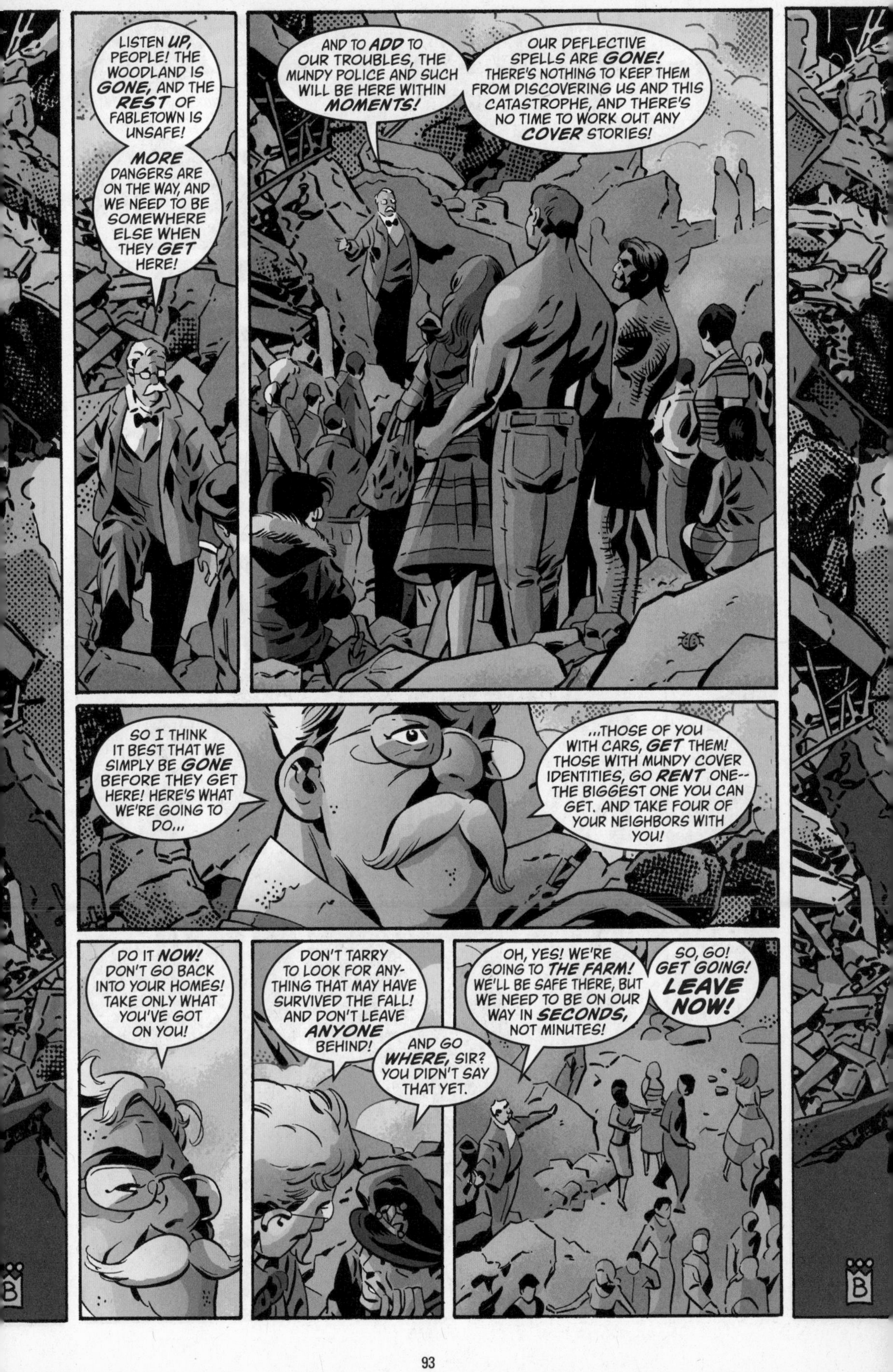
LISTEN UP, PEOPLE! THE WOODLAND IS GONE, AND THE REST OF FABLETOWN IS UNSAFE!
MORE DANGERS ARE ON THE WAY, AND WE NEED TO BE SOMEWHERE ELSE WHEN THEY GET HERE!
AND TO ADD TO OUR TROUBLES, THE MUNDY POLICE AND SUCH WILL BE HERE WITHIN MOMENTS!
OUR DEFLECTIVE SPELLS ARE GONE! THERE'S NOTHING TO KEEP THEM FROM DISCOVERING US AND THIS CATASTROPHE, AND THERE'S NO TIME TO WORK OUT ANY COVER STORIES!
SO I THINK IT BEST THAT WE SIMPLY BE GONE BEFORE THEY GET HERE! HERE'S WHAT WE'RE GOING TO DO...
...THOSE OF YOU WITH CARS, GET THEM! THOSE WITH MUNDY COVER IDENTITIES, GO RENT ONE-- THE BIGGEST ONE YOU CAN GET. AND TAKE FOUR OF YOUR NEIGHBORS WITH YOU!
DO IT NOW! DON'T GO BACK INTO YOUR HOMES! TAKE ONLY WHAT YOU'VE GOT ON YOU!
DON'T TARRY TO LOOK FOR ANY-THING THAT MAY HAVE SURVIVED THE FALL! AND DON'T LEAVE ANYONE BEHIND!
AND GO WHERE, SIR? YOU DIDN'T SAY THAT YET.
OH, YES! WE'RE GOING TO THE FARM! WE'LL BE SAFE THERE, BUT WE NEED TO BE ON OUR WAY IN SECONDS, NOT MINUTES!
SO, GO! GET GOING! LEAVE NOW!

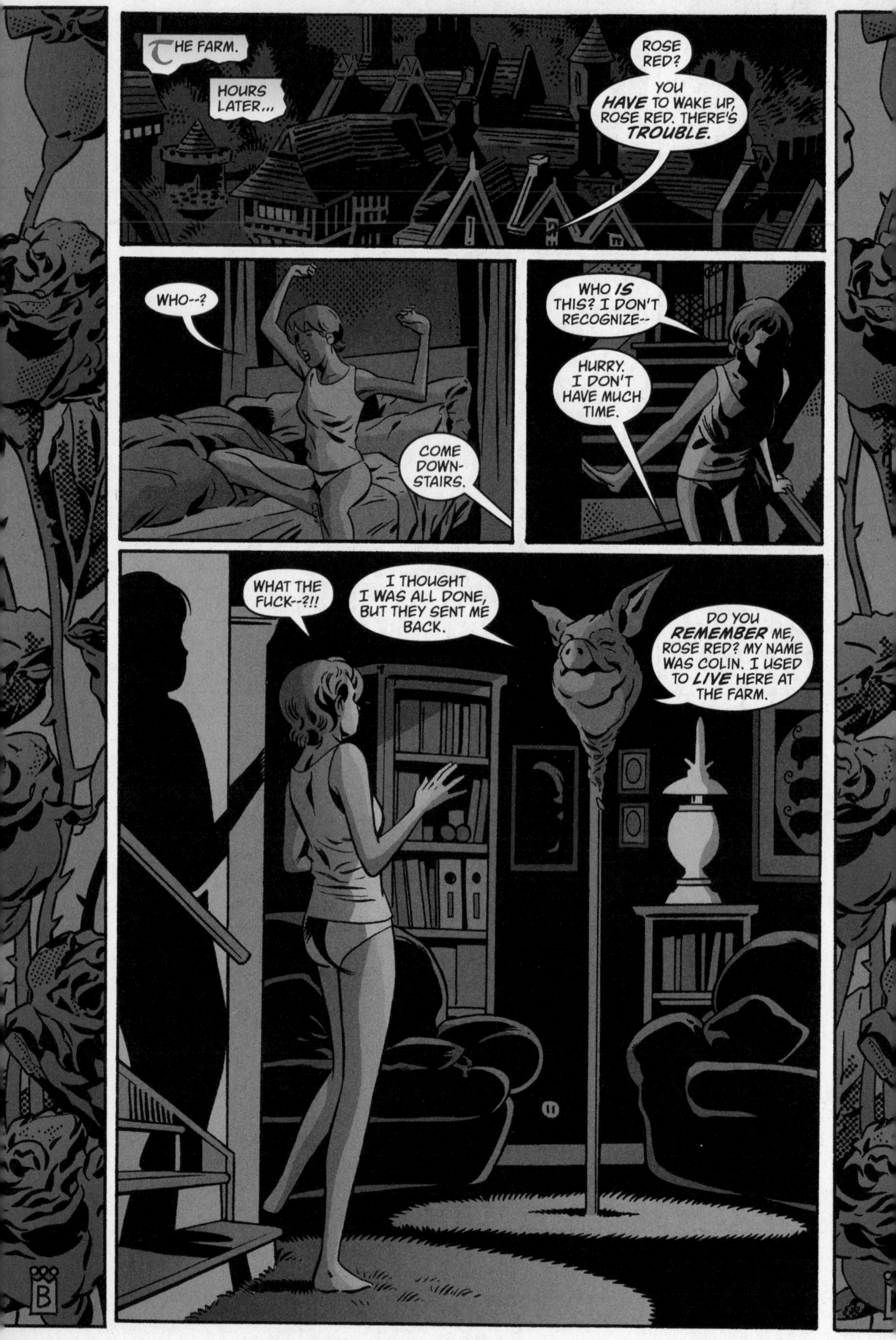
THE FARM.
HOURS LATER...
ROSE RED?
YOU HAVE TO WAKE UP, ROSE RED. THERE'S TROUBLE.
WHO--?
COME DOWN-STAIRS.
WHO IS THIS? I DON'T RECOGNIZE--
HURRY. I DON'T HAVE MUCH TIME.
WHAT THE FUCK--?!!
I THOUGHT I WAS ALL DONE, BUT THEY SENT ME BACK.
DO YOU REMEMBER ME, ROSE RED? MY NAME WAS COLIN. I USED TO LIVE HERE AT THE FARM.

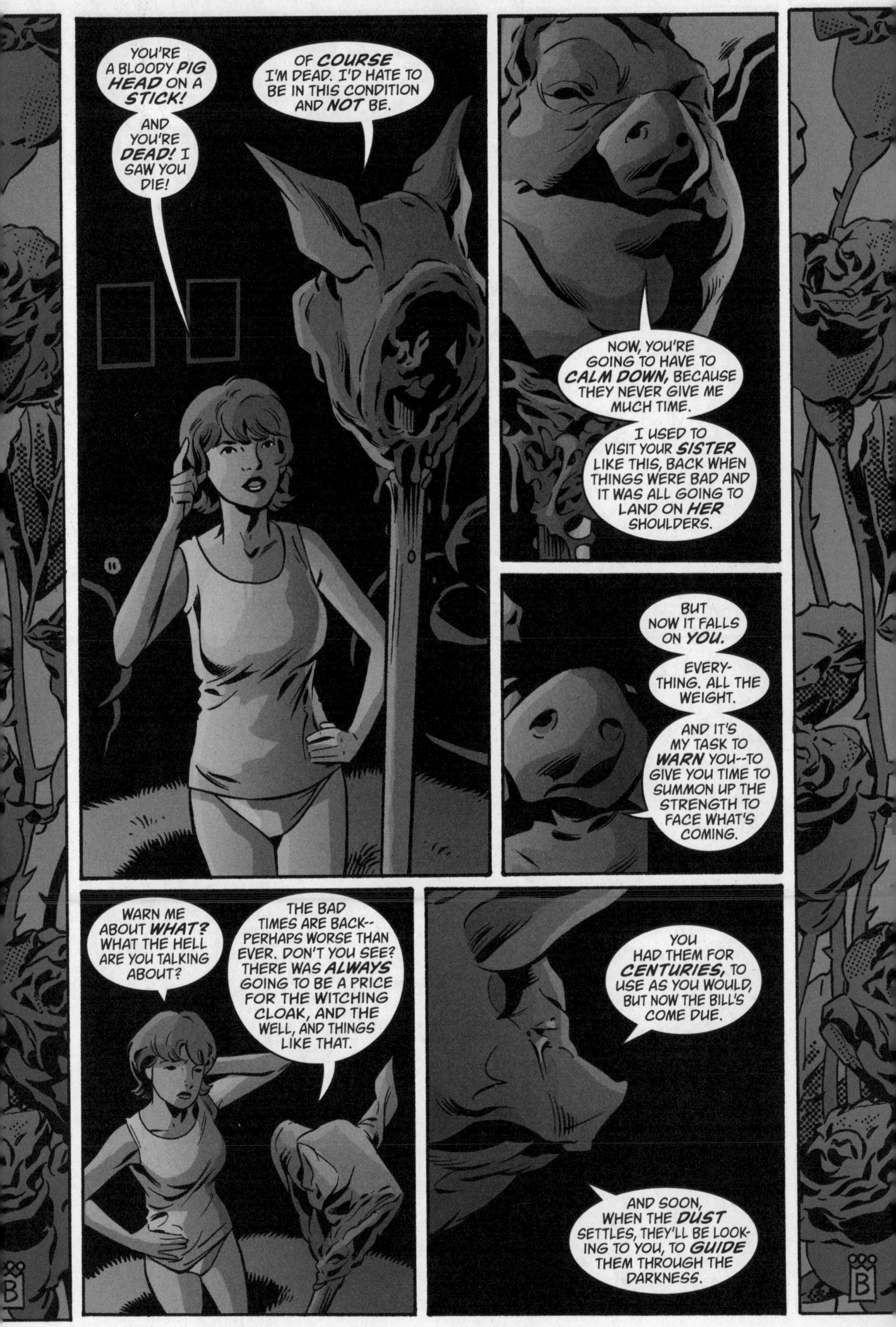
YOU'RE A BLOODY PIG HEAD ON A STICK!
AND YOU'RE DEAD! I SAW YOU DIE!
OF COURSE I'M DEAD. I'D HATE TO BE IN THIS CONDITION AND NOT BE.
NOW, YOU'RE GOING TO HAVE TO CALM DOWN, BECAUSE THEY NEVER GIVE ME MUCH TIME.
I USED TO VISIT YOUR SISTER LIKE THIS, BACK WHEN THINGS WERE BAD AND IT WAS ALL GOING TO LAND ON HER SHOULDERS.
BUT NOW IT FALLS ON YOU.
EVERY-THING. ALL THE WEIGHT.
AND IT'S MY TASK TO WARN YOU--TO GIVE YOU TIME TO SUMMON UP THE STRENGTH TO FACE WHAT'S COMING.
WARN ME ABOUT WHAT? WHAT THE HELL ARE YOU TALKING ABOUT?
THE BAD TIMES ARE BACK--PERHAPS WORSE THAN EVER. DON'T YOU SEE? THERE WAS ALWAYS GOING TO BE A PRICE FOR THE WITCHING CLOAK, AND THE WELL, AND THINGS LIKE THAT.
YOU HAD THEM FOR CENTURIES, TO USE AS YOU WOULD, BUT NOW THE BILL'S COME DUE.
AND SOON, WHEN THE DUST SETTLES, THEY'LL BE LOOK-ING TO YOU, TO GUIDE THEM THROUGH THE DARKNESS.

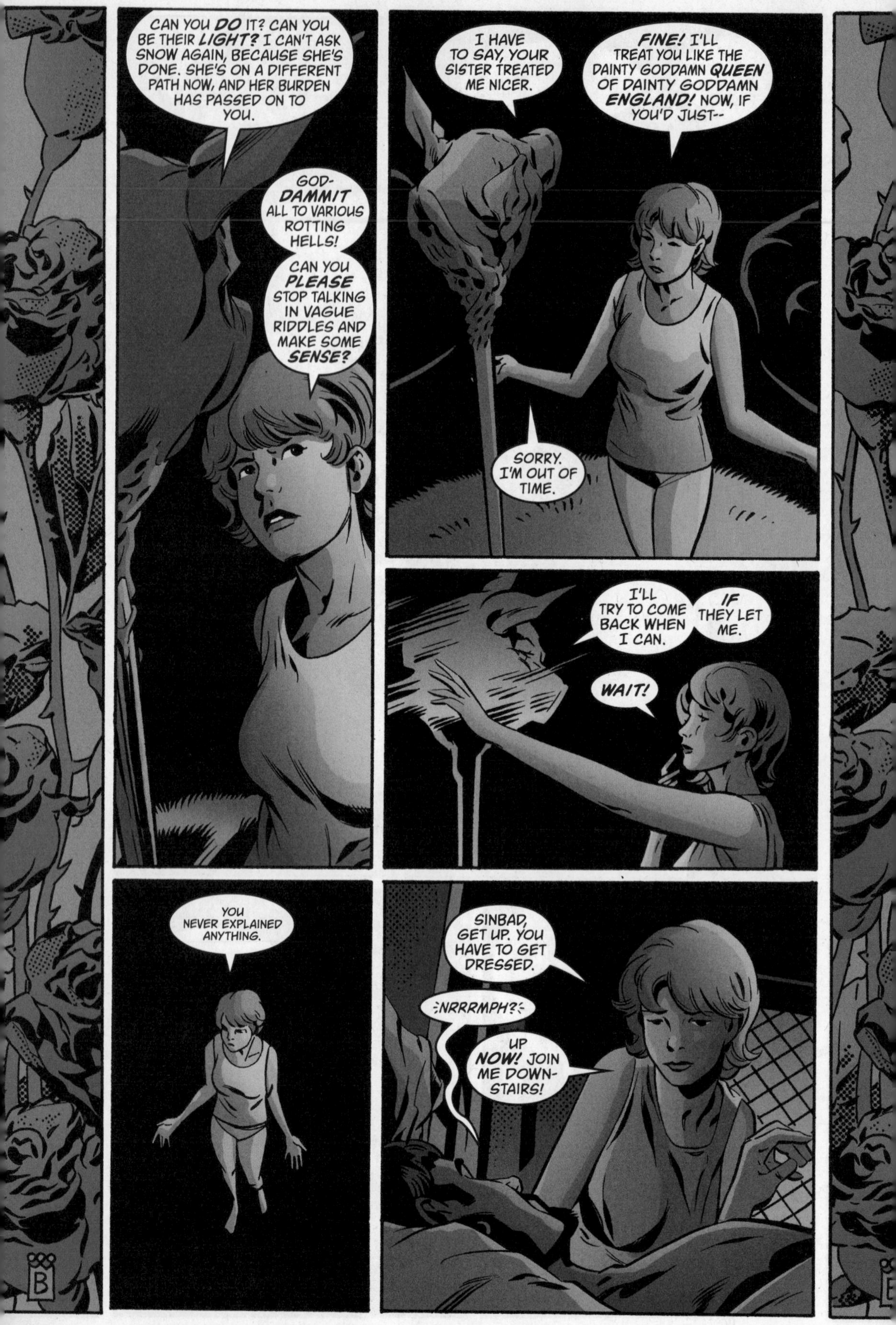
CAN YOU DO IT? CAN YOU BE THEIR LIGHT? I CAN'T ASK SNOW AGAIN, BECAUSE SHE'S DONE. SHE'S ON A DIFFERENT PATH NOW, AND HER BURDEN HAS PASSED ON TO YOU.
GOD-DAMMIT ALL TO VARIOUS ROTTING HELLS!
CAN YOU PLEASE STOP TALKING IN VAGUE RIDDLES AND MAKE SOME SENSE?
I HAVE TO SAY, YOUR SISTER TREATED ME NICER.
FINE! I'LL TREAT YOU LIKE THE DAINTY GODDAMN QUEEN OF DAINTY GODDAMN ENGLAND! NOW, IF YOU'D JUST--
SORRY. I'M OUT OF TIME.
I'LL TRY TO COME BACK WHEN I CAN.
IF THEY LET ME.
WAIT!
YOU NEVER EXPLAINED ANYTHING.
SINBAD, GET UP. YOU HAVE TO GET DRESSED.
NRRRMPH?
UP NOW! JOIN ME DOWN-STAIRS!

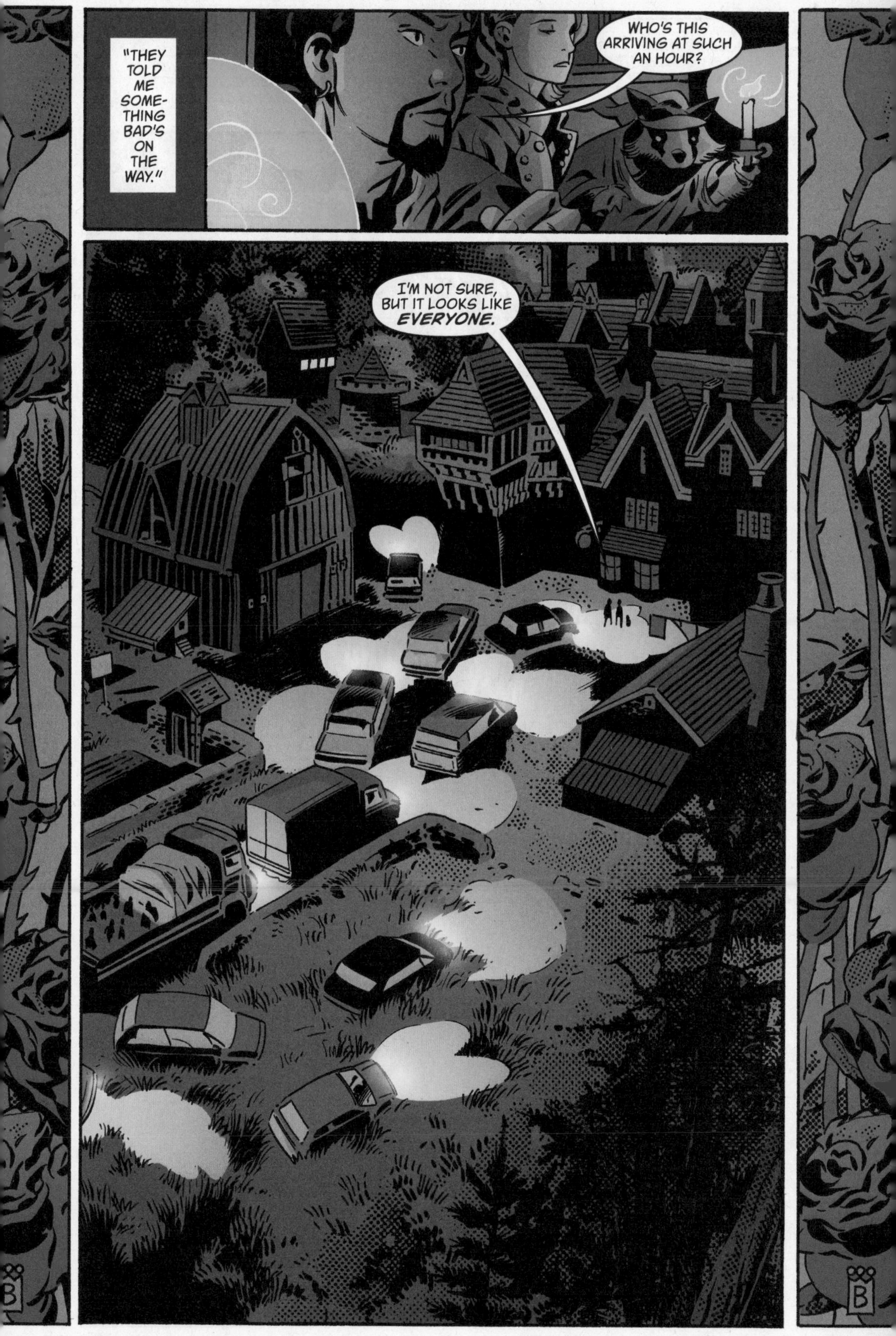
"THEY TOLD ME SOMETHING BAD'S ON THE WAY."
WHO'S THIS ARRIVING AT SUCH AN HOUR?
I'M NOT SURE, BUT IT LOOKS LIKE **EVERYONE.**

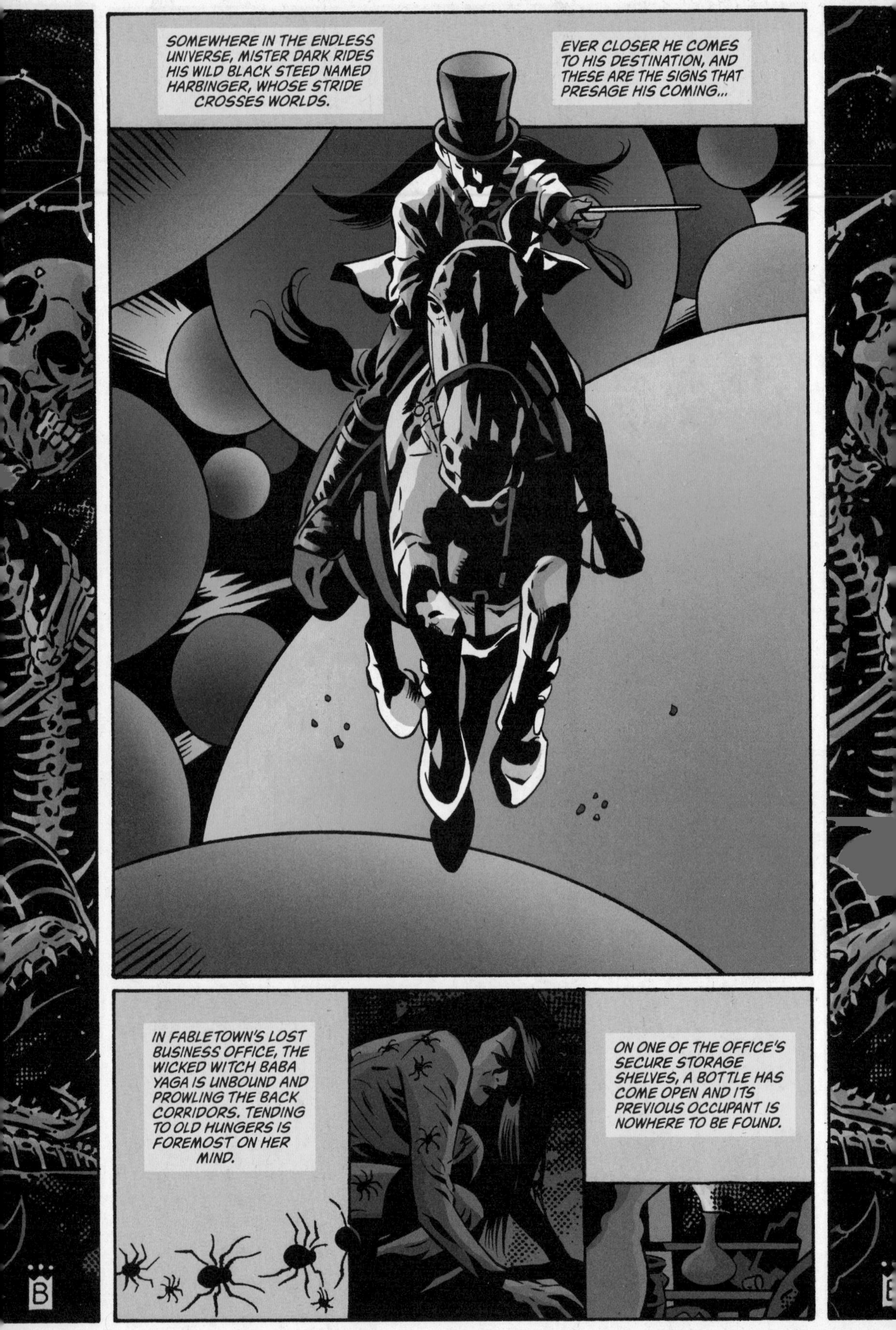
SOMEWHERE IN THE ENDLESS UNIVERSE, MISTER DARK RIDES HIS WILD BLACK STEED NAMED HARBINGER, WHOSE STRIDE CROSSES WORLDS.
EVER CLOSER HE COMES TO HIS DESTINATION, AND THESE ARE THE SIGNS THAT PRESAGE HIS COMING...
IN FABLETOWN'S LOST BUSINESS OFFICE, THE WICKED WITCH BABA YAGA IS UNBOUND AND PROWLING THE BACK CORRIDORS. TENDING TO OLD HUNGERS IS FOREMOST ON HER MIND.
ON ONE OF THE OFFICE'S SECURE STORAGE SHELVES, A BOTTLE HAS COME OPEN AND ITS PREVIOUS OCCUPANT IS NOWHERE TO BE FOUND.

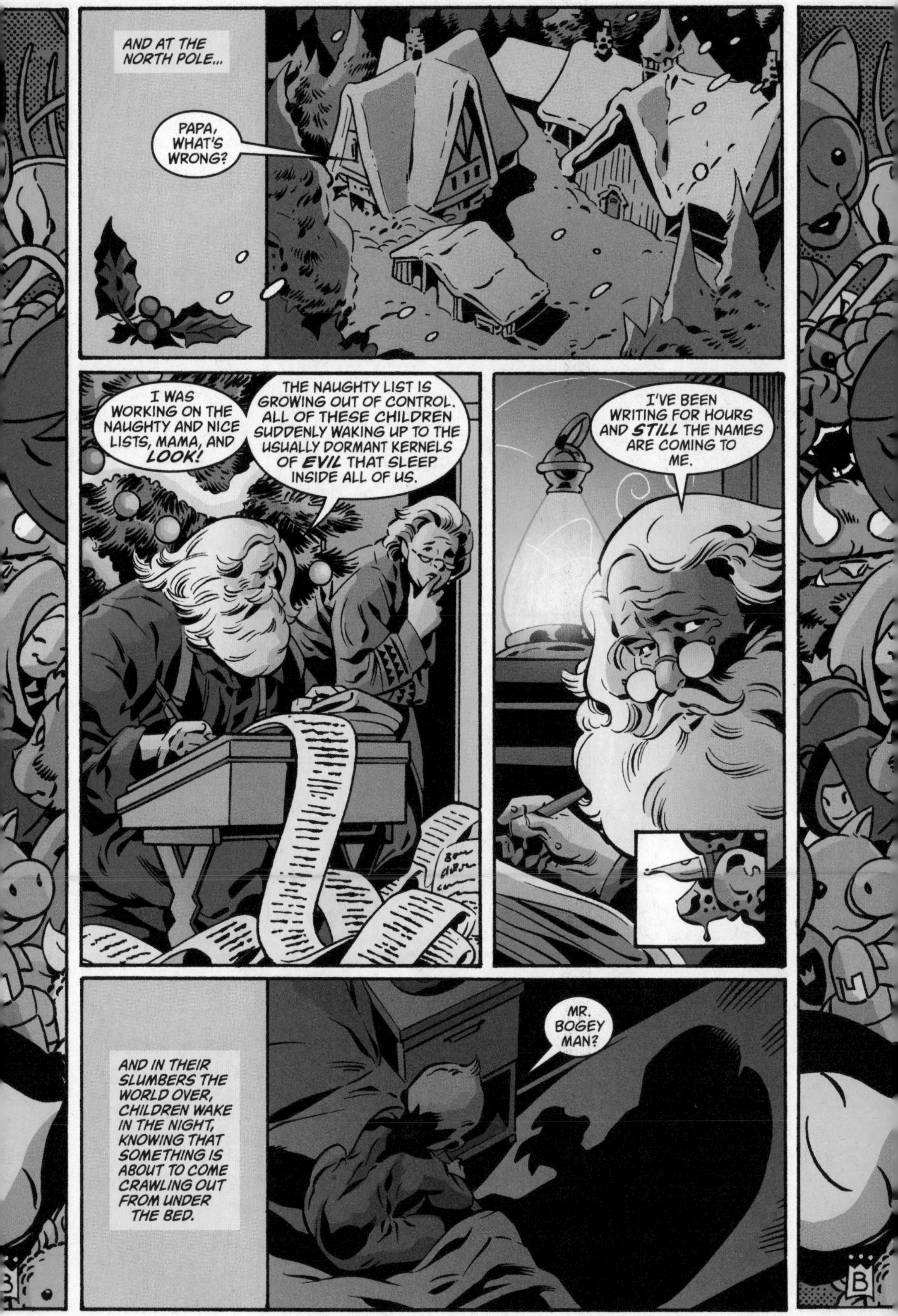
AND AT THE NORTH POLE...
PAPA, WHAT'S WRONG?
I WAS WORKING ON THE NAUGHTY AND NICE LISTS, MAMA, AND LOOK!
THE NAUGHTY LIST IS GROWING OUT OF CONTROL. ALL OF THESE CHILDREN SUDDENLY WAKING UP TO THE USUALLY DORMANT KERNELS OF EVIL THAT SLEEP INSIDE ALL OF US.
I'VE BEEN WRITING FOR HOURS AND STILL THE NAMES ARE COMING TO ME.
AND IN THEIR SLUMBERS THE WORLD OVER, CHILDREN WAKE IN THE NIGHT, KNOWING THAT SOMETHING IS ABOUT TO COME CRAWLING OUT FROM UNDER THE BED.
MR. BOGEY MAN?

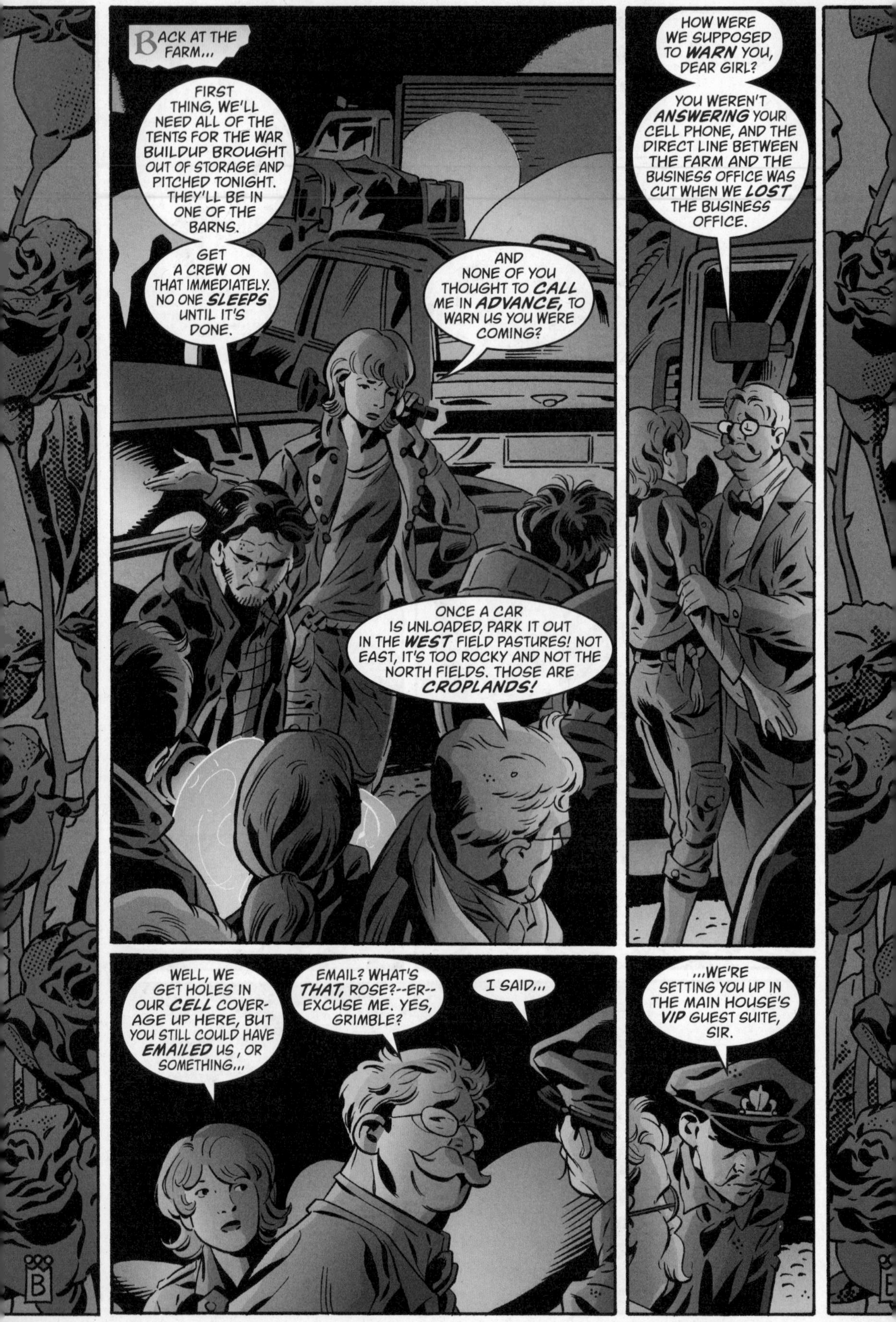
BACK AT THE FARM...
FIRST THING, WE'LL NEED ALL OF THE TENTS FOR THE WAR BUILDUP BROUGHT OUT OF STORAGE AND PITCHED TONIGHT. THEY'LL BE IN ONE OF THE BARNS.
GET A CREW ON THAT IMMEDIATELY. NO ONE SLEEPS UNTIL IT'S DONE.
AND NONE OF YOU THOUGHT TO CALL ME IN ADVANCE, TO WARN US YOU WERE COMING?
ONCE A CAR IS UNLOADED, PARK IT OUT IN THE WEST FIELD PASTURES! NOT EAST, IT'S TOO ROCKY AND NOT THE NORTH FIELDS. THOSE ARE CROPLANDS!
HOW WERE WE SUPPOSED TO WARN YOU, DEAR GIRL?
YOU WEREN'T ANSWERING YOUR CELL PHONE, AND THE DIRECT LINE BETWEEN THE FARM AND THE BUSINESS OFFICE WAS CUT WHEN WE LOST THE BUSINESS OFFICE.
WELL, WE GET HOLES IN OUR CELL COVERAGE UP HERE, BUT YOU STILL COULD HAVE EMAILED US , OR SOMETHING...
EMAIL? WHAT'S THAT, ROSE?--ER--EXCUSE ME. YES, GRIMBLE?
I SAID...
...WE'RE SETTING YOU UP IN THE MAIN HOUSE'S VIP GUEST SUITE, SIR.

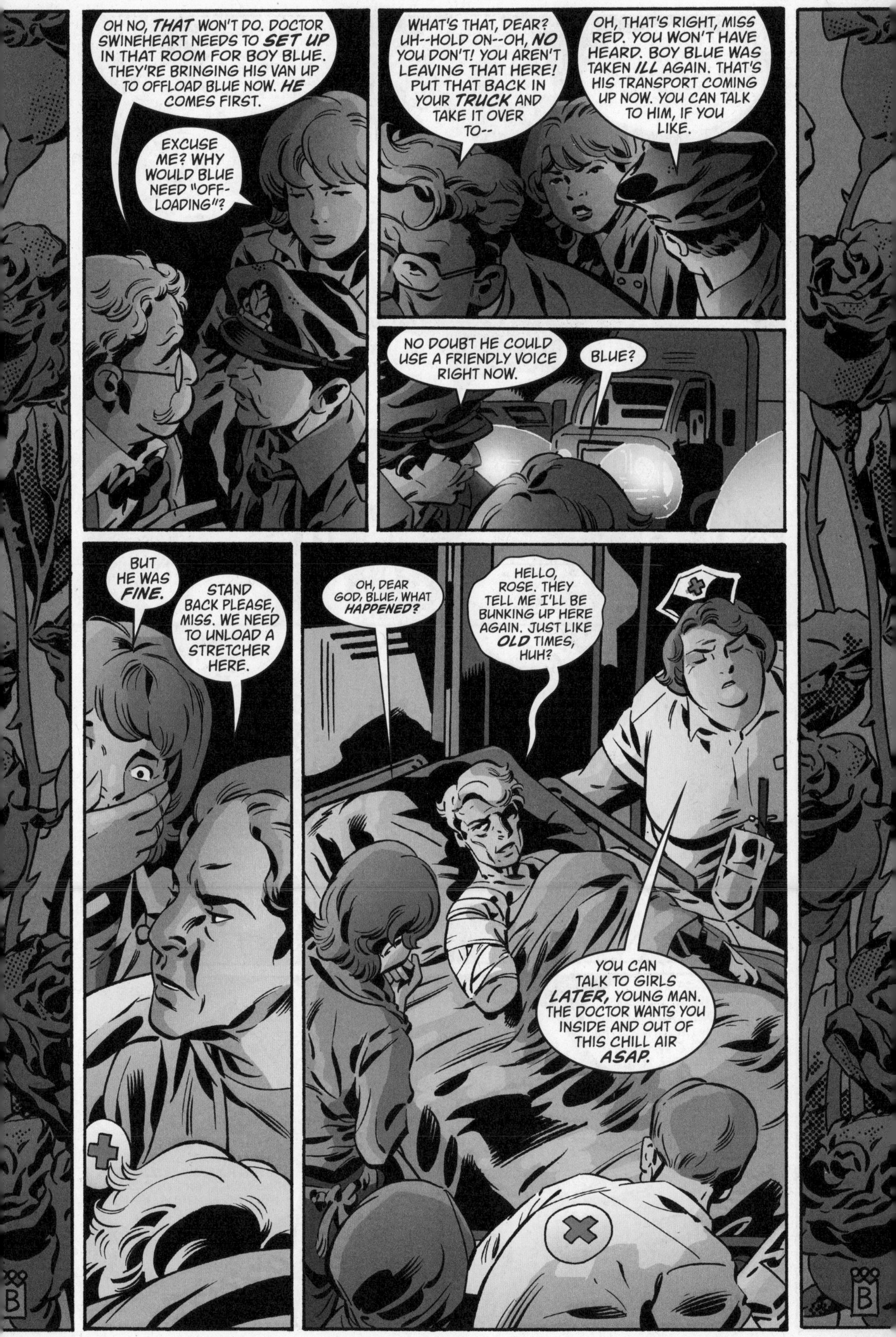
OH NO, THAT WON'T DO. DOCTOR SWINEHEART NEEDS TO SET UP IN THAT ROOM FOR BOY BLUE. THEY'RE BRINGING HIS VAN UP TO OFFLOAD BLUE NOW. HE COMES FIRST.
EXCUSE ME? WHY WOULD BLUE NEED "OFF-LOADING"?
WHAT'S THAT, DEAR? UH--HOLD ON--OH, NO YOU DON'T! YOU AREN'T LEAVING THAT HERE! PUT THAT BACK IN YOUR TRUCK AND TAKE IT OVER TO--
OH, THAT'S RIGHT, MISS RED. YOU WON'T HAVE HEARD. BOY BLUE WAS TAKEN ILL AGAIN. THAT'S HIS TRANSPORT COMING UP NOW. YOU CAN TALK TO HIM, IF YOU LIKE.
NO DOUBT HE COULD USE A FRIENDLY VOICE RIGHT NOW.
BLUE?
BUT HE WAS FINE.
STAND BACK PLEASE, MISS. WE NEED TO UNLOAD A STRETCHER HERE.
OH, DEAR GOD, BLUE, WHAT HAPPENED?
HELLO, ROSE. THEY TELL ME I'LL BE BUNKING UP HERE AGAIN. JUST LIKE OLD TIMES, HUH?
YOU CAN TALK TO GIRLS LATER, YOUNG MAN. THE DOCTOR WANTS YOU INSIDE AND OUT OF THIS CHILL AIR ASAP.

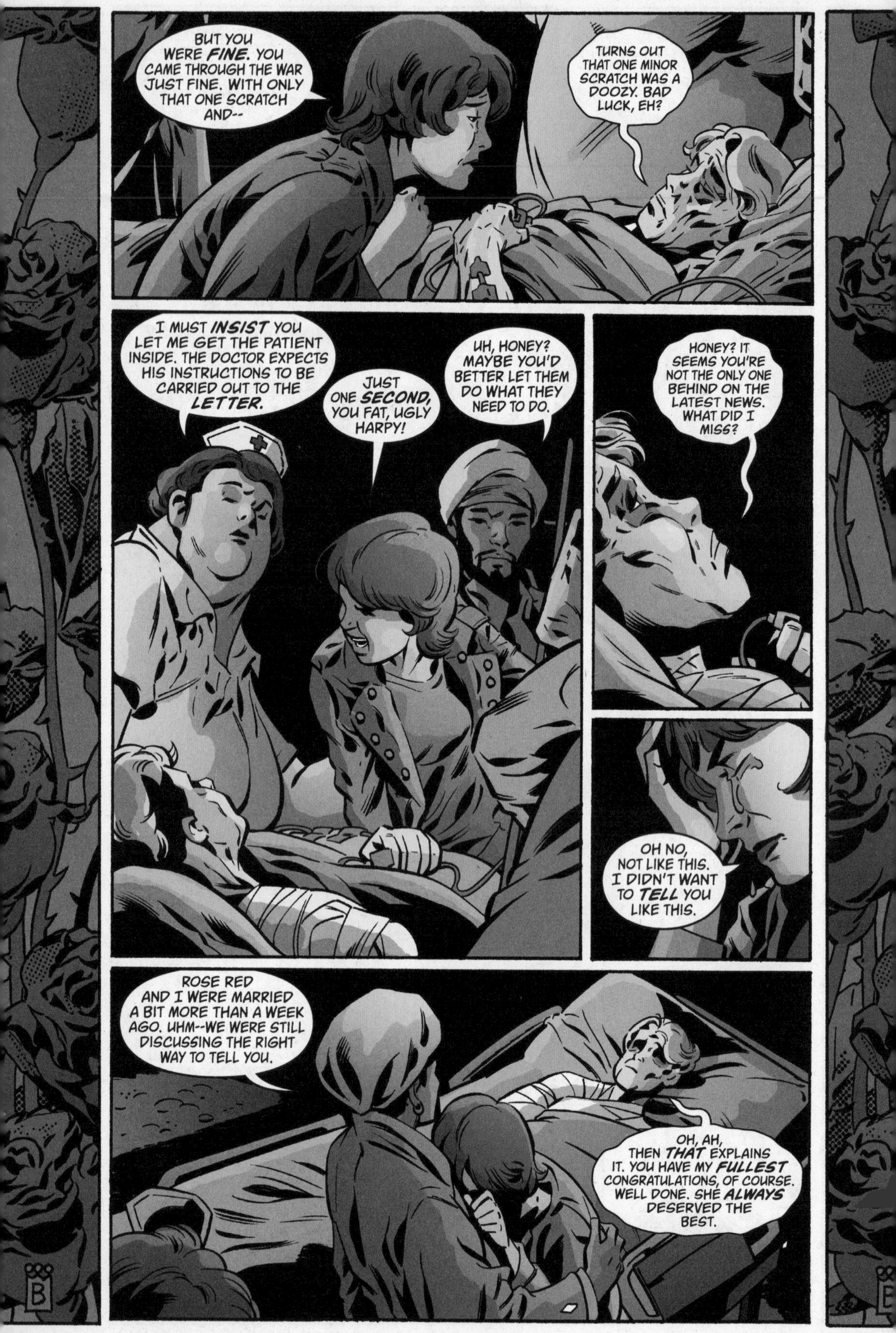
BUT YOU WERE FINE. YOU CAME THROUGH THE WAR JUST FINE. WITH ONLY THAT ONE SCRATCH AND--
TURNS OUT THAT ONE MINOR SCRATCH WAS A DOOZY. BAD LUCK, EH?
I MUST INSIST YOU LET ME GET THE PATIENT INSIDE. THE DOCTOR EXPECTS HIS INSTRUCTIONS TO BE CARRIED OUT TO THE LETTER.
JUST ONE SECOND, YOU FAT, UGLY HARPY!
UH, HONEY? MAYBE YOU'D BETTER LET THEM DO WHAT THEY NEED TO DO.
HONEY? IT SEEMS YOU'RE NOT THE ONLY ONE BEHIND ON THE LATEST NEWS. WHAT DID I MISS?
OH NO, NOT LIKE THIS. I DIDN'T WANT TO TELL YOU LIKE THIS.
ROSE RED AND I WERE MARRIED A BIT MORE THAN A WEEK AGO. UHM--WE WERE STILL DISCUSSING THE RIGHT WAY TO TELL YOU.
OH, AH, THEN THAT EXPLAINS IT. YOU HAVE MY FULLEST CONGRATULATIONS, OF COURSE. WELL DONE. SHE ALWAYS DESERVED THE BEST.

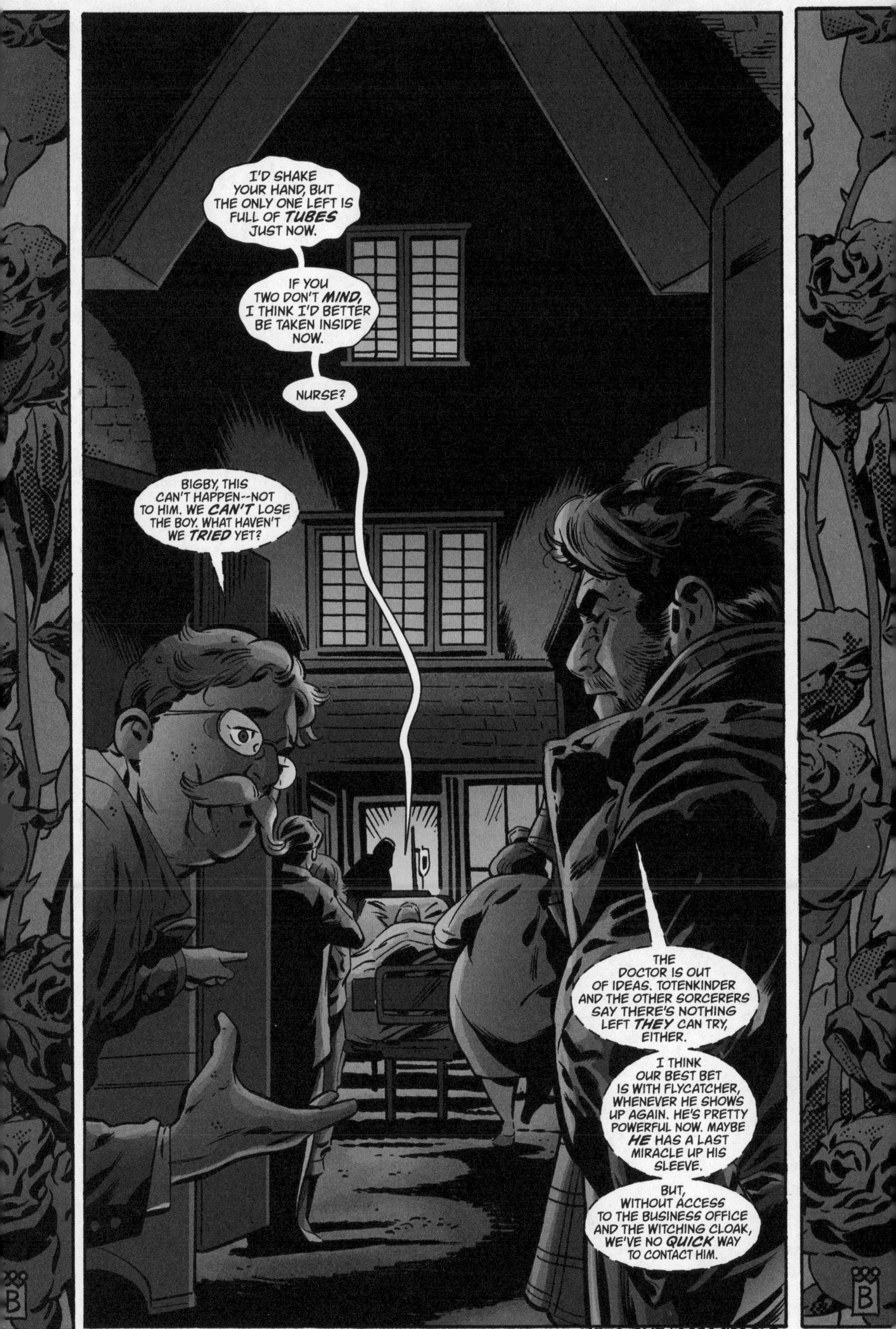
I'D SHAKE YOUR HAND, BUT THE ONLY ONE LEFT IS FULL OF TUBES JUST NOW.
IF YOU TWO DON'T MIND, I THINK I'D BETTER BE TAKEN INSIDE NOW.
NURSE?
BIGBY, THIS CAN'T HAPPEN--NOT TO HIM. WE CAN'T LOSE THE BOY. WHAT HAVEN'T WE TRIED YET?
THE DOCTOR IS OUT OF IDEAS. TOTENKINDER AND THE OTHER SORCERERS SAY THERE'S NOTHING LEFT THEY CAN TRY, EITHER.
I THINK OUR BEST BET IS WITH FLYCATCHER, WHENEVER HE SHOWS UP AGAIN. HE'S PRETTY POWERFUL NOW. MAYBE HE HAS A LAST MIRACLE UP HIS SLEEVE.
BUT, WITHOUT ACCESS TO THE BUSINESS OFFICE AND THE WITCHING CLOAK, WE'VE NO QUICK WAY TO CONTACT HIM.

NEXT: ONE LAST MIRACLE

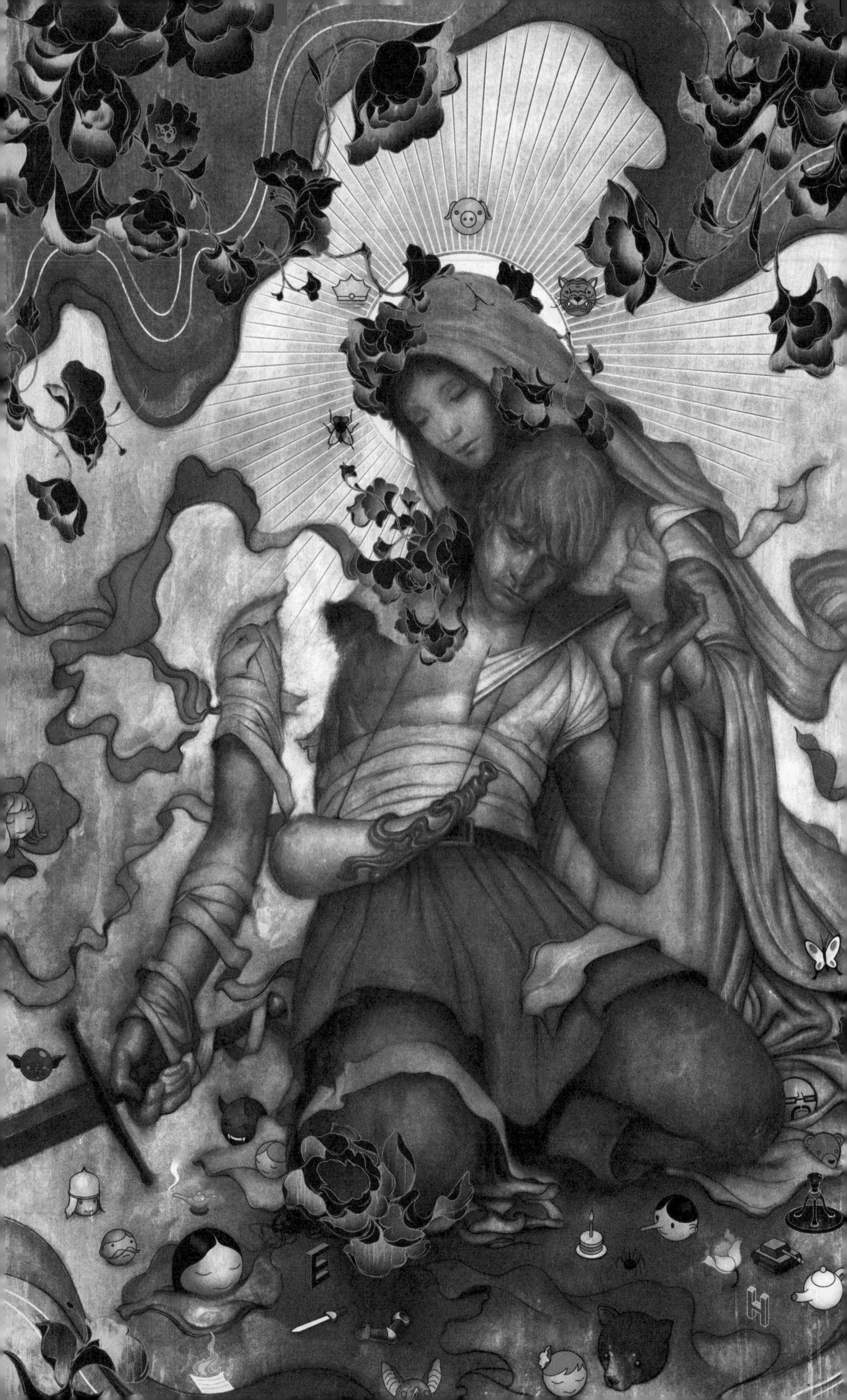

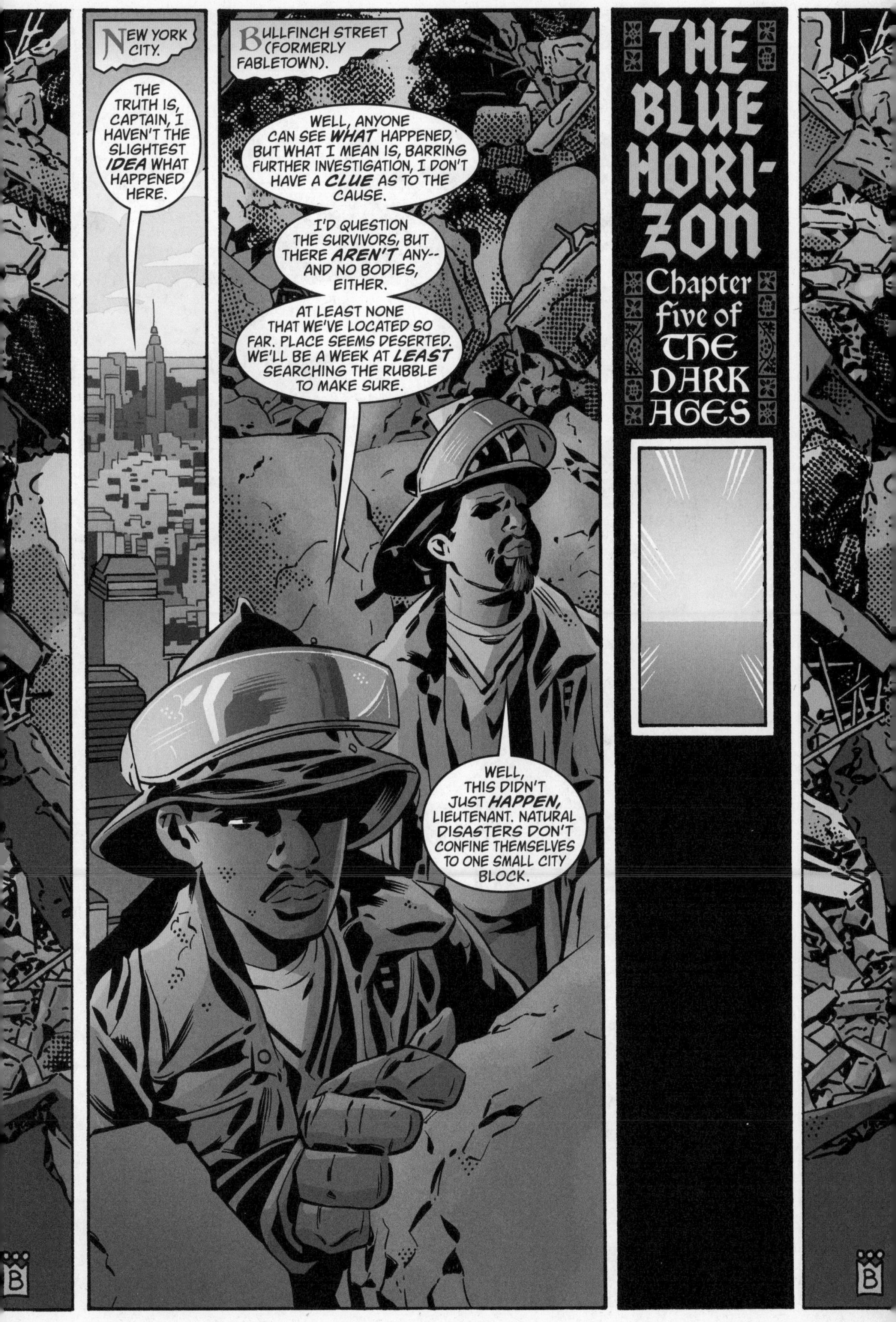

NEW YORK CITY.
THE TRUTH IS, CAPTAIN, I HAVEN'T THE SLIGHTEST IDEA WHAT HAPPENED HERE.
BULLFINCH STREET (FORMERLY FABLETOWN).
WELL, ANYONE CAN SEE WHAT HAPPENED, BUT WHAT I MEAN IS, BARRING FURTHER INVESTIGATION, I DON'T HAVE A CLUE AS TO THE CAUSE.
I'D QUESTION THE SURVIVORS, BUT THERE AREN'T ANY-- AND NO BODIES, EITHER.
AT LEAST NONE THAT WE'VE LOCATED SO FAR. PLACE SEEMS DESERTED. WE'LL BE A WEEK AT LEAST SEARCHING THE RUBBLE TO MAKE SURE.
WELL, THIS DIDN'T JUST HAPPEN, LIEUTENANT. NATURAL DISASTERS DON'T CONFINE THEMSELVES TO ONE SMALL CITY BLOCK.
THE BLUE HORI-ZON
Chapter five of THE DARK AGES

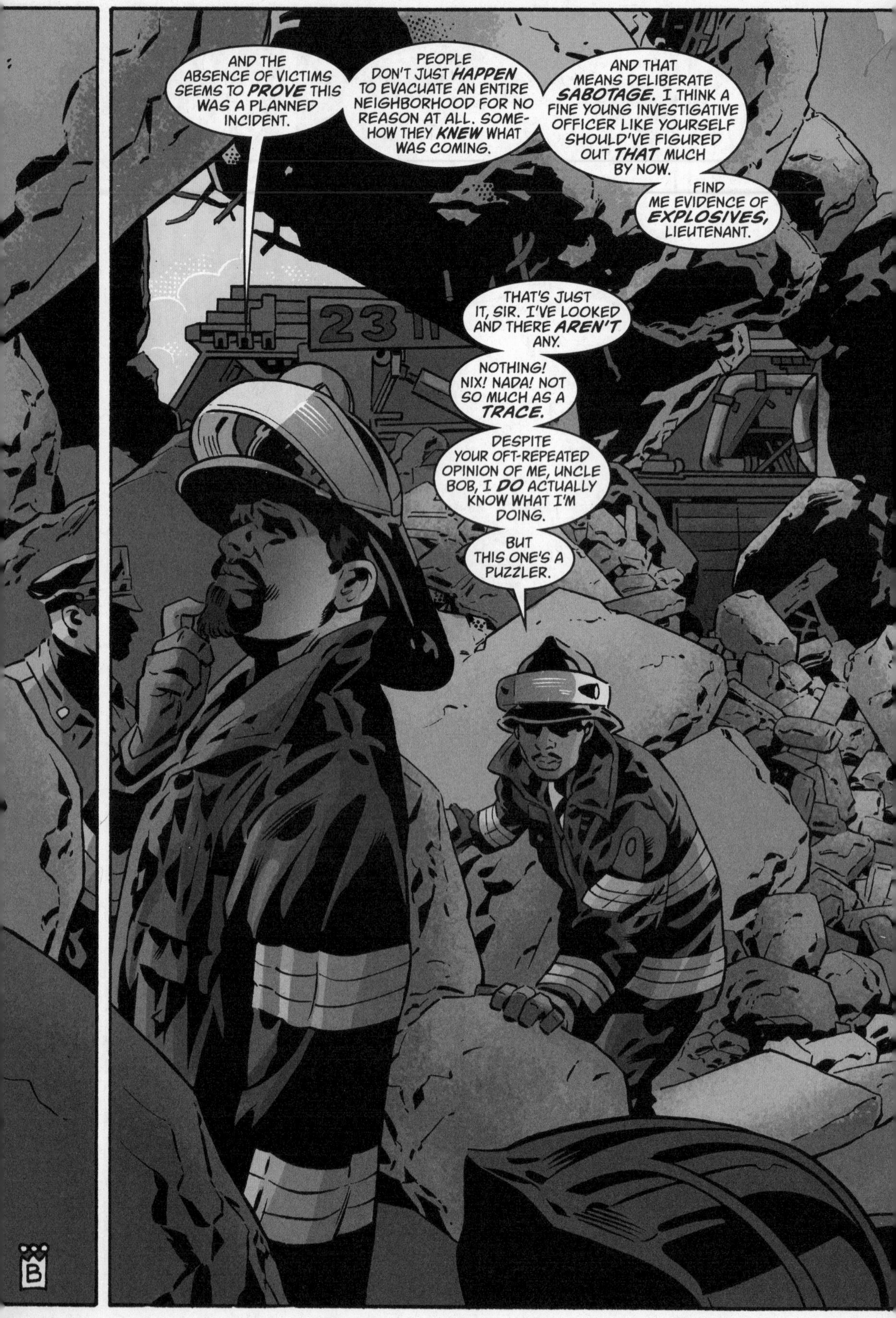
AND THE ABSENCE OF VICTIMS SEEMS TO PROVE THIS WAS A PLANNED INCIDENT.
PEOPLE DON'T JUST HAPPEN TO EVACUATE AN ENTIRE NEIGHBORHOOD FOR NO REASON AT ALL. SOMEHOW THEY KNEW WHAT WAS COMING.
AND THAT MEANS DELIBERATE SABOTAGE. I THINK A FINE YOUNG INVESTIGATIVE OFFICER LIKE YOURSELF SHOULD'VE FIGURED OUT THAT MUCH BY NOW.
FIND ME EVIDENCE OF EXPLOSIVES, LIEUTENANT.
THAT'S JUST IT, SIR. I'VE LOOKED AND THERE AREN'T ANY.
NOTHING! NIX! NADA! NOT SO MUCH AS A TRACE.
DESPITE YOUR OFT-REPEATED OPINION OF ME, UNCLE BOB, I DO ACTUALLY KNOW WHAT I'M DOING.
BUT THIS ONE'S A PUZZLER.
23

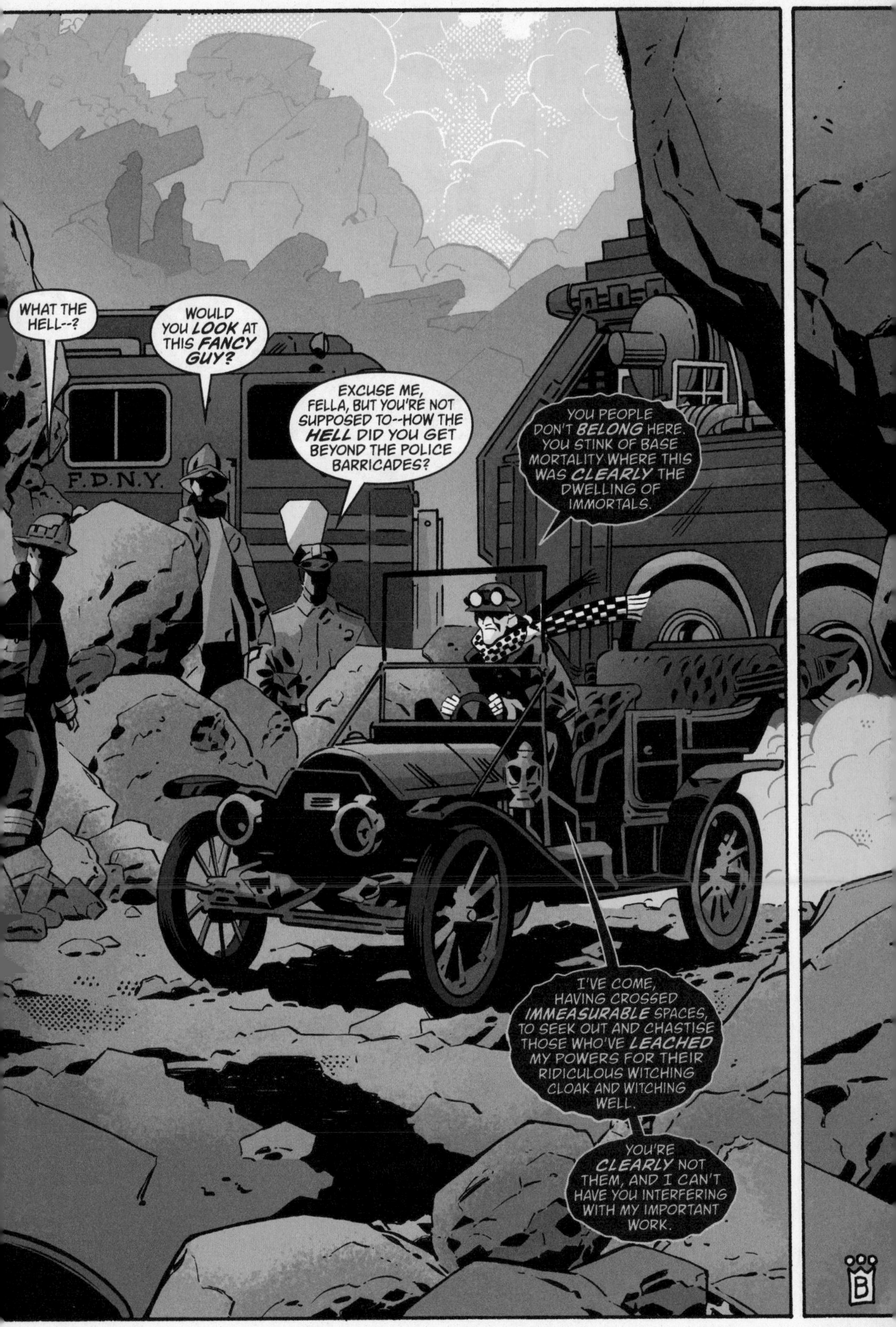
WHAT THE HELL--?
WOULD YOU LOOK AT THIS FANCY GUY?
EXCUSE ME, FELLA, BUT YOU'RE NOT SUPPOSED TO--HOW THE HELL DID YOU GET BEYOND THE POLICE BARRICADES?
F.D.N.Y.
YOU PEOPLE DON'T BELONG HERE. YOU STINK OF BASE MORTALITY WHERE THIS WAS CLEARLY THE DWELLING OF IMMORTALS.
I'VE COME, HAVING CROSSED IMMEASURABLE SPACES, TO SEEK OUT AND CHASTISE THOSE WHO'VE LEACHED MY POWERS FOR THEIR RIDICULOUS WITCHING CLOAK AND WITCHING WELL.
YOU'RE CLEARLY NOT THEM, AND I CAN'T HAVE YOU INTERFERING WITH MY IMPORTANT WORK.

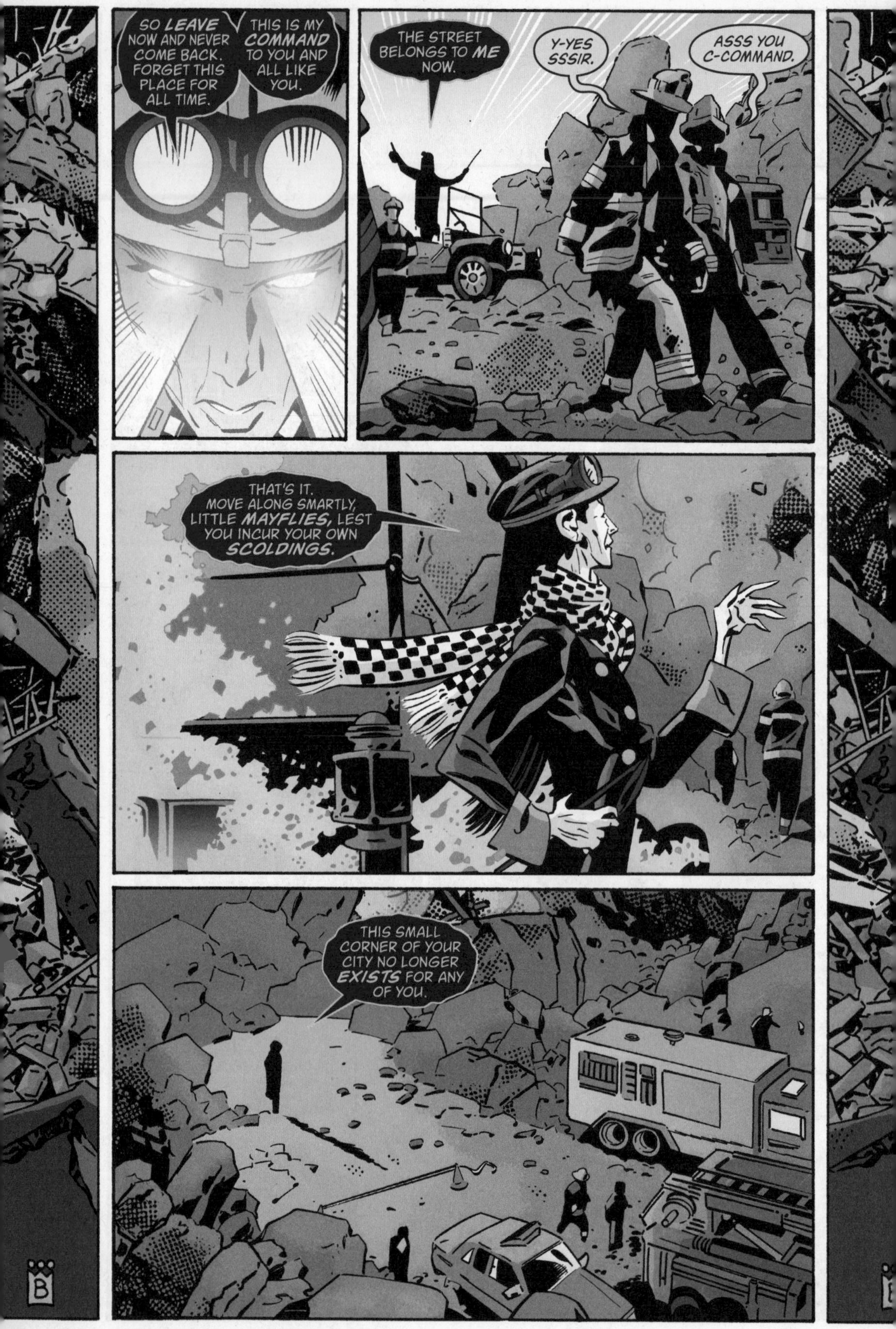
SO LEAVE NOW AND NEVER COME BACK. FORGET THIS PLACE FOR ALL TIME.
THIS IS MY COMMAND TO YOU AND ALL LIKE YOU.
THE STREET BELONGS TO ME NOW.
Y-YES SSSIR.
ASSS YOU C-COMMAND.
THAT'S IT. MOVE ALONG SMARTLY, LITTLE MAYFLIES, LEST YOU INCUR YOUR OWN SCOLDINGS.
THIS SMALL CORNER OF YOUR CITY NO LONGER EXISTS FOR ANY OF YOU.

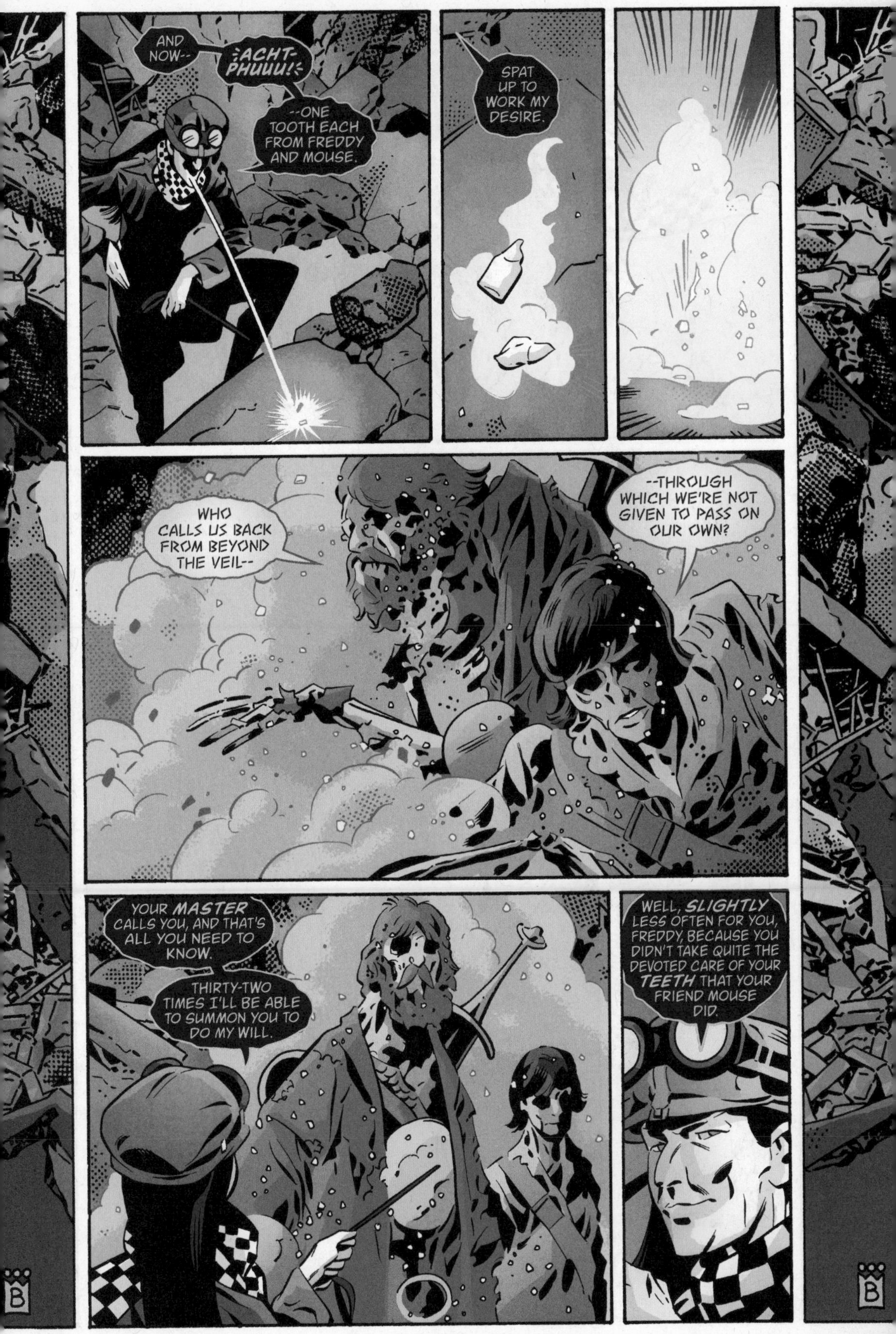
AND NOW--
ACHT-PHUUU!
--ONE TOOTH EACH FROM FREDDY AND MOUSE.
SPAT UP TO WORK MY DESIRE.
WHO CALLS US BACK FROM BEYOND THE VEIL--
--THROUGH WHICH WE'RE NOT GIVEN TO PASS ON OUR OWN?
YOUR MASTER CALLS YOU, AND THAT'S ALL YOU NEED TO KNOW.
THIRTY-TWO TIMES I'LL BE ABLE TO SUMMON YOU TO DO MY WILL.
WELL, SLIGHTLY LESS OFTEN FOR YOU, FREDDY, BECAUSE YOU DIDN'T TAKE QUITE THE DEVOTED CARE OF YOUR TEETH THAT YOUR FRIEND MOUSE DID.

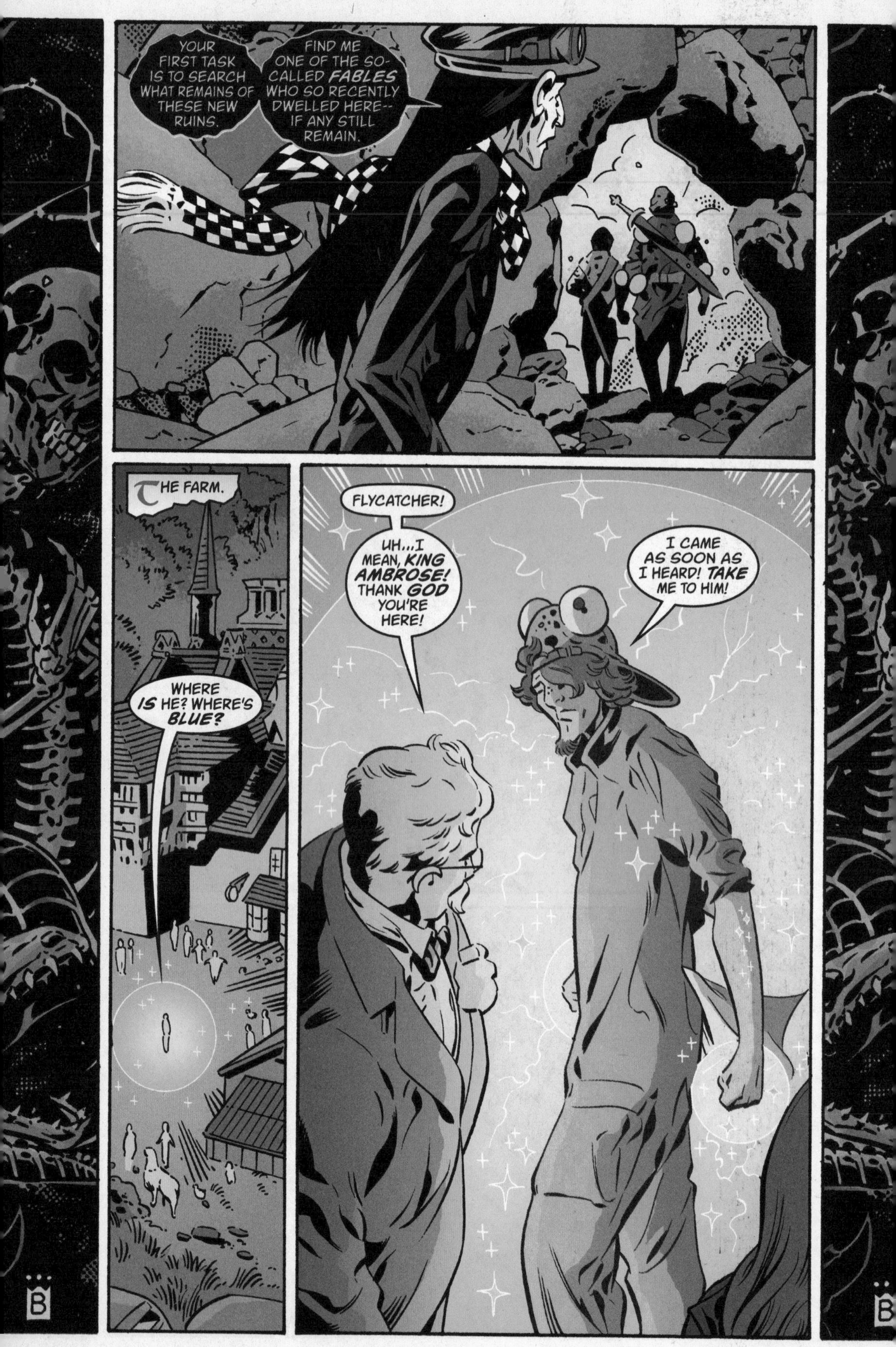
YOUR FIRST TASK IS TO SEARCH WHAT REMAINS OF THESE NEW RUINS.
FIND ME ONE OF THE SO-CALLED FABLES WHO SO RECENTLY DWELLED HERE-- IF ANY STILL REMAIN.
THE FARM.
WHERE IS HE? WHERE'S BLUE?
FLYCATCHER!
UH...I MEAN, KING AMBROSE! THANK GOD YOU'RE HERE!
I CAME AS SOON AS I HEARD! TAKE ME TO HIM!

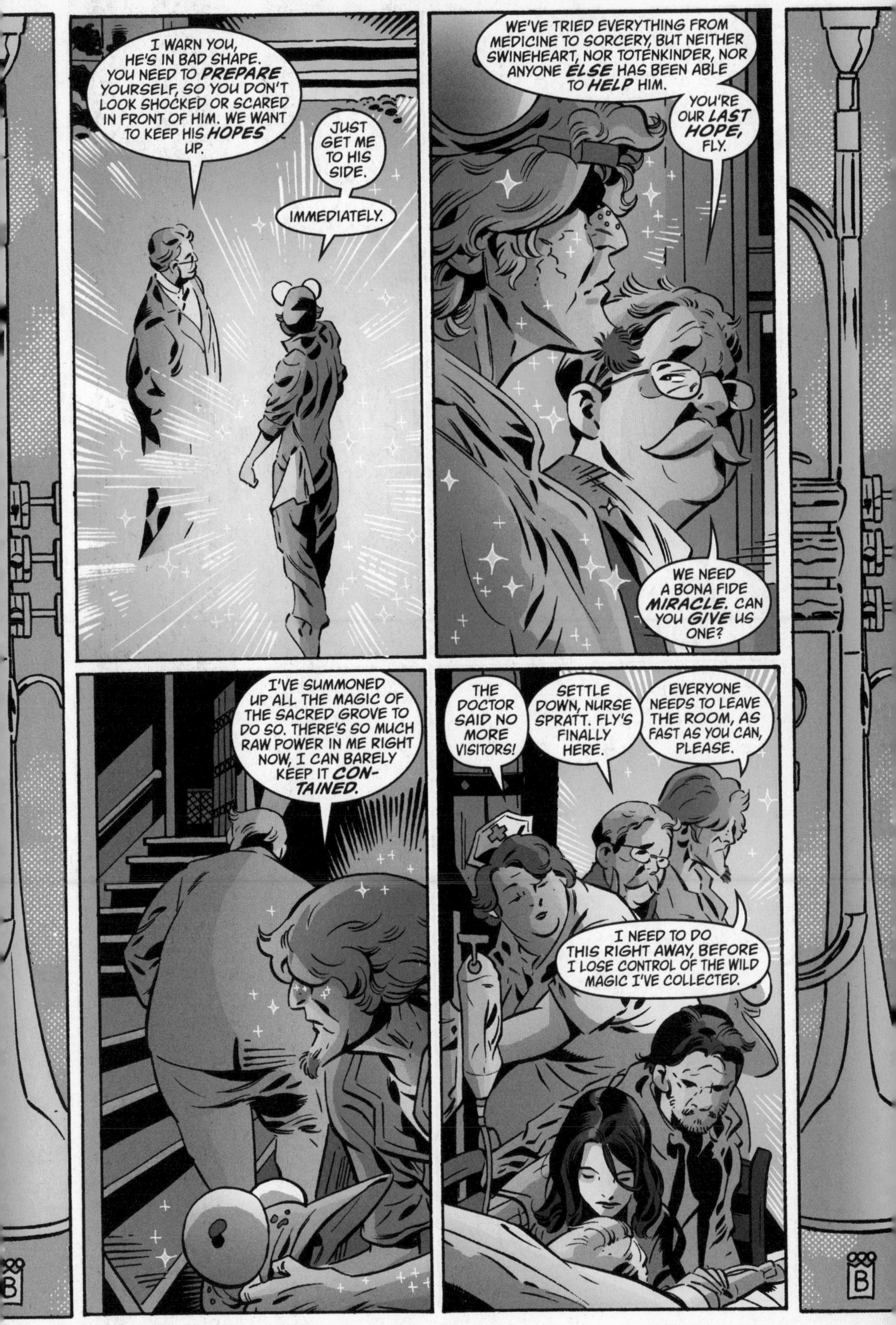
I WARN YOU, HE'S IN BAD SHAPE. YOU NEED TO PREPARE YOURSELF, SO YOU DON'T LOOK SHOCKED OR SCARED IN FRONT OF HIM. WE WANT TO KEEP HIS HOPES UP.
JUST GET ME TO HIS SIDE.
IMMEDIATELY.
WE'VE TRIED EVERYTHING FROM MEDICINE TO SORCERY, BUT NEITHER SWINEHEART, NOR TOTENKINDER, NOR ANYONE ELSE HAS BEEN ABLE TO HELP HIM.
YOU'RE OUR LAST HOPE, FLY.
WE NEED A BONA FIDE MIRACLE. CAN YOU GIVE US ONE?
I'VE SUMMONED UP ALL THE MAGIC OF THE SACRED GROVE TO DO SO. THERE'S SO MUCH RAW POWER IN ME RIGHT NOW, I CAN BARELY KEEP IT CONTAINED.
THE DOCTOR SAID NO MORE VISITORS!
SETTLE DOWN, NURSE SPRATT. FLY'S FINALLY HERE.
EVERYONE NEEDS TO LEAVE THE ROOM, AS FAST AS YOU CAN, PLEASE.
I NEED TO DO THIS RIGHT AWAY, BEFORE I LOSE CONTROL OF THE WILD MAGIC I'VE COLLECTED.

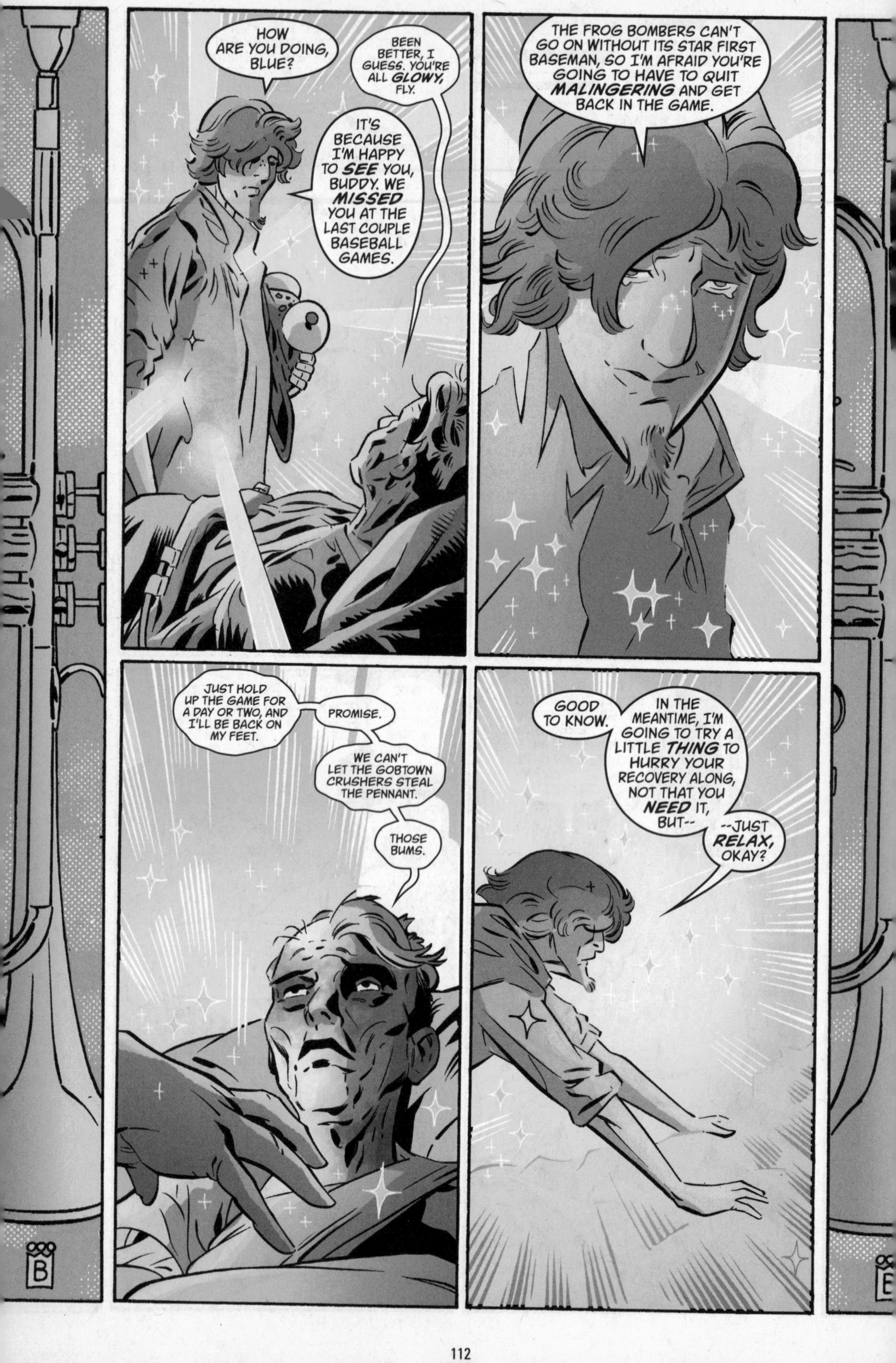

HOW ARE YOU DOING, BLUE?
BEEN BETTER, I GUESS. YOU'RE ALL GLOWY, FLY.
IT'S BECAUSE I'M HAPPY TO SEE YOU, BUDDY. WE MISSED YOU AT THE LAST COUPLE BASEBALL GAMES.
THE FROG BOMBERS CAN'T GO ON WITHOUT ITS STAR FIRST BASEMAN, SO I'M AFRAID YOU'RE GOING TO HAVE TO QUIT MALINGERING AND GET BACK IN THE GAME.
JUST HOLD UP THE GAME FOR A DAY OR TWO, AND I'LL BE BACK ON MY FEET.
PROMISE.
WE CAN'T LET THE GOBTOWN CRUSHERS STEAL THE PENNANT.
THOSE BUMS.
GOOD TO KNOW.
IN THE MEANTIME, I'M GOING TO TRY A LITTLE THING TO HURRY YOUR RECOVERY ALONG, NOT THAT YOU NEED IT, BUT--
--JUST RELAX, OKAY?

BACK ON BULLFINCH STREET...

WHO'S *THIS* BROKEN RAGDOLL?

SAYS HIS NAME IS *KAY*.

FOUND HIM IN BUILDING. UNDER SOME RUBBLE.

WELL, I CAN *SEE* YOU'RE A FABLE, BUT WHY ARE YOU ALONE? WHERE ARE YOUR *FRIENDS*, KAY?

I DON'T KNOW. I WAS ALONE IN BED, STILL RECOVER-ING FROM....

...FROM WHAT I DID TO MY *EYES*.

AND THE NEXT THING I KNOW, THESE CREATURES WERE DIGGING ME OUT FROM UNDER MY COLLAPSED BEDROOM CEILING.

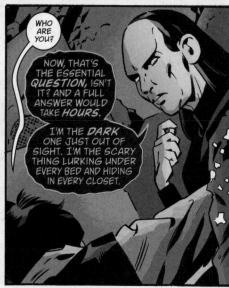

WHO ARE YOU?

NOW, THAT'S THE ESSENTIAL *QUESTION*, ISN'T IT? AND A FULL ANSWER WOULD TAKE *HOURS*.

I'M THE *DARK* ONE JUST OUT OF SIGHT. I'M THE SCARY THING LURKING UNDER EVERY BED AND HIDING IN EVERY CLOSET.

MORE TO THE *POINT*, I'M SOMEONE WHO HAS NO FURTHER *USE* FOR YOU, SINCE YOU CAN'T ANSWER MY QUESTIONS.

NO! NO!

OH DEAR GOD, NO!

WHAT ARE YOU *DOING* TO ME?!

HAND ME HIS SKULL.

I WANT HIS *TEETH*.

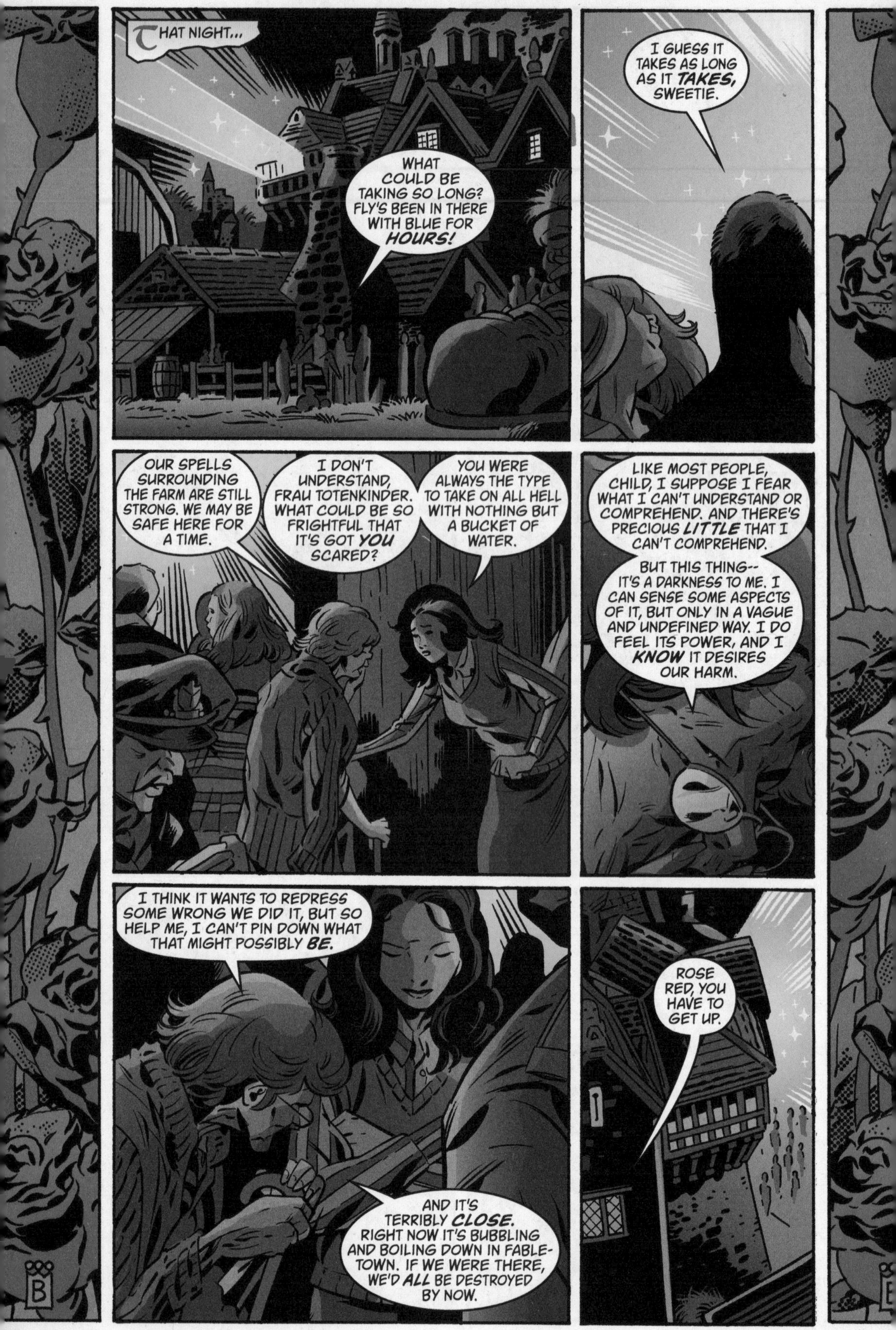
THAT NIGHT...
WHAT COULD BE TAKING SO LONG? FLY'S BEEN IN THERE WITH BLUE FOR HOURS!
I GUESS IT TAKES AS LONG AS IT TAKES, SWEETIE.
OUR SPELLS SURROUNDING THE FARM ARE STILL STRONG. WE MAY BE SAFE HERE FOR A TIME.
I DON'T UNDERSTAND, FRAU TOTENKINDER. WHAT COULD BE SO FRIGHTFUL THAT IT'S GOT YOU SCARED?
YOU WERE ALWAYS THE TYPE TO TAKE ON ALL HELL WITH NOTHING BUT A BUCKET OF WATER.
LIKE MOST PEOPLE, CHILD, I SUPPOSE I FEAR WHAT I CAN'T UNDERSTAND OR COMPREHEND. AND THERE'S PRECIOUS LITTLE THAT I CAN'T COMPREHEND.
BUT THIS THING-- IT'S A DARKNESS TO ME. I CAN SENSE SOME ASPECTS OF IT, BUT ONLY IN A VAGUE AND UNDEFINED WAY. I DO FEEL ITS POWER, AND I KNOW IT DESIRES OUR HARM.
I THINK IT WANTS TO REDRESS SOME WRONG WE DID IT, BUT SO HELP ME, I CAN'T PIN DOWN WHAT THAT MIGHT POSSIBLY BE.
AND IT'S TERRIBLY CLOSE. RIGHT NOW IT'S BUBBLING AND BOILING DOWN IN FABLE-TOWN. IF WE WERE THERE, WE'D ALL BE DESTROYED BY NOW.
ROSE RED, YOU HAVE TO GET UP.

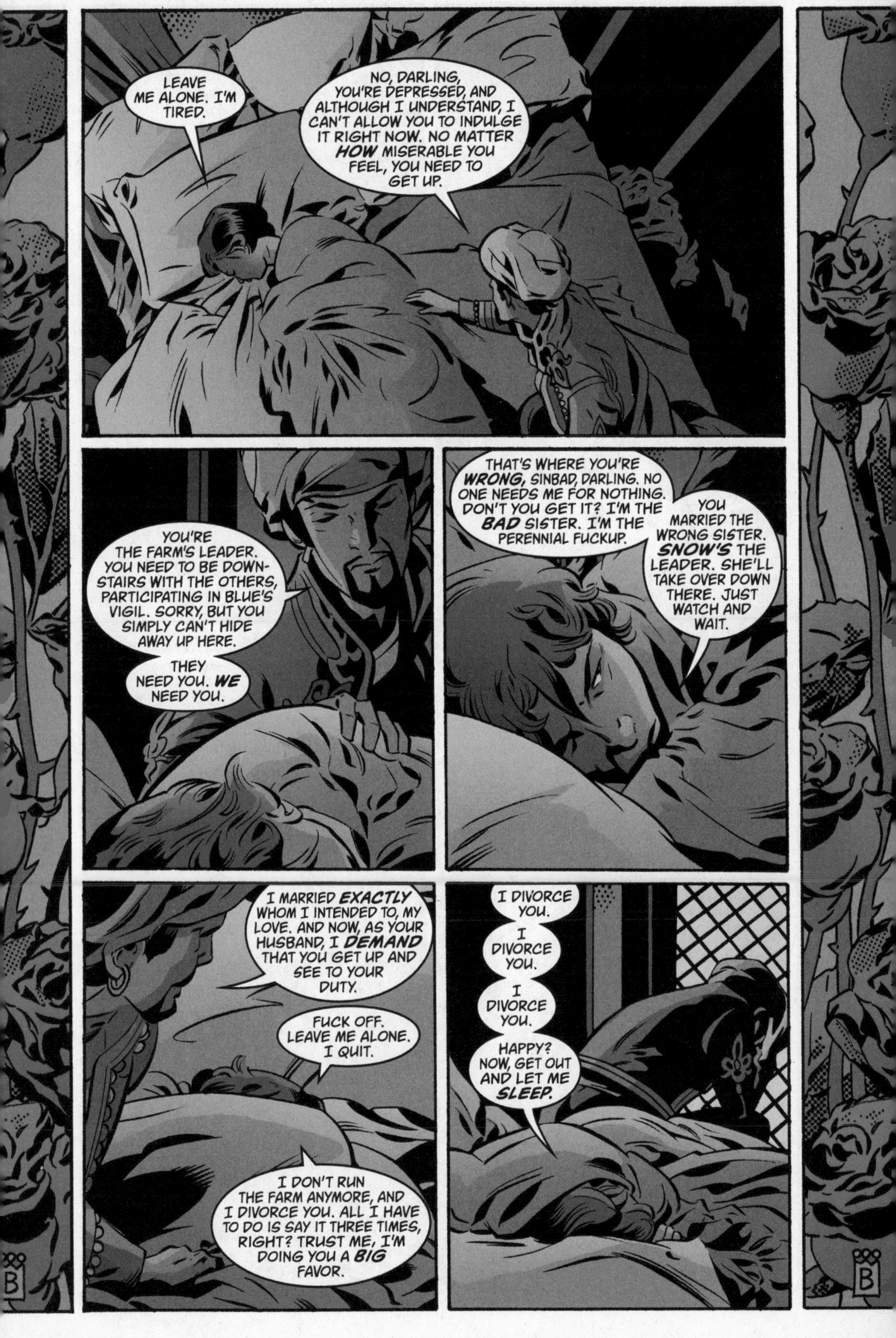
LEAVE ME ALONE. I'M TIRED.
NO, DARLING, YOU'RE DEPRESSED, AND ALTHOUGH I UNDERSTAND, I CAN'T ALLOW YOU TO INDULGE IT RIGHT NOW. NO MATTER HOW MISERABLE YOU FEEL, YOU NEED TO GET UP.
YOU'RE THE FARM'S LEADER. YOU NEED TO BE DOWNSTAIRS WITH THE OTHERS, PARTICIPATING IN BLUE'S VIGIL. SORRY, BUT YOU SIMPLY CAN'T HIDE AWAY UP HERE.
THEY NEED YOU. WE NEED YOU.
THAT'S WHERE YOU'RE WRONG, SINBAD, DARLING. NO ONE NEEDS ME FOR NOTHING. DON'T YOU GET IT? I'M THE BAD SISTER. I'M THE PERENNIAL FUCKUP.
YOU MARRIED THE WRONG SISTER. SNOW'S THE LEADER. SHE'LL TAKE OVER DOWN THERE. JUST WATCH AND WAIT.
I MARRIED EXACTLY WHOM I INTENDED TO, MY LOVE. AND NOW, AS YOUR HUSBAND, I DEMAND THAT YOU GET UP AND SEE TO YOUR DUTY.
FUCK OFF. LEAVE ME ALONE. I QUIT.
I DON'T RUN THE FARM ANYMORE, AND I DIVORCE YOU. ALL I HAVE TO DO IS SAY IT THREE TIMES, RIGHT? TRUST ME, I'M DOING YOU A BIG FAVOR.
I DIVORCE YOU.
I DIVORCE YOU.
I DIVORCE YOU.
HAPPY? NOW, GET OUT AND LET ME SLEEP.

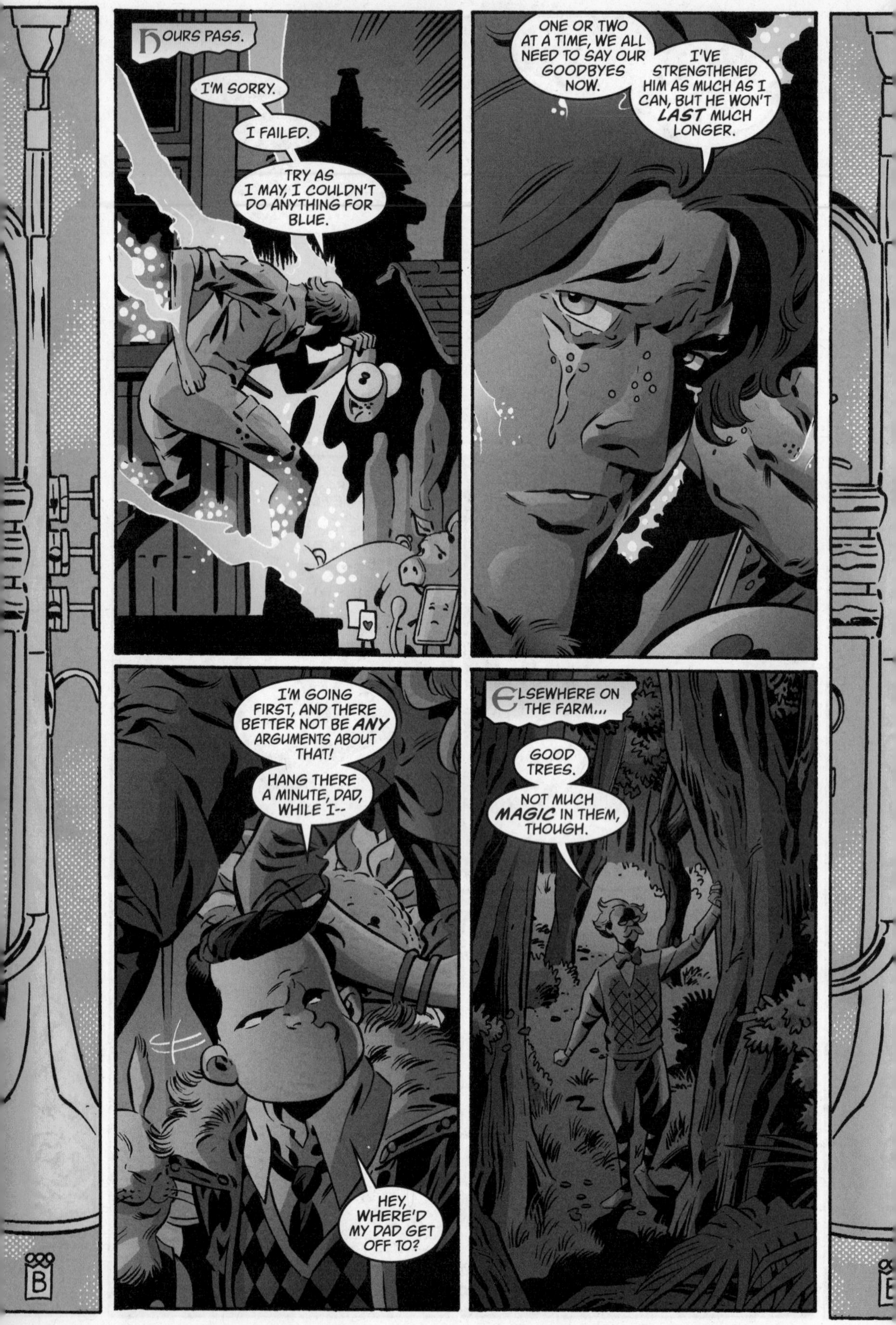
HOURS PASS.
I'M SORRY.
I FAILED.
TRY AS I MAY, I COULDN'T DO ANYTHING FOR BLUE.
ONE OR TWO AT A TIME, WE ALL NEED TO SAY OUR GOODBYES NOW.
I'VE STRENGTHENED HIM AS MUCH AS I CAN, BUT HE WON'T LAST MUCH LONGER.
I'M GOING FIRST, AND THERE BETTER NOT BE ANY ARGUMENTS ABOUT THAT!
HANG THERE A MINUTE, DAD, WHILE I--
HEY, WHERE'D MY DAD GET OFF TO?
ELSEWHERE ON THE FARM...
GOOD TREES.
NOT MUCH MAGIC IN THEM, THOUGH.

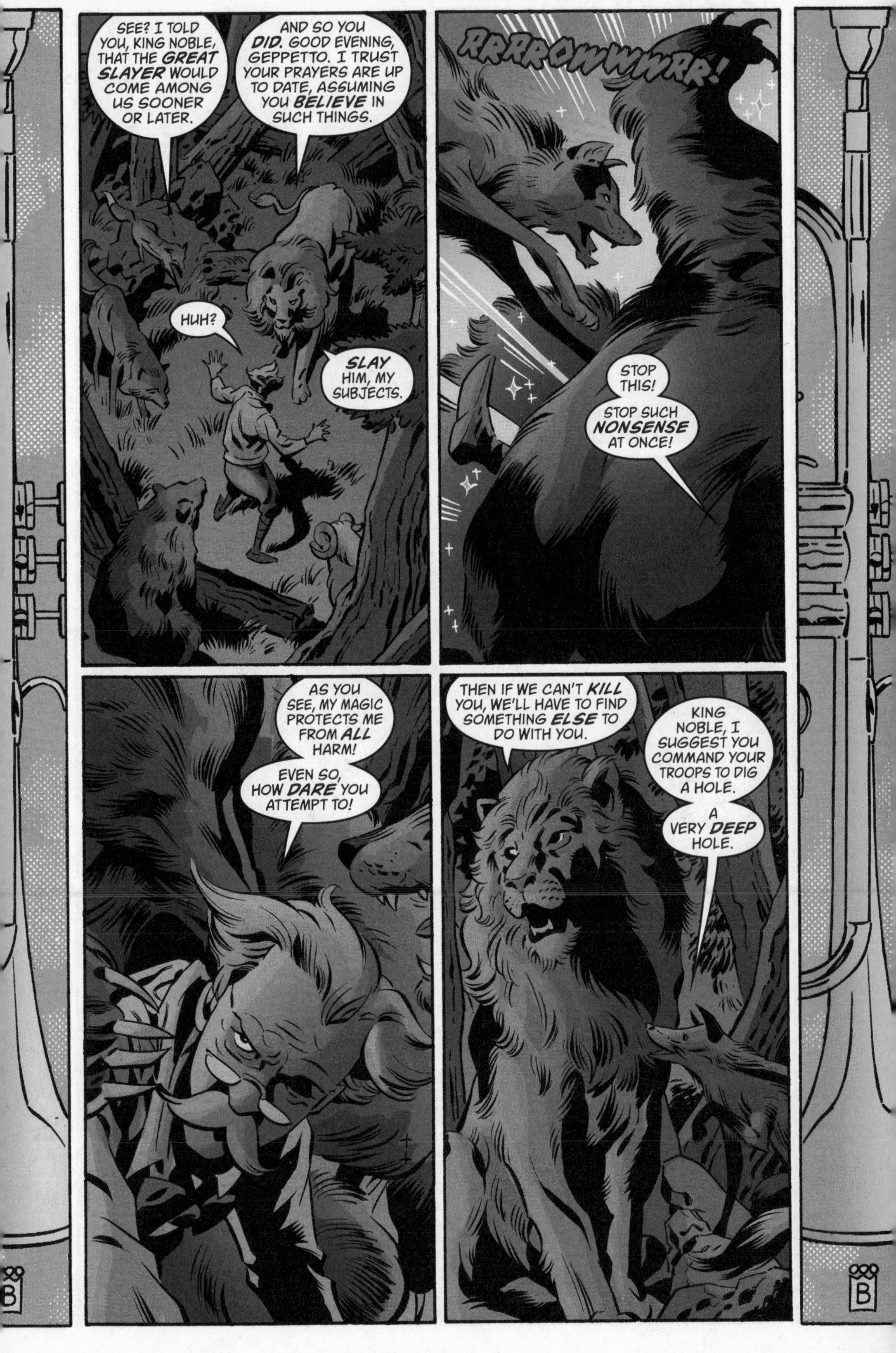
SEE? I TOLD YOU, KING NOBLE, THAT THE GREAT SLAYER WOULD COME AMONG US SOONER OR LATER.
AND SO YOU DID. GOOD EVENING, GEPPETTO. I TRUST YOUR PRAYERS ARE UP TO DATE, ASSUMING YOU BELIEVE IN SUCH THINGS.
HUH?
SLAY HIM, MY SUBJECTS.
RRRROWWWRR!
STOP THIS!
STOP SUCH NONSENSE AT ONCE!
AS YOU SEE, MY MAGIC PROTECTS ME FROM ALL HARM!
EVEN SO, HOW DARE YOU ATTEMPT TO!
THEN IF WE CAN'T KILL YOU, WE'LL HAVE TO FIND SOMETHING ELSE TO DO WITH YOU.
KING NOBLE, I SUGGEST YOU COMMAND YOUR TROOPS TO DIG A HOLE.
A VERY DEEP HOLE.

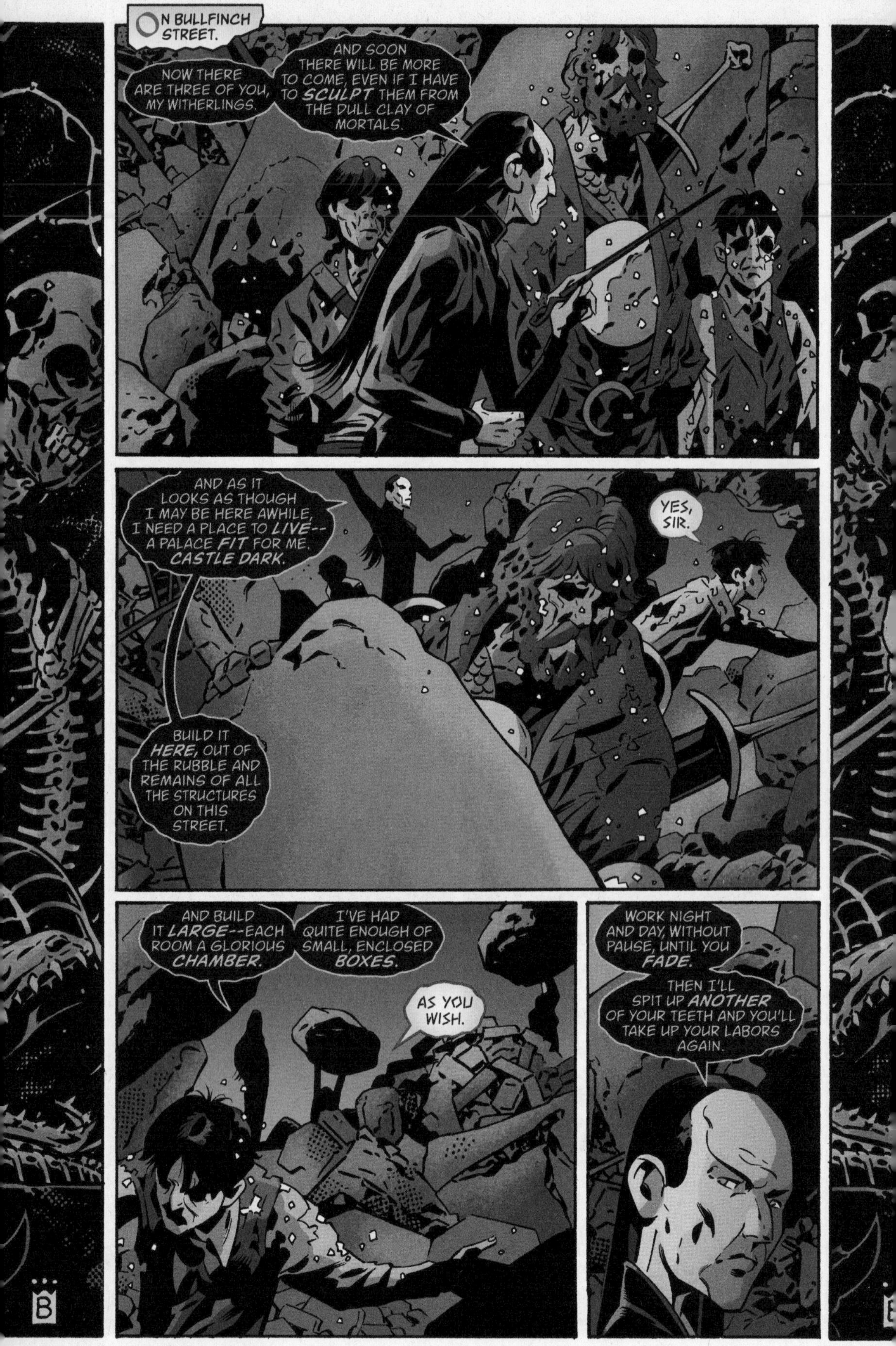
ON BULLFINCH STREET.
NOW THERE ARE THREE OF YOU, MY WITHERLINGS.
AND SOON THERE WILL BE MORE TO COME, EVEN IF I HAVE TO SCULPT THEM FROM THE DULL CLAY OF MORTALS.
AND AS IT LOOKS AS THOUGH I MAY BE HERE AWHILE, I NEED A PLACE TO LIVE-- A PALACE FIT FOR ME. CASTLE DARK.
BUILD IT HERE, OUT OF THE RUBBLE AND REMAINS OF ALL THE STRUCTURES ON THIS STREET.
YES, SIR.
AND BUILD IT LARGE--EACH ROOM A GLORIOUS CHAMBER.
I'VE HAD QUITE ENOUGH OF SMALL, ENCLOSED BOXES.
AS YOU WISH.
WORK NIGHT AND DAY, WITHOUT PAUSE, UNTIL YOU FADE.
THEN I'LL SPIT UP ANOTHER OF YOUR TEETH AND YOU'LL TAKE UP YOUR LABORS AGAIN.

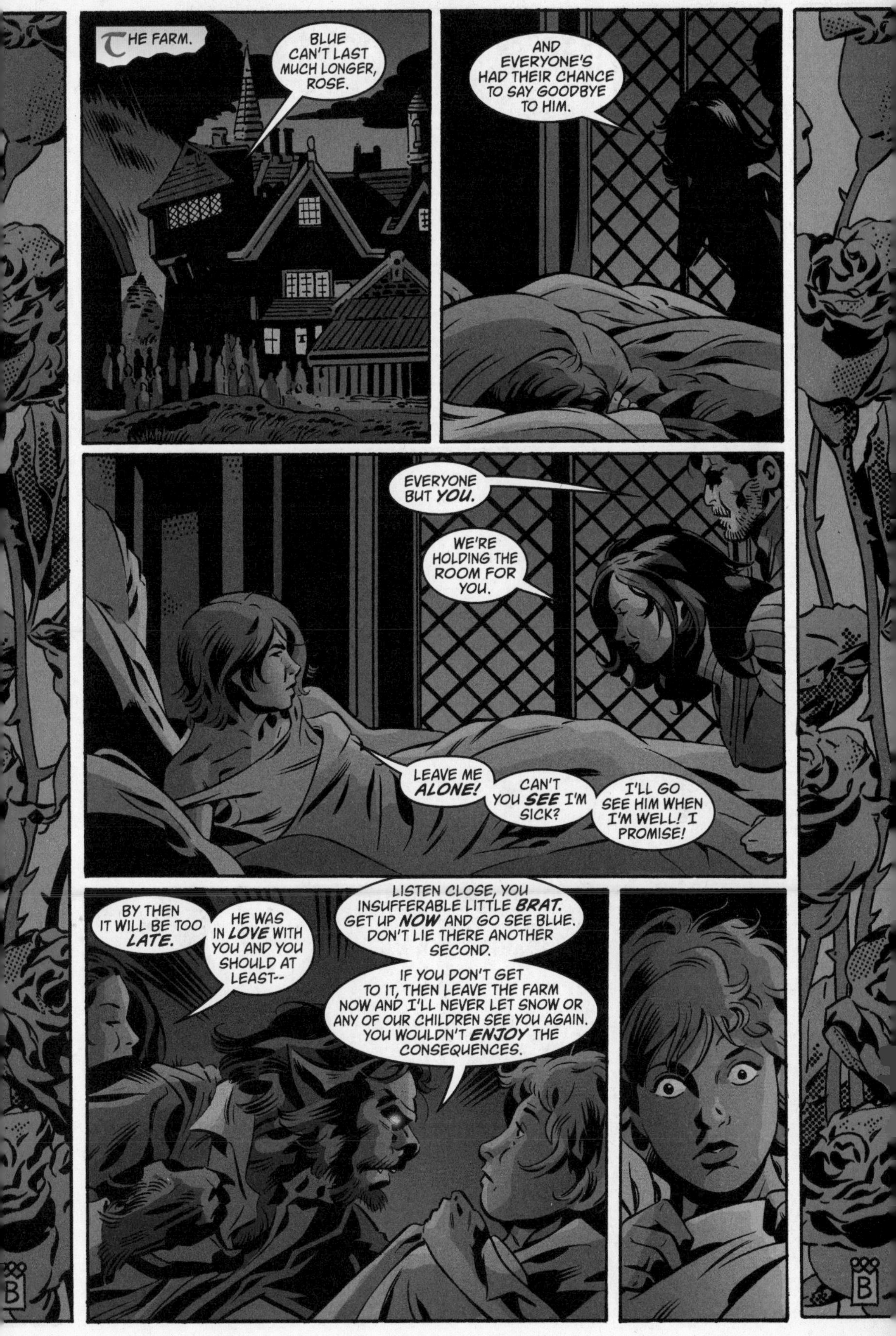
THE FARM.
BLUE CAN'T LAST MUCH LONGER, ROSE.
AND EVERYONE'S HAD THEIR CHANCE TO SAY GOODBYE TO HIM.
EVERYONE BUT YOU.
WE'RE HOLDING THE ROOM FOR YOU.
LEAVE ME ALONE!
CAN'T YOU SEE I'M SICK?
I'LL GO SEE HIM WHEN I'M WELL! I PROMISE!
BY THEN IT WILL BE TOO LATE.
HE WAS IN LOVE WITH YOU AND YOU SHOULD AT LEAST--
LISTEN CLOSE, YOU INSUFFERABLE LITTLE BRAT. GET UP NOW AND GO SEE BLUE. DON'T LIE THERE ANOTHER SECOND.
IF YOU DON'T GET TO IT, THEN LEAVE THE FARM NOW AND I'LL NEVER LET SNOW OR ANY OF OUR CHILDREN SEE YOU AGAIN. YOU WOULDN'T ENJOY THE CONSEQUENCES.

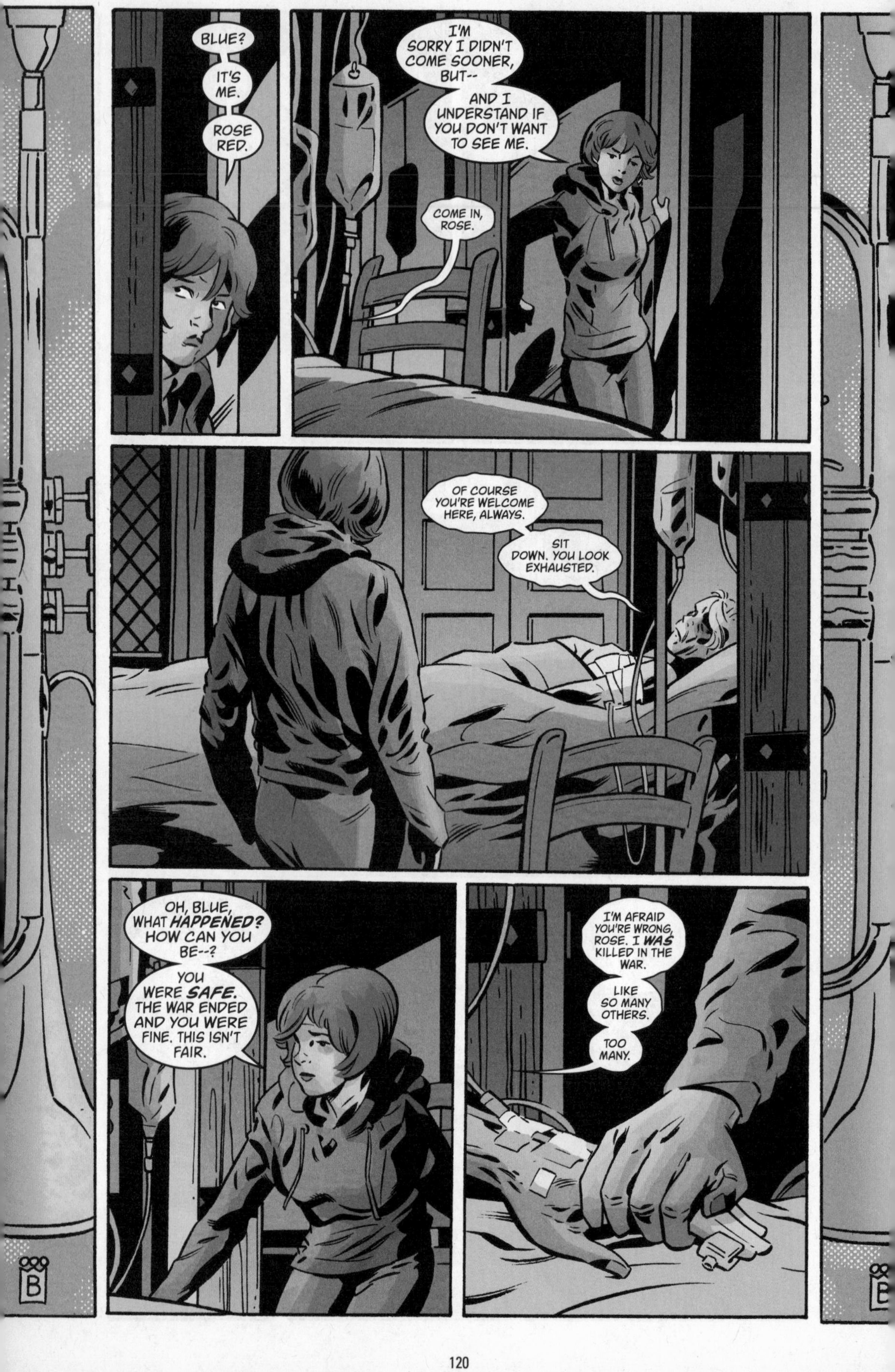
BLUE?
IT'S ME.
ROSE RED.
I'M SORRY I DIDN'T COME SOONER, BUT--
AND I UNDERSTAND IF YOU DON'T WANT TO SEE ME.
COME IN, ROSE.
OF COURSE YOU'RE WELCOME HERE, ALWAYS.
SIT DOWN. YOU LOOK EXHAUSTED.
OH, BLUE, WHAT HAPPENED? HOW CAN YOU BE--?
YOU WERE SAFE. THE WAR ENDED AND YOU WERE FINE. THIS ISN'T FAIR.
I'M AFRAID YOU'RE WRONG, ROSE. I WAS KILLED IN THE WAR.
LIKE SO MANY OTHERS.
TOO MANY.

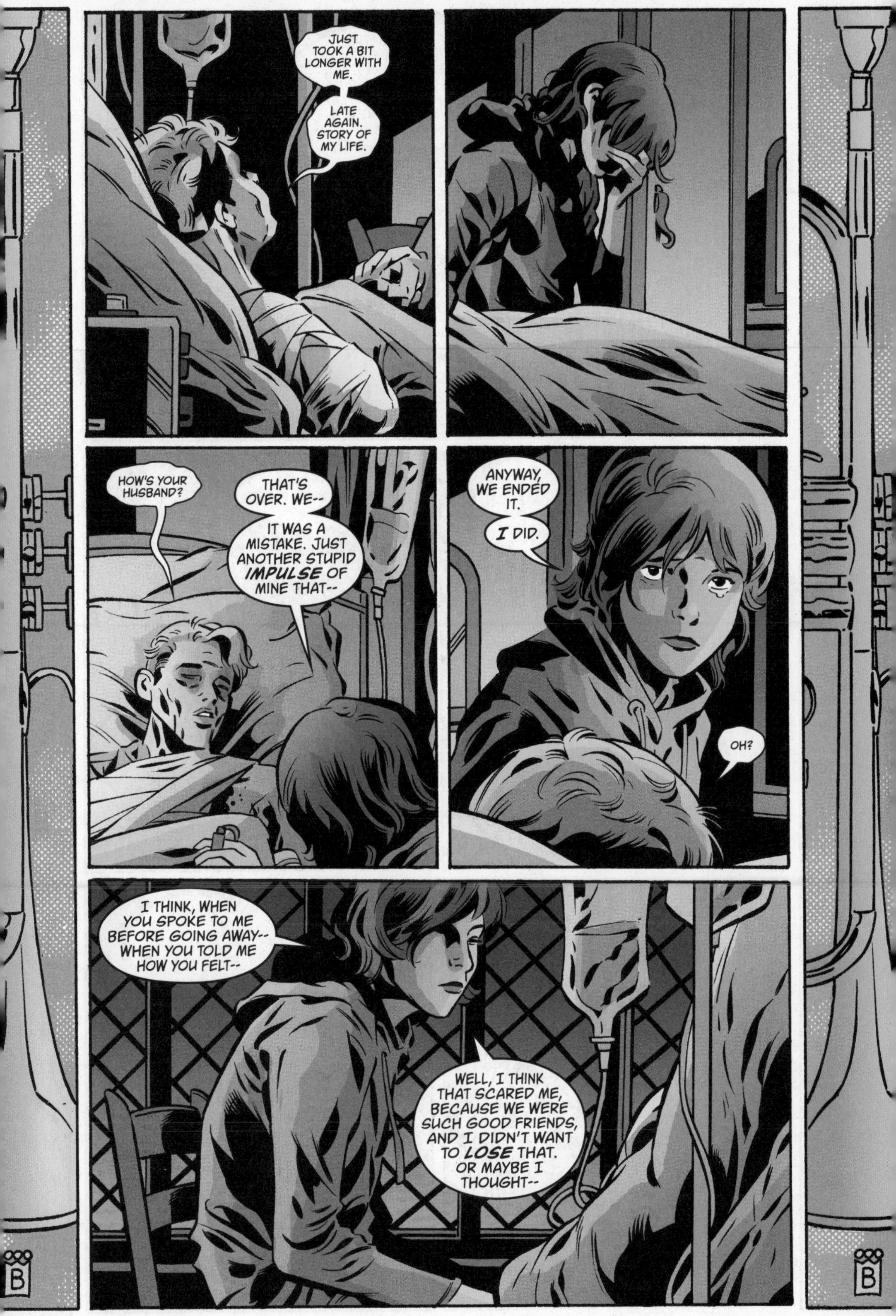
JUST TOOK A BIT LONGER WITH ME.
LATE AGAIN. STORY OF MY LIFE.
HOW'S YOUR HUSBAND?
THAT'S OVER. WE--
IT WAS A MISTAKE. JUST ANOTHER STUPID IMPULSE OF MINE THAT--
ANYWAY, WE ENDED IT.
I DID.
OH?
I THINK, WHEN YOU SPOKE TO ME BEFORE GOING AWAY-- WHEN YOU TOLD ME HOW YOU FELT--
WELL, I THINK THAT SCARED ME, BECAUSE WE WERE SUCH GOOD FRIENDS, AND I DIDN'T WANT TO LOSE THAT. OR MAYBE I THOUGHT--

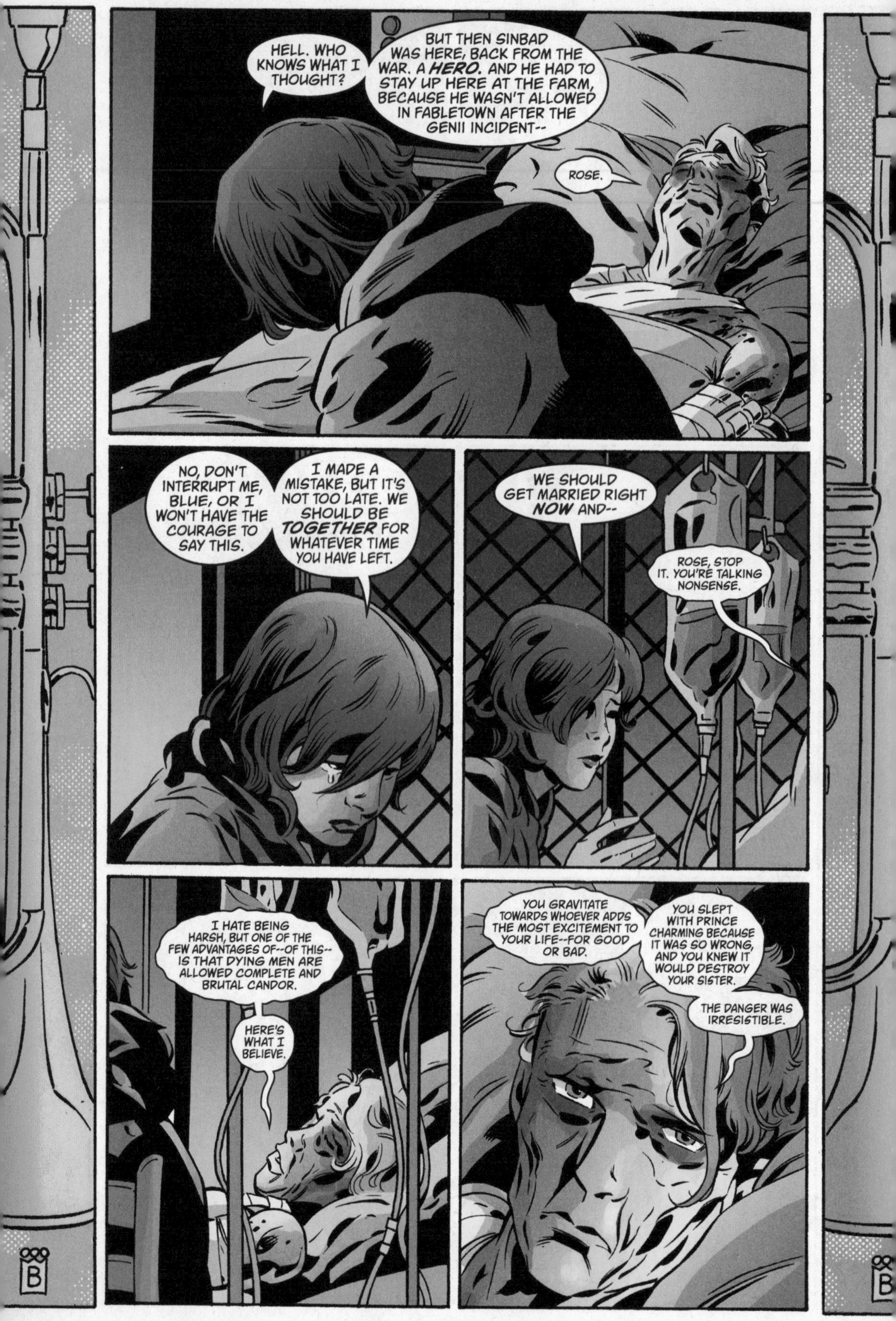
HELL. WHO KNOWS WHAT I THOUGHT?
BUT THEN SINBAD WAS HERE, BACK FROM THE WAR. A **HERO.** AND HE HAD TO STAY UP HERE AT THE FARM, BECAUSE HE WASN'T ALLOWED IN FABLETOWN AFTER THE GENII INCIDENT--
ROSE.
NO, DON'T INTERRUPT ME, BLUE, OR I WON'T HAVE THE COURAGE TO SAY THIS.
I MADE A MISTAKE, BUT IT'S NOT TOO LATE. WE SHOULD BE ***TOGETHER*** FOR WHATEVER TIME YOU HAVE LEFT.
WE SHOULD GET MARRIED RIGHT ***NOW*** AND--
ROSE, STOP IT. YOU'RE TALKING NONSENSE.
I HATE BEING HARSH, BUT ONE OF THE FEW ADVANTAGES OF--OF THIS--IS THAT DYING MEN ARE ALLOWED COMPLETE AND BRUTAL CANDOR.
HERE'S WHAT I BELIEVE.
YOU GRAVITATE TOWARDS WHOEVER ADDS THE MOST EXCITEMENT TO YOUR LIFE--FOR GOOD OR BAD.
YOU SLEPT WITH PRINCE CHARMING BECAUSE IT WAS SO WRONG, AND YOU KNEW IT WOULD DESTROY YOUR SISTER.
THE DANGER WAS IRRESISTIBLE.

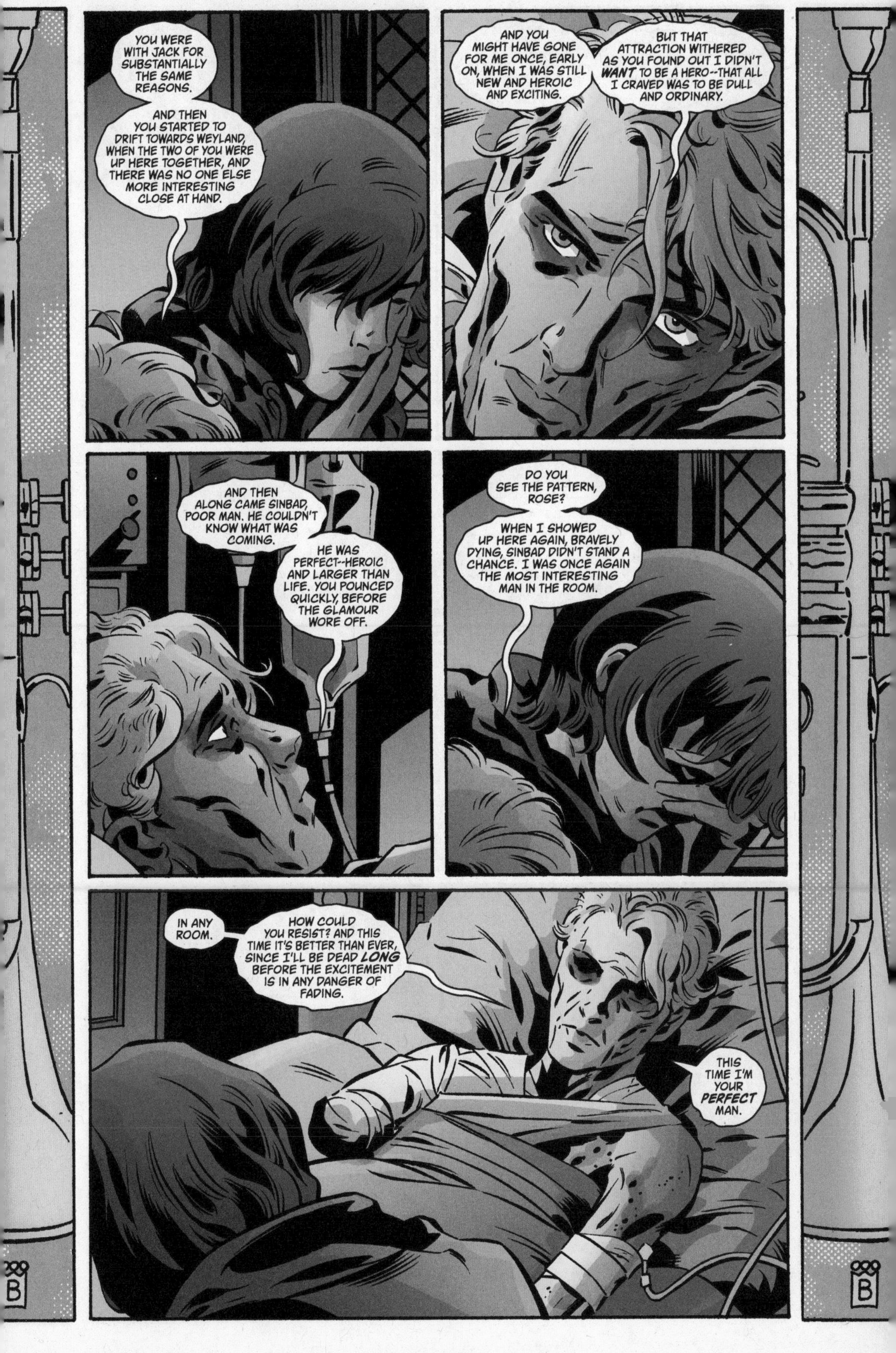
YOU WERE WITH JACK FOR SUBSTANTIALLY THE SAME REASONS.
AND THEN YOU STARTED TO DRIFT TOWARDS WEYLAND, WHEN THE TWO OF YOU WERE UP HERE TOGETHER, AND THERE WAS NO ONE ELSE MORE INTERESTING CLOSE AT HAND.
AND YOU MIGHT HAVE GONE FOR ME ONCE, EARLY ON, WHEN I WAS STILL NEW AND HEROIC AND EXCITING.
BUT THAT ATTRACTION WITHERED AS YOU FOUND OUT I DIDN'T *WANT* TO BE A HERO--THAT ALL I CRAVED WAS TO BE DULL AND ORDINARY.
AND THEN ALONG CAME SINBAD, POOR MAN. HE COULDN'T KNOW WHAT WAS COMING.
HE WAS PERFECT--HEROIC AND LARGER THAN LIFE. YOU POUNCED QUICKLY, BEFORE THE GLAMOUR WORE OFF.
DO YOU SEE THE PATTERN, ROSE?
WHEN I SHOWED UP HERE AGAIN, BRAVELY DYING, SINBAD DIDN'T STAND A CHANCE. I WAS ONCE AGAIN THE MOST INTERESTING MAN IN THE ROOM.
IN ANY ROOM.
HOW COULD YOU RESIST? AND THIS TIME IT'S BETTER THAN EVER, SINCE I'LL BE DEAD *LONG* BEFORE THE EXCITEMENT IS IN ANY DANGER OF FADING.
THIS TIME I'M YOUR *PERFECT* MAN.

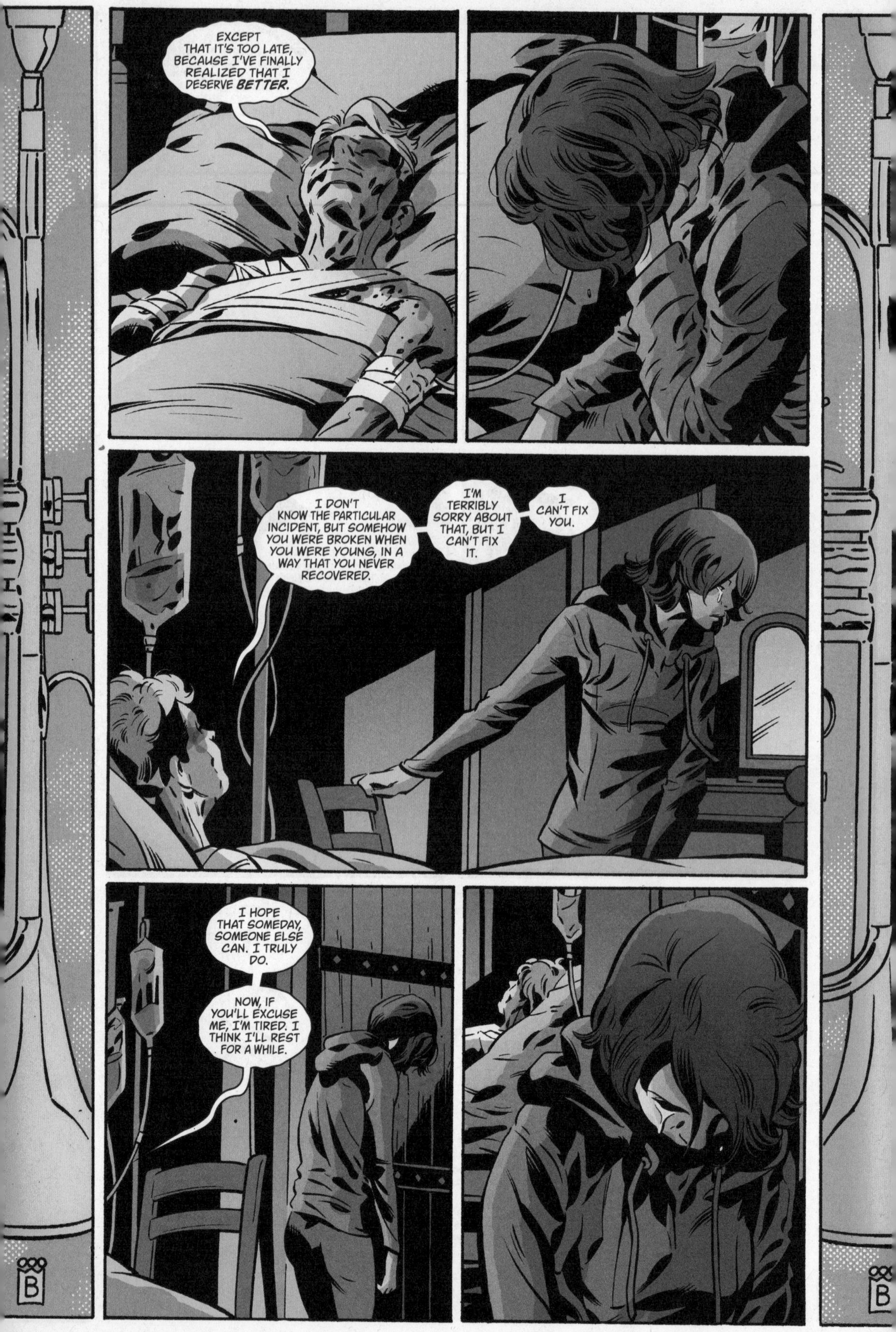
EXCEPT THAT IT'S TOO LATE, BECAUSE I'VE FINALLY REALIZED THAT I DESERVE BETTER.
I DON'T KNOW THE PARTICULAR INCIDENT, BUT SOMEHOW YOU WERE BROKEN WHEN YOU WERE YOUNG, IN A WAY THAT YOU NEVER RECOVERED.
I'M TERRIBLY SORRY ABOUT THAT, BUT I CAN'T FIX IT.
I CAN'T FIX YOU.
I HOPE THAT SOMEDAY, SOMEONE ELSE CAN. I TRULY DO.
NOW, IF YOU'LL EXCUSE ME, I'M TIRED. I THINK I'LL REST FOR A WHILE.

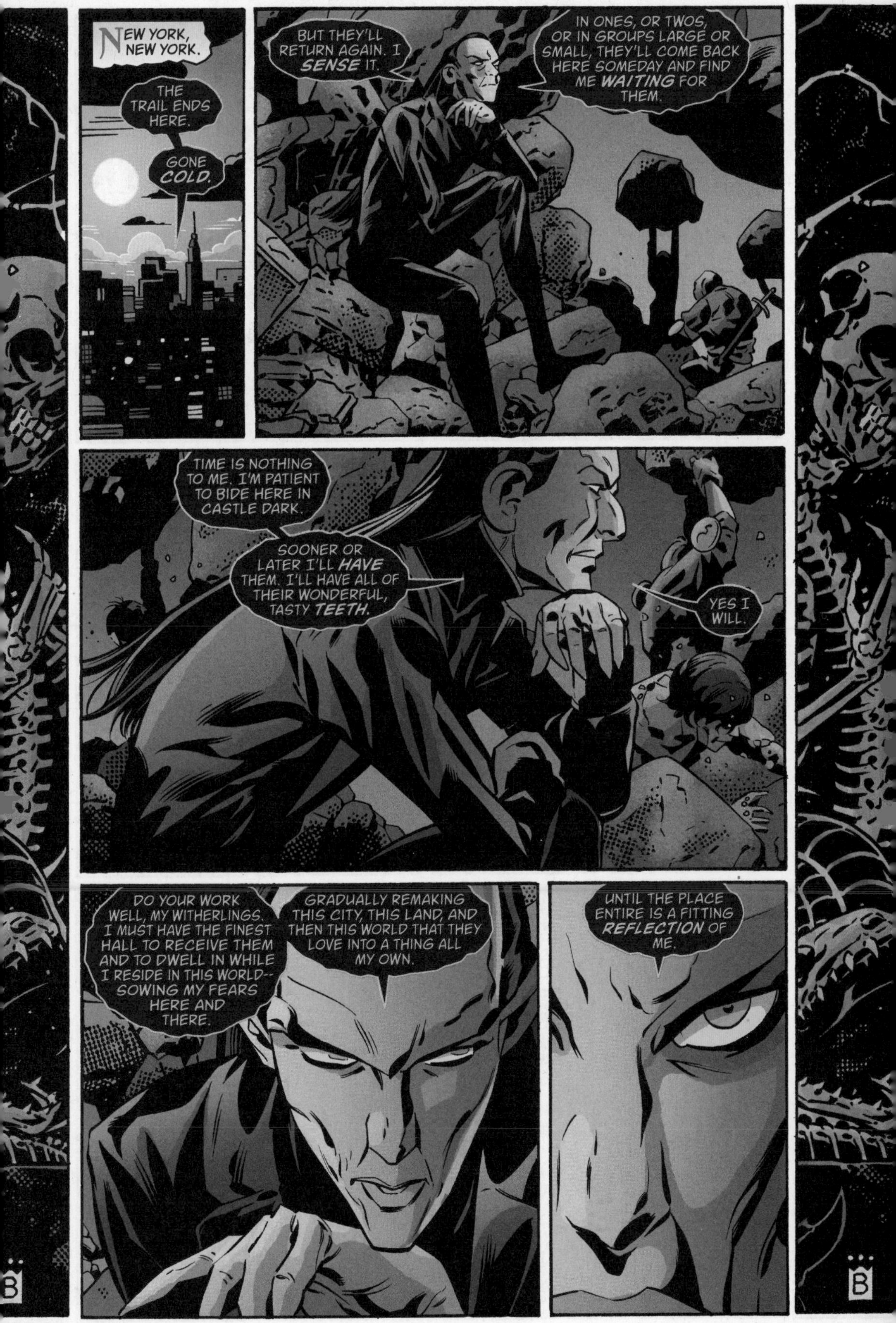
NEW YORK, NEW YORK.
THE TRAIL ENDS HERE.
GONE COLD.
BUT THEY'LL RETURN AGAIN. I SENSE IT.
IN ONES, OR TWOS, OR IN GROUPS LARGE OR SMALL, THEY'LL COME BACK HERE SOMEDAY AND FIND ME WAITING FOR THEM.
TIME IS NOTHING TO ME. I'M PATIENT TO BIDE HERE IN CASTLE DARK.
SOONER OR LATER I'LL HAVE THEM. I'LL HAVE ALL OF THEIR WONDERFUL, TASTY TEETH.
YES I WILL.
DO YOUR WORK WELL, MY WITHERLINGS. I MUST HAVE THE FINEST HALL TO RECEIVE THEM AND TO DWELL IN WHILE I RESIDE IN THIS WORLD-- SOWING MY FEARS HERE AND THERE.
GRADUALLY REMAKING THIS CITY, THIS LAND, AND THEN THIS WORLD THAT THEY LOVE INTO A THING ALL MY OWN.
UNTIL THE PLACE ENTIRE IS A FITTING REFLECTION OF ME.

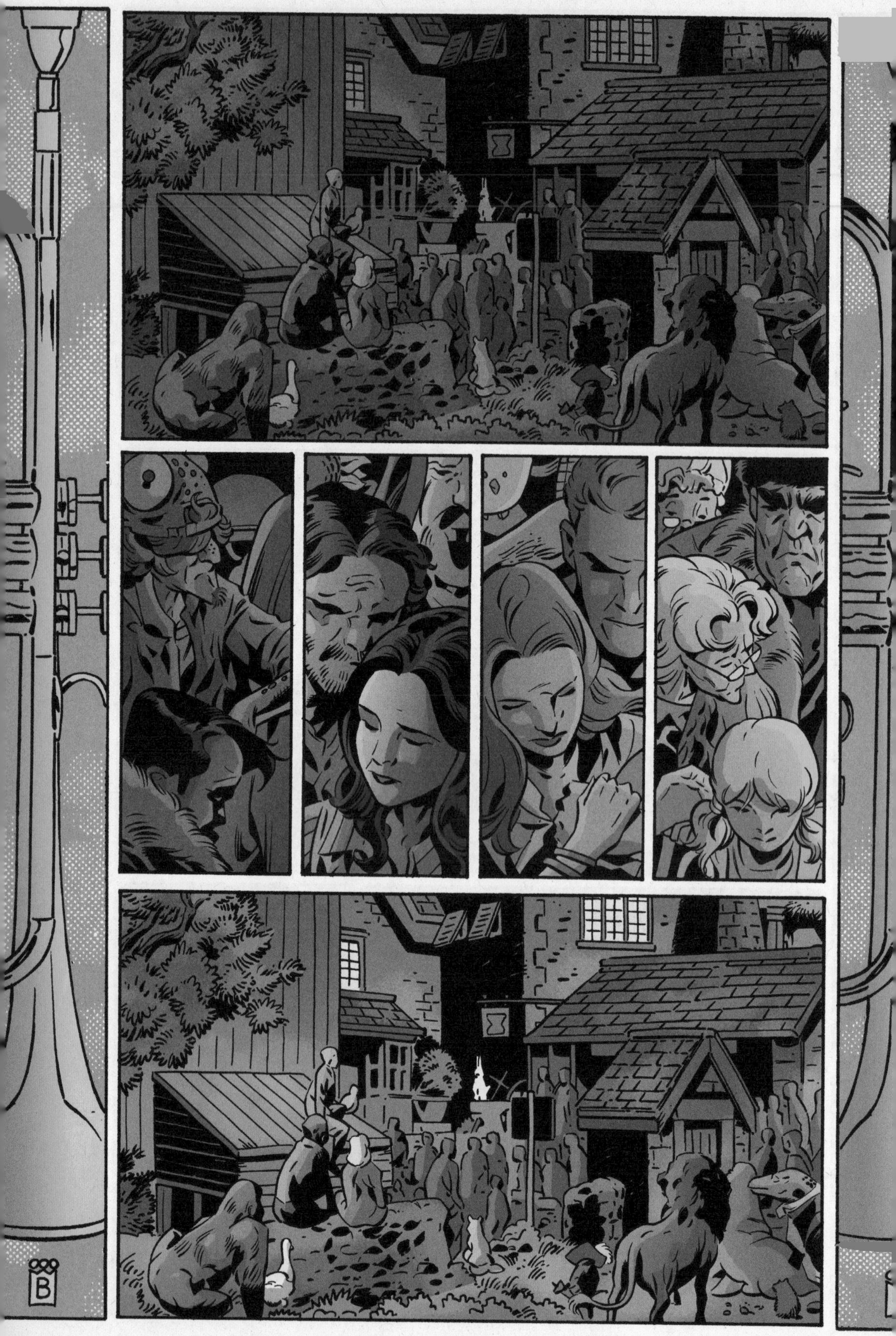

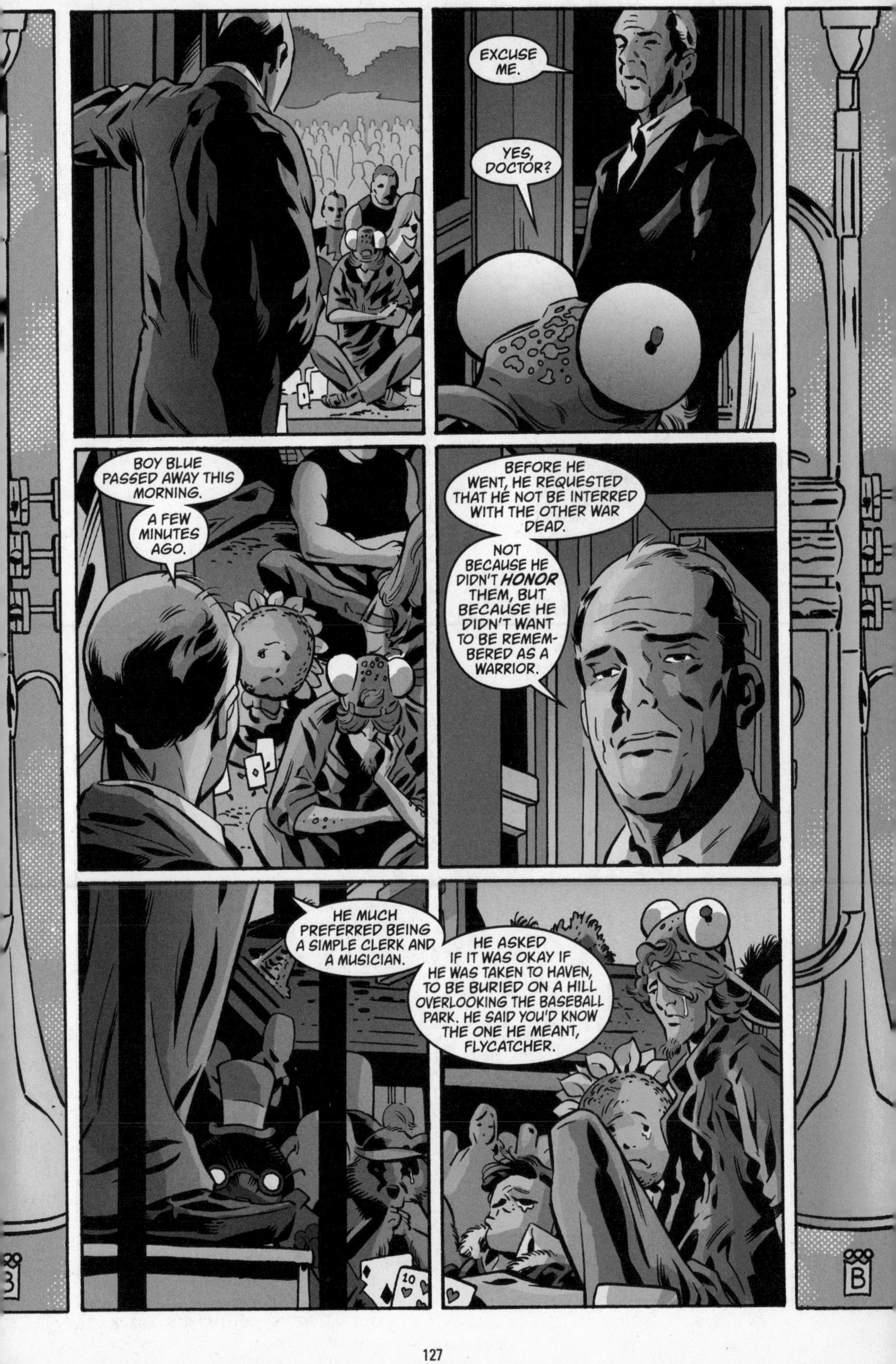
EXCUSE ME.
YES, DOCTOR?
BOY BLUE PASSED AWAY THIS MORNING.
A FEW MINUTES AGO.
BEFORE HE WENT, HE REQUESTED THAT HE NOT BE INTERRED WITH THE OTHER WAR DEAD.
NOT BECAUSE HE DIDN'T HONOR THEM, BUT BECAUSE HE DIDN'T WANT TO BE REMEMBERED AS A WARRIOR.
HE MUCH PREFERRED BEING A SIMPLE CLERK AND A MUSICIAN.
HE ASKED IF IT WAS OKAY IF HE WAS TAKEN TO HAVEN, TO BE BURIED ON A HILL OVERLOOKING THE BASEBALL PARK. HE SAID YOU'D KNOW THE ONE HE MEANT, FLYCATCHER.

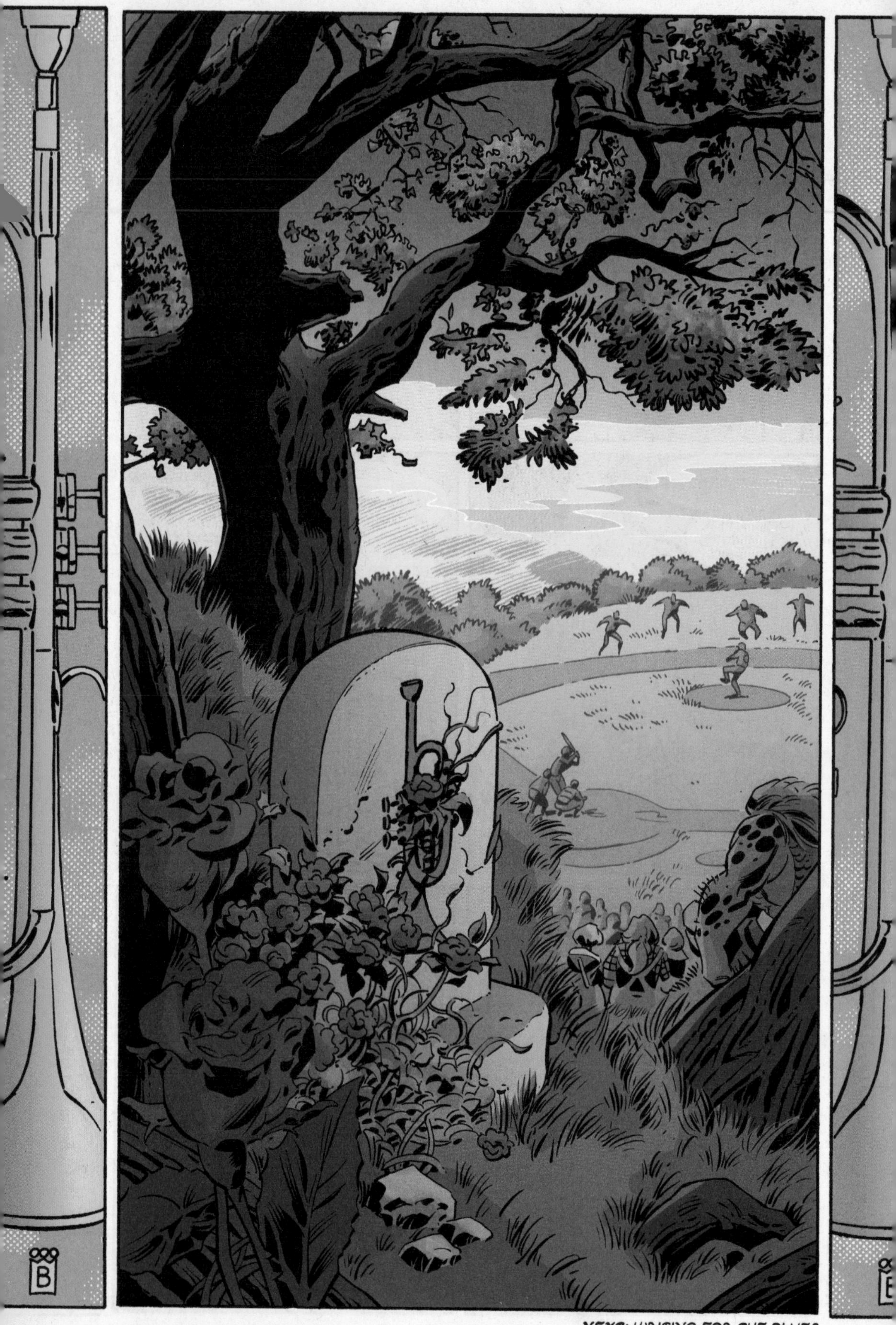

NEXT: WAITING FOR THE BLUES

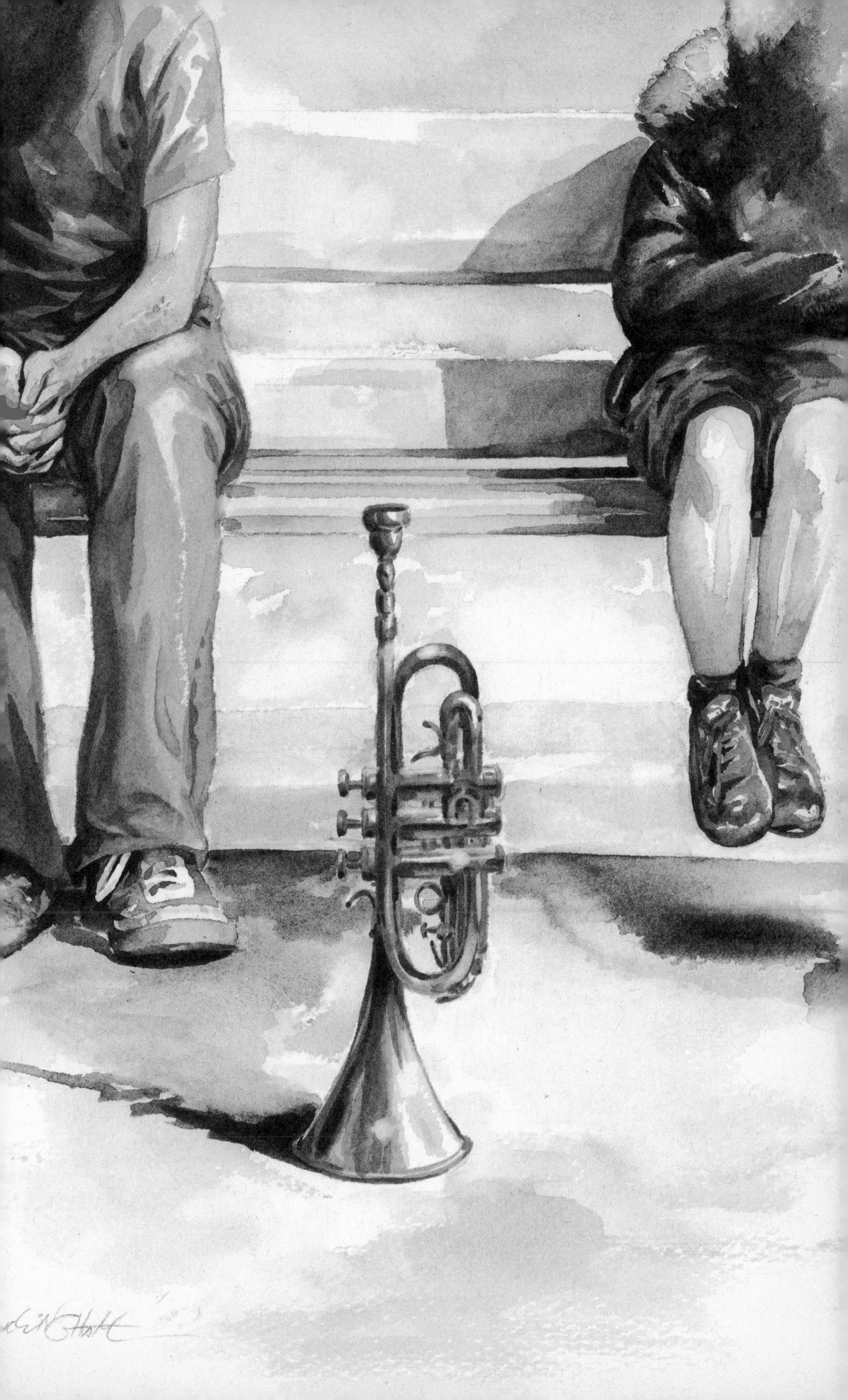

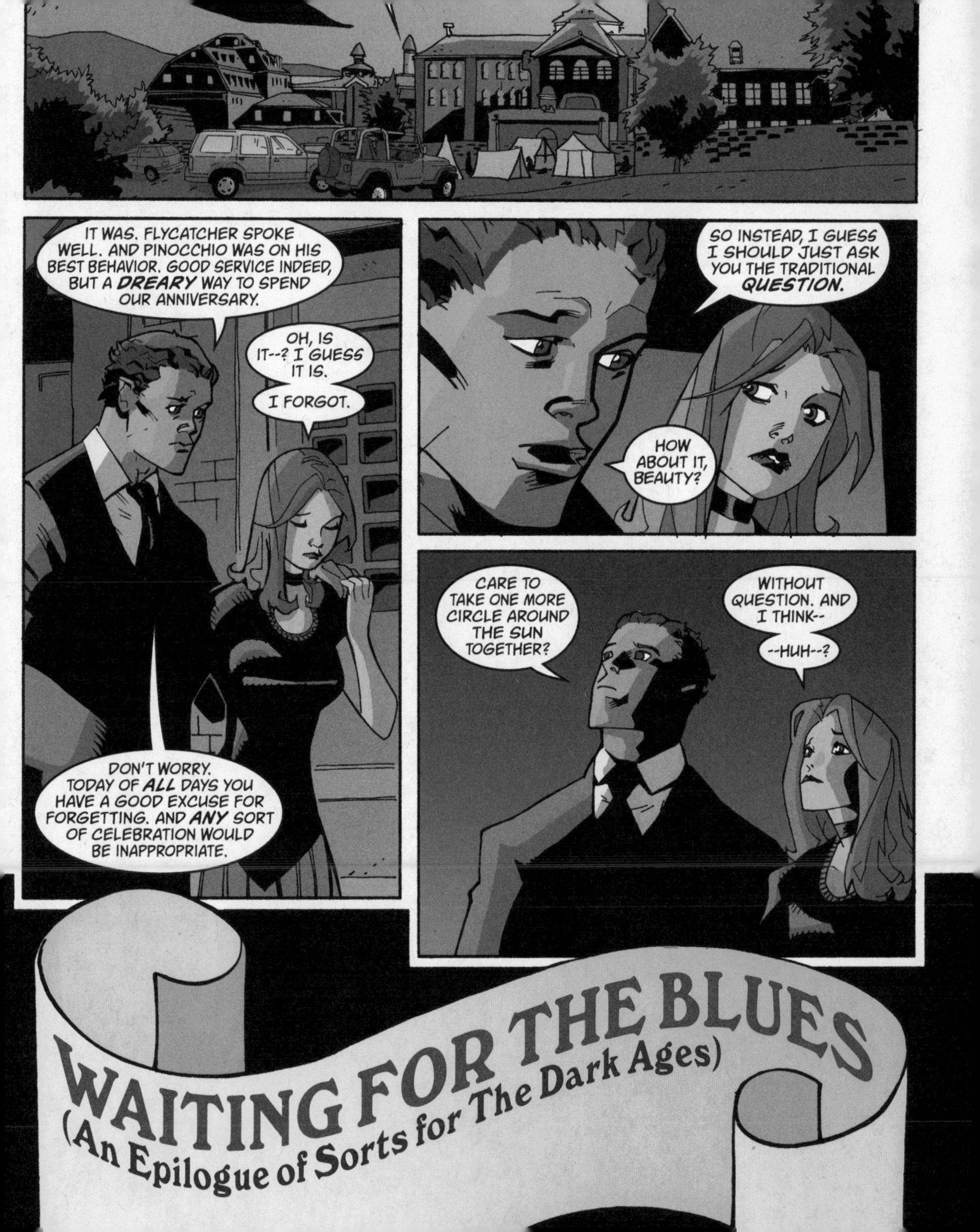
IT WAS. FLYCATCHER SPOKE WELL. AND PINOCCHIO WAS ON HIS BEST BEHAVIOR. GOOD SERVICE INDEED, BUT A DREARY WAY TO SPEND OUR ANNIVERSARY.
OH, IS IT--? I GUESS IT IS.
I FORGOT.
DON'T WORRY. TODAY OF ALL DAYS YOU HAVE A GOOD EXCUSE FOR FORGETTING. AND ANY SORT OF CELEBRATION WOULD BE INAPPROPRIATE.
SO INSTEAD, I GUESS I SHOULD JUST ASK YOU THE TRADITIONAL QUESTION.
HOW ABOUT IT, BEAUTY?
CARE TO TAKE ONE MORE CIRCLE AROUND THE SUN TOGETHER?
WITHOUT QUESTION. AND I THINK--
--HUH--?
WAITING FOR THE BLUES
(An Epilogue of Sorts for The Dark Ages)

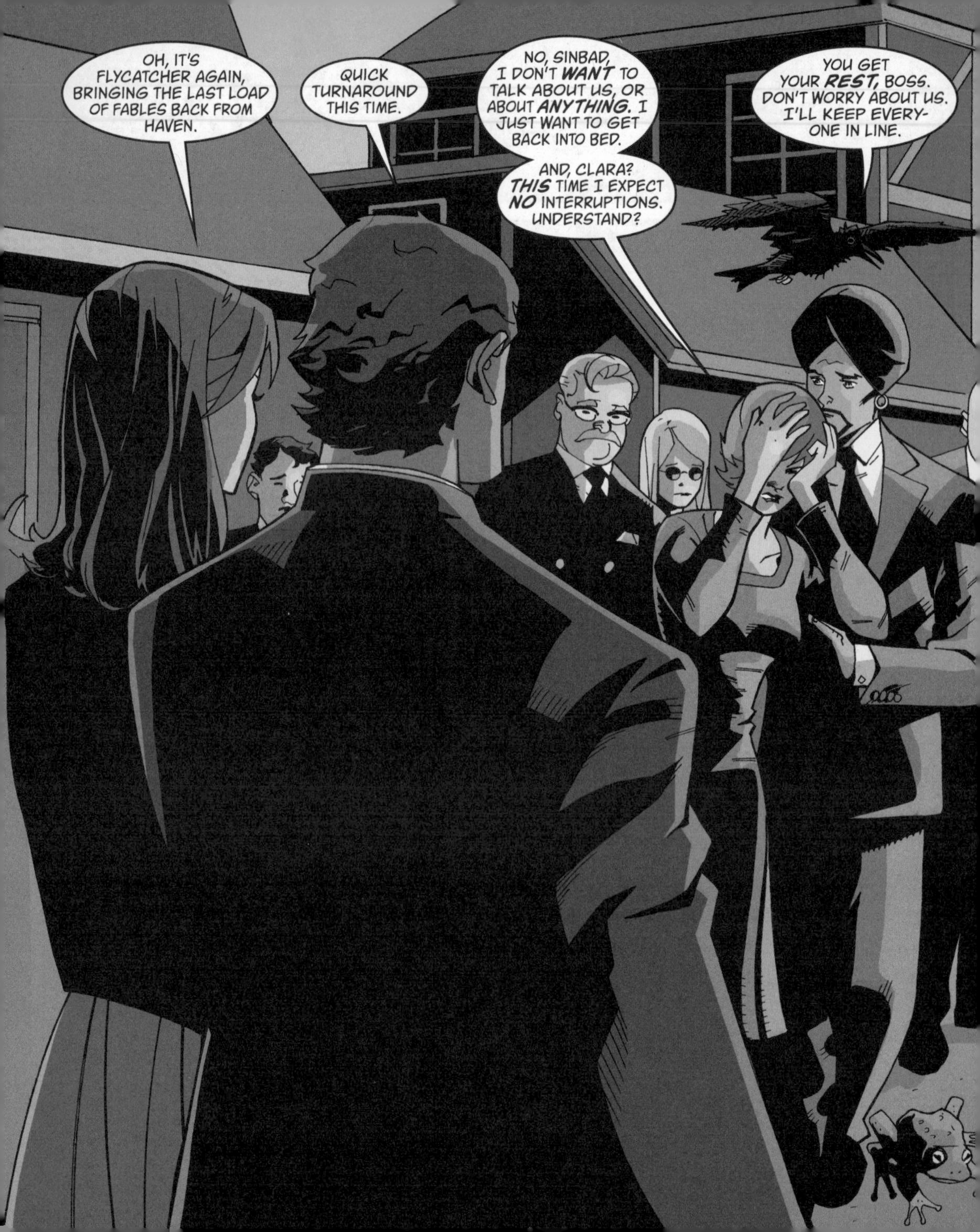
OH, IT'S FLYCATCHER AGAIN, BRINGING THE LAST LOAD OF FABLES BACK FROM HAVEN.
QUICK TURNAROUND THIS TIME.
NO, SINBAD, I DON'T WANT TO TALK ABOUT US, OR ABOUT ANYTHING. I JUST WANT TO GET BACK INTO BED.
AND, CLARA? THIS TIME I EXPECT NO INTERRUPTIONS. UNDERSTAND?
YOU GET YOUR REST, BOSS. DON'T WORRY ABOUT US. I'LL KEEP EVERY-ONE IN LINE.

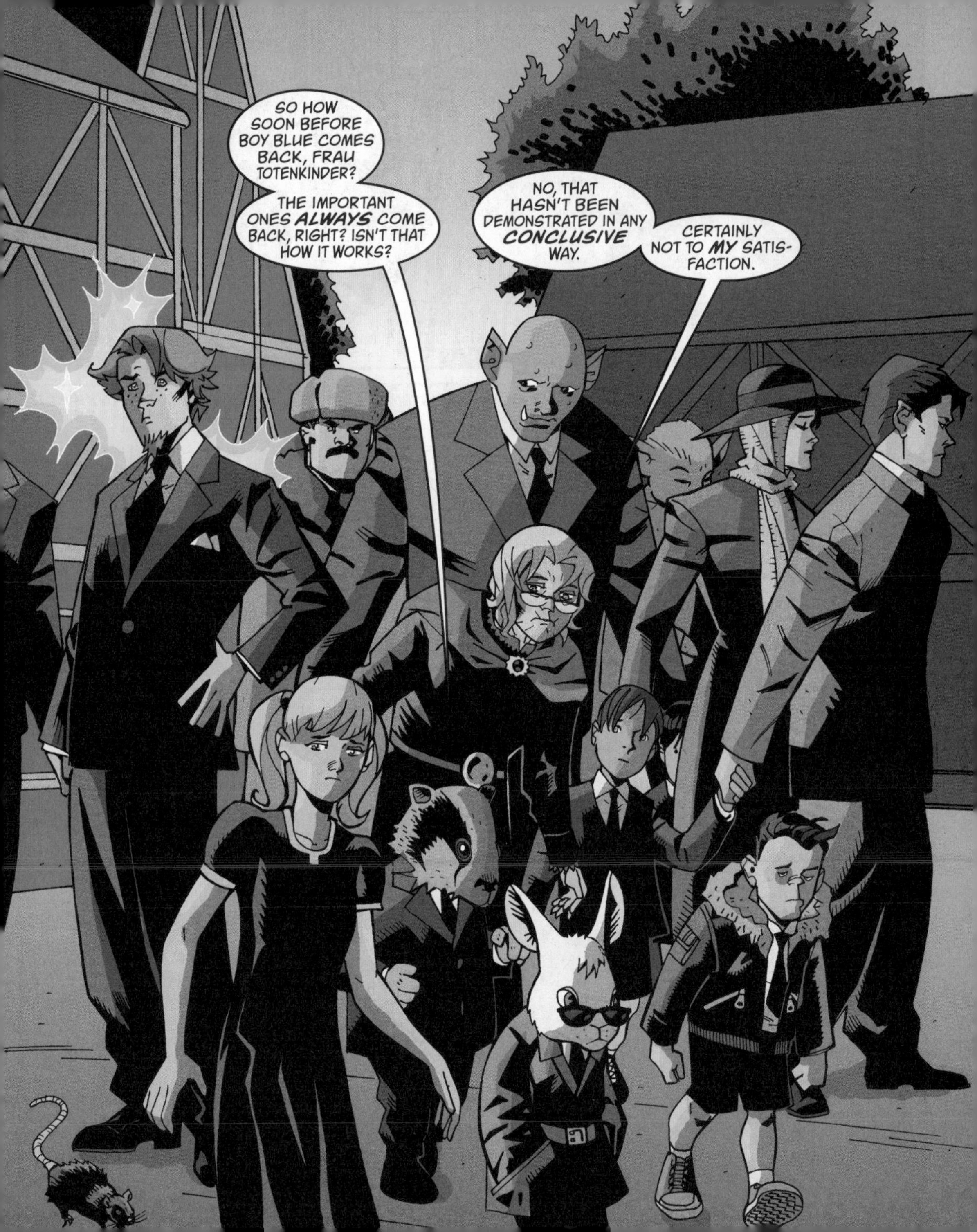
SO HOW SOON BEFORE BOY BLUE COMES BACK, FRAU TOTENKINDER?
THE IMPORTANT ONES ALWAYS COME BACK, RIGHT? ISN'T THAT HOW IT WORKS?
NO, THAT HASN'T BEEN DEMONSTRATED IN ANY CONCLUSIVE WAY.
CERTAINLY NOT TO MY SATIS-FACTION.

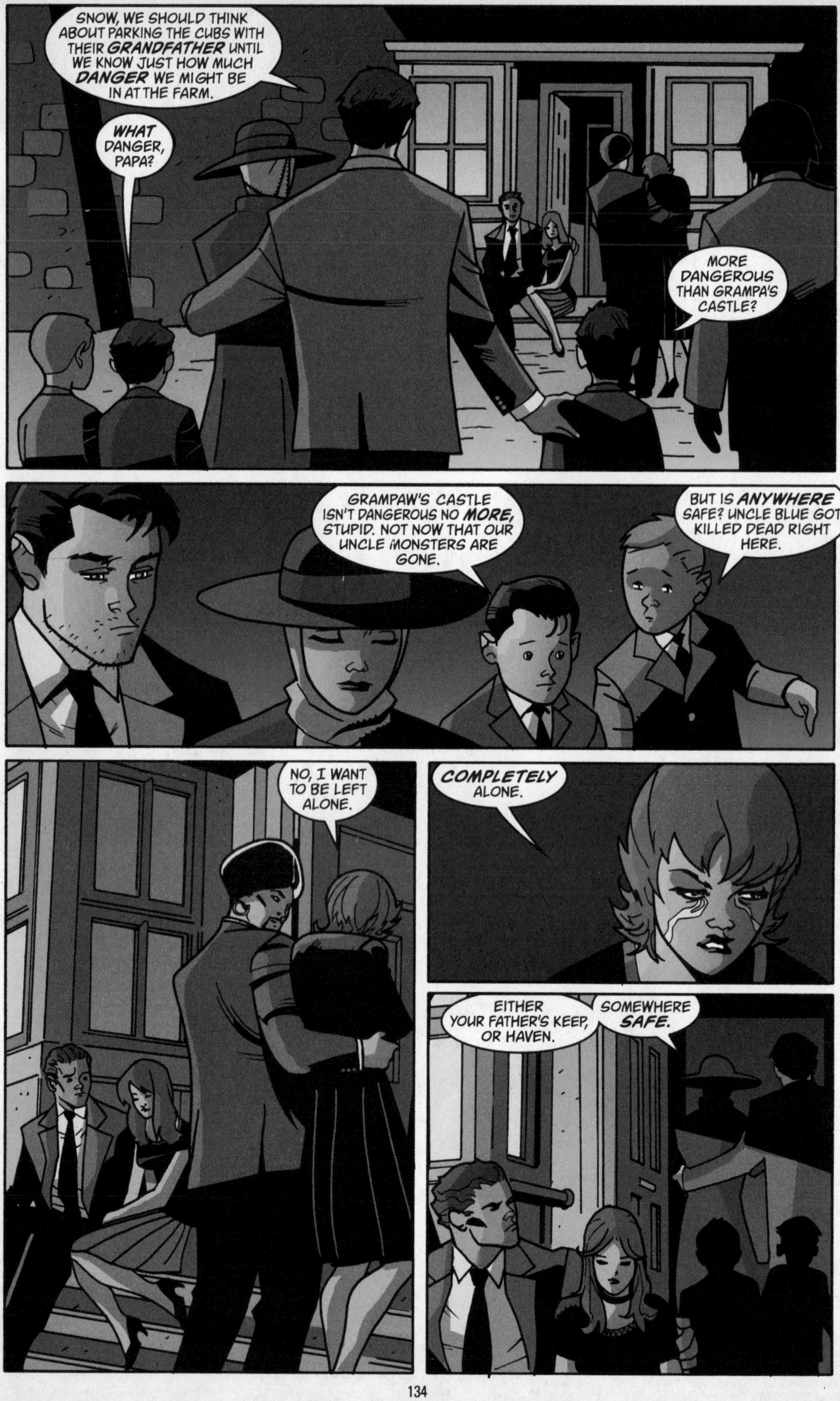
SNOW, WE SHOULD THINK ABOUT PARKING THE CUBS WITH THEIR GRANDFATHER UNTIL WE KNOW JUST HOW MUCH DANGER WE MIGHT BE IN AT THE FARM.
WHAT DANGER, PAPA?
MORE DANGEROUS THAN GRAMPA'S CASTLE?
GRAMPAW'S CASTLE ISN'T DANGEROUS NO MORE, STUPID. NOT NOW THAT OUR UNCLE MONSTERS ARE GONE.
BUT IS ANYWHERE SAFE? UNCLE BLUE GOT KILLED DEAD RIGHT HERE.
NO, I WANT TO BE LEFT ALONE.
COMPLETELY ALONE.
EITHER YOUR FATHER'S KEEP, OR HAVEN.
SOMEWHERE SAFE.

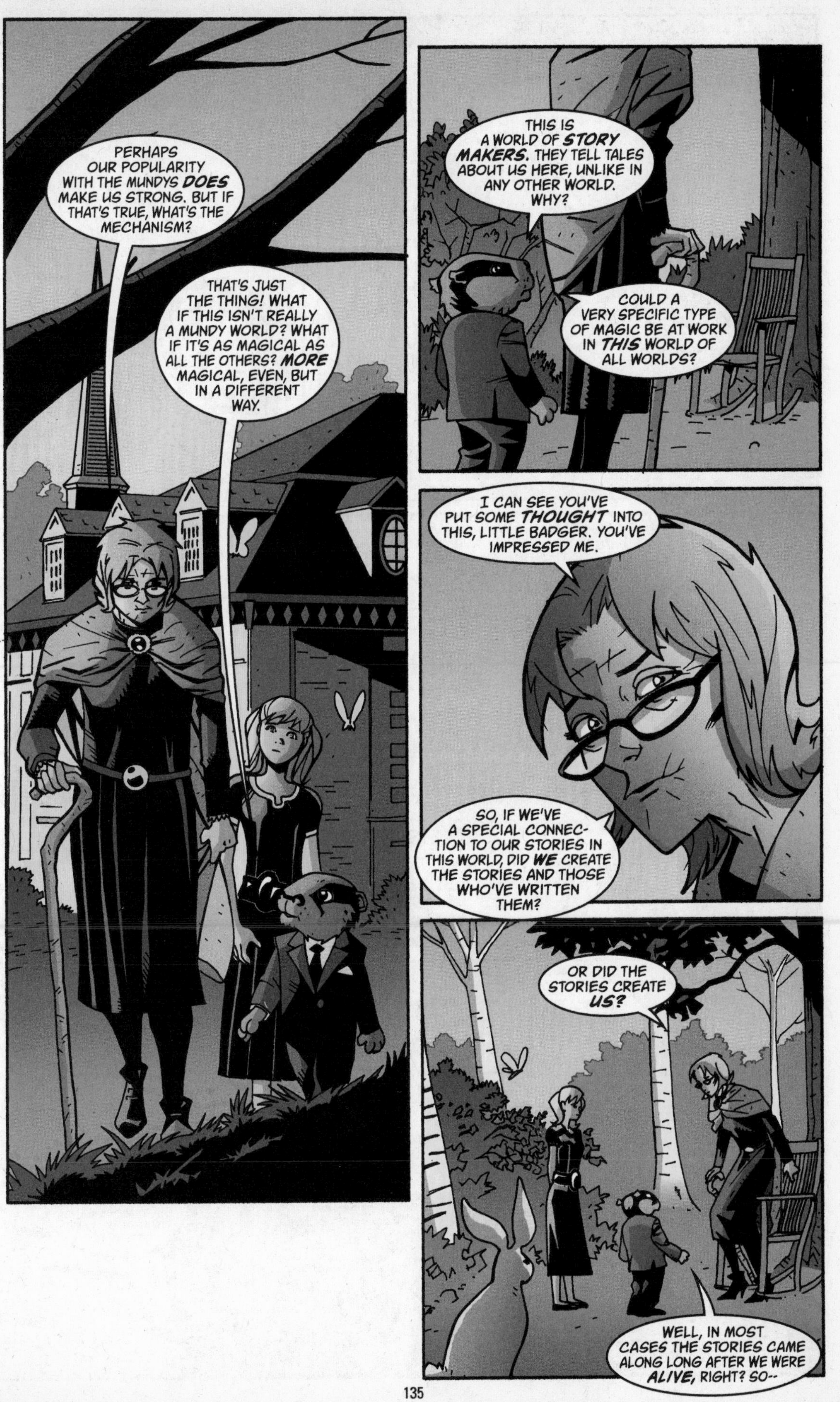

PERHAPS OUR POPULARITY WITH THE MUNDYS DOES MAKE US STRONG. BUT IF THAT'S TRUE, WHAT'S THE MECHANISM?
THAT'S JUST THE THING! WHAT IF THIS ISN'T REALLY A MUNDY WORLD? WHAT IF IT'S AS MAGICAL AS ALL THE OTHERS? MORE MAGICAL, EVEN, BUT IN A DIFFERENT WAY.
THIS IS A WORLD OF STORY MAKERS. THEY TELL TALES ABOUT US HERE, UNLIKE IN ANY OTHER WORLD. WHY?
COULD A VERY SPECIFIC TYPE OF MAGIC BE AT WORK IN THIS WORLD OF ALL WORLDS?
I CAN SEE YOU'VE PUT SOME THOUGHT INTO THIS, LITTLE BADGER. YOU'VE IMPRESSED ME.
SO, IF WE'VE A SPECIAL CONNECTION TO OUR STORIES IN THIS WORLD, DID WE CREATE THE STORIES AND THOSE WHO'VE WRITTEN THEM?
OR DID THE STORIES CREATE US?
WELL, IN MOST CASES THE STORIES CAME ALONG LONG AFTER WE WERE ALIVE, RIGHT? SO--

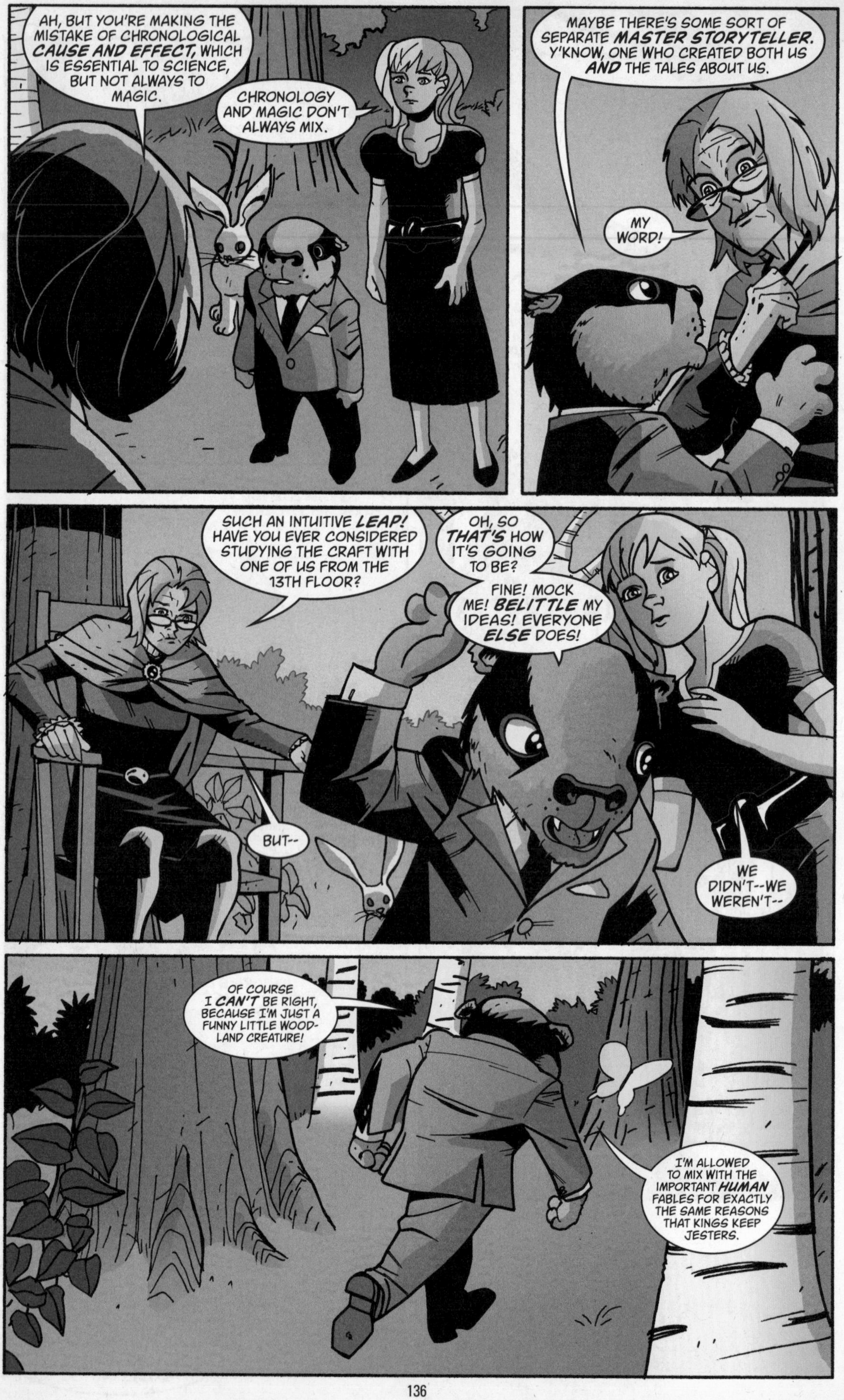
AH, BUT YOU'RE MAKING THE MISTAKE OF CHRONOLOGICAL CAUSE AND EFFECT, WHICH IS ESSENTIAL TO SCIENCE, BUT NOT ALWAYS TO MAGIC.
CHRONOLOGY AND MAGIC DON'T ALWAYS MIX.
MAYBE THERE'S SOME SORT OF SEPARATE MASTER STORYTELLER. Y'KNOW, ONE WHO CREATED BOTH US AND THE TALES ABOUT US.
MY WORD!
SUCH AN INTUITIVE LEAP! HAVE YOU EVER CONSIDERED STUDYING THE CRAFT WITH ONE OF US FROM THE 13TH FLOOR?
OH, SO THAT'S HOW IT'S GOING TO BE?
FINE! MOCK ME! BELITTLE MY IDEAS! EVERYONE ELSE DOES!
BUT--
WE DIDN'T--WE WEREN'T--
OF COURSE I CAN'T BE RIGHT, BECAUSE I'M JUST A FUNNY LITTLE WOOD-LAND CREATURE!
I'M ALLOWED TO MIX WITH THE IMPORTANT HUMAN FABLES FOR EXACTLY THE SAME REASONS THAT KINGS KEEP JESTERS.

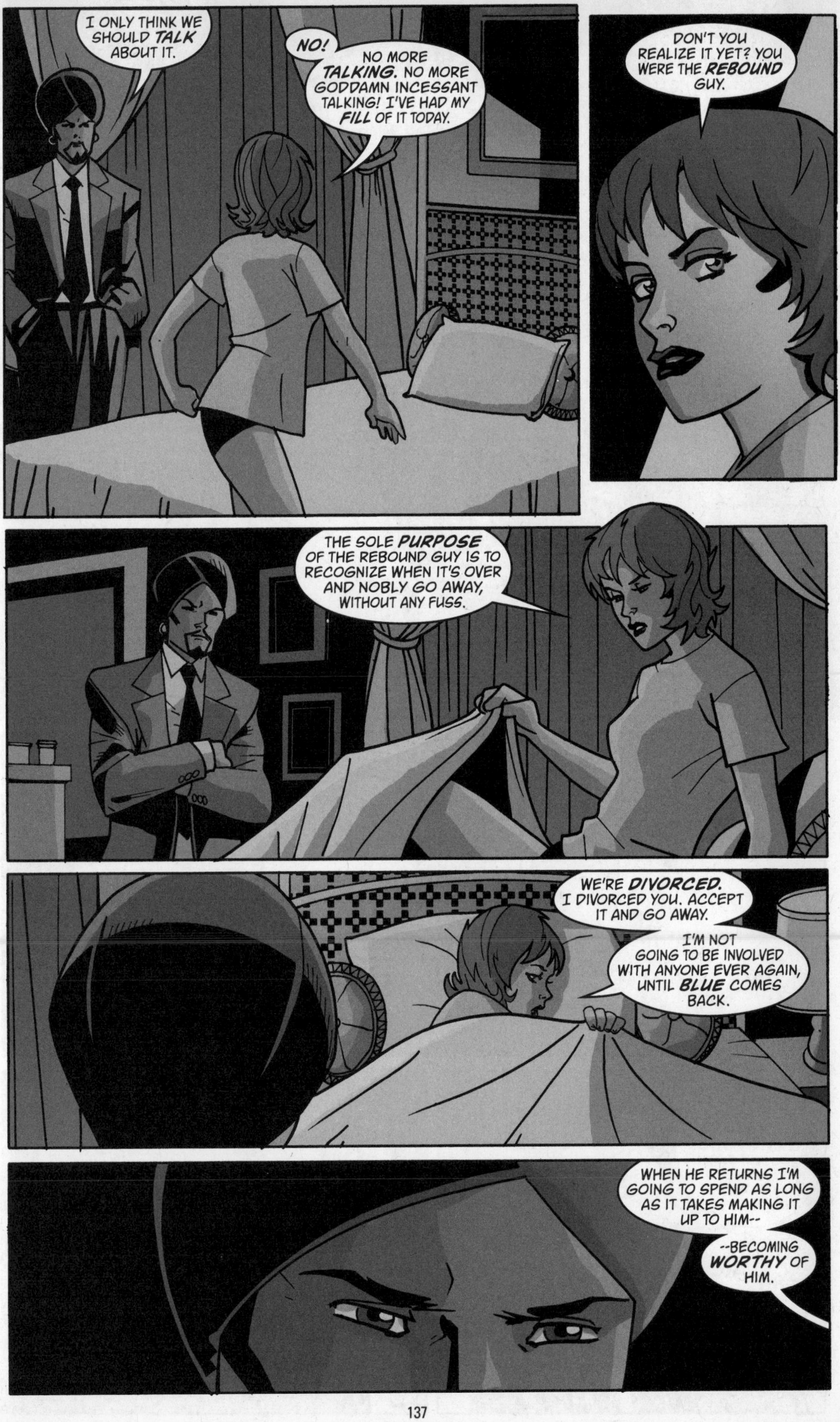

I ONLY THINK WE SHOULD TALK ABOUT IT.
NO!
NO MORE TALKING. NO MORE GODDAMN INCESSANT TALKING! I'VE HAD MY FILL OF IT TODAY.
DON'T YOU REALIZE IT YET? YOU WERE THE REBOUND GUY.
THE SOLE PURPOSE OF THE REBOUND GUY IS TO RECOGNIZE WHEN IT'S OVER AND NOBLY GO AWAY, WITHOUT ANY FUSS.
WE'RE DIVORCED. I DIVORCED YOU. ACCEPT IT AND GO AWAY.
I'M NOT GOING TO BE INVOLVED WITH ANYONE EVER AGAIN, UNTIL BLUE COMES BACK.
WHEN HE RETURNS I'M GOING TO SPEND AS LONG AS IT TAKES MAKING IT UP TO HIM--
--BECOMING WORTHY OF HIM.

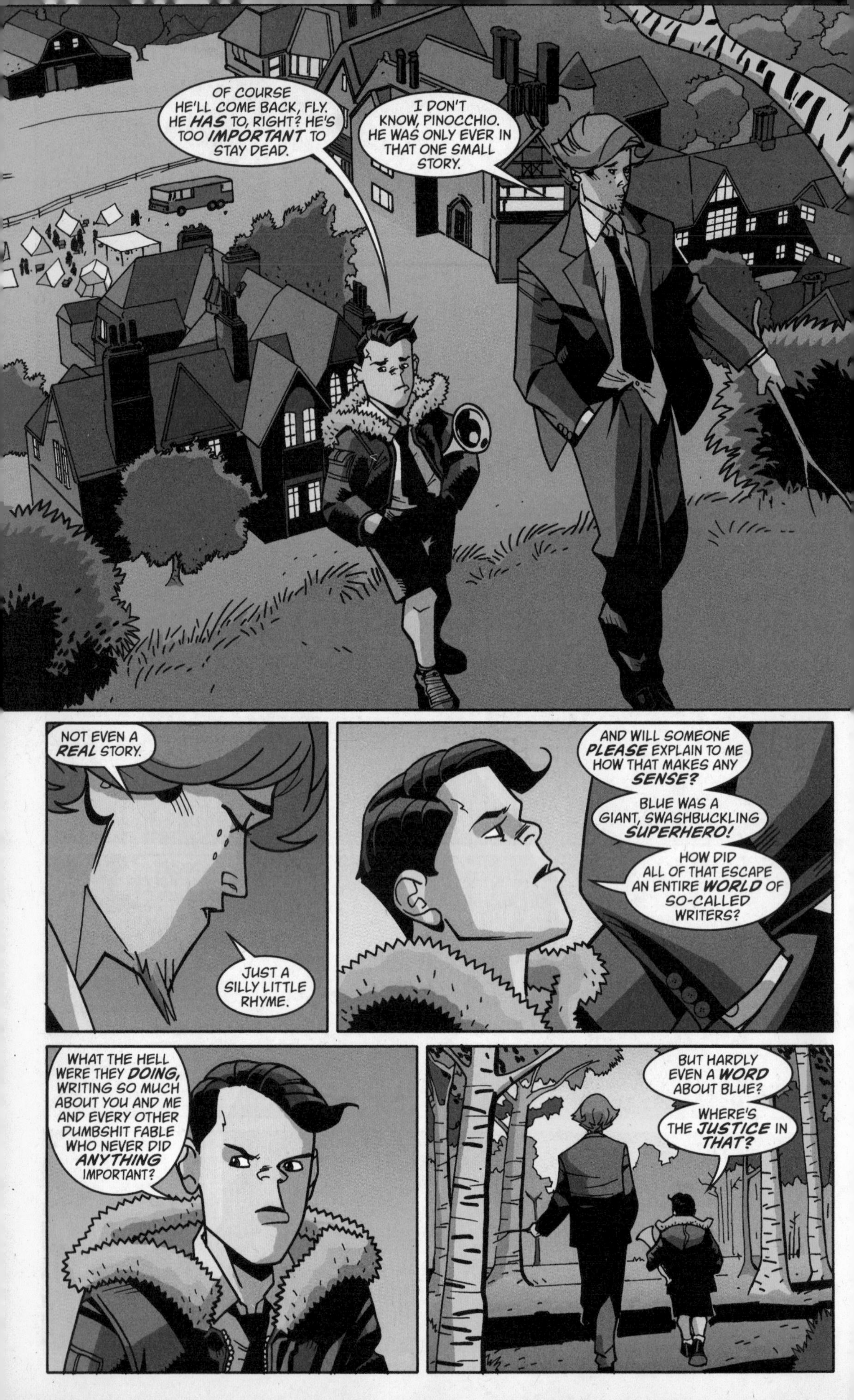

OF COURSE HE'LL COME BACK, FLY. HE HAS TO, RIGHT? HE'S TOO IMPORTANT TO STAY DEAD.
I DON'T KNOW, PINOCCHIO. HE WAS ONLY EVER IN THAT ONE SMALL STORY.
NOT EVEN A REAL STORY.
JUST A SILLY LITTLE RHYME.
AND WILL SOMEONE PLEASE EXPLAIN TO ME HOW THAT MAKES ANY SENSE?
BLUE WAS A GIANT, SWASHBUCKLING SUPERHERO!
HOW DID ALL OF THAT ESCAPE AN ENTIRE WORLD OF SO-CALLED WRITERS?
WHAT THE HELL WERE THEY DOING, WRITING SO MUCH ABOUT YOU AND ME AND EVERY OTHER DUMBSHIT FABLE WHO NEVER DID ANYTHING IMPORTANT?
BUT HARDLY EVEN A WORD ABOUT BLUE?
WHERE'S THE JUSTICE IN THAT?

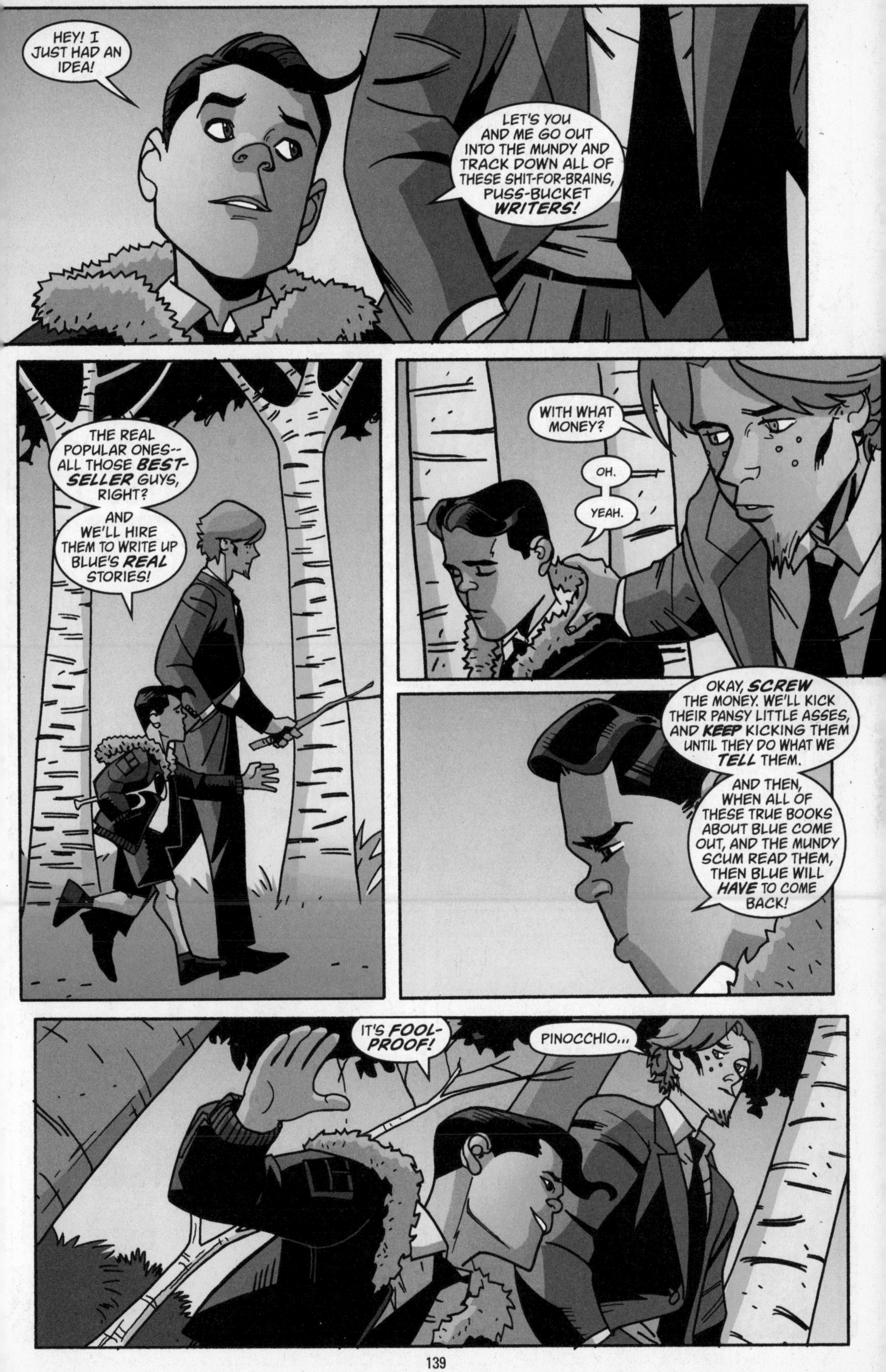
HEY! I JUST HAD AN IDEA!
LET'S YOU AND ME GO OUT INTO THE MUNDY AND TRACK DOWN ALL OF THESE SHIT-FOR-BRAINS, PUSS-BUCKET WRITERS!
THE REAL POPULAR ONES--ALL THOSE BEST-SELLER GUYS, RIGHT?
AND WE'LL HIRE THEM TO WRITE UP BLUE'S REAL STORIES!
WITH WHAT MONEY?
OH.
YEAH.
OKAY, SCREW THE MONEY. WE'LL KICK THEIR PANSY LITTLE ASSES, AND KEEP KICKING THEM UNTIL THEY DO WHAT WE TELL THEM.
AND THEN, WHEN ALL OF THESE TRUE BOOKS ABOUT BLUE COME OUT, AND THE MUNDY SCUM READ THEM, THEN BLUE WILL HAVE TO COME BACK!
IT'S FOOL-PROOF!
PINOCCHIO...

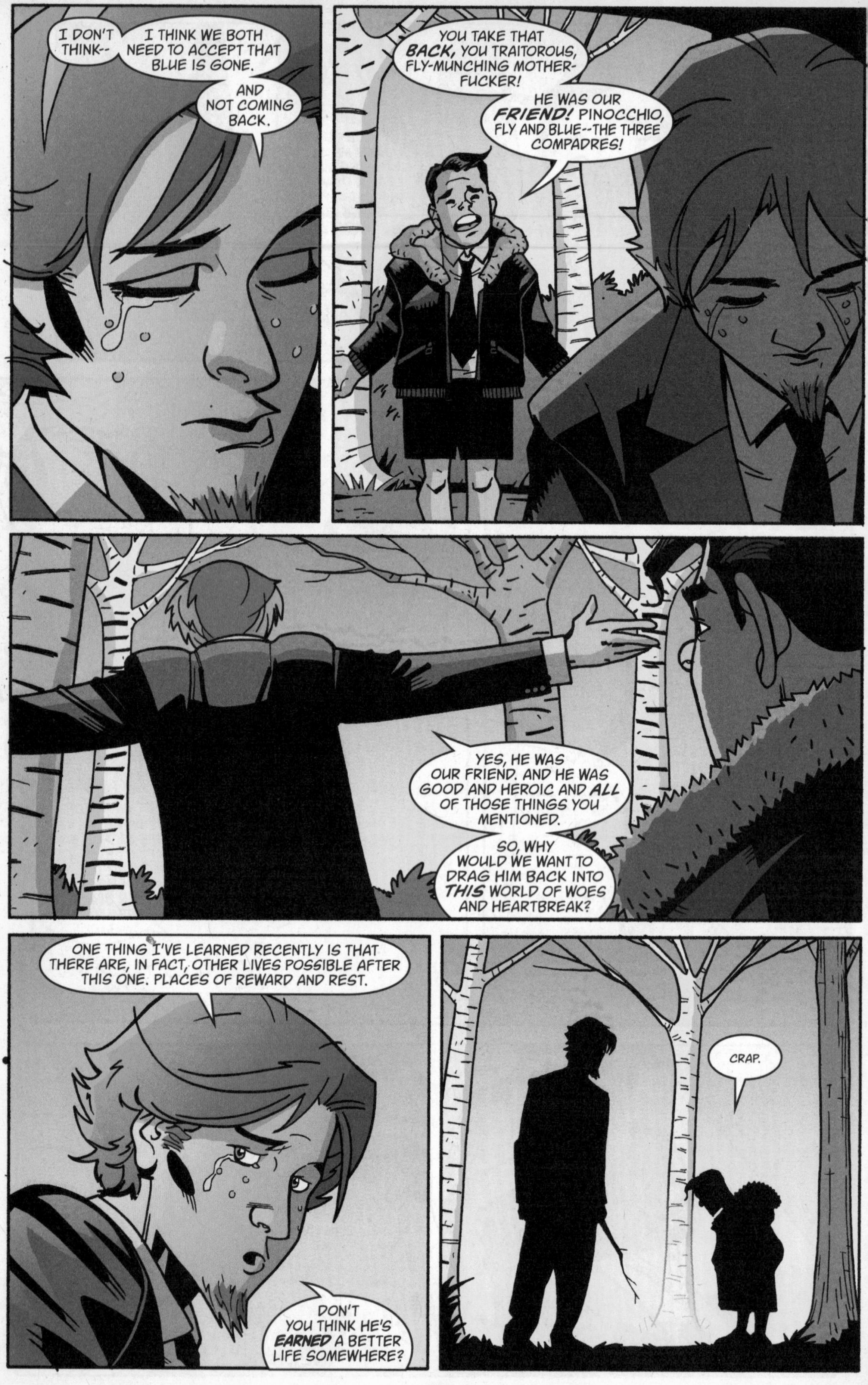
I DON'T THINK--
I THINK WE BOTH NEED TO ACCEPT THAT BLUE IS GONE.
AND NOT COMING BACK.
YOU TAKE THAT BACK, YOU TRAITOROUS, FLY-MUNCHING MOTHER-FUCKER!
HE WAS OUR FRIEND! PINOCCHIO, FLY AND BLUE--THE THREE COMPADRES!
YES, HE WAS OUR FRIEND. AND HE WAS GOOD AND HEROIC AND ALL OF THOSE THINGS YOU MENTIONED.
SO, WHY WOULD WE WANT TO DRAG HIM BACK INTO THIS WORLD OF WOES AND HEARTBREAK?
ONE THING I'VE LEARNED RECENTLY IS THAT THERE ARE, IN FACT, OTHER LIVES POSSIBLE AFTER THIS ONE. PLACES OF REWARD AND REST.
DON'T YOU THINK HE'S EARNED A BETTER LIFE SOMEWHERE?
CRAP.

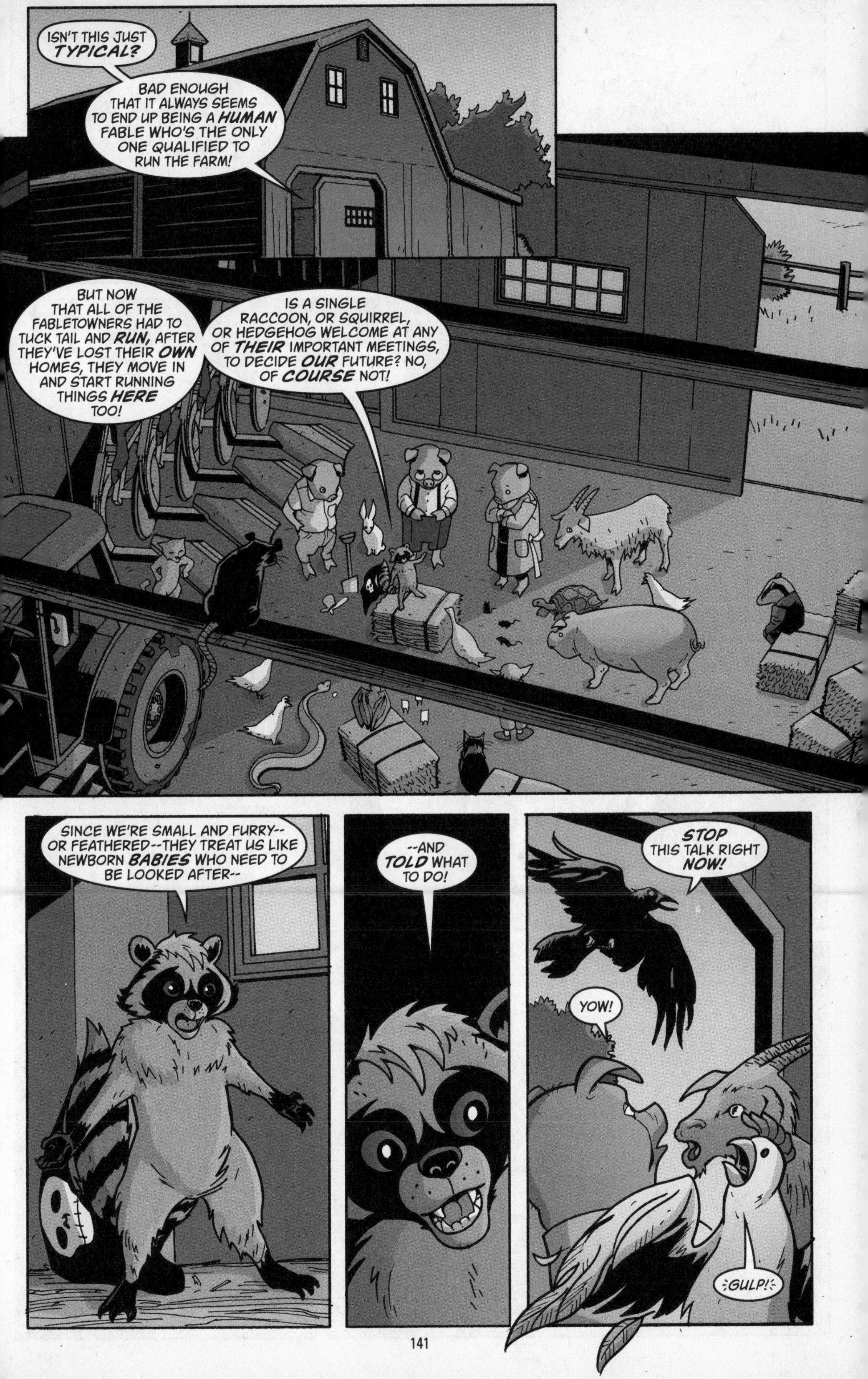
ISN'T THIS JUST TYPICAL?
BAD ENOUGH THAT IT ALWAYS SEEMS TO END UP BEING A HUMAN FABLE WHO'S THE ONLY ONE QUALIFIED TO RUN THE FARM!
BUT NOW THAT ALL OF THE FABLETOWNERS HAD TO TUCK TAIL AND RUN, AFTER THEY'VE LOST THEIR OWN HOMES, THEY MOVE IN AND START RUNNING THINGS HERE TOO!
IS A SINGLE RACCOON, OR SQUIRREL, OR HEDGEHOG WELCOME AT ANY OF THEIR IMPORTANT MEETINGS, TO DECIDE OUR FUTURE? NO, OF COURSE NOT!
SINCE WE'RE SMALL AND FURRY--OR FEATHERED--THEY TREAT US LIKE NEWBORN BABIES WHO NEED TO BE LOOKED AFTER--
--AND TOLD WHAT TO DO!
STOP THIS TALK RIGHT NOW!
YOW!
GULP!

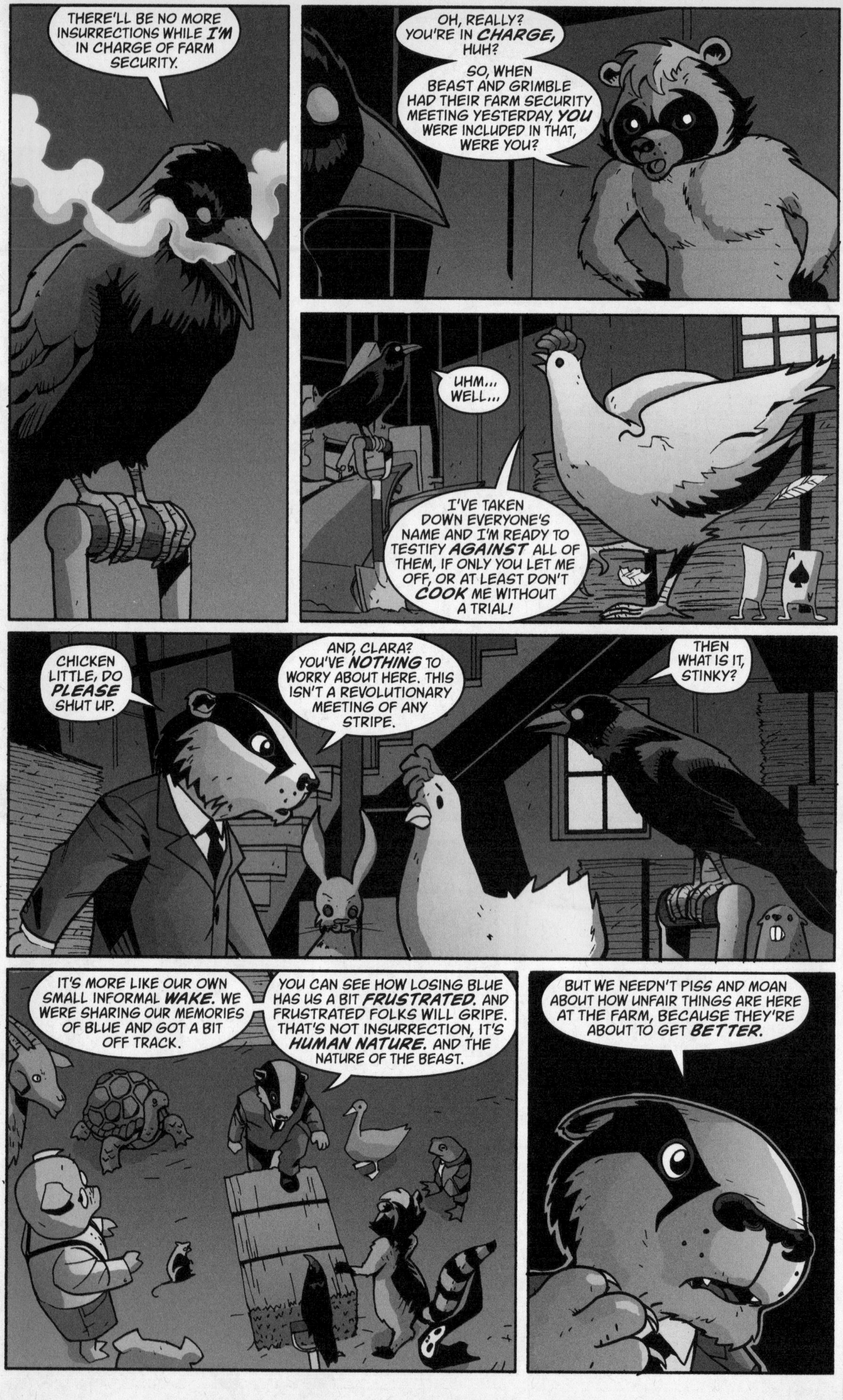
THERE'LL BE NO MORE INSURRECTIONS WHILE I'M IN CHARGE OF FARM SECURITY.
OH, REALLY? YOU'RE IN CHARGE, HUH?
SO, WHEN BEAST AND GRIMBLE HAD THEIR FARM SECURITY MEETING YESTERDAY, YOU WERE INCLUDED IN THAT, WERE YOU?
UHM... WELL...
I'VE TAKEN DOWN EVERYONE'S NAME AND I'M READY TO TESTIFY AGAINST ALL OF THEM, IF ONLY YOU LET ME OFF, OR AT LEAST DON'T COOK ME WITHOUT A TRIAL!
CHICKEN LITTLE, DO PLEASE SHUT UP.
AND, CLARA? YOU'VE NOTHING TO WORRY ABOUT HERE. THIS ISN'T A REVOLUTIONARY MEETING OF ANY STRIPE.
THEN WHAT IS IT, STINKY?
IT'S MORE LIKE OUR OWN SMALL INFORMAL WAKE. WE WERE SHARING OUR MEMORIES OF BLUE AND GOT A BIT OFF TRACK.
YOU CAN SEE HOW LOSING BLUE HAS US A BIT FRUSTRATED. AND FRUSTRATED FOLKS WILL GRIPE. THAT'S NOT INSURRECTION, IT'S HUMAN NATURE. AND THE NATURE OF THE BEAST.
BUT WE NEEDN'T PISS AND MOAN ABOUT HOW UNFAIR THINGS ARE HERE AT THE FARM, BECAUSE THEY'RE ABOUT TO GET BETTER.

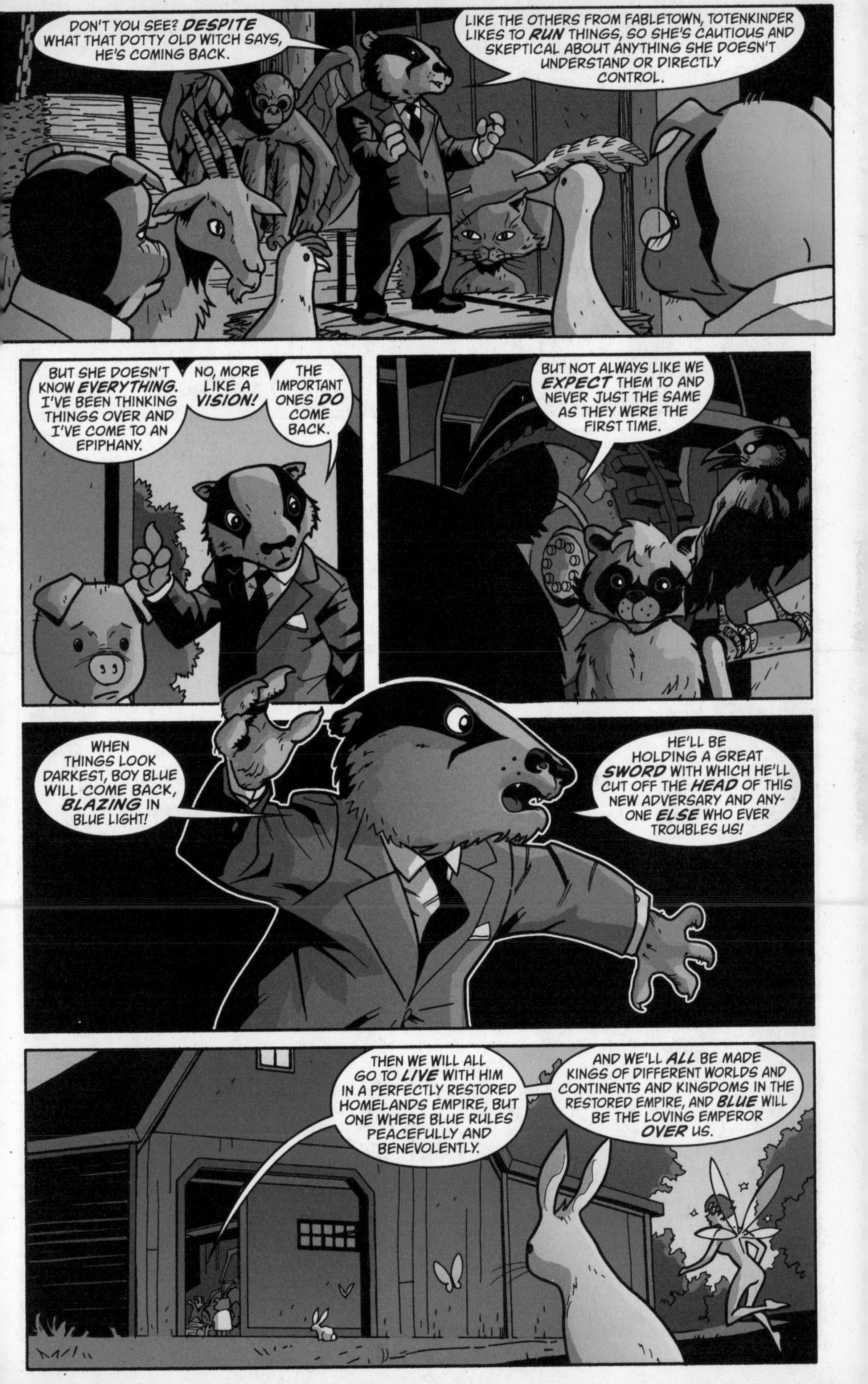
DON'T YOU SEE? DESPITE WHAT THAT DOTTY OLD WITCH SAYS, HE'S COMING BACK.
LIKE THE OTHERS FROM FABLETOWN, TOTENKINDER LIKES TO RUN THINGS, SO SHE'S CAUTIOUS AND SKEPTICAL ABOUT ANYTHING SHE DOESN'T UNDERSTAND OR DIRECTLY CONTROL.
BUT SHE DOESN'T KNOW EVERYTHING. I'VE BEEN THINKING THINGS OVER AND I'VE COME TO AN EPIPHANY.
NO, MORE LIKE A VISION!
THE IMPORTANT ONES DO COME BACK.
BUT NOT ALWAYS LIKE WE EXPECT THEM TO AND NEVER JUST THE SAME AS THEY WERE THE FIRST TIME.
WHEN THINGS LOOK DARKEST, BOY BLUE WILL COME BACK, BLAZING IN BLUE LIGHT!
HE'LL BE HOLDING A GREAT SWORD WITH WHICH HE'LL CUT OFF THE HEAD OF THIS NEW ADVERSARY AND ANY-ONE ELSE WHO EVER TROUBLES US!
THEN WE WILL ALL GO TO LIVE WITH HIM IN A PERFECTLY RESTORED HOMELANDS EMPIRE, BUT ONE WHERE BLUE RULES PEACEFULLY AND BENEVOLENTLY.
AND WE'LL ALL BE MADE KINGS OF DIFFERENT WORLDS AND CONTINENTS AND KINGDOMS IN THE RESTORED EMPIRE, AND BLUE WILL BE THE LOVING EMPEROR OVER US.

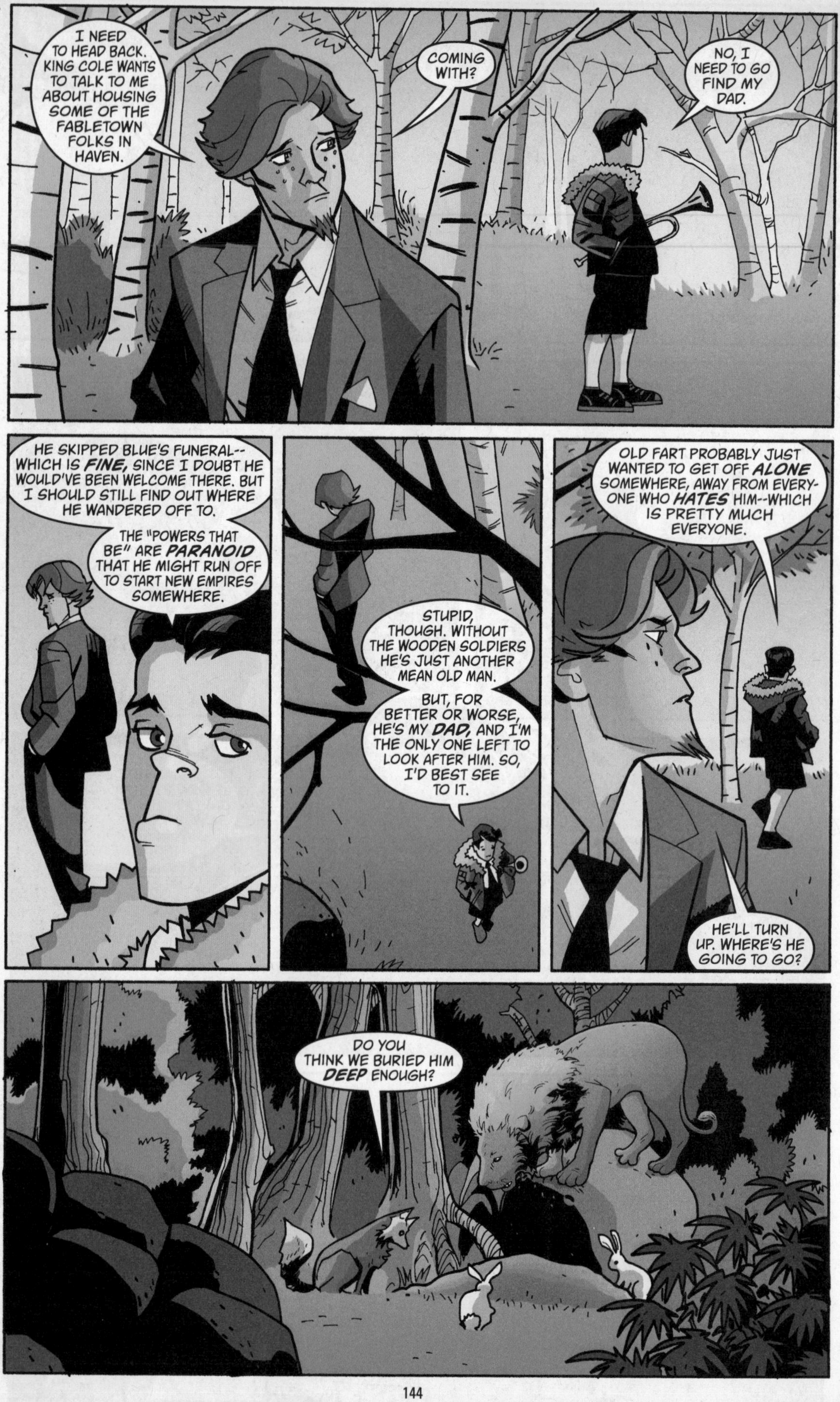

I NEED TO HEAD BACK. KING COLE WANTS TO TALK TO ME ABOUT HOUSING SOME OF THE FABLETOWN FOLKS IN HAVEN.
COMING WITH?
NO, I NEED TO GO FIND MY DAD.
HE SKIPPED BLUE'S FUNERAL-- WHICH IS FINE, SINCE I DOUBT HE WOULD'VE BEEN WELCOME THERE. BUT I SHOULD STILL FIND OUT WHERE HE WANDERED OFF TO.
THE "POWERS THAT BE" ARE PARANOID THAT HE MIGHT RUN OFF TO START NEW EMPIRES SOMEWHERE.
STUPID, THOUGH. WITHOUT THE WOODEN SOLDIERS HE'S JUST ANOTHER MEAN OLD MAN.
BUT, FOR BETTER OR WORSE, HE'S MY DAD, AND I'M THE ONLY ONE LEFT TO LOOK AFTER HIM. SO, I'D BEST SEE TO IT.
OLD FART PROBABLY JUST WANTED TO GET OFF ALONE SOMEWHERE, AWAY FROM EVERYONE WHO HATES HIM--WHICH IS PRETTY MUCH EVERYONE.
HE'LL TURN UP. WHERE'S HE GOING TO GO?
DO YOU THINK WE BURIED HIM DEEP ENOUGH?

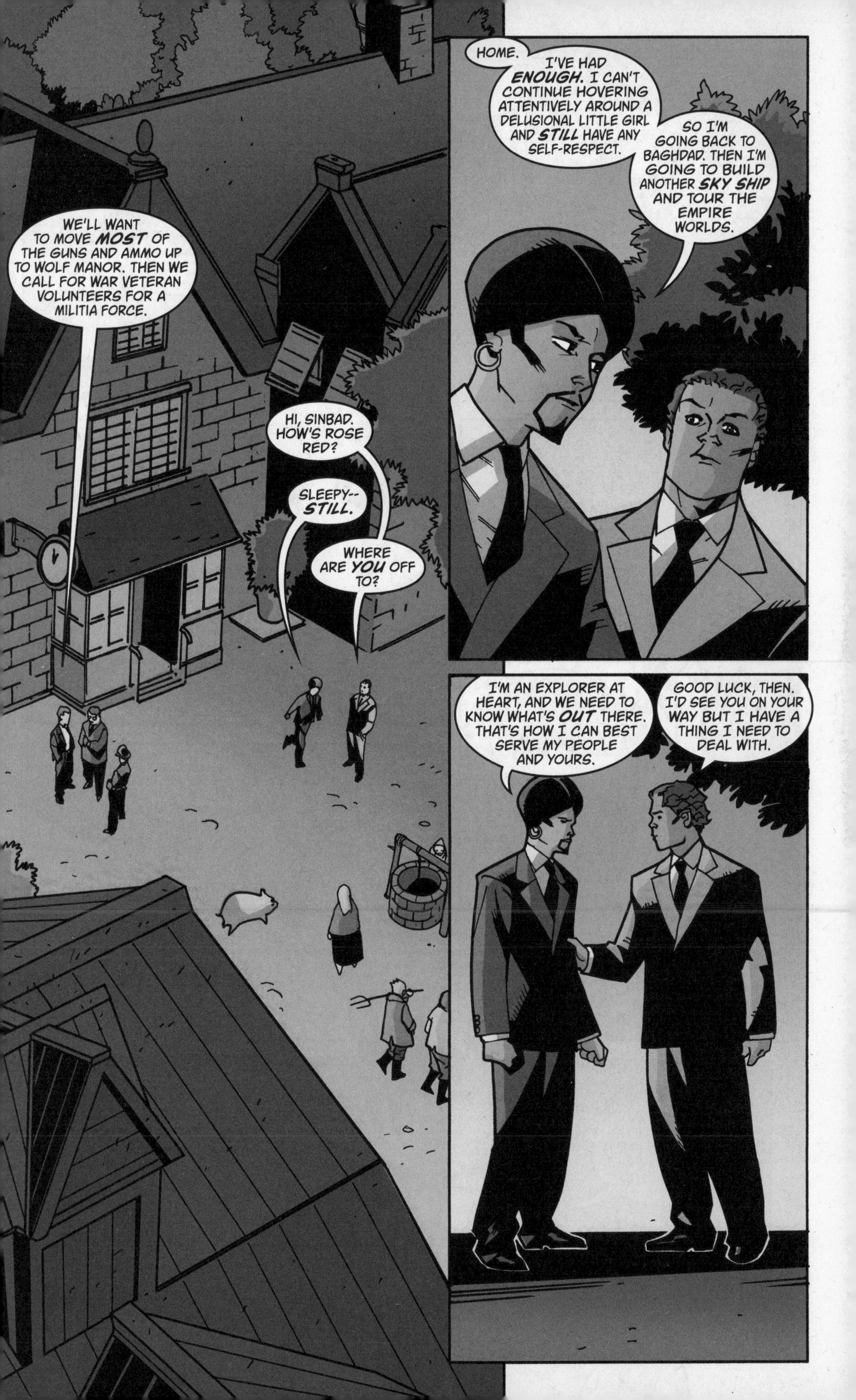
WE'LL WANT TO MOVE MOST OF THE GUNS AND AMMO UP TO WOLF MANOR. THEN WE CALL FOR WAR VETERAN VOLUNTEERS FOR A MILITIA FORCE.
HI, SINBAD. HOW'S ROSE RED?
SLEEPY-- STILL.
WHERE ARE YOU OFF TO?
HOME.
I'VE HAD ENOUGH. I CAN'T CONTINUE HOVERING ATTENTIVELY AROUND A DELUSIONAL LITTLE GIRL AND STILL HAVE ANY SELF-RESPECT.
SO I'M GOING BACK TO BAGHDAD. THEN I'M GOING TO BUILD ANOTHER SKY SHIP AND TOUR THE EMPIRE WORLDS.
I'M AN EXPLORER AT HEART, AND WE NEED TO KNOW WHAT'S OUT THERE. THAT'S HOW I CAN BEST SERVE MY PEOPLE AND YOURS.
GOOD LUCK, THEN. I'D SEE YOU ON YOUR WAY BUT I HAVE A THING I NEED TO DEAL WITH.

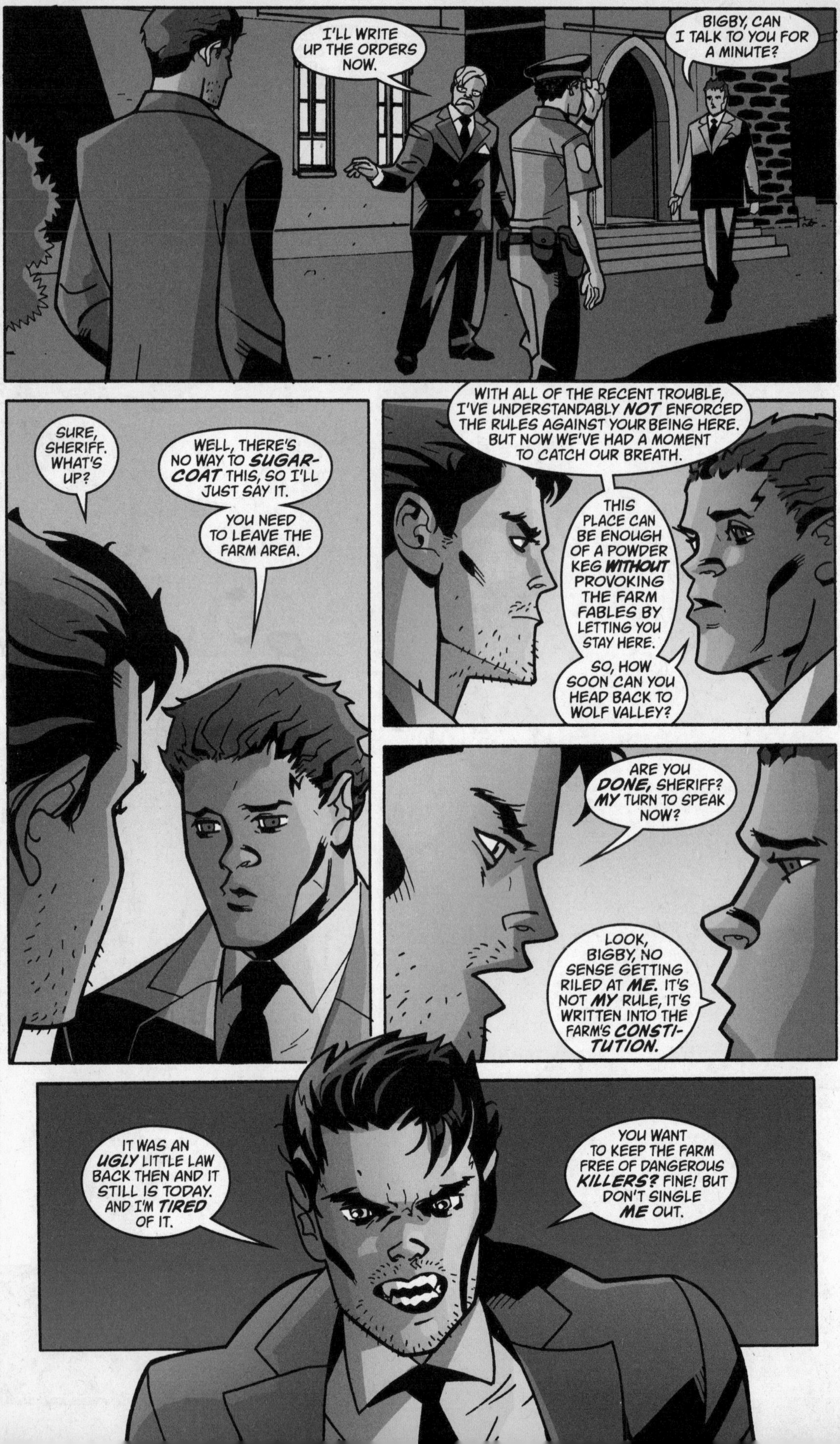
I'LL WRITE UP THE ORDERS NOW.
BIGBY, CAN I TALK TO YOU FOR A MINUTE?
SURE, SHERIFF. WHAT'S UP?
WELL, THERE'S NO WAY TO SUGAR-COAT THIS, SO I'LL JUST SAY IT.
YOU NEED TO LEAVE THE FARM AREA.
WITH ALL OF THE RECENT TROUBLE, I'VE UNDERSTANDABLY NOT ENFORCED THE RULES AGAINST YOUR BEING HERE. BUT NOW WE'VE HAD A MOMENT TO CATCH OUR BREATH.
THIS PLACE CAN BE ENOUGH OF A POWDER KEG WITHOUT PROVOKING THE FARM FABLES BY LETTING YOU STAY HERE.
SO, HOW SOON CAN YOU HEAD BACK TO WOLF VALLEY?
ARE YOU DONE, SHERIFF? MY TURN TO SPEAK NOW?
LOOK, BIGBY, NO SENSE GETTING RILED AT ME. IT'S NOT MY RULE, IT'S WRITTEN INTO THE FARM'S CONSTI-TUTION.
IT WAS AN UGLY LITTLE LAW BACK THEN AND IT STILL IS TODAY. AND I'M TIRED OF IT.
YOU WANT TO KEEP THE FARM FREE OF DANGEROUS KILLERS? FINE! BUT DON'T SINGLE ME OUT.

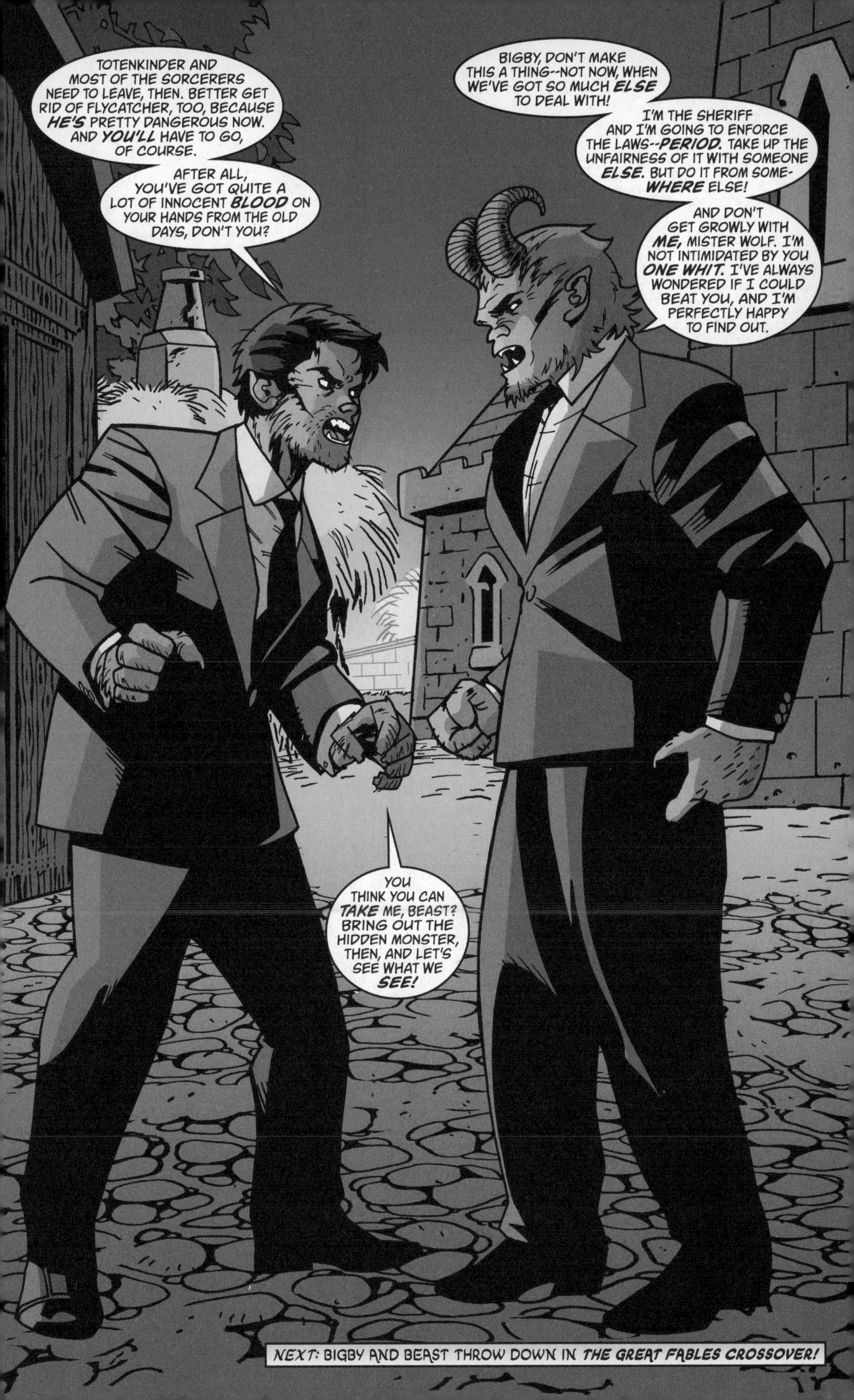
TOTENKINDER AND MOST OF THE SORCERERS NEED TO LEAVE, THEN. BETTER GET RID OF FLYCATCHER, TOO, BECAUSE HE'S PRETTY DANGEROUS NOW. AND YOU'LL HAVE TO GO, OF COURSE.
AFTER ALL, YOU'VE GOT QUITE A LOT OF INNOCENT BLOOD ON YOUR HANDS FROM THE OLD DAYS, DON'T YOU?
BIGBY, DON'T MAKE THIS A THING--NOT NOW, WHEN WE'VE GOT SO MUCH ELSE TO DEAL WITH!
I'M THE SHERIFF AND I'M GOING TO ENFORCE THE LAWS--PERIOD. TAKE UP THE UNFAIRNESS OF IT WITH SOMEONE ELSE. BUT DO IT FROM SOME-WHERE ELSE!
AND DON'T GET GROWLY WITH ME, MISTER WOLF. I'M NOT INTIMIDATED BY YOU ONE WHIT. I'VE ALWAYS WONDERED IF I COULD BEAT YOU, AND I'M PERFECTLY HAPPY TO FIND OUT.
YOU THINK YOU CAN TAKE ME, BEAST? BRING OUT THE HIDDEN MONSTER, THEN, AND LET'S SEE WHAT WE SEE!
NEXT: BIGBY AND BEAST THROW DOWN IN THE GREAT FABLES CROSSOVER!

RETURN TO THE JUNGLE BOOK

A Tale of Mowgli

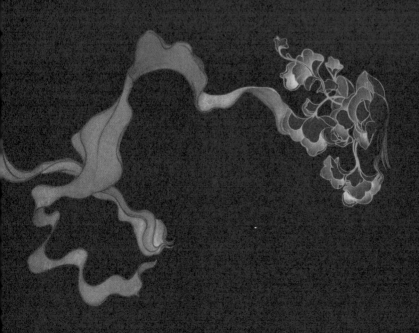

HOMELAND RECOVERY PART ONE OF FIVE

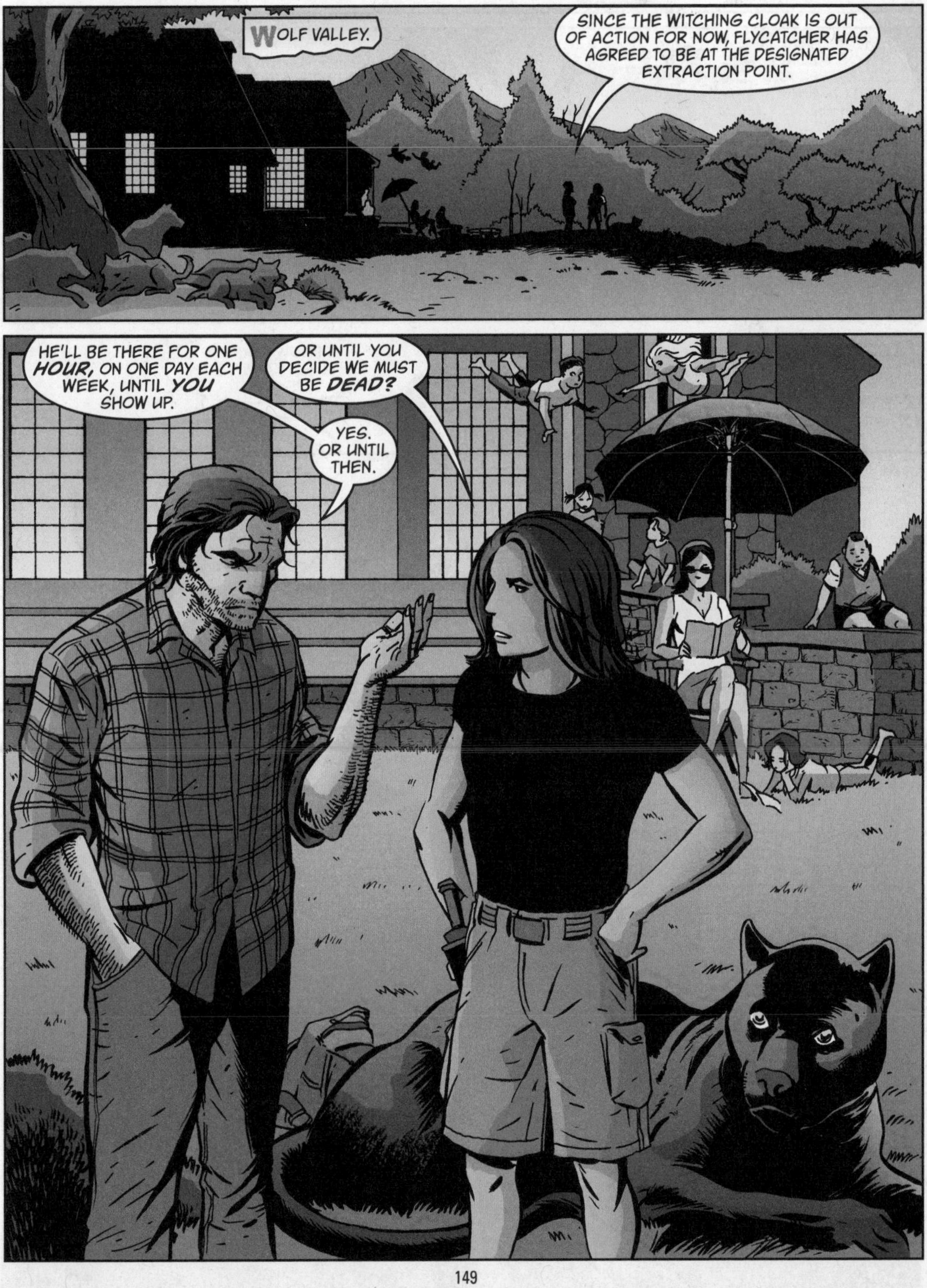

WOLF VALLEY.
SINCE THE WITCHING CLOAK IS OUT OF ACTION FOR NOW, FLYCATCHER HAS AGREED TO BE AT THE DESIGNATED EXTRACTION POINT.
HE'LL BE THERE FOR ONE **HOUR,** ON ONE DAY EACH WEEK, UNTIL **YOU** SHOW UP.
OR UNTIL YOU DECIDE WE MUST BE **DEAD?**
YES. OR UNTIL THEN.

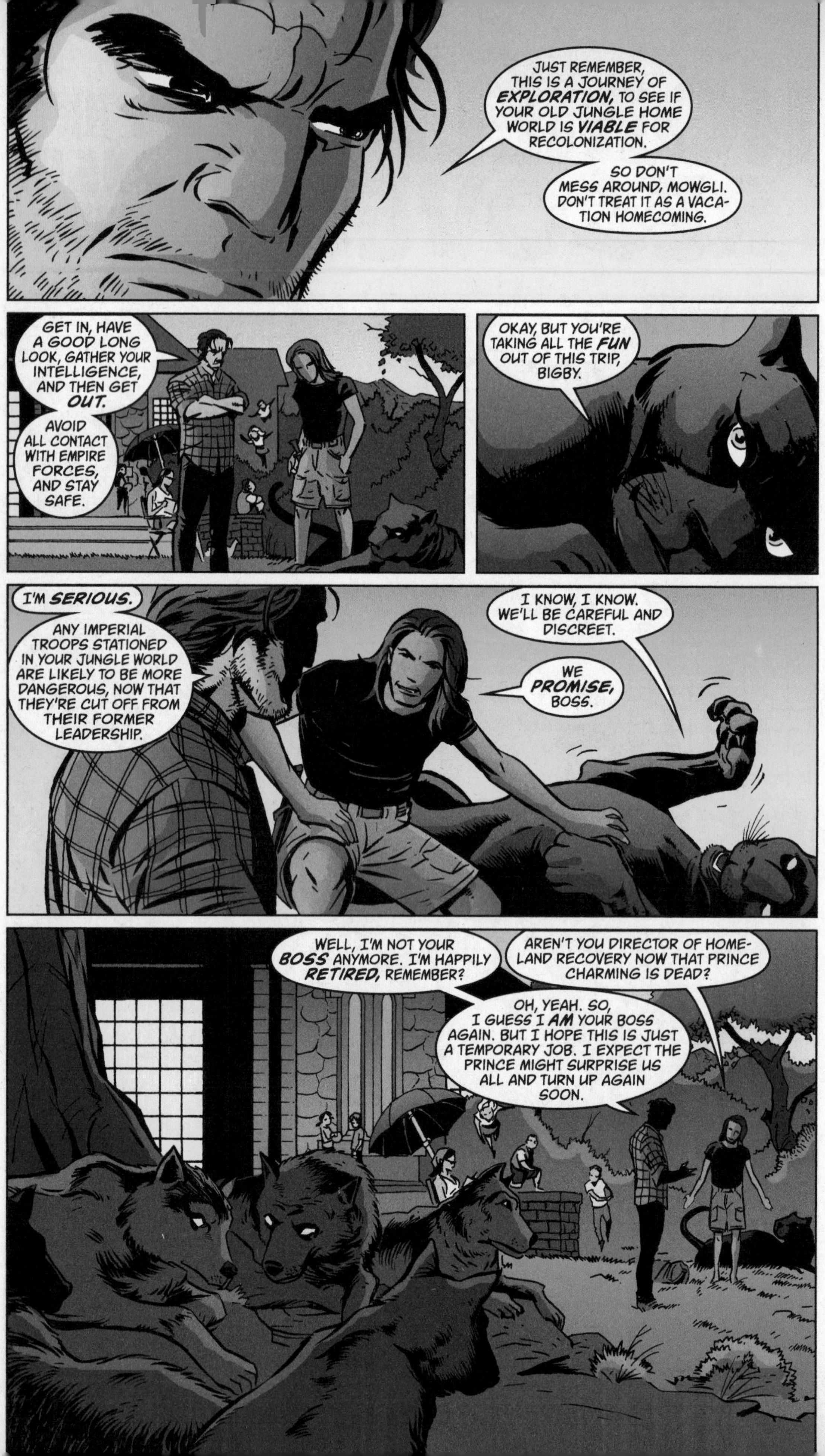
JUST REMEMBER, THIS IS A JOURNEY OF EXPLORATION, TO SEE IF YOUR OLD JUNGLE HOME WORLD IS VIABLE FOR RECOLONIZATION.
SO DON'T MESS AROUND, MOWGLI. DON'T TREAT IT AS A VACATION HOMECOMING.
GET IN, HAVE A GOOD LONG LOOK, GATHER YOUR INTELLIGENCE, AND THEN GET OUT.
AVOID ALL CONTACT WITH EMPIRE FORCES, AND STAY SAFE.
OKAY, BUT YOU'RE TAKING ALL THE FUN OUT OF THIS TRIP, BIGBY.
I'M SERIOUS.
ANY IMPERIAL TROOPS STATIONED IN YOUR JUNGLE WORLD ARE LIKELY TO BE MORE DANGEROUS, NOW THAT THEY'RE CUT OFF FROM THEIR FORMER LEADERSHIP.
I KNOW, I KNOW. WE'LL BE CAREFUL AND DISCREET.
WE PROMISE, BOSS.
WELL, I'M NOT YOUR BOSS ANYMORE. I'M HAPPILY RETIRED, REMEMBER?
AREN'T YOU DIRECTOR OF HOMELAND RECOVERY NOW THAT PRINCE CHARMING IS DEAD?
OH, YEAH. SO, I GUESS I AM YOUR BOSS AGAIN. BUT I HOPE THIS IS JUST A TEMPORARY JOB. I EXPECT THE PRINCE MIGHT SURPRISE US ALL AND TURN UP AGAIN SOON.

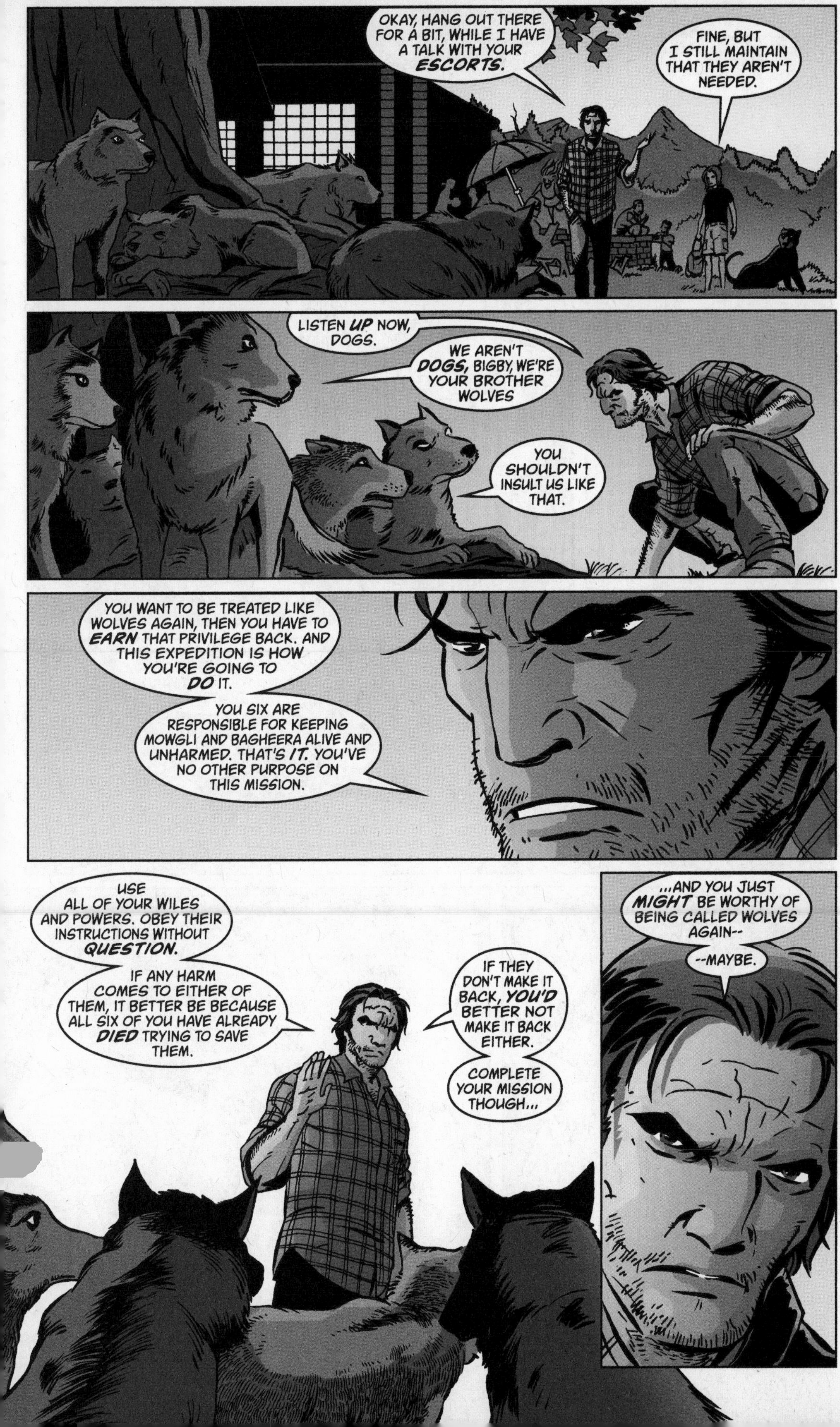
OKAY, HANG OUT THERE FOR A BIT, WHILE I HAVE A TALK WITH YOUR ESCORTS.
FINE, BUT I STILL MAINTAIN THAT THEY AREN'T NEEDED.
LISTEN UP NOW, DOGS.
WE AREN'T DOGS, BIGBY, WE'RE YOUR BROTHER WOLVES
YOU SHOULDN'T INSULT US LIKE THAT.
YOU WANT TO BE TREATED LIKE WOLVES AGAIN, THEN YOU HAVE TO EARN THAT PRIVILEGE BACK. AND THIS EXPEDITION IS HOW YOU'RE GOING TO DO IT.
YOU SIX ARE RESPONSIBLE FOR KEEPING MOWGLI AND BAGHEERA ALIVE AND UNHARMED. THAT'S IT. YOU'VE NO OTHER PURPOSE ON THIS MISSION.
USE ALL OF YOUR WILES AND POWERS. OBEY THEIR INSTRUCTIONS WITHOUT QUESTION.
IF ANY HARM COMES TO EITHER OF THEM, IT BETTER BE BECAUSE ALL SIX OF YOU HAVE ALREADY DIED TRYING TO SAVE THEM.
IF THEY DON'T MAKE IT BACK, YOU'D BETTER NOT MAKE IT BACK EITHER.
COMPLETE YOUR MISSION THOUGH...
...AND YOU JUST MIGHT BE WORTHY OF BEING CALLED WOLVES AGAIN--
--MAYBE.

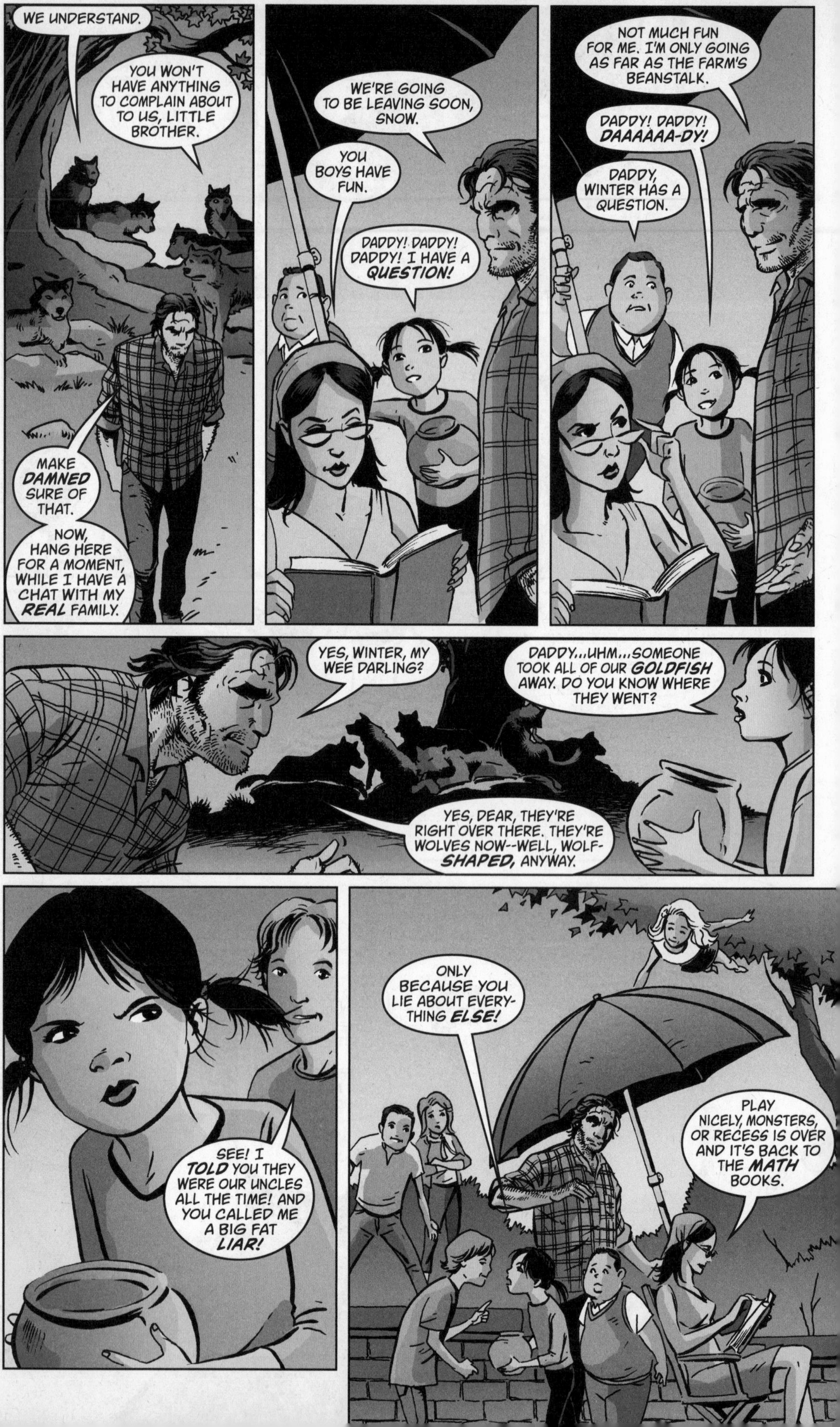
WE UNDERSTAND.
YOU WON'T HAVE ANYTHING TO COMPLAIN ABOUT TO US, LITTLE BROTHER.
MAKE *DAMNED* SURE OF THAT.
NOW, HANG HERE FOR A MOMENT, WHILE I HAVE A CHAT WITH MY *REAL* FAMILY.
WE'RE GOING TO BE LEAVING SOON, SNOW.
YOU BOYS HAVE FUN.
DADDY! DADDY! DADDY! I HAVE A *QUESTION!*
NOT MUCH FUN FOR ME. I'M ONLY GOING AS FAR AS THE FARM'S BEANSTALK.
DADDY! DADDY! *DAAAAAA-DY!*
DADDY, WINTER HAS A QUESTION.
YES, WINTER, MY WEE DARLING?
DADDY...UHM...SOMEONE TOOK ALL OF OUR *GOLDFISH* AWAY. DO YOU KNOW WHERE THEY WENT?
YES, DEAR, THEY'RE RIGHT OVER THERE. THEY'RE WOLVES NOW--WELL, WOLF-*SHAPED,* ANYWAY.
SEE! I *TOLD* YOU THEY WERE OUR UNCLES ALL THE TIME! AND YOU CALLED ME A BIG FAT *LIAR!*
ONLY BECAUSE YOU LIE ABOUT EVERY-THING *ELSE!*
PLAY NICELY, MONSTERS, OR RECESS IS OVER AND IT'S BACK TO THE *MATH* BOOKS.

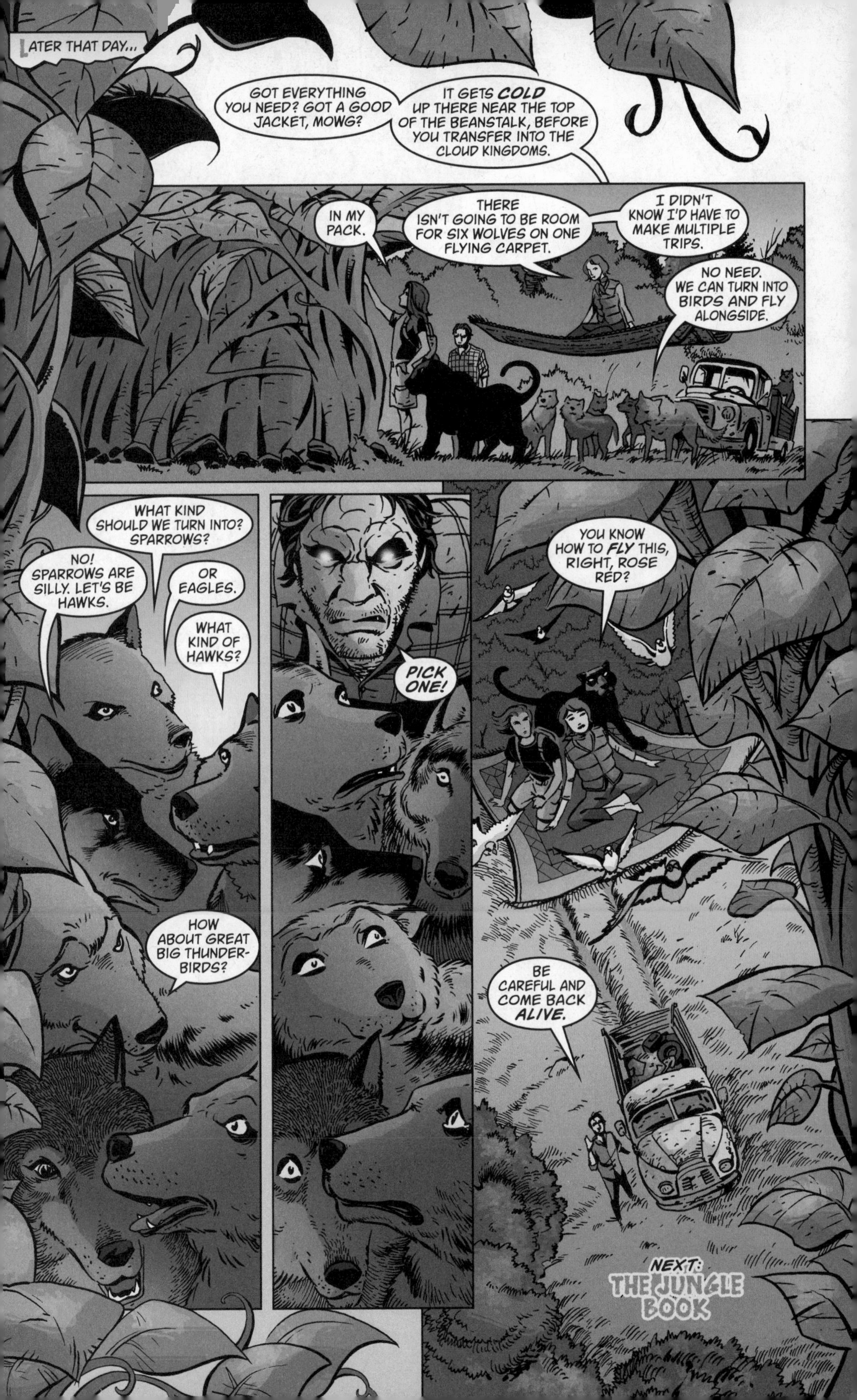
LATER THAT DAY...
GOT EVERYTHING YOU NEED? GOT A GOOD JACKET, MOWG?
IT GETS COLD UP THERE NEAR THE TOP OF THE BEANSTALK, BEFORE YOU TRANSFER INTO THE CLOUD KINGDOMS.
IN MY PACK.
THERE ISN'T GOING TO BE ROOM FOR SIX WOLVES ON ONE FLYING CARPET.
I DIDN'T KNOW I'D HAVE TO MAKE MULTIPLE TRIPS.
NO NEED. WE CAN TURN INTO BIRDS AND FLY ALONGSIDE.
WHAT KIND SHOULD WE TURN INTO? SPARROWS?
NO! SPARROWS ARE SILLY. LET'S BE HAWKS.
OR EAGLES.
WHAT KIND OF HAWKS?
HOW ABOUT GREAT BIG THUNDER-BIRDS?
PICK ONE!
YOU KNOW HOW TO FLY THIS, RIGHT, ROSE RED?
BE CAREFUL AND COME BACK ALIVE.
NEXT: THE JUNGLE BOOK

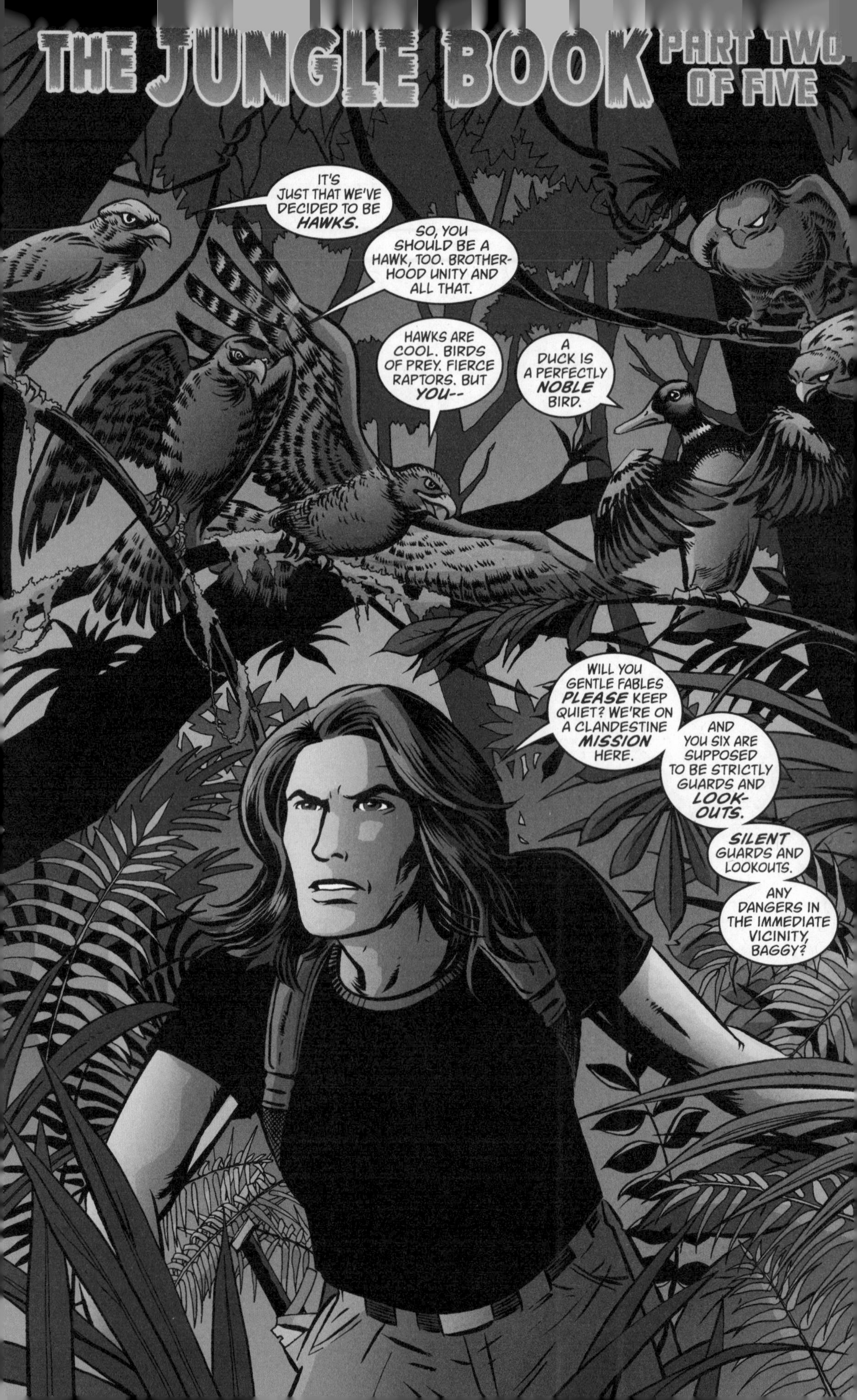
THE JUNGLE BOOK PART TWO OF FIVE
IT'S JUST THAT WE'VE DECIDED TO BE HAWKS.
SO, YOU SHOULD BE A HAWK, TOO. BROTHER-HOOD UNITY AND ALL THAT.
HAWKS ARE COOL. BIRDS OF PREY. FIERCE RAPTORS. BUT YOU--
A DUCK IS A PERFECTLY NOBLE BIRD.
WILL YOU GENTLE FABLES PLEASE KEEP QUIET? WE'RE ON A CLANDESTINE MISSION HERE.
AND YOU SIX ARE SUPPOSED TO BE STRICTLY GUARDS AND LOOK-OUTS.
SILENT GUARDS AND LOOKOUTS.
ANY DANGERS IN THE IMMEDIATE VICINITY, BAGGY?

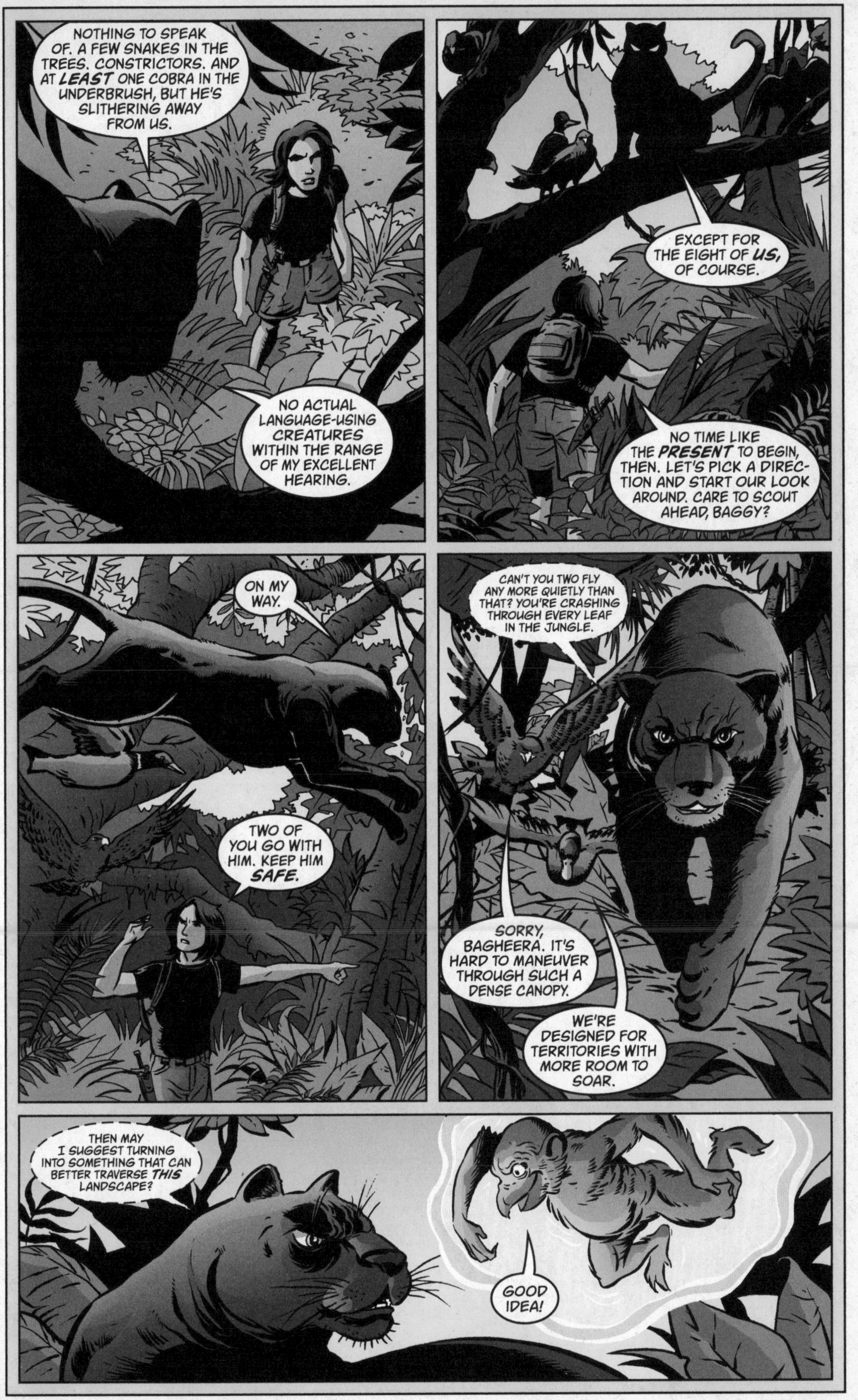
NOTHING TO SPEAK OF. A FEW SNAKES IN THE TREES. CONSTRICTORS. AND AT LEAST ONE COBRA IN THE UNDERBRUSH, BUT HE'S SLITHERING AWAY FROM US.
NO ACTUAL LANGUAGE-USING CREATURES WITHIN THE RANGE OF MY EXCELLENT HEARING.
EXCEPT FOR THE EIGHT OF US, OF COURSE.
NO TIME LIKE THE PRESENT TO BEGIN, THEN. LET'S PICK A DIRECTION AND START OUR LOOK AROUND. CARE TO SCOUT AHEAD, BAGGY?
ON MY WAY.
TWO OF YOU GO WITH HIM. KEEP HIM SAFE.
CAN'T YOU TWO FLY ANY MORE QUIETLY THAN THAT? YOU'RE CRASHING THROUGH EVERY LEAF IN THE JUNGLE.
SORRY, BAGHEERA. IT'S HARD TO MANEUVER THROUGH SUCH A DENSE CANOPY.
WE'RE DESIGNED FOR TERRITORIES WITH MORE ROOM TO SOAR.
THEN MAY I SUGGEST TURNING INTO SOMETHING THAT CAN BETTER TRAVERSE THIS LANDSCAPE?
GOOD IDEA!

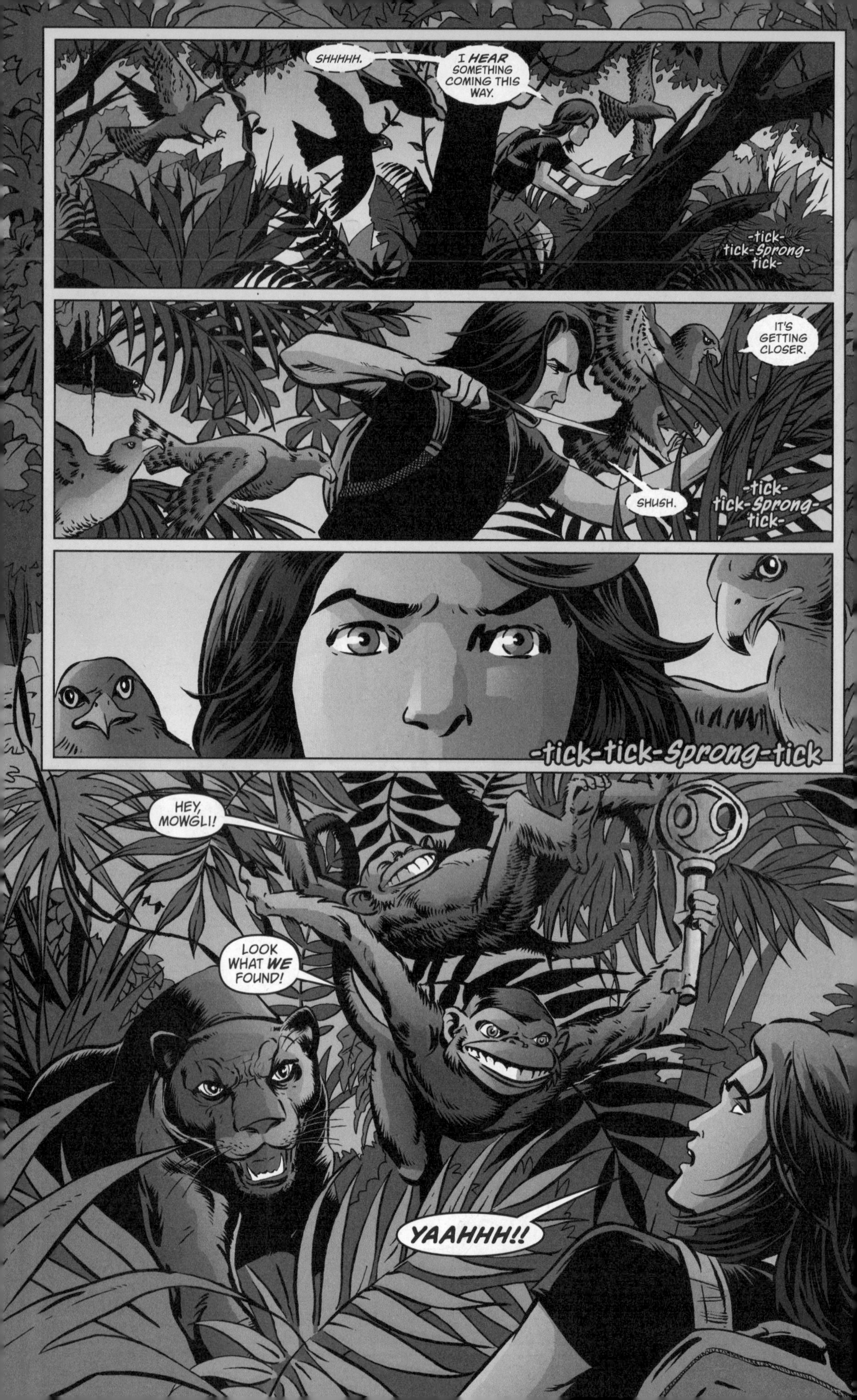
SHHHHH.
I HEAR SOMETHING COMING THIS WAY.
-tick-tick-Sprong-tick-
IT'S GETTING CLOSER.
SHUSH.
-tick-tick-Sprong-tick-
-tick-tick-Sprong-tick
HEY, MOWGLI!
LOOK WHAT WE FOUND!
YAAHHH!!

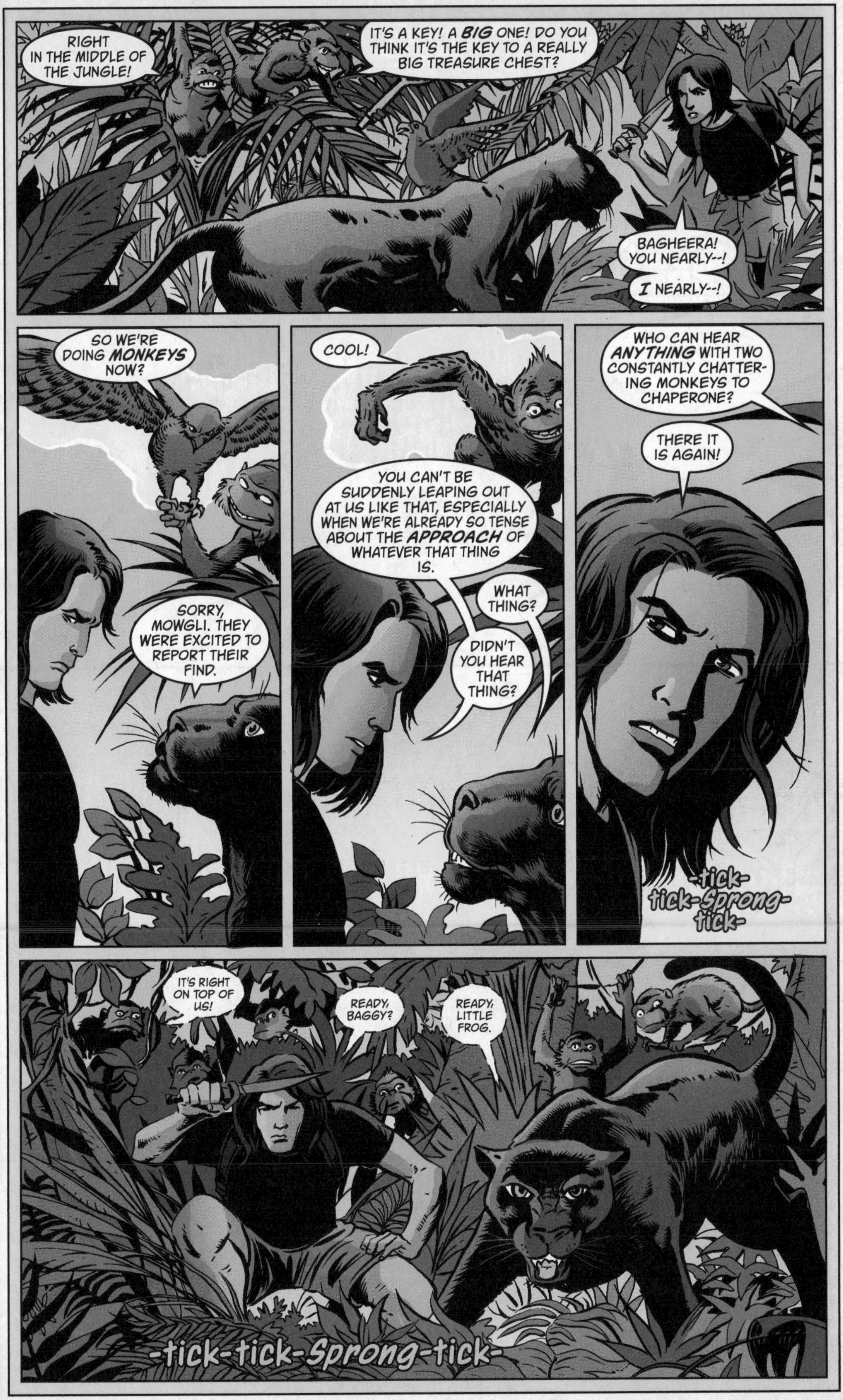
RIGHT IN THE MIDDLE OF THE JUNGLE!
IT'S A KEY! A BIG ONE! DO YOU THINK IT'S THE KEY TO A REALLY BIG TREASURE CHEST?
BAGHEERA! YOU NEARLY--!
I NEARLY--!
SO WE'RE DOING MONKEYS NOW?
SORRY, MOWGLI. THEY WERE EXCITED TO REPORT THEIR FIND.
COOL!
YOU CAN'T BE SUDDENLY LEAPING OUT AT US LIKE THAT, ESPECIALLY WHEN WE'RE ALREADY SO TENSE ABOUT THE APPROACH OF WHATEVER THAT THING IS.
WHAT THING?
DIDN'T YOU HEAR THAT THING?
WHO CAN HEAR ANYTHING WITH TWO CONSTANTLY CHATTERING MONKEYS TO CHAPERONE?
THERE IT IS AGAIN!
-tick-tick-Sprong-tick-
IT'S RIGHT ON TOP OF US!
READY, BAGGY?
READY, LITTLE FROG.
-tick-tick-Sprong-tick-

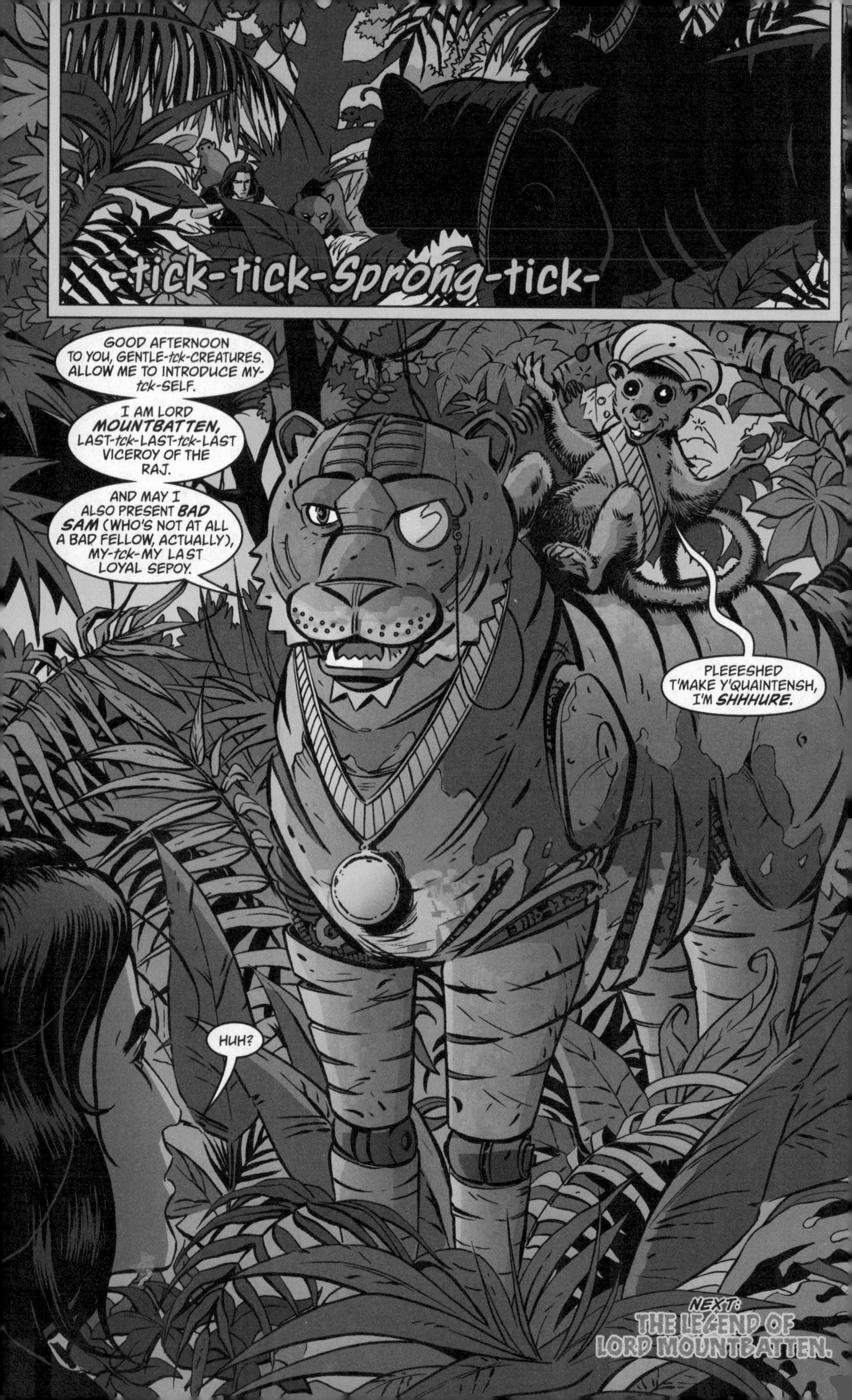
-tick-tick-Sprong-tick-
GOOD AFTERNOON TO YOU, GENTLE-tck-CREATURES. ALLOW ME TO INTRODUCE MY-tck-SELF.
I AM LORD MOUNTBATTEN, LAST-tck-LAST-tck-LAST VICEROY OF THE RAJ.
AND MAY I ALSO PRESENT BAD SAM (WHO'S NOT AT ALL A BAD FELLOW, ACTUALLY), MY-tck-MY LAST LOYAL SEPOY.
PLEEESHED T'MAKE Y'QUAINTENSH, I'M SHHHURE.
HUH?
NEXT:
THE LEGEND OF LORD MOUNTBATTEN.

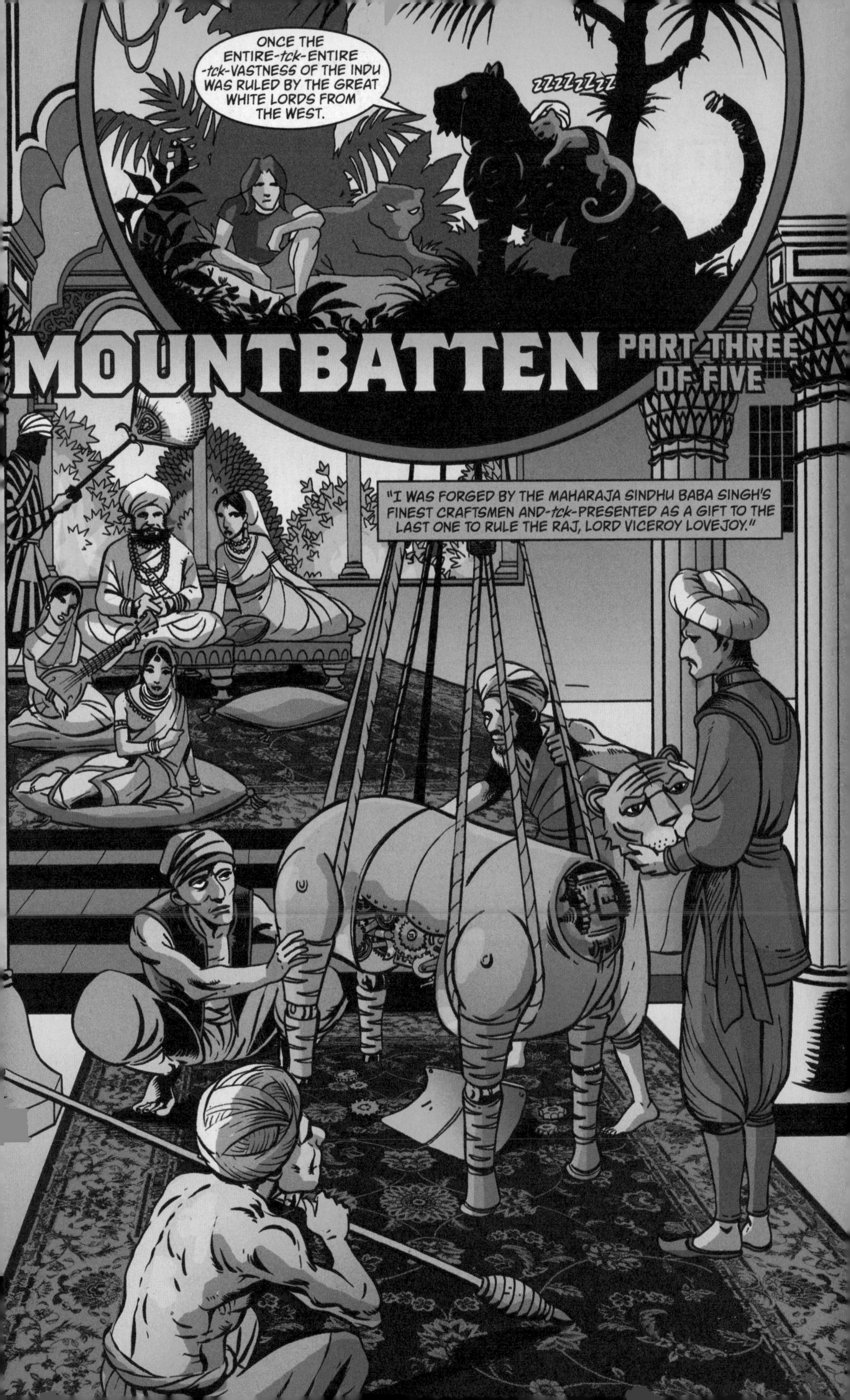
ONCE THE ENTIRE-tck-ENTIRE -tck-VASTNESS OF THE INDU WAS RULED BY THE GREAT WHITE LORDS FROM THE WEST.
ZZZZZZZZ
MOUNTBATTEN PART THREE OF FIVE
"I WAS FORGED BY THE MAHARAJA SINDHU BABA SINGH'S FINEST CRAFTSMEN AND-tck-PRESENTED AS A GIFT TO THE LAST ONE TO RULE THE RAJ, LORD VICEROY LOVEJOY."

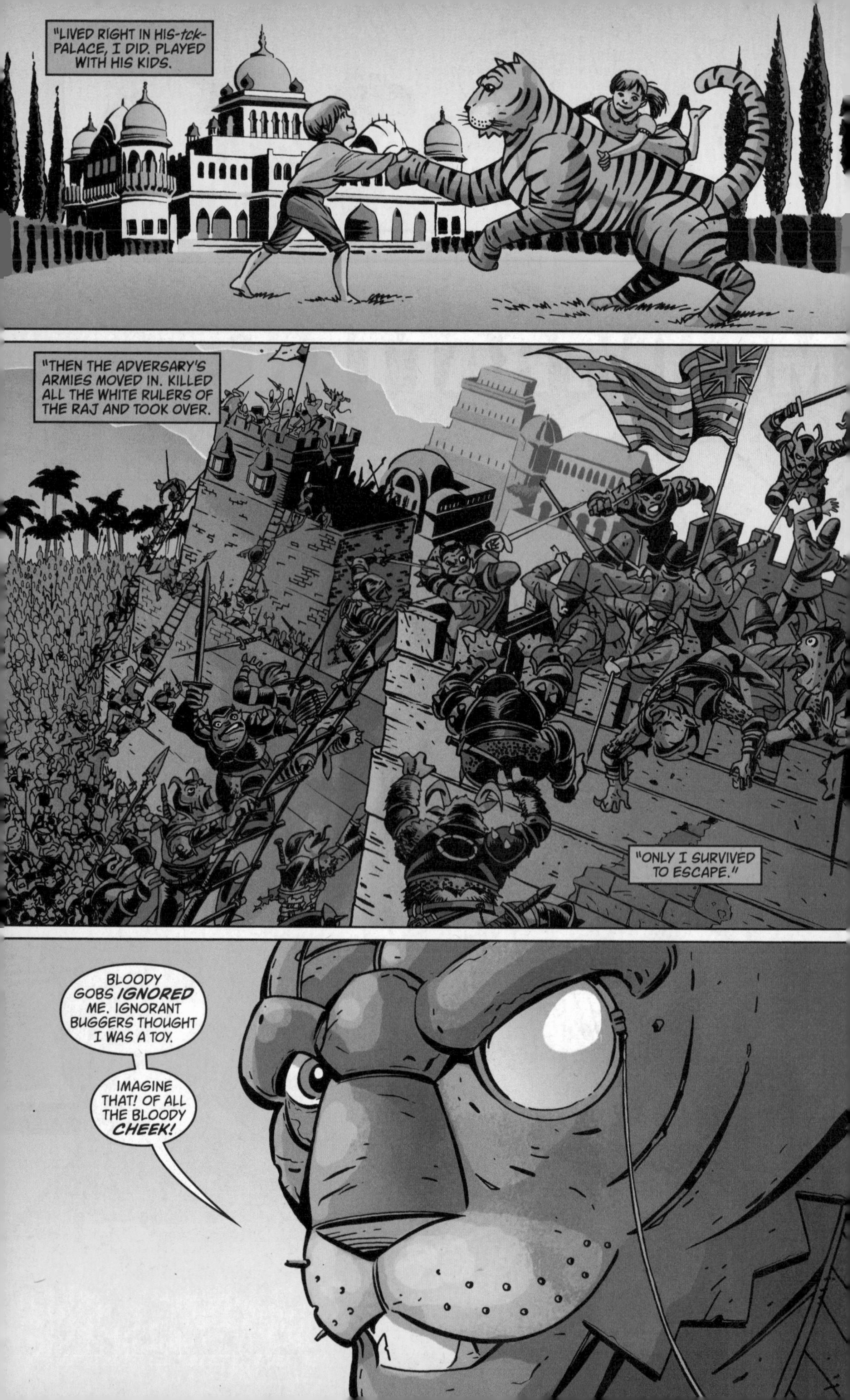
"LIVED RIGHT IN HIS-tck- PALACE, I DID. PLAYED WITH HIS KIDS.
"THEN THE ADVERSARY'S ARMIES MOVED IN. KILLED ALL THE WHITE RULERS OF THE RAJ AND TOOK OVER.
"ONLY I SURVIVED TO ESCAPE."
BLOODY GOBS IGNORED ME. IGNORANT BUGGERS THOUGHT I WAS A TOY.
IMAGINE THAT! OF ALL THE BLOODY CHEEK!

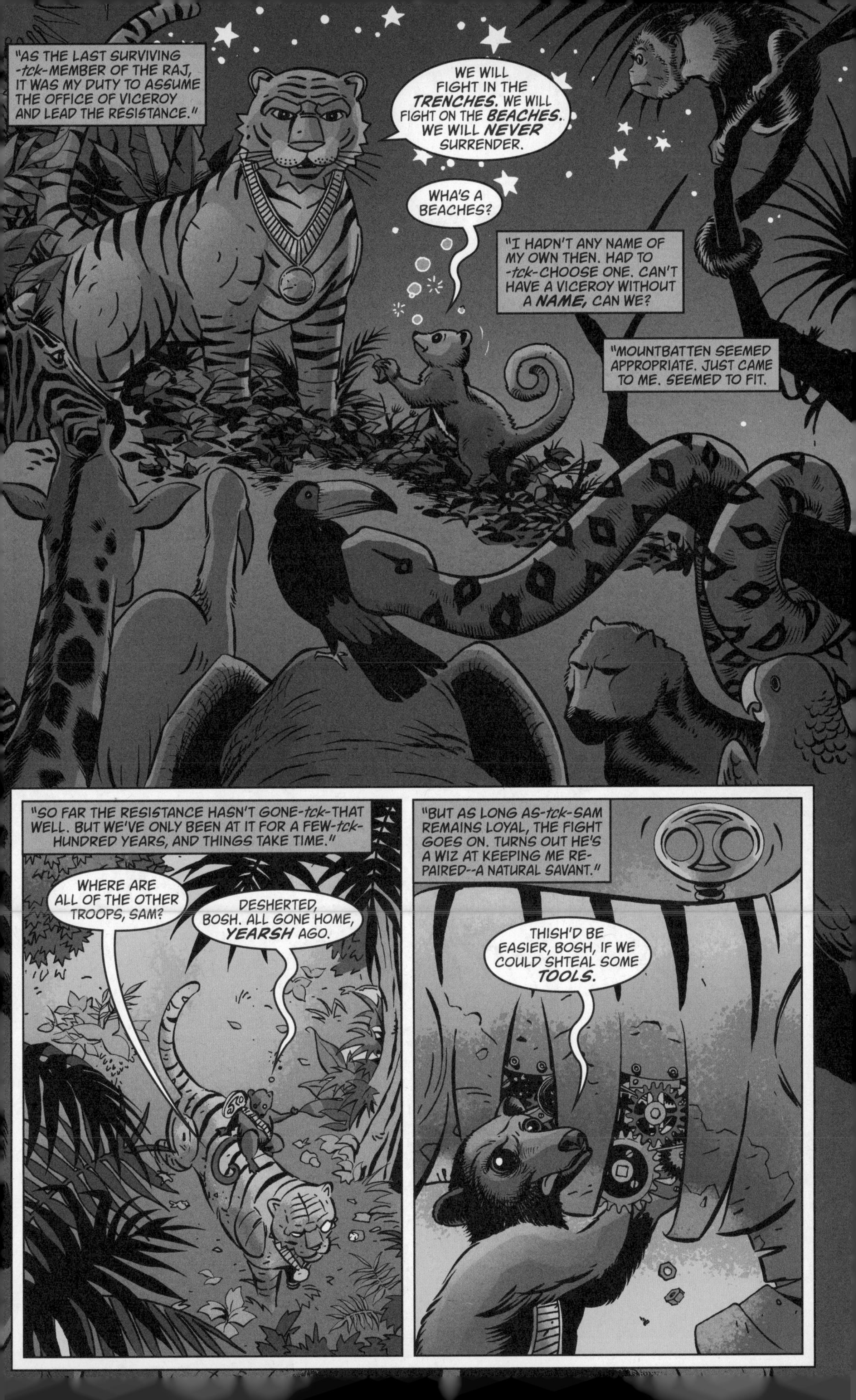
"AS THE LAST SURVIVING -tck- MEMBER OF THE RAJ, IT WAS MY DUTY TO ASSUME THE OFFICE OF VICEROY AND LEAD THE RESISTANCE."
WE WILL FIGHT IN THE TRENCHES. WE WILL FIGHT ON THE BEACHES. WE WILL NEVER SURRENDER.
WHA'S A BEACHES?
"I HADN'T ANY NAME OF MY OWN THEN. HAD TO -tck- CHOOSE ONE. CAN'T HAVE A VICEROY WITHOUT A NAME, CAN WE?
"MOUNTBATTEN SEEMED APPROPRIATE. JUST CAME TO ME. SEEMED TO FIT.
"SO FAR THE RESISTANCE HASN'T GONE -tck- THAT WELL. BUT WE'VE ONLY BEEN AT IT FOR A FEW -tck- HUNDRED YEARS, AND THINGS TAKE TIME."
WHERE ARE ALL OF THE OTHER TROOPS, SAM?
DESHERTED, BOSH. ALL GONE HOME, YEARSH AGO.
"BUT AS LONG AS -tck- SAM REMAINS LOYAL, THE FIGHT GOES ON. TURNS OUT HE'S A WIZ AT KEEPING ME RE-PAIRED--A NATURAL SAVANT."
THISH'D BE EASIER, BOSH, IF WE COULD SHTEAL SOME TOOLS.

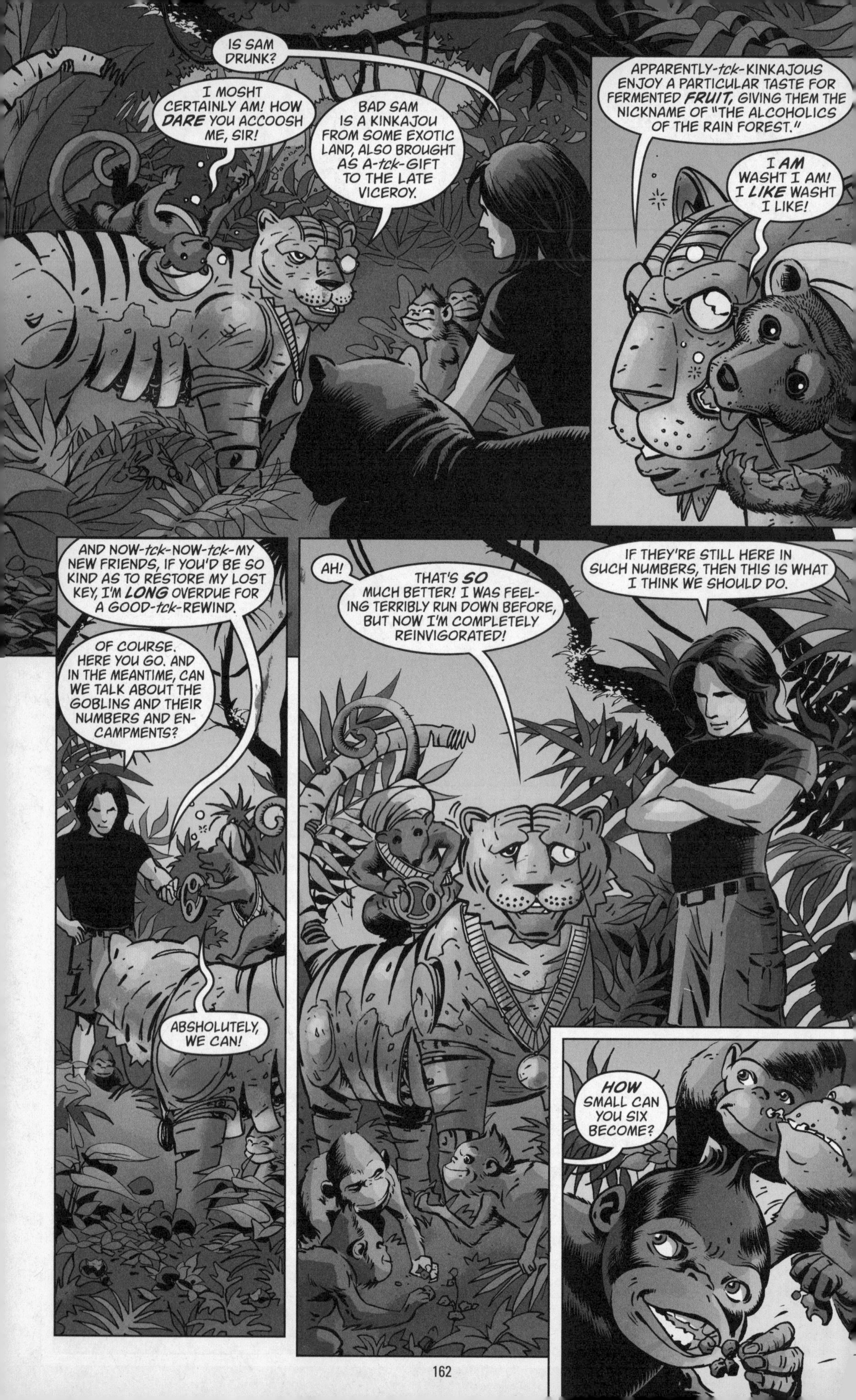
IS SAM DRUNK?
I MOSHT CERTAINLY AM! HOW DARE YOU ACCOOSH ME, SIR!
BAD SAM IS A KINKAJOU FROM SOME EXOTIC LAND, ALSO BROUGHT AS A-tck-GIFT TO THE LATE VICEROY.
APPARENTLY-tck-KINKAJOUS ENJOY A PARTICULAR TASTE FOR FERMENTED FRUIT, GIVING THEM THE NICKNAME OF "THE ALCOHOLICS OF THE RAIN FOREST."
I AM WASHT I AM! I LIKE WASHT I LIKE!
AND NOW-tck-NOW-tck-MY NEW FRIENDS, IF YOU'D BE SO KIND AS TO RESTORE MY LOST KEY, I'M LONG OVERDUE FOR A GOOD-tck-REWIND.
OF COURSE. HERE YOU GO. AND IN THE MEANTIME, CAN WE TALK ABOUT THE GOBLINS AND THEIR NUMBERS AND ENCAMPMENTS?
ABSHOLUTELY, WE CAN!
AH!
THAT'S SO MUCH BETTER! I WAS FEELING TERRIBLY RUN DOWN BEFORE, BUT NOW I'M COMPLETELY REINVIGORATED!
IF THEY'RE STILL HERE IN SUCH NUMBERS, THEN THIS IS WHAT I THINK WE SHOULD DO.
HOW SMALL CAN YOU SIX BECOME?

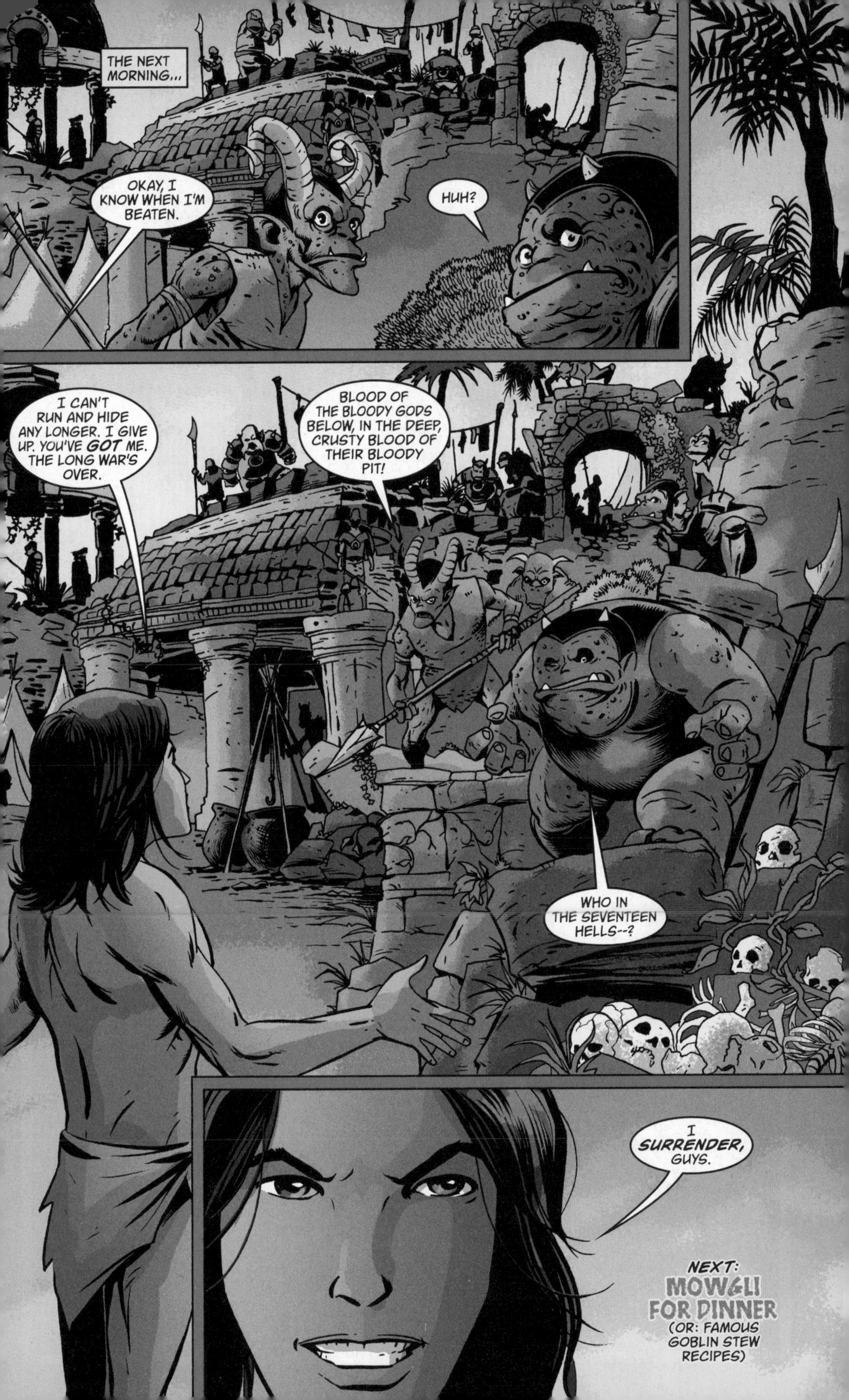
THE NEXT MORNING...
OKAY, I KNOW WHEN I'M BEATEN.
HUH?
I CAN'T RUN AND HIDE ANY LONGER. I GIVE UP. YOU'VE GOT ME. THE LONG WAR'S OVER.
BLOOD OF THE BLOODY GODS BELOW, IN THE DEEP, CRUSTY BLOOD OF THEIR BLOODY PIT!
WHO IN THE SEVENTEEN HELLS--?
I SURRENDER, GUYS.
NEXT: MOWGLI FOR DINNER
(OR: FAMOUS GOBLIN STEW RECIPES)

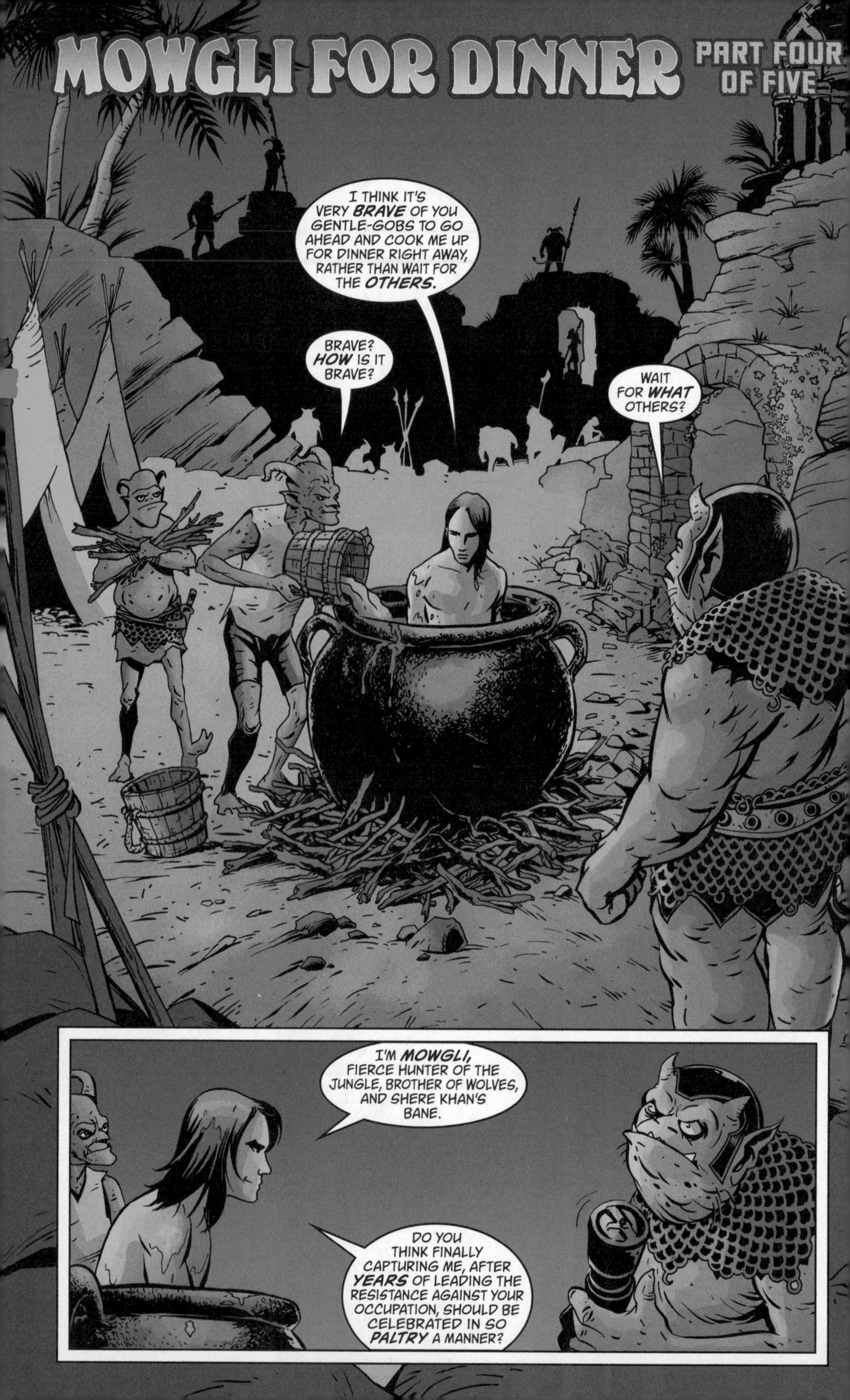
MOWGLI FOR DINNER
PART FOUR OF FIVE
I THINK IT'S VERY BRAVE OF YOU GENTLE-GOBS TO GO AHEAD AND COOK ME UP FOR DINNER RIGHT AWAY, RATHER THAN WAIT FOR THE OTHERS.
BRAVE? HOW IS IT BRAVE?
WAIT FOR WHAT OTHERS?
I'M MOWGLI, FIERCE HUNTER OF THE JUNGLE, BROTHER OF WOLVES, AND SHERE KHAN'S BANE.
DO YOU THINK FINALLY CAPTURING ME, AFTER YEARS OF LEADING THE RESISTANCE AGAINST YOUR OCCUPATION, SHOULD BE CELEBRATED IN SO PALTRY A MANNER?

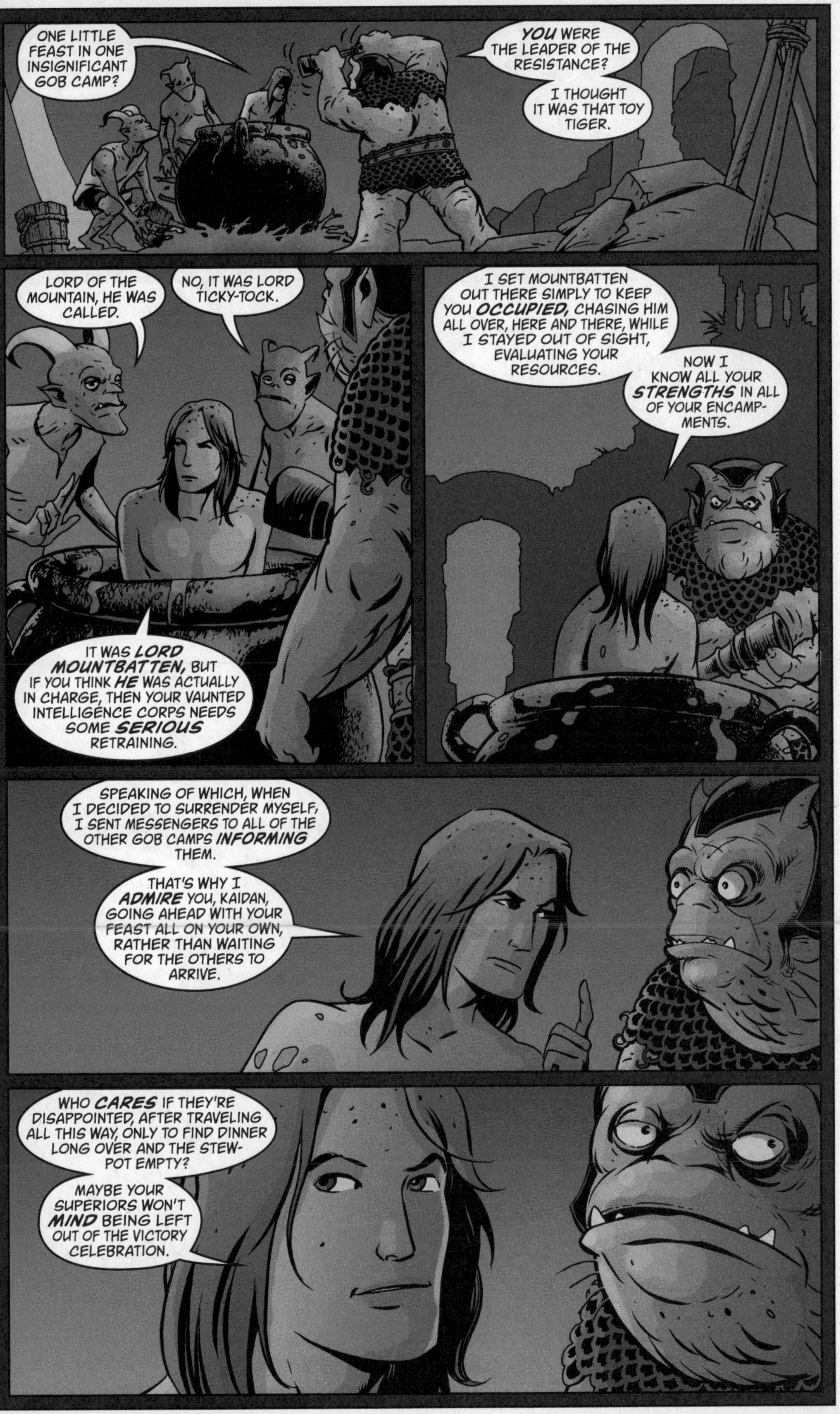
ONE LITTLE FEAST IN ONE INSIGNIFICANT GOB CAMP?
YOU WERE THE LEADER OF THE RESISTANCE?
I THOUGHT IT WAS THAT TOY TIGER.
LORD OF THE MOUNTAIN, HE WAS CALLED.
NO, IT WAS LORD TICKY-TOCK.
IT WAS LORD MOUNTBATTEN, BUT IF YOU THINK HE WAS ACTUALLY IN CHARGE, THEN YOUR VAUNTED INTELLIGENCE CORPS NEEDS SOME SERIOUS RETRAINING.
I SET MOUNTBATTEN OUT THERE SIMPLY TO KEEP YOU OCCUPIED, CHASING HIM ALL OVER, HERE AND THERE, WHILE I STAYED OUT OF SIGHT, EVALUATING YOUR RESOURCES.
NOW I KNOW ALL YOUR STRENGTHS IN ALL OF YOUR ENCAMPMENTS.
SPEAKING OF WHICH, WHEN I DECIDED TO SURRENDER MYSELF, I SENT MESSENGERS TO ALL OF THE OTHER GOB CAMPS INFORMING THEM.
THAT'S WHY I ADMIRE YOU, KAIDAN, GOING AHEAD WITH YOUR FEAST ALL ON YOUR OWN, RATHER THAN WAITING FOR THE OTHERS TO ARRIVE.
WHO CARES IF THEY'RE DISAPPOINTED, AFTER TRAVELING ALL THIS WAY, ONLY TO FIND DINNER LONG OVER AND THE STEW-POT EMPTY?
MAYBE YOUR SUPERIORS WON'T MIND BEING LEFT OUT OF THE VICTORY CELEBRATION.

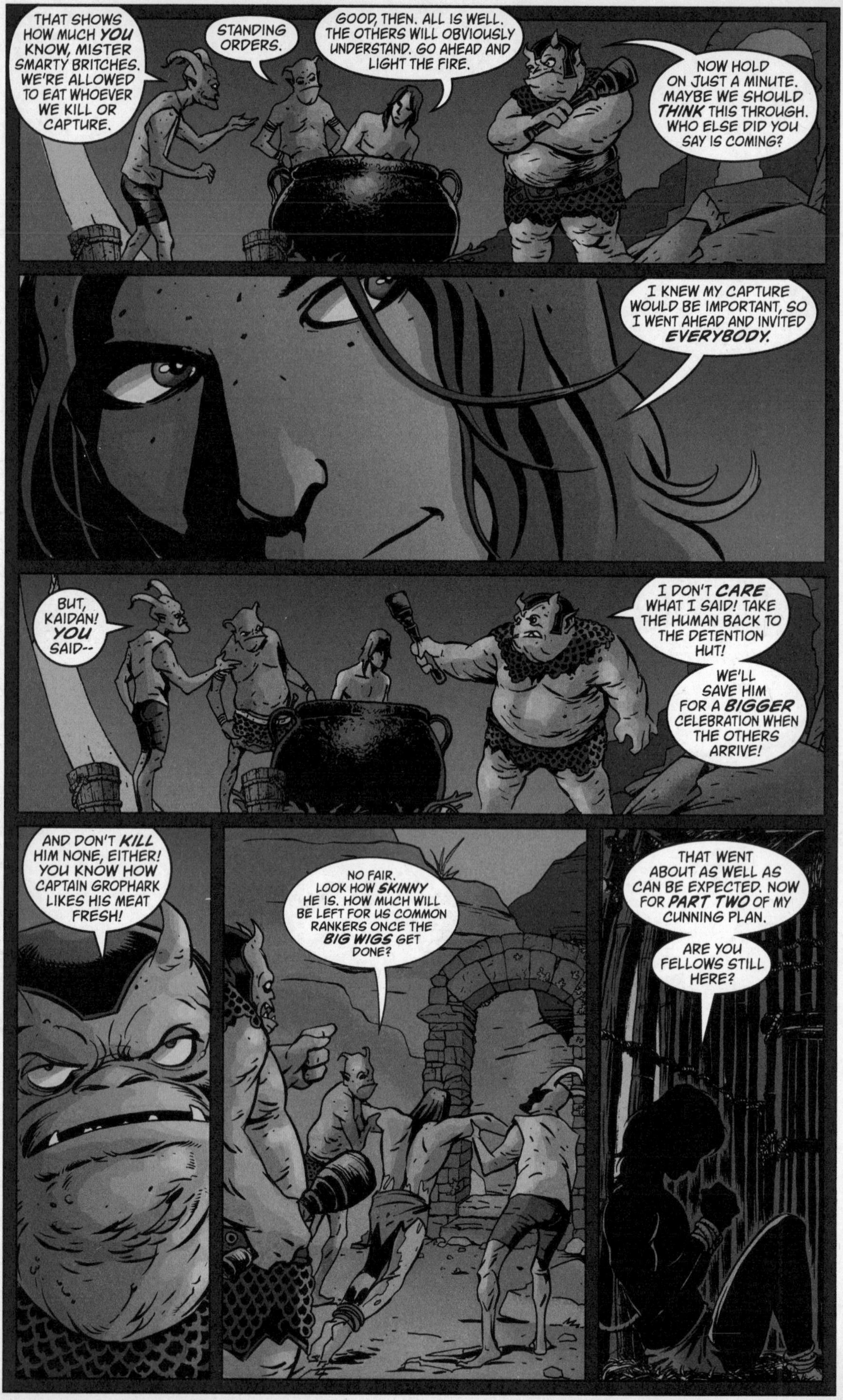
THAT SHOWS HOW MUCH YOU KNOW, MISTER SMARTY BRITCHES. WE'RE ALLOWED TO EAT WHOEVER WE KILL OR CAPTURE.
STANDING ORDERS.
GOOD, THEN. ALL IS WELL. THE OTHERS WILL OBVIOUSLY UNDERSTAND. GO AHEAD AND LIGHT THE FIRE.
NOW HOLD ON JUST A MINUTE. MAYBE WE SHOULD THINK THIS THROUGH. WHO ELSE DID YOU SAY IS COMING?
I KNEW MY CAPTURE WOULD BE IMPORTANT, SO I WENT AHEAD AND INVITED EVERYBODY.
BUT, KAIDAN! YOU SAID--
I DON'T CARE WHAT I SAID! TAKE THE HUMAN BACK TO THE DETENTION HUT!
WE'LL SAVE HIM FOR A BIGGER CELEBRATION WHEN THE OTHERS ARRIVE!
AND DON'T KILL HIM NONE, EITHER! YOU KNOW HOW CAPTAIN GROPHARK LIKES HIS MEAT FRESH!
NO FAIR. LOOK HOW SKINNY HE IS. HOW MUCH WILL BE LEFT FOR US COMMON RANKERS ONCE THE BIG WIGS GET DONE?
THAT WENT ABOUT AS WELL AS CAN BE EXPECTED. NOW FOR PART TWO OF MY CUNNING PLAN.
ARE YOU FELLOWS STILL HERE?

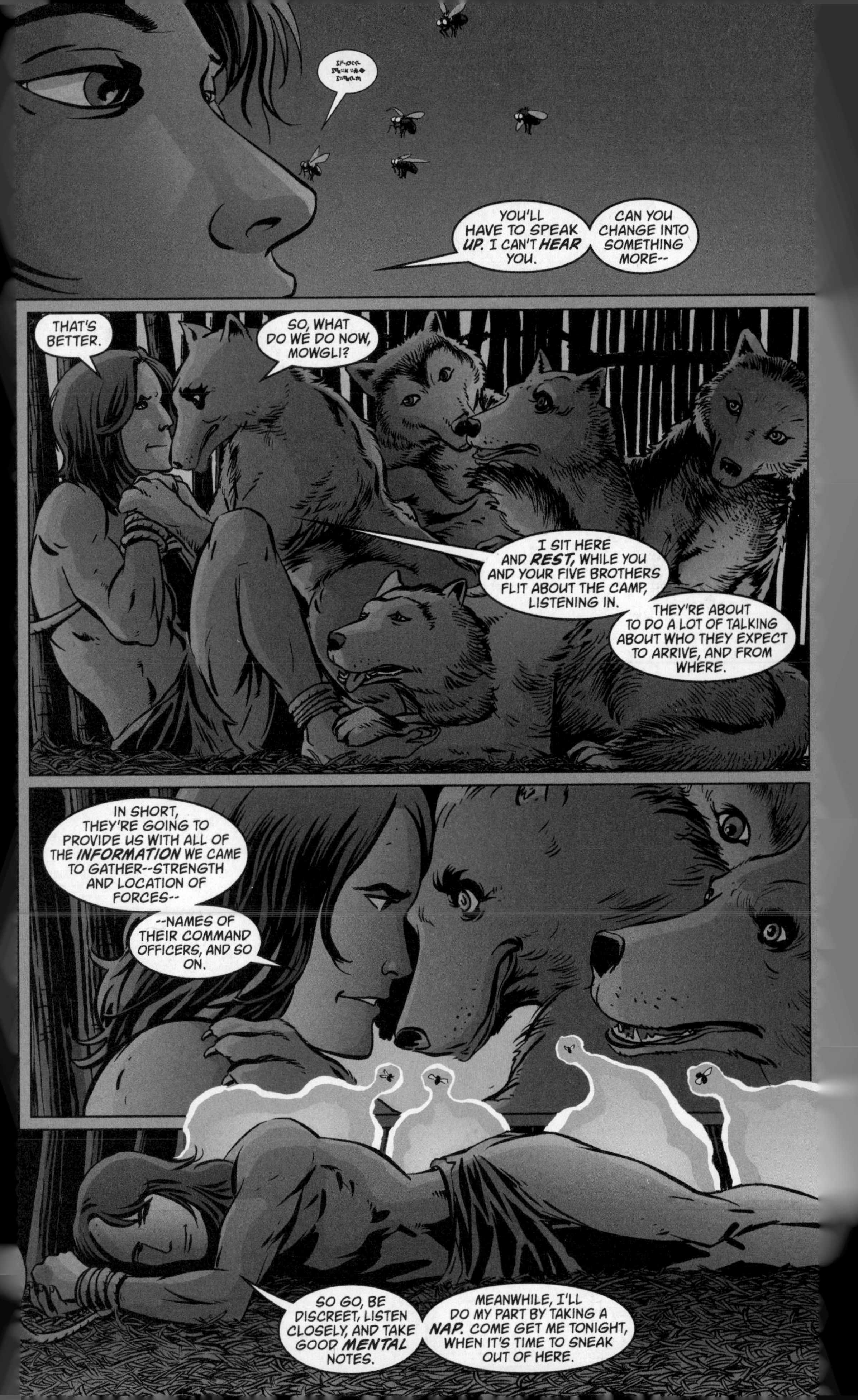
YOU'LL HAVE TO SPEAK UP. I CAN'T HEAR YOU.
CAN YOU CHANGE INTO SOMETHING MORE--
THAT'S BETTER.
SO, WHAT DO WE DO NOW, MOWGLI?
I SIT HERE AND REST, WHILE YOU AND YOUR FIVE BROTHERS FLIT ABOUT THE CAMP, LISTENING IN.
THEY'RE ABOUT TO DO A LOT OF TALKING ABOUT WHO THEY EXPECT TO ARRIVE, AND FROM WHERE.
IN SHORT, THEY'RE GOING TO PROVIDE US WITH ALL OF THE INFORMATION WE CAME TO GATHER--STRENGTH AND LOCATION OF FORCES--
--NAMES OF THEIR COMMAND OFFICERS, AND SO ON.
SO GO, BE DISCREET, LISTEN CLOSELY, AND TAKE GOOD MENTAL NOTES.
MEANWHILE, I'LL DO MY PART BY TAKING A NAP. COME GET ME TONIGHT, WHEN IT'S TIME TO SNEAK OUT OF HERE.

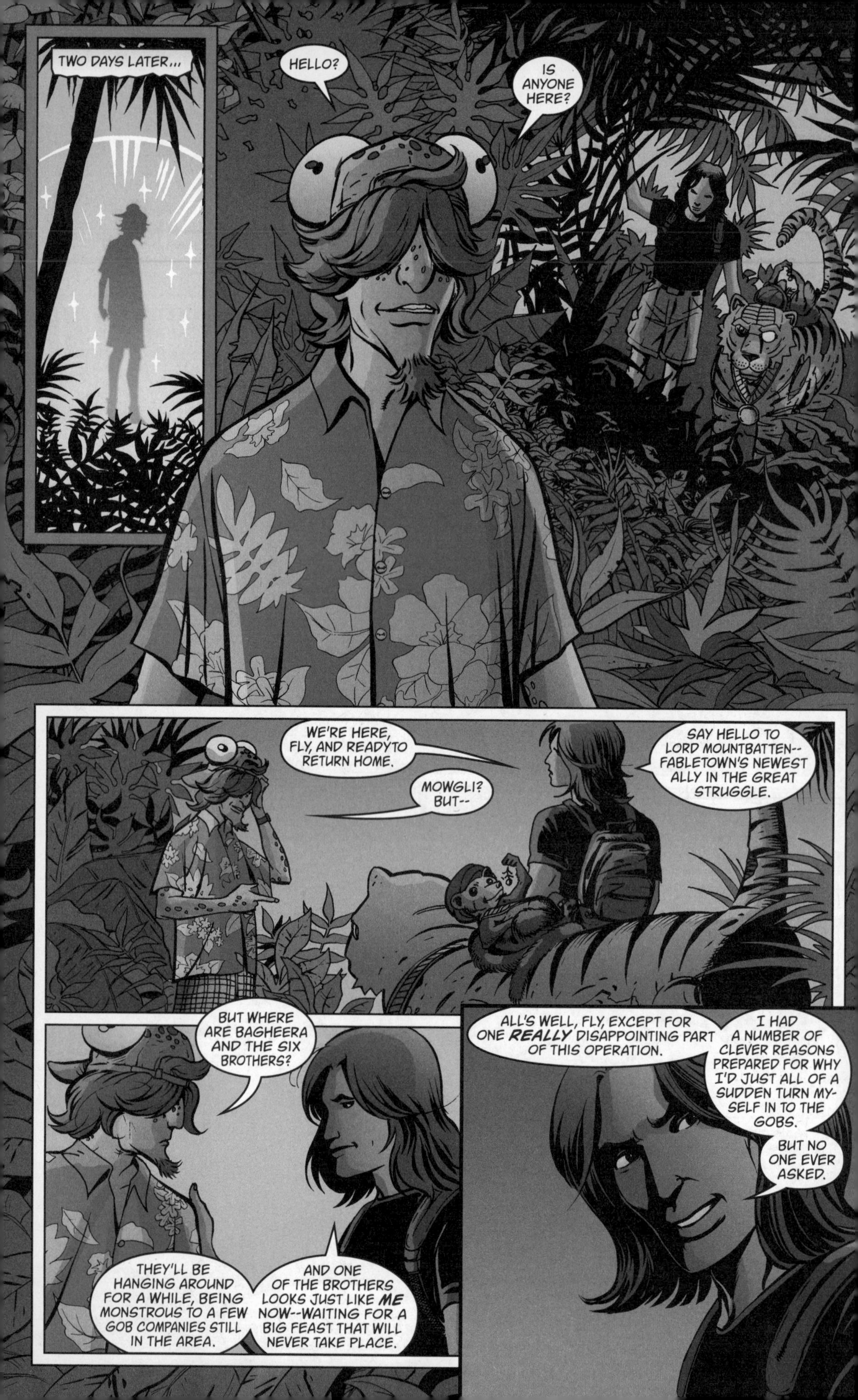
TWO DAYS LATER...
HELLO?
IS ANYONE HERE?
WE'RE HERE, FLY, AND READY TO RETURN HOME.
MOWGLI? BUT--
SAY HELLO TO LORD MOUNTBATTEN--FABLETOWN'S NEWEST ALLY IN THE GREAT STRUGGLE.
BUT WHERE ARE BAGHEERA AND THE SIX BROTHERS?
THEY'LL BE HANGING AROUND FOR A WHILE, BEING MONSTROUS TO A FEW GOB COMPANIES STILL IN THE AREA.
AND ONE OF THE BROTHERS LOOKS JUST LIKE ME NOW--WAITING FOR A BIG FEAST THAT WILL NEVER TAKE PLACE.
ALL'S WELL, FLY, EXCEPT FOR ONE REALLY DISAPPOINTING PART OF THIS OPERATION.
I HAD A NUMBER OF CLEVER REASONS PREPARED FOR WHY I'D JUST ALL OF A SUDDEN TURN MYSELF IN TO THE GOBS.
BUT NO ONE EVER ASKED.

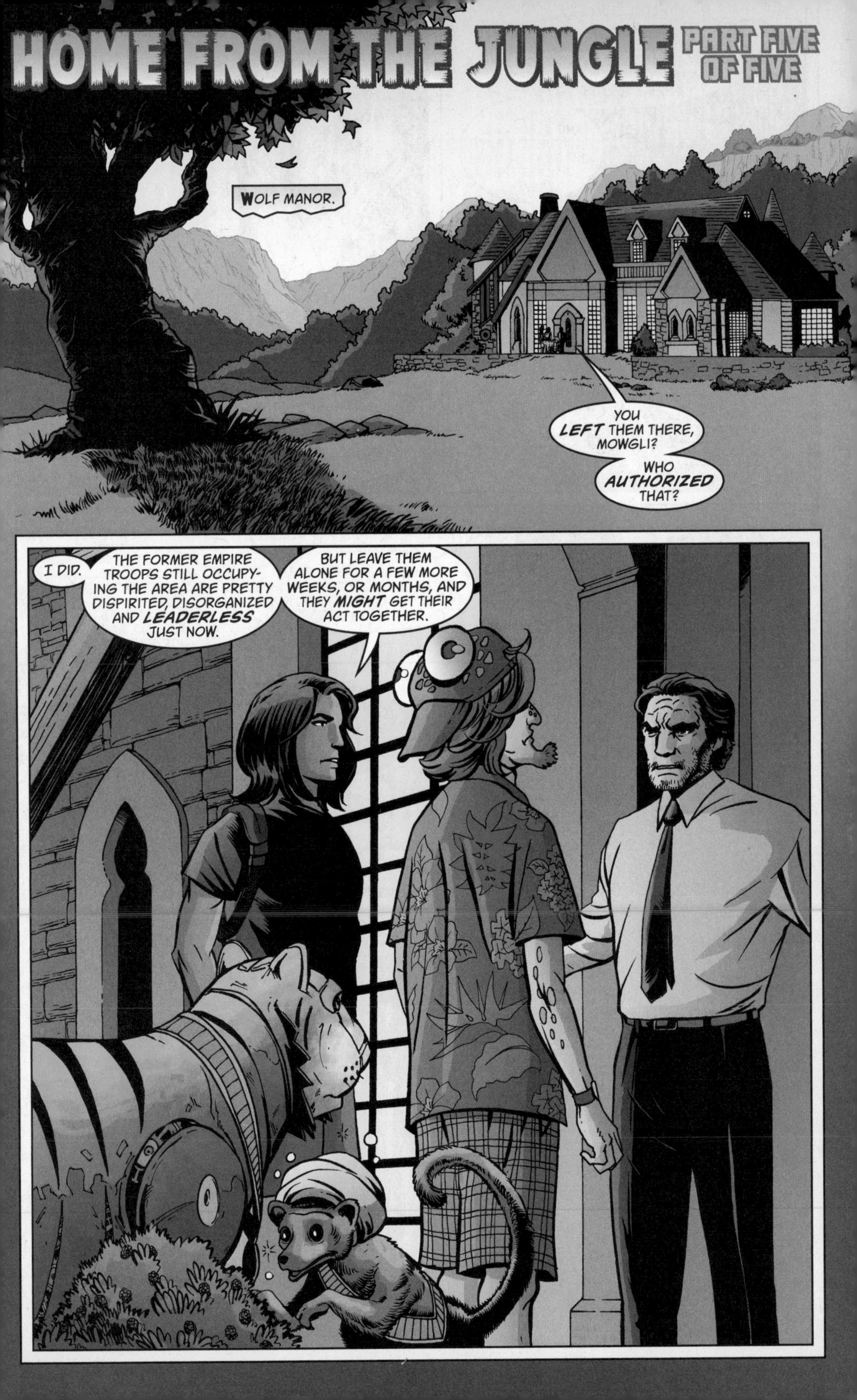
HOME FROM THE JUNGLE PART FIVE OF FIVE
WOLF MANOR.
YOU LEFT THEM THERE, MOWGLI?
WHO AUTHORIZED THAT?
I DID.
THE FORMER EMPIRE TROOPS STILL OCCUPYING THE AREA ARE PRETTY DISPIRITED, DISORGANIZED AND LEADERLESS JUST NOW.
BUT LEAVE THEM ALONE FOR A FEW MORE WEEKS, OR MONTHS, AND THEY MIGHT GET THEIR ACT TOGETHER.

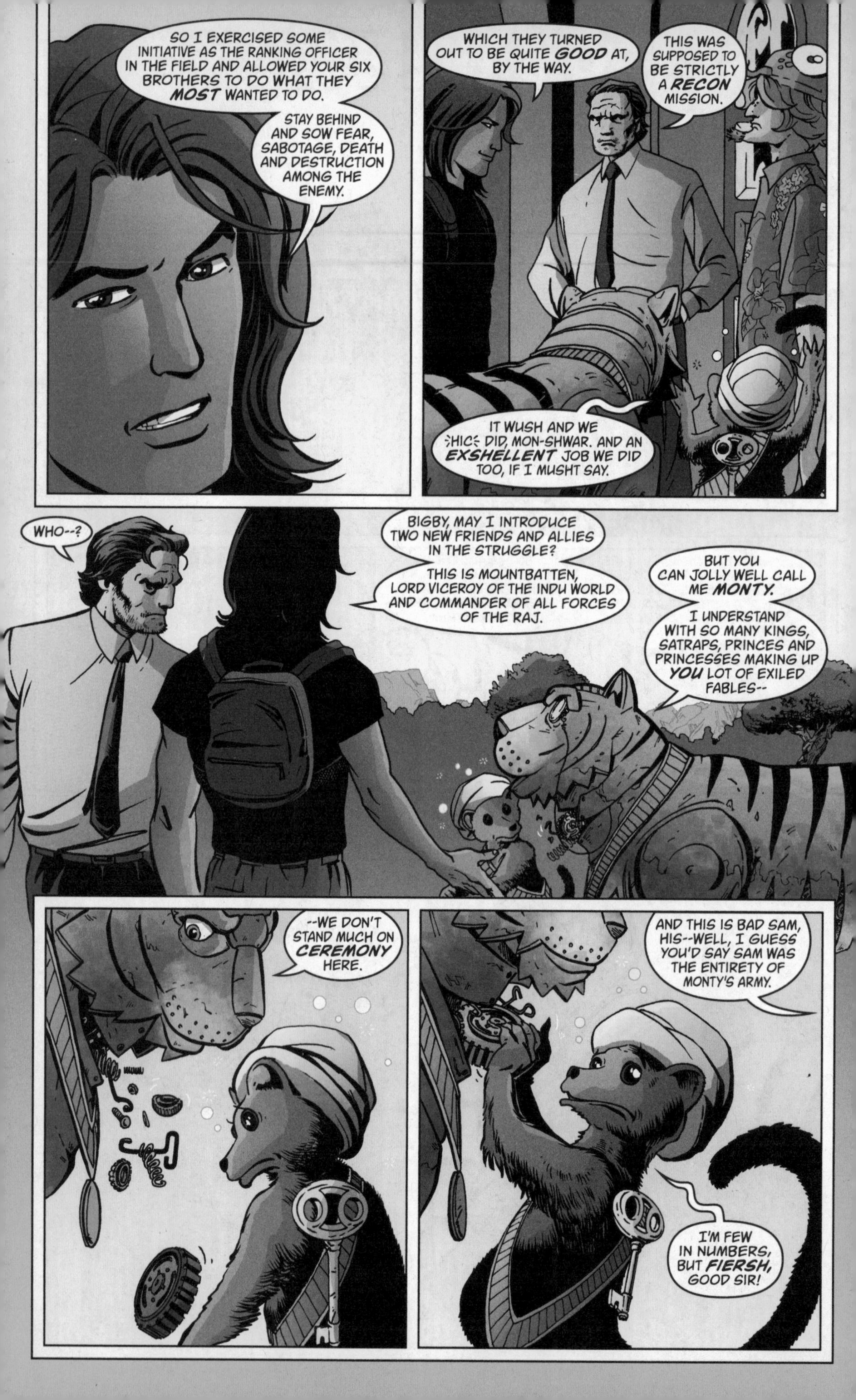

SO I EXERCISED SOME INITIATIVE AS THE RANKING OFFICER IN THE FIELD AND ALLOWED YOUR SIX BROTHERS TO DO WHAT THEY *MOST* WANTED TO DO.
STAY BEHIND AND SOW FEAR, SABOTAGE, DEATH AND DESTRUCTION AMONG THE ENEMY.
WHICH THEY TURNED OUT TO BE QUITE *GOOD* AT, BY THE WAY.
THIS WAS SUPPOSED TO BE STRICTLY A *RECON* MISSION.
IT WUSH AND WE ≶HIC≶ DID, MON-SHWAR. AND AN *EXSHELLENT* JOB WE DID TOO, IF I MUSHT SAY.
WHO--?
BIGBY, MAY I INTRODUCE TWO NEW FRIENDS AND ALLIES IN THE STRUGGLE?
THIS IS MOUNTBATTEN, LORD VICEROY OF THE INDU WORLD AND COMMANDER OF ALL FORCES OF THE RAJ.
BUT YOU CAN JOLLY WELL CALL ME *MONTY.*
I UNDERSTAND WITH SO MANY KINGS, SATRAPS, PRINCES AND PRINCESSES MAKING UP *YOU* LOT OF EXILED FABLES--
--WE DON'T STAND MUCH ON *CEREMONY* HERE.
AND THIS IS BAD SAM, HIS--WELL, I GUESS YOU'D SAY SAM WAS THE ENTIRETY OF MONTY'S ARMY.
I'M FEW IN NUMBERS, BUT *FIERSH,* GOOD SIR!

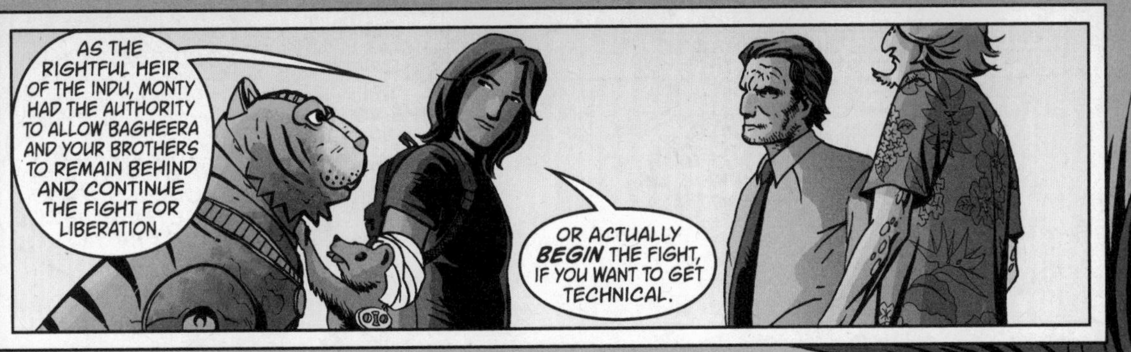
AS THE RIGHTFUL HEIR OF THE INDU, MONTY HAD THE AUTHORITY TO ALLOW BAGHEERA AND YOUR BROTHERS TO REMAIN BEHIND AND CONTINUE THE FIGHT FOR LIBERATION.
OR ACTUALLY BEGIN THE FIGHT, IF YOU WANT TO GET TECHNICAL.

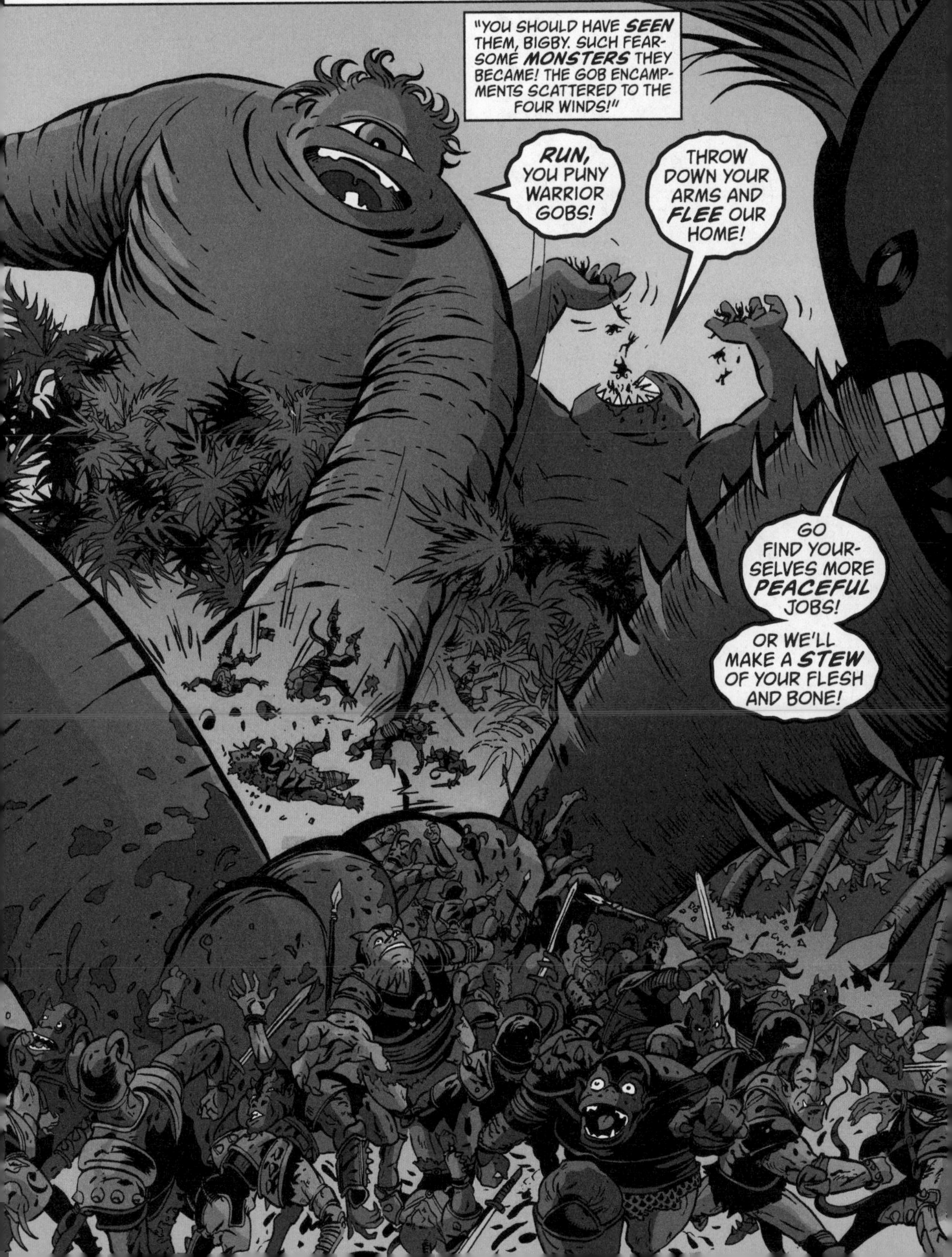
"YOU SHOULD HAVE SEEN THEM, BIGBY. SUCH FEAR-SOME MONSTERS THEY BECAME! THE GOB ENCAMP-MENTS SCATTERED TO THE FOUR WINDS!"
RUN, YOU PUNY WARRIOR GOBS!
THROW DOWN YOUR ARMS AND FLEE OUR HOME!
GO FIND YOUR-SELVES MORE PEACEFUL JOBS!
OR WE'LL MAKE A STEW OF YOUR FLESH AND BONE!

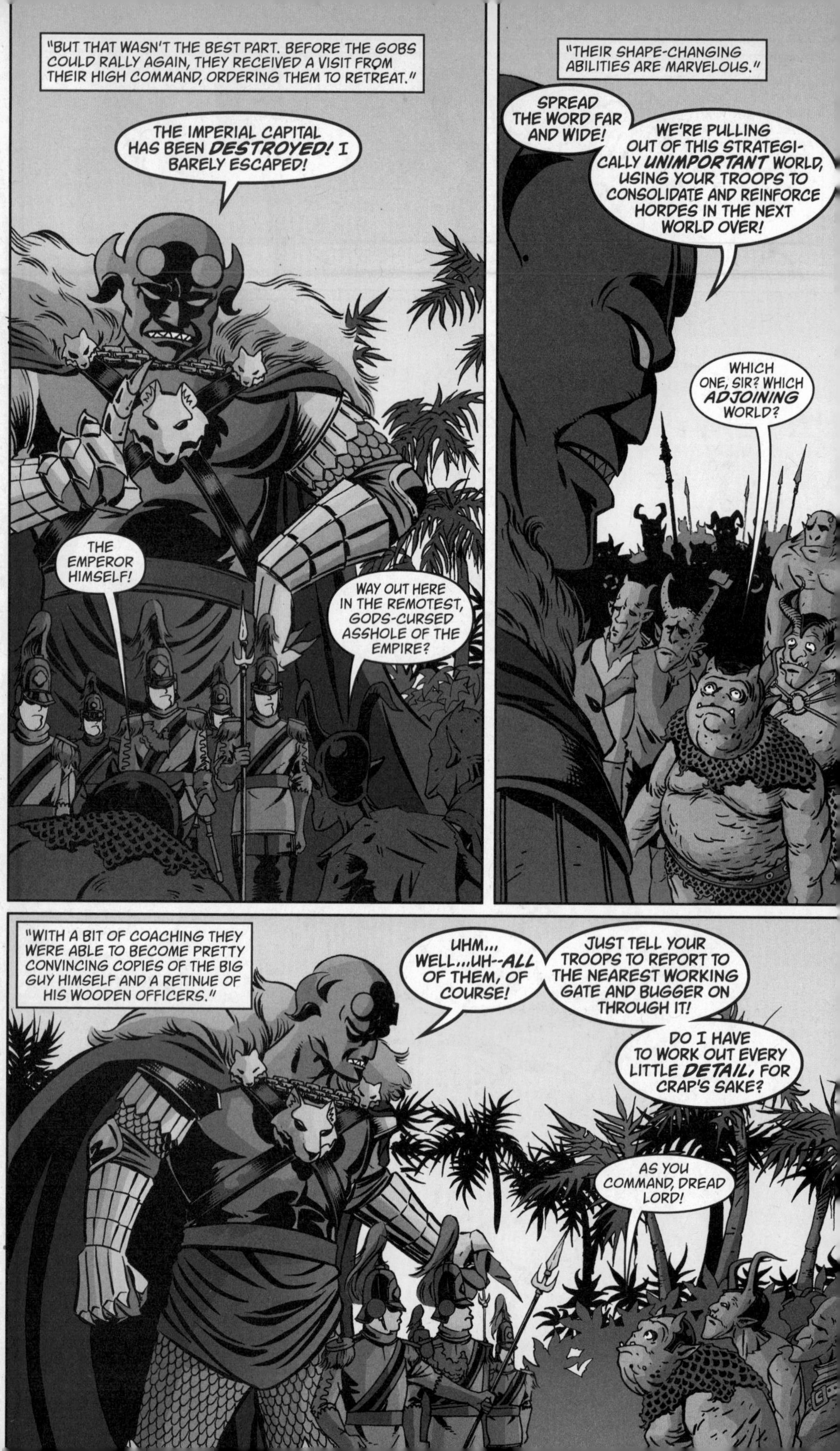
"BUT THAT WASN'T THE BEST PART. BEFORE THE GOBS COULD RALLY AGAIN, THEY RECEIVED A VISIT FROM THEIR HIGH COMMAND, ORDERING THEM TO RETREAT."
THE IMPERIAL CAPITAL HAS BEEN DESTROYED! I BARELY ESCAPED!
THE EMPEROR HIMSELF!
WAY OUT HERE IN THE REMOTEST, GODS-CURSED ASSHOLE OF THE EMPIRE?
"THEIR SHAPE-CHANGING ABILITIES ARE MARVELOUS."
SPREAD THE WORD FAR AND WIDE!
WE'RE PULLING OUT OF THIS STRATEGI-CALLY UNIMPORTANT WORLD, USING YOUR TROOPS TO CONSOLIDATE AND REINFORCE HORDES IN THE NEXT WORLD OVER!
WHICH ONE, SIR? WHICH ADJOINING WORLD?
"WITH A BIT OF COACHING THEY WERE ABLE TO BECOME PRETTY CONVINCING COPIES OF THE BIG GUY HIMSELF AND A RETINUE OF HIS WOODEN OFFICERS."
UHM... WELL...UH--ALL OF THEM, OF COURSE!
JUST TELL YOUR TROOPS TO REPORT TO THE NEAREST WORKING GATE AND BUGGER ON THROUGH IT!
DO I HAVE TO WORK OUT EVERY LITTLE DETAIL, FOR CRAP'S SAKE?
AS YOU COMMAND, DREAD LORD!

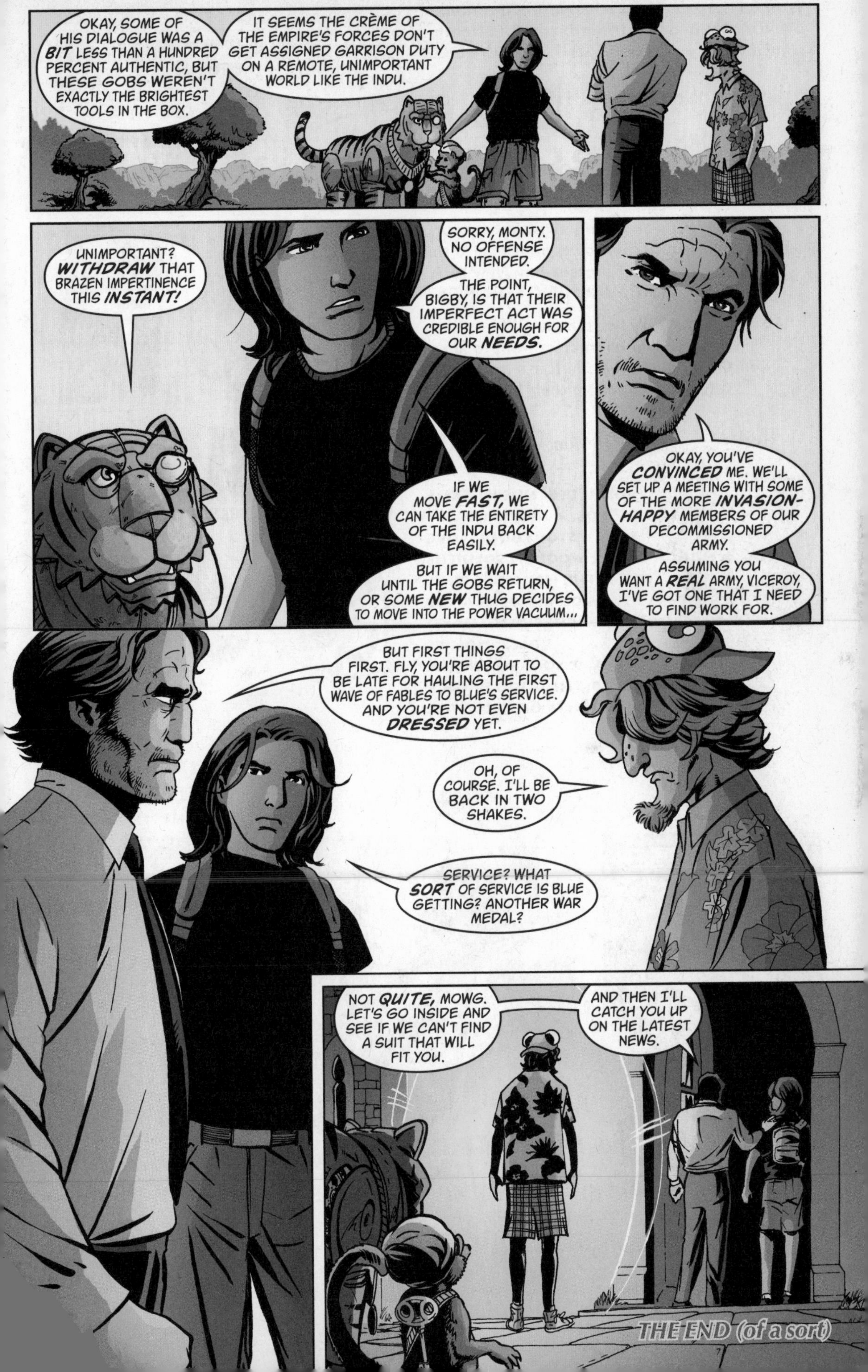
OKAY, SOME OF HIS DIALOGUE WAS A BIT LESS THAN A HUNDRED PERCENT AUTHENTIC, BUT THESE GOBS WEREN'T EXACTLY THE BRIGHTEST TOOLS IN THE BOX.
IT SEEMS THE CRÈME OF THE EMPIRE'S FORCES DON'T GET ASSIGNED GARRISON DUTY ON A REMOTE, UNIMPORTANT WORLD LIKE THE INDU.
UNIMPORTANT? WITHDRAW THAT BRAZEN IMPERTINENCE THIS INSTANT!
SORRY, MONTY. NO OFFENSE INTENDED.
THE POINT, BIGBY, IS THAT THEIR IMPERFECT ACT WAS CREDIBLE ENOUGH FOR OUR NEEDS.
IF WE MOVE FAST, WE CAN TAKE THE ENTIRETY OF THE INDU BACK EASILY.
BUT IF WE WAIT UNTIL THE GOBS RETURN, OR SOME NEW THUG DECIDES TO MOVE INTO THE POWER VACUUM...
OKAY, YOU'VE CONVINCED ME. WE'LL SET UP A MEETING WITH SOME OF THE MORE INVASION-HAPPY MEMBERS OF OUR DECOMMISSIONED ARMY.
ASSUMING YOU WANT A REAL ARMY, VICEROY, I'VE GOT ONE THAT I NEED TO FIND WORK FOR.
BUT FIRST THINGS FIRST. FLY, YOU'RE ABOUT TO BE LATE FOR HAULING THE FIRST WAVE OF FABLES TO BLUE'S SERVICE. AND YOU'RE NOT EVEN DRESSED YET.
OH, OF COURSE. I'LL BE BACK IN TWO SHAKES.
SERVICE? WHAT SORT OF SERVICE IS BLUE GETTING? ANOTHER WAR MEDAL?
NOT QUITE, MOWG. LET'S GO INSIDE AND SEE IF WE CAN'T FIND A SUIT THAT WILL FIT YOU.
AND THEN I'LL CATCH YOU UP ON THE LATEST NEWS.
THE END (of a sort)

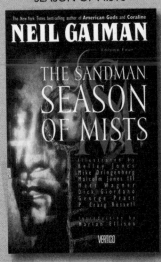

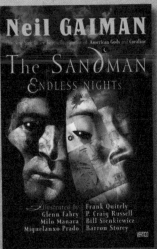